1 cup uncooked grain, rinsed

Grain	Cups water	Tsp. Salt	Cooking time	Standing time	Cups Yield	Comments
Amaranth	1½	½	20 min.	—	2	Add salt after cooking
Pearl Barley	2⅔	1	40 min.	5 min.	3½	
Buckwheat (kasha)	2	1	12 min.	7 min.	3½	
Bulgar (medium grain)	2	¾	20 min.	5 min.	3 cups	
Job's Tears	3	½	1 hour + 40 min.	5 min.	3⅓	Discard discolored grains
Millet	2	½	30 min.	5 min.	4	
Whole Grain Oats	2	½	1 hour	10 min.	2½	
Quinoa	2	1	15 min.	5 min.	3½	Rinse grain very thoroughly before cooking
Rice, white long grain	2	1	20 min.	5 min.	3	Don't rinse
Rice, brown long grain	2¼	1	45 min.	10 min.	3½	Use ¼ cup more water for fluffier rice
Whole Grain Rye	2½	½	2 hours + 15 min.	10 min.	3⅓	
Teff	3	½	15 min.	—	3	Don't rinse
Whole Grain Triticale	2½	½	1 hour + 45 min.	10 min.	2½	Add salt only after cooking
Whole Grain Wheat	2½	½	2 hours	15 min.	2¾	Add salt only after cooking
Wild Rice	2½	¾	55 min.	10 min.	3⅔	

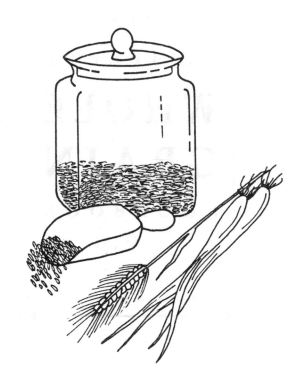

THE

COMPLETE

WHOLE

GRAIN

COOKBOOK

CAROL GELLES

DONALD I. FINE, INC.
NEW YORK

Library of Congress Cataloging-in-Publication Data

Gelles, Carol.
  The complete whole grain cookbook / by Carol Gelles.
    p.   cm.
  Includes bibliographical references.
  ISBN 1-55611-155-X
  1. Cookery (Cereals)   I. Title.
TX808.G45   1989   89-45344
641.6′31—dc20   CIP

Manufactured in the United States of America

10   9   8   7   6   5   4   3   2   1

DESIGNED BY STANLEY S. DRATE/FOLIO GRAPHICS COMPANY, INC.

Contents

v

Acknowledgments

This book would have been impossible to complete without the help of many, many people: those who worked directly on the manuscript, others who provided technical information and advice, and, finally, all my friends and neighbors who tasted and critiqued the recipes.

My first thanks are to the worker bees: Holly Garrison, the best food editor a cookbook author could ever hope for, who was constantly there for me, checking up on all the details, bringing her creative talents to the project, and mostly for being such a good friend. And I can't neglect to mention Holly's husband, Gerry Repp, who cheerfully sat through endless meals consisting of one grain dish after another, and answered the phone a million times without once saying, "You again?" My parents, Charlotte and Ernest Gelles, who toiled for hours calculating the nutritional values for each and every recipe, and, of course, for just being all-around terrific parents and people. Roger Vergnes at Donald I. Fine, Inc., who worked to turn my manuscript into the book I had hoped for.

And thanks, too, to the tasters; above all, my sister, Sherry, who is a wonderful cook herself and who ate more grain dishes in a short period of time than anyone should ever have to. Her ideas and suggestions added so much. The entire chapter on millet, that most "difficult" of grains, should probably be dedicated to Danusia and Elliot Cohen, who were excellent tasters and good sports as well. Marie and Bob Riesel and Michele Pigliavento, who were my muffin and bread tasters. Paula Rudolph, Kevin Reed, Jesse, Erica and Leah Weissman, who were always so willing to come into the city on the spur of the moment for an impromptu tasting. The night staff at Proskauer Rose Goetz & Mendelsohn.

And thanks to the technical advisers: Rebecca Wood, who was very generous with her time, as well as contributing her recipe for injera. The many people at the Kansas Wheat Commission and

Kansas State University. The staffs at Arrowhead Mills and Eden Foods.

And, finally, very special thanks to all my good friends, who were always there to lend an ear and who kept the faith through all my "brilliant" ideas.

*To my mother and father
for their unending love and support.*

BUCKWHEAT

OATS

**LEGEND
TO
JACKET
GRAINS**

BASMATI
BROWN RICE

SOFT GRAIN
BROWN RICE

POT BARLEY

CORN

BASMATI
WHITE RICE

ARTICULATED
PEA

MILLET

QUIBOA

OAT BRAN

HARD WHEAT

AMARANTH

OATMEAL

TEFF

WHOLE GRAIN
RYE

SOFT
WHEAT

KASHA
(ROASTED
BUCKWHEAT)

Foreword

The idea for this book started about three years ago when I went on vacation with my friend, Lysa (Randy) Kraft. At her suggestion, we spent five days at the Norwich Inn & Spa in Connecticut which serves absolutely delicious food that emphasizes high complex carbohydrates, low sodium, and low fat. Of all the many wonderful dishes we enjoyed, whole-wheat berries and kasha salad were my very favorites.

As soon as I got home, I dashed to the nearest health-food store and scooped up grains from nearly every bin. I brought them home and only then did it hit me: here I was, sitting with a bunch of bags, all filled with good stuff, and I had no idea how to cook any of it. And so this book began.

When I started seeking cookbooks and other reference sources to help me understand and prepare my little collection of grains, I found that there wasn't a single, all-in-one reference book that answered even a small number of my questions. The need for one complete book on the subject, with the kinds of recipes I wanted to cook and eat, became obvious.

I chose to make the recipes in this book as specific as possible and included separate sections about things that I think are important. I was specific about amounts called for, pan sizes, and cooking times, so that even inexperienced cooks would have no difficulty following the recipes, and I could feel comfortable knowing that the results would be the same as mine. Old hands in the kitchen may prefer recipes that are less exact. They will undoubtedly take the liberty of just chopping up a small carrot instead of measuring out the half cup chopped carrot that I call for, for example, and will adjust the seasonings to suit themselves.

For the most part, the recipes also reflect the kinds of food that I enjoy (which is just about everything, come to think of it), and the seasonings are, more or less, to my taste. For example, as you use the book, you will find that I have a preference for spicy (although not fiery) food, and the first time you cook some of these foods you may want to start with just half the amount of these seasonings.

I believe that the recipes in this book will appeal to a large number of people with diverse tastes. I have tried to include things that will appeal both to the gourmet as well as to those who like simple, down-home food. Vegetarians are not neglected, nor are meat eaters. And parents will find lots of recipes that kids will like.

I strongly believe that grains are an important food for the future, and have great value as part of the human diet, monetarily, nutritionally, and simply as good food. So, it is my fondest hope that this book will awaken your interest (not to mention your taste buds) in this fascinating subject.

PART

I

◊

INTRODUCTION TO GRAIN COOKING: GETTING STARTED

◊

What Is Grain?
Grain Terminology
Milling
Buying Grains
Storing Grains
About Cooking Grains
Microwaving Grains
Alternate Cooking Methods
Freezing
Ingredients Used in These Recipes
Equipment
Nutritional Analysis
Health Tips
Vegetarian Recipes
Sprouting
Sources

What Is Grain?

Grains are grasses that bear edible seeds. Both the plant and the seed (kernel) are referred to as grain. Grains are also known as cereals (usually when referred to in nutritional terms). The seeds are the fruit of the grain, and, like all seeds, they are the vehicles of reproduction and are the part of the plant that contain the most nutrients.

Each kernel of grain is composed of four parts:

Outer husk or hull: This is the inedible seed covering, which is removed from grains that are intended for human consumption. In some grains, such as barley, the hull clings tightly to the grain and must be removed by grinding or pearling. Other grains, such as wheat, have hulls that are loosely attached and can be removed by threshing. Then there are some grains that are "naked" and don't have any hull at all. A grain that has had the outer hull removed is considered a whole grain if the bran and germ are still intact.

Bran: This is the protective covering on the grain and is several layers thick. The inner layers are called the aleurone layers. Bran is rich in B vitamins and minerals and is an excellent source of dietary fiber. It is the bran layer, plus the germ, that is removed from the grain when it is polished to produce "white" products such as white rice or pearled barley.

Germ: The germ is the embryo of the seed and is responsible for germination. It is this part of the kernel that produces the sprout; it is rich in enzymes, fat, and protein, as well as certain vitamins and minerals. Germ is also polished away when grains are refined.

Endosperm: This is the starchy center of the grain. It is high in carbohydrates and its purpose is to nourish the seed after it sprouts. White rice, pearled barley, and that part of the wheat that is made into white flour are all endosperms.

GRAIN KERNEL
(cross section)

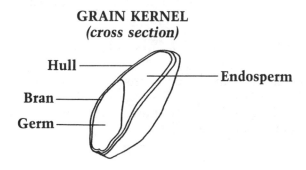

Hull — Endosperm

Bran

Germ

Grain Terminology

Berry: The whole grain with just the outer hull removed. Whole grains that have loosely attached hulls and require very little mechanical processing (wheat, for instance) are called berries. Grains that have tightly attached hulls and need milling to remove them are called groats. It is not unusual to use the terms berry and groat interchangeably, since the product is still the whole grain with the bran and germ intact.

Bleached: After the endosperm has been ground into white flour, it can be treated chemically to make it even whiter. White flour is available bleached or unbleached.

Converted: This is a term used by the makers of Uncle Ben's rice and refers to a process in which the rice is steamed and then dried before the bran is removed. The process supposedly "seals in" more of the rice's nutrients.

Enriched: Because so many of the nutrients in grain are lost when the bran and germ are removed, many processors put vitamins back into the grains. This is especially true of long-grain white rice and breads. In the case of long-grain white rice, avoid rinsing before cooking or you will wash away the added vitamins.

Fiber: This is sometimes referred to as *roughage* or *bulk*, and is the cellular structure of the plant (*all* plants, as a matter of fact), which humans cannot digest. The fiber in grains is found primarily in the bran and the germ, those parts of the grain that are so often discarded during milling. There are two types of fiber: water insoluble and water soluble. Wheat bran is an insoluble fiber, and it is this type of fiber that provides bulk in the diet and is now thought to help prevent certain kinds of cancer and other less serious intestinal disorders. Oat bran, on the other hand, is water soluble, and it is this kind of fiber that is currently being studied for its ability to lower blood cholesterol. Both kinds of fiber are necessary in a healthy diet.

Flakes: When hulled grains are steamed and flattened between rollers, they are called flakes. The major advantage of flakes is that they cook faster than whole grains.

Flour: Finely ground hulled grains. Flour can be ground from the whole grain, including the bran and germ, but whole-grain flour does become rancid more quickly than flour made of just the endosperm (white flour).

Grits: Although the word hominy (which means hulled corn) comes to mind in connection with grits, grits are simply any coarsely ground, hulled grain. Any grain can be ground into grits.

Groat: A whole grain with only the outer hull removed. A groat differs from a berry in that its hull has been removed by polishing, a more abrasive process than threshing.

Meal: Very coarsely ground flour. Any grain can be made into meal.

Pearling: The process by which the outer hull is removed by grinding. For example, pot barley has been pearled until the hull is removed, but the bran is still intact. Further pearling will remove the bran and germ, resulting in pearl (or pearled) barley.

Polish: This is a term for both the process of grinding off the hull and also for a by-product of that process. Polish is a flour that still retains some of the bran and some of the wheat.

Rolled: The process of steaming grains and then pressing them between large metal rollers. Flakes tend to be thicker than those designated as rolled. For example, oat flakes are thicker than rolled oats.

Sprout: A young plant shoot. Sprouts are good sources of nutrition and can be eaten raw or cooked. Any grain or bean can be sprouted when the proper techniques are used. (See Sprouting, page 20.)

Threshing: The method used to separate the hull from the grain by beating, rather than by polishing or grinding.

Whole grain: Usually refers to a groat or a berry that has had neither the bran or germ removed. The term is also often used to describe products made with whole grains. Technically, it could also mean an unhulled grain.

Milling

Milling is the process of separating the various parts of the grain. It can start in the field when the grains are cut and put through a thresher, which, for grains with loose husks (wheat, rye, triticale, and hulless barley), will separate the grain from the husk very easily. Then all that remains to be done is to remove the debris and these grains are ready for further milling. Grains that have husks that adhere more tightly will have to be ground or pearled, a more abrasive process than threshing. These husking and sifting processes, as well as the further processing used to remove the bran and the germ, are correctly called decortication. Other milling processes will grind endosperm or whole grains into flour, steam and roll grain into flakes, or crack whole grain into pieces.

Occasionally you may note the term *stone ground* on a package. This means that the grain was ground with a stone mill rather than steel mill. Since stone grinders are gentler and more precise than steel grinders, they are less likely to overgrind the grain. And since there is also less chance of the germ being damaged by this method, stone-ground products will not become rancid as quickly as steel-ground products. Products that are stone ground will always say so on the package. They are also more expensive than steel-ground grains.

Buying Grains

The number of options you have when it comes to buying grains depends largely upon what kind of grain you want to buy. All of the popular grains are available, neatly packaged, at the supermarket. You can count on the fact that these grains have been pretty well picked over and cleaned before packaging.

However, if organically grown products are important to you, you might consider doing your grain shopping at a health-food store, where the selection will be wide and you will probably also have the option to buy in bulk. The advantage of buying in bulk is obvious: you save money, and you can also buy exactly what you need. If the health-food store is new to you, have a look around before you buy anything. Make sure that the general environment is clean and appetizing and that the storage bins are covered. Also, look carefully at the bin you are ready to buy from and make sure there are no insects moving around in the grain. (No store that I can think of would intentionally carry insect-laden grains, but even the best of stores can occasionally have a problem.)

If a health-food store is not available to you, then you can consider buying your grains from a mail-order source that is usually direct from the growers and/or distributors.

It is also possible, if you live in a rural area, to purchase grains directly from a feed mill. However, although these grains may be perfectly wholesome and edible, since they are not intended for human consumption they may not be very well cleaned. And, since picking out this extraneous material is a long and laborious task, you may decide it's better to go to conventional sources for your grains.

Seed houses are another possible source *that I would strongly advise against,* unless you are absolutely sure that the grains being sold are not treated with fungicides, pesticides, or other chemicals that would make them dangerous for human consumption.

Storing Grains

The germ of whole grains contain oils that can turn rancid, especially if the grain is improperly stored. Rancid foods give off a most unpleasant odor, and I generally use my nose to tell me whether or not a grain is still fresh and usable.

Ideally, all grains should be refrigerated to retard spoilage. This is especially true for whole-grain products, which tend to have a shorter shelf life than processed grains. Given that most people do not have endless refrigeration space, the next best thing is to place the grains in containers with tight-fitting lids and store them in a cool, dry spot. Even under ideal storage conditions, it is entirely possible that an insect egg or two may have found its way into your grain. By keeping each grain in a tightly sealed container, you can at least contain the infestation to that one grain.

Dampness is another enemy of grains, since they absorb moisture readily and can quickly turn moldly.

As a rule of thumb, whole-grain products should be stored at room temperature for no longer than one month. If you wish to store them for much longer, they should be refrigerated. Untoasted wheat and other grain germs, because they contain high levels of oil, should always be stored in the refrigerator. Toasted germs can be stored at room temperature.

About Cooking Grains

If the grains that are the basis for every single recipe in this book are not cooked properly, it's unlikely that the dish you are preparing will turn out successfully. There are so many variables in cooking grains that absolute cooking instructions are impossible. On the whole, I found the cooking instructions given on the packages of most grains to be very unreliable. I suggest that you follow my cooking instructions, regardless of what the package says. Here are a few of the major factors that figure into the perfectly cooked grain:

Type of cookware used: Grains should be cooked in a reasonably heavy saucepan with a tight-fitting lid. I used Farberware-brand cookware, which is comparable to the cookware most people own, for testing the recipes in this book. The lids, though certainly tight fitting, do allow a little steam to escape. If your pans have lids that fit tighter and don't allow any steam to escape, you may need a little less cooking water. Or you may need more water if your lids allow more steam to escape.

Temperature of cooking water: Although I call for the grains to be cooked in simmering water, our ideas of simmering may be slightly different. If your grains simmer more quickly than mine did, they will probably cook in a little less time, or at least the water will evaporate more quickly. It's always best to check near the end of cooking time to make sure the grains are not overcooking. Or the water may have evaporated, but the grains are still undercooked. In this case you will have to add a little boiling water and allow the grain to cook longer. If you are cooking at a lower simmer, then it may take a little longer for all of the water to be absorbed. In this case, you may find the cooked grain to be a little sticky.

Age of the grain: As grains grow older they also dry out. Freshly harvested grain may need less water to cook than grain that has been around a while. Unfortunately, there's no way of knowing how old your grain is, so if it has cooked the prescribed amount of time and you find that it is still undercooked, simply add a little boiling water and let it continue to simmer.

Personal preference: I prefer my grain the same way I do my pasta— al dente, or slightly chewy. If you like your grains softer, then you will require a little more water and a little more cooking time.

Bearing in mind these factors, here is the basic method for the preparation and cooking of all grains.

Sorting: If you've purchased loose grains, you may find that they are not as well cleaned as the popular packaged brands. So look them over and pick out any obvious foreign objects.

Measuring: Measure out the grains in a nested measuring cup (not a glass measuring cup that is intended for liquids), filling it to the top, then leveling it off.

Rinsing: For the most part, rinsing whole grains is optional. I feel that if the grain is not so small that it would fall through the strainer, and so long as it is not enriched, rinsing it to remove dust and debris is not a bad idea. However, some experts contend that rinsing washes away some of the valuable nutrients, so it's up to you.

If you choose to rinse, put the measured grain into a strainer and run it under cold tap water, then let it drain. Never rinse grains before storing them or they will mold. Rinse just before cooking.

I should note here that some grains require elaborate rinsing procedures. Specific directions for rinsing are given with those particular grains.

Cracked, rolled or other processed grains don't need rinsing.

Measuring the cooking liquid: Measure in a glass measuring cup, checking the measurement at eye level.

Adding salt: Each grain reacts a little differently to salt in the cooking water. Most grains cook well in salted water, and for those grains you can add salt to the saucepan when you add the water.

Some grains (amaranth, wheat berries, triticale, and Waheni brown rice) do not absorb liquid properly if it is salted, and they should be salted after cooking. The result of cooking these grains in salted water will be undercooked grains and only half of the liquid absorbed by the end of cooking time. Also, you will probably need to add less salt after cooking than if you were to add it before cooking for the same degree of saltiness. Needless to say, if you are watching your sodium intake, then cook the grains without adding any salt.

Adding the grain and simmering: When the water or other cooking liquid has come to a full boil, stir in the grain and then wait for the water to return to a boil. Reduce the heat so that the mixture is just simmering. Cover and start timing.

If you're cooking on an electric range, reduce the heat to low as soon as the grain is added, since the burner will remain hot long enough for the mixture to return to boiling.

On a gas range, keep the flame high until the water boils, then reduce the heat to the lowest possible setting, adjusting it upward until the mixture simmers.

The exact setting to achieve a simmer will vary from range to range, and even from one burner to another. What you are looking for is for the surface of the water to remain calm with just a few bubbles breaking the surface.

Sometimes gas ranges can't maintain a low enough flame for cooking grains at a simmer without going out. In that case, invest in an inexpensive simmering pad which will allow you to simmer at a higher temperature.

Checking for doneness: All things being equal, the grain should be cooked when almost all of the liquid is absorbed. There are three methods for determining if the grain is done:

1. Remove the lid and tilt the saucepan. If you don't see any water running out from the grain, then you can safely assume that it has evaporated. Let the saucepan stand, covered, on the cool burner for 5 to 10 minutes to allow any small amount of water that may be left on the bottom to be absorbed.
2. Lift the lid toward the end of cooking time. When holes appear between the grains, all of the water has been absorbed. (I prefer the first method of removing the pan from the heat, which is just before the holes appear, because then I am reasonably assured that the grain has not begun to stick to the bottom of the pan.)
3. Taste a few grains. Are they the consistency that you like? If so, the grain is ready, and you can simply drain off any water that remains in the pan.

Fluffing: Grain should not be stirred during cooking, because it will bruise the grains and make them sticky. After cooking, you can use a fork to fluff the grains, if you like, and you can also add salt to those grains that must have the salt added after cooking.

Microwaving Grains

Microwave instructions are given in the basic cooking directions for each grain.

Except for those grains that require very long cooking times, microwaving will not save a lot of time. It does, however, have the important advantage of producing consistent results, and all those varying factors of cooking grains on the stovetop are eliminated. In addition, many of the grains come out with a better texture

I usually recommend using the microwave only for cooking grains that will be needed, precooked, for a recipe. The microwave instructions in this book are for 600–700 watt microwave ovens. Smaller ovens will require longer cooking times.

Alternate Cooking Methods

Stove-top and microwave cooking methods are given with each grain in this book. However, for those who find themselves discouraged by the long cooking times required for some of the grains, here are some shortcut cooking strategies that work quite well:

Precooking: If the recipe you are planning to use calls for cooked grain, cook the grain a day or two in advance, and then follow the directions given for reheating it.

Slow cooker: This method is good for cooking grains that will be needed, precooked, for a recipe. Place both grain and liquid into a slow cooker (crock pot), and allow it to cook slowly during the day. When you get home at night, the grain should be cooked. (Please note that crock pots are no longer recommended for recipes that include meat.) You may find that grains cooked in a crock pot will absorb less liquid, so just drain off any excess.

Soaking: Following the general cooking directions, measure out the grain and the water and place them in the saucepan. Cover the pan and allow the grain to soak overnight or all day. Then cook for ⅓ less time than given in the general directions.

Pressure cooker: A pressure cooker will reduce the cooking time for grains, but you must be careful that you do not cook too much grain at one time. The starches given off during cooking can bubble up and clog the pressure gauge. Read the instructions that come with your pressure cooker, and call the manufacturer (nowadays, most manufacturers have telephone numbers for consumers to call with questions about their products) for specific information about cooking grains.

Freezing

I have found that cooked grains that have been frozen tend to become waterlogged and lose their al dente consistency. However, it is nice to have cooked grains on hand in the freezer, so you can try it and make the final judgment yourself. However, soups and stews that contain cooked grains freeze very well. For other dishes containing grains, here again it's a matter of personal preference as to whether or not you find the thawed and reheated grain dishes acceptable.

Ingredients Used in These Recipes

Eggs are always large.

Butter is always lightly salted.

Specific amounts of **salt** and **pepper** are given only as a guide. Feel free to alter them to suit your own taste.

Can sizes may be approximate. For instance, if the recipe calls for a 15-ounce can, and you have one that is 14 to 16 ounces, go ahead and use it.

Unless otherwise stated, **canned broths** are the ready-to-use variety, that come in can sizes of either 13¾ ounces or 14½ ounces.

Dried **herbs** are used in whole form, not ground.

Spices, when not specified as ground, are used whole, except for black pepper.

When the recipe calls for minced **garlic,** you can put the garlic through a press if you don't feel like mincing it.

Red-wine **vinegar** can be substituted in equal parts for any type of vinegar specified in a recipe.

Fresh **lemon juice** is always used in these recipes. Reconstituted lemon juice has a chemical flavor I don't like.

Fresh chopped **parsley** (either curly or flat) is always used. If necessary you can substitute 1 teaspoon of dried parsley for 1 tablespoon fresh parsley.

Scallions are also known as green or spring onions in certain regions.

Heavy cream and whipping cream are different terms for the same product.

Yeast: There are a number of recipes in this book that call for yeast. I almost always use the packets of active dry yeast that are usually sold in strips of three, but you can also use the little bricks of compressed (fresh) yeast, if you prefer.

Yeast is alive—a one-cell fungus—therefore it's important to use yeast by the expiration date on the package. When fed with the flour and sometimes the sugar that it is mixed with it, the yeast will begin to divide and to convert the carbohydrates in the flour into alcohol and carbon dioxide. It is this gas that gives dough its typical "yeasty aroma" and makes it swell and rise. (The alcohol will evaporate as the bread bakes.)

Most complete cookbooks devote at least one chapter, and lots of pictures, to the topic of baking with yeast. And by now there are undoubtedly videotapes available on the subject, too, so you can actually *see* what risen dough looks like, and how to knead, for instance. The old-fashioned direct approach is another way to learn this skill: ask a friend who has baked with yeast to show you how to do it.

Equipment

You probably already own most of the equipment necessary for preparing the recipes in this book. The following are what I consider essential for any well-equipped kitchen:

Good pots: For these recipes you will need a 2-quart saucepan with a tight-fitting lid (most of the grains are cooked in this size saucepan), a large skillet, a large saucepot (for soups and such) with a lid, a heavy 4-quart saucepan or a Dutch oven with a tight-fitting lid, and a double boiler (to prevent delicate sauces and other foods from overcooking). You can usually rig up a double boiler by resting a small pan into a larger one, but the real thing is best.

Sharp knives: They make the difference between easy work and hard labor. You can get along nicely with a 10-inch chef's knife (for chopping), a long serrated bread knife (for slicing breads), and a paring knife.

Measuring utensils: Use glass measuring cups for measuring liquids. Pour the liquid into the cup and then check the cup at eye level to make sure that the measurement is exact.
Use nested measuring cups for measuring dry ingredients. These metal or plastic cups are nested in four sizes: ¼ cup, ⅓ cup, ½ cup, and 1 cup; sometimes there are ⅛-cup or 2-cup measures, as well. To use these cups correctly, dip the measuring cup into the dry ingredient and lift out a generously full cup. Using a flat utensil, such as the back of a knife, level the top, returning the excess to the package or canister. When measuring brown sugar, press it firmly into the cup. Dry ingredients can also be spooned into the measuring cup if it's not possible to scoop them.
Remember that glass and nested measuring cups are not interchangeable. The general rule is that if it pours use the glass measuring cup. If it plops, or is dry, use the nested cups.
Standard measuring spoons are necessary for small amounts of either dry or liquid ingredients.

3 teaspoons	=	1 tablespoon
4 tablespoons	=	¼ cup
5 tablespoons plus 1 teaspoon	=	⅓ cup
8 tablespoons	=	½ cup
2 cups	=	1 pint
4 cups (or 2 pints)	=	1 quart

Simmering pad: In the old days this would have been an asbestos pad. Now it is a metal circle with a cardboardlike material inserted in the center. You insert this gadget between the flame and your pot if you find that you cannot adjust the heat source to maintain an even, slow simmer.

Mixing bowls: One large, one medium, and one small.

Colander: Essential for thorough draining.

Vegetable peeler: Although you can peel vegetables and fruits with a paring knife, this gadget saves time and, unless you're a real expert, doesn't waste as much of the flesh.

Strainer: A large one for rinsing grains before cooking.

Timer: Otherwise it's easy to forget when you put something on the stove or in the oven.

Spatulas: At least one rubber spatula for scraping mixtures out of bowls, and one wide metal spatula for turning pancakes and the like.

Wooden spoons: The professional cook's choice for stirring.

Whisk: For stirring ingredients that would otherwise lump; for use as a beater, if you don't own an electric mixer.

Grater: Preferably a four-sided grater that can shred as well as grate.

Oven thermometer: Preferably a mercury or a spring-type thermometer. The correct oven temperature can make the difference between an outstanding dish and a dismal failure. An oven thermometer will enable you to check the calibration of your oven.

Baking pans: For baked goods, especially cakes, muffins, and breads, it's important that you use the size pan called for, otherwise baking times will not be accurate.

Strongly Suggested Equipment

Blender and/or **food processor:** I use the blender for processing liquids and the processor for chopping and shredding.

Microwave oven: You will find the microwave is great for cooking and reheating grains. It is also incredibly helpful for small jobs such as melting butter and chocolate, bringing cream cheese and butter to room temperature, and heating milk.

Electric mixer: Either stand-alone or hand-held, an electric mixer will produce a much better baked product than one beaten with a spoon or a whisk, and it saves a lot of time and elbow grease, too.

Nonstick cookware: If you're watching your fat intake, this cookware is a god-send; it allows you to decrease the fat in your cooking significantly. It also minimizes sticking if you accidentally overcook your grain.

Pastry blender: Although you can cut shortening into flour with two knives, this gadget is much easier to use and much more efficient.

Garlic press: When you are too hurried to mince garlic by hand, a press (especially a self-cleaning one) makes quick work of this task.

Instant-read thermometer: If you're going to do much baking with yeast (this thermometer is wonderful for taking the temperature of the water in which the yeast is dissolved), or if you're just picky about exactly how done your meat is, this gadget is a dream come true. Just insert it into the food to get an accurate temperature reading within seconds. Don't leave the thermometer in the roast as it bakes or you will ruin the thermometer.

Steamer: Whether you select an Oriental bamboo steamer or a metal one, these are wonderful for reheating grains, as well as for cooking short-grain rice and vegetables to perfection.

Crock pot or **slow cooker:** See Alternate Cooking Methods on page 11.

Equipment That's Nice to Own, But Not Essential

For the most part, these are large, and sometimes expensive, single-use gadgets. If you do a lot of whatever it does (or if you have a lot of spare storage space) you might consider purchasing one or more of them:

Wok: You can certainly use a large skillet for stir-frying, but a wok does a better job. If you like lots of vegetables in your diet, all cooked tender-crisp, or if you intend to do much Oriental cooking, a wok is a good investment.

Rice cooker: In some parts of the world where rice is eaten every day and at almost every meal, owning a rice cooker is like owning a toaster. A rice cooker makes perfect rice every time with no fuss or bother, so if you eat a lot of rice you may want to consider buying one.

Waffle iron: Everybody loves waffles; they're a great way to enjoy many whole-grain products, and this book includes a number of recipes for them. Waffle irons come in various sizes, and nonstick coatings make waffles that stick to the iron a thing of the past.

Couscousiere: This is a rather large two-tiered pot. Holes in the top part allow you to cook the couscous over the stew. (Obviously, it cooks couscous better than anything else in the world.)

Tortilla press and comal: These are necessary for making authentic tortillas. If you have the press, you might as well have the comal (the cast iron griddle used for cooking tortillas) or vice versa.

Pizza-making equipment: If you just love homemade pizza, having a peel, which is a big wooden paddle used to slide the pizza in and out of the oven, may be an important item. A pizza wheel will cut very neat slices, but a sharp knife works almost as well. The stones that are used to line the oven will superheat it, which results in a very crisp crust, quickly. (Although, using these stones, I have occasionally ended up with a crust that was burnt to a crisp.) My method for preheating a baking sheet, as described in the pizza recipe on page 63, works just fine.

Pasta machine: There are two types of pasta machines available. One is hand cranked and will roll out the pasta dough and cut it into different widths. The second type is an electric machine that will mix, knead, and then extrude the dough into many different shapes. I suggest buying the less expensive hand-cranked model first in case the thrill of pasta making wears thin.

Bread-making machine: This is similar to the electric pasta machine and also very expensive. You put the ingredients into the machine and it mixes, kneads, proofs, and then bakes the bread all by itself. The quality of the bread it makes depends largely on the ingredients you put into it. Because I do so much baking in my work, I use one of these machines to mix and knead the dough, but then I shape it and bake the bread myself.

Grain mills: These appliances or attachments will grind your grains into flour. Most are fairly expensive and on the large side, but the obvious advantage is that you will always have fresh whole-grain flour when you want it. My feeling is that with so many fresh flours available, you probably don't need this machine unless you are a truly ardent baker. Many other kitchen appliances will do the same job. An unused spice or coffee grinder can be used; a blender will also do the job, but it's tedious to grind and sift out the flour, returning the coarse meal to the machine to be ground even finer.

Nutritional Analysis

The figures given for the nutritional content of the recipes in this book were calculated using "The Food Processor II" software developed by ESHA Research in Salem, Oregon. However, the figures for some of the more unusual grains were provided by Arrowhead Mills, Inc., of Hereford, Texas.

These calculations are for the estimated values of the ingredients. The figures can vary, depending on the brands used and variations in ingredients. In some cases, such as deep-fried foods, the amount of oil actually absorbed had to be approximated. But if you use these figures simply as guidelines, you should be able to find recipes that are compatible with your dietary goals.

Remember that nutritional figures given for these recipes (or any recipes, for that matter) have little or no meaning by themselves, but are imporant as part of a whole dietary program. Listed below are the United States Department of Agriculture's recommended dietary allowances for an average 26-year-old woman and man. If you have specific dietary restrictions, your needs will probably vary from the charts. Consult your physician or dietitian if you have any questions.

RECOMMENDED DIETARY ALLOWANCES

RDA for: Jane Doe   **Age: 26 yrs 0 mo**   **Sex: Female**
Weight: 125 lbs   **Height: 5 ft 4 in**   **Lightly active**

Calories	1973	*	Pyridoxine—B6	2.00 Mg	
Protein	45.5 G		Cobalamin—B12	3.00 Mcg	
Carbohydrates	286 G	**	Folacin	400 Mcg	
Dietary Fiber	19.7 G	#	Pantothenic	7.00 Mg	*
Fat—Total	65.8 G	**	Vitamin C	60.0 Mg	
Fat—Saturated	21.9 G	**	Vitamin E	8.00 Mg	
Fat—Mono	21.9 G	**	Calcium	800 Mg	
Fat—Poly	21.9 G	**	Copper	2.50 Mg	*
Cholesterol	300 Mg	**	Iron	18.0 Mg	
Vit A—Carotene	RE		Magnesium	300 Mg	
Vit A—Preformed	RE		Phosphorus	800 Mg	
Vitamin A—Total	800 RE		Potassium	3750 Mg	*
Thiamin—B1	1.00 Mg		Selenium	125 Mcg	*
Riboflavin—B2	1.20 Mg		Sodium	2200 Mg	*
Niacin—B3	13.0 Mg		Zinc	15.0 Mg	

*Suggested values; within recommended ranges
**Dietary goals   # Fiber = 1gram/100 kcal

RECOMMENDED DIETARY ALLOWANCES

RDA for: John Doe		Age: 26 yrs 0 mo		Sex: Male	
Weight: 170 lbs		Height: 5 ft 10 in		Lightly active	
Calories	2644 *	Pyridoxine—B6	2.20 Mg		
Protein	61.9 G	Cobalamin—B12	3.00 Mcg		
Carbohydrates	383 G **	Folacin	400 Mcg		
Dietary Fiber	26.4 G #	Pantothenic	7.00 Mg *		
Fat—Total	88.2 G **	Vitamin C	60.0 Mg		
Fat—Saturated	29.4 G **	Vitamin E	10.0 Mg		
Fat—Mono	29.4 G **	Calcium	800 Mg		
Fat—Poly	29.4 G **	Copper	2.50 Mg *		
Cholesterol	300 Mg **	Iron	10.0 Mg		
Vit A—Carotene	RE	Magnesium	350 Mg		
Vit A—Preformed	RE	Phosphorus	800 Mg		
Vitamin A—Total	1000 RE	Potassium	3750 Mg *		
Thiamin—B1	1.32 Mg	Selenium	125 Mcg *		
Riboflavin—B2	1.59 Mg	Sodium	2200 Mg *		
Niacin—B3	17.5 Mg	Zinc	15.0 Mg		

*Suggested values; within recommended ranges
**Dietary goals   # Fiber = 1 gram/100 kcal

CALORIC CONTENT OF 1 CUP COOKED GRAIN

Grain	Calories
Amaranth	300
Pearled Barley	228
Whole Roasted Buckwheat	162
Bulgur	246
Job's Tears	194
Millet	135
Whole-grain Oats	264
Quinoa	171
White Rice	223
Brown Rice	232
Whole-grain Rye	171
Teff	266
Triticale	228
Whole-grain Wheat	276
Wild Rice	184

Health Tips

When calculating sodium values, I've assumed that the salt has also been omitted from precooked grains if they are called for in the recipe.

The health tips for each recipe are merely a guide to help you alter the recipes for your own special needs, and you can use any of the tips you want or need to. In many recipes in which the health tip is to reduce fat, I have not completely eliminated fat from the recipe. My feeling is that a little fat enhances flavor. If you feel that you want to reduce the fat even more, use skim milk where whole milk is called for, for example, and coat nonstick skillets and saucepans with vegetable-oil cooking spray.

There is one further health tip that applies to almost every recipe. Watch your portion size. Most recipes in this book provide more-than-ample serving sizes. Use your own good sense to determine whether or not you want to eat that much.

Vegetarian Recipes

Many of the recipes in this book are strict vegetarian (vegan) or lacto-ovo vegetarian. Other recipes include suggestions for vegetarian adaptations in the introduction or in the health tips. For instance, in many cases the only meat called for in a recipe will be the broth. For those recipes, it's easy enough to simply substitute vegetable broth.

You can make up a large quantity of the homemade vegetable broth given below and then freeze it in 1¾-cup portions, the standard substitution for a can of beef or chicken broth. If you prefer not to bother (although the result is well worth the effort), you can make a reasonably tasty facsimile from packets or cubes of dried vegetable broth.

———————— ◇ ————————

Vegetable Broth

12 cups (3 quarts) water
¼ head cabbage (about ½ pound)
4 medium carrots, peeled
4 ribs celery
3 medium leeks (both white and green parts), trimmed and well rinsed
3 medium parsnips, peeled
2 medium kohlrabi, peeled
2 white turnips, peeled
1 large tomato
1 large onion, peeled
1 small celeriac, peeled
1 bunch parsley
1 tablespoon lemon juice
¾ teaspoon salt

Place the water, cabbage, carrots, celery, leeks, parsnips, kohlrabi, turnips, tomato, onion, and celeriac in a large saucepot. Bring to a boil over high heat. Reduce heat and simmer, uncovered, for 1 hour and 45 minutes. Add parsley, lemon juice, and salt. Simmer for 30 minutes longer. Strain broth through a colander, pressing the vegetables with the back of a spoon to extract all of their essence before discarding.

Freeze broth in 1¾ cup portions.

MAKES ABOUT 5 CUPS.
CALORIES: 30   CHOLESTEROL: 0 mg   SODIUM: 95 mg   FIBER: 0g

Health tip:
Omit salt.
CALORIES: 30   CHOLESTEROL: 0 mg   SODIUM: 0 mg   FIBER: 0g

Sprouting

Sprouting is the process of soaking and draining whole grains until a shoot appears. Although all kinds of sprouts are generally available these days, even at the supermarket, it's still fun to make your own.

You will need a 1-quart jar, cheesecloth, and two rubberbands.

Place 3 tablespoons of whole grains into the jar (only use 2 tablespoons for the smaller grains, such as teff) and fill it half full with water. Let stand, uncovered, for about 8 hours, but not much longer, or until doubled in size. Drain off the water. (Although it won't look terribly appetizing, it's now rich in minerals and you can use this nutritious water for cooking or for watering your plants.)

Rinse the grains thoroughly in fresh water and drain well. Put the grains back in the jar. Cover the top of the jar with a piece of cheesecloth and fasten it with rubberbands. Lay the jar on its side in a spot that is dark, or at least dim. It's best if you elevate the back of the jar so that any excess water can drain off. Repeat this procedure three times a day until the grains have sprouted. It's important that during this time the grains are not too damp or too dry. If the grains are too wet they will rot (you'll know by the smell), and if they're too dry they will shrivel and die.

When the sprouts are about as long as the grain (this will take about three days, but the time can vary, depending on the temperature and even on the grain itself) they are ready to be eaten either raw or cooked.

Sources

Here are some addresses for sources of unusual and hard-to-find foods and equipment. They all do mail order.

Grains:

Arrowhead Mills
P.O. Box 2059
Hereford, TX 79045
Grains, cereals, beans

Deer Valley Farm
R.D. 1
Guilford, NY 13780
Grains, beans, baked goods, and health-food items (organic)

Eden Foods, Inc.
701 Tecumseh Road
Clinton, MI 49236
*Grains, beans, baked goods, Japanese products, pastas, snacks,
    lima products from Belgium*

Garden Spot Distributors
438 White Oak Road
New Holland, PA 17557
*Grains, breads, beans, nuts, seeds, dried fruits, herbs, and
    health-food items*

Walnut Acres
Penns Creek, PA 17862
*Grains, beans, prepared foods, baked goods, equipment
    including grain mills)*

Gourmet and Ethnic Foods and Equipment:

Balducci's
424 Sixth Avenue
New York, NY 10011
Unusual produce, meats, cheeses, Italian specialty foods

Dean and DeLuca
560 Broadway
New York, NY 10012
Fresh produce, grains, beans, herbs, cheeses, kitchen equipment

Kam Man Food Products
200 Canal Street
New York, NY 10012
Chinese products

Foods of India
121 Lexington Avenue
New York, NY 10016
Specialty rices, bulgur, spices, and Indian goods

Spice and Sweet Mahal
135 Lexington Avenue
New York, NY 10016
Specialty rices, bulgur, spices, and Indian goods

Maskal Forages, Inc.
1318 Willow
Caldwell, ID 83605
Teff Growers

Wild Rice:

Fall River Wild Rice
HC-01
Osprey Drive
Fall River Mills, CA 96028

Gibbs Wild Rice
10400 Billings Road
Live Oak, CA 95053

St. Maries Wild Rice
P.O. Box 293
St. Maries, ID 83861

——— ◇ ———

MAJOR GRAINS:
THE CHOSEN ONES

——— ◇ ———

Wheat
Rice
Corn

I can't think of a single person who does not like at least some forms of wheat, rice, and corn, which may account for why these are the grains of choice for most cultures, both ancient and modern, and are the grains that feed the largest populations in the world today.

Initially, the determining factors for a so-called native grain that would become the diet staple for a particular civilization, were the climate and growing conditions. But as time went on, and trade routes became established and personal wealth grew, flavor and other considerations became more important. So, where barley was once the main grain of China, rye, the staple of Scandinavia, and oats, the native grain of both Scotland and Ireland, all of these countries now use more wheat or rice than they do those original grains. (The use of corn, incidentally, has never really caught on in Europe, with the exception of cornmeal for polenta in Italy.) The same is true of many of the other minor grains, as well. As the major grains became available, the wealthy would convert to them, abandoning the native grains as food for the poor. The poor, in turn, hoping to imitate the rich, would also abandon the old grain for new as soon as it was financially possible.

The most unfortunate part of this mass conversion was that in addition to adopting the new grains, processed grains eventually became a status symbol. When white flour and white rice became fashionable, for instance, many of the nutritional advantages of the grains were lost.

To some extent, the grain staple of a country or region is still determined by local growing conditions. For example, in northern India and China, where wheat grows well, the staple foods of these countries are bread in India and noodles in China. In the south, both countries use rice. The southwestern part of North America and Central America still base their diets on corn. But it is still the "big three" that dominate the scene for all developed countries.

I expect that most people in the United States are familiar with at least some form of these three grains. You would have to look far and wide to find someone who has never tasted white bread, long-grain white rice, or corn. On the other hand, the great majority of these people have probably never tasted wheat berries, short-grain rice, or corn bran.

This section includes recipes for many of the classic uses for these grains, as well as new uses for their less-familiar forms.

WHEAT

(Triticum)

I t is of little wonder that wheat is still referred to as the staff of life, for it is the most widely grown and consumed grain in the world. Although it is available in many forms, flour is the wheat form most commonly used, usually for noodles, breads, and other baked goods.

Wheat comes in hundreds of different varieties, but the types used in the United States are red (really a reddish brown) and white (really a golden color).

Hard and *soft* refers to the physical hardness of the wheat. Technically, either hard or soft wheat can be high in gluten, a plant protein which, when kneaded, develops elasticity that allows dough to rise. As far as the consumer is concerned, hard wheat means the high-gluten wheat that is generally used as bread flour, and soft wheat is the low-gluten wheat used for pastry flour.

Durum wheat is a very hard spring wheat. It is used to make semolina and semolina flour, which is important in pasta making. Durum wheat is also used for making couscous.

Winter wheat, and spring wheat (sometimes called summer wheat), refer to the time of year the wheat is planted. Spring wheat tends to have a higher gluten content than winter wheat.

Types of Wheat Products Available

Whole-grain wheat (wheat berries): The whole kernel with just the hull removed. When it is cooked, it can be used in the same manner as rice, as a side dish or in salads.

Cracked wheat: This is exactly what the name implies: wheat cracked into varying degrees of coarseness, generally coarse, medium, and fine. It can be made from red or white wheat and can be distinguished from bulgur by the white uncooked center of the cracked kernels. Cracked wheat still has the bran and germ intact and so is high in fiber. If you cannot find cracked wheat, but have access to wheat berries, you can make you own by placing the berries in an electric blender container and processing until coarsely ground. Sift out the very fine flour, and the remaining coarse pieces are cracked wheat.

27

Bulgur (bulghur or bulgar): Wheat berries that are pearled (the bran is removed), cooked (steamed), and dried. After drying, the berries are cracked into varying degrees of coarseness. Bulgur is uniform in color, differentiating it from cracked wheat. It requires less cooking time than cracked wheat, since it has already been cooked once. The fine grind is the one most commonly used for packaged mixes, such as tabouli (tabooli). The medium grind is the more common form of bulgur, and usually the one found in bins at health-food stores. Indian and Pakistani stores are more likely to carry four grinds. You can make your own bulgur by cooking wheat berries (see Basic Cooking Instructions), then spreading them in a single layer on a large baking sheet. Bake at 250° F for about an hour, or until completely dried. Cool, then process in a blender or food processor until broken into pieces. Place in a strainer to remove the particles that have been ground too finely.

Couscous: The bran and germ have been removed from durum wheat and the endosperm (the semolina) has been steamed, agglomerated (that means that the small pieces have been pressed together to make bigger ones), and dried. Couscous comes in fine, medium, and coarse grinds, but is most commonly available in a medium grind.

Wheat germ: As the name suggests, this is the germ (embryo) of the wheat. It is available raw, but the type with which we are most familiar has been toasted, sometimes with honey. Wheat germ has a high fat content and will turn rancid quickly unless stored in the refrigerator. (If the germ has been vacuum packed, it won't need refrigeration until after it has been opened.) Wheat germ is usually sprinkled on cereal or yogurt, or added to baked goods to boost the fiber and nutrition content.

Wheat bran (miller's bran/unprocessed wheat bran): The hard layer of the wheat kernel found under the hull. It is fiber rich and comes finely or coarsely ground. Wheat bran is valued for its high fiber content and is rarely used by itself, but rather as a nutrition booster in baked goods, cereals, meat loaves, and other cooked foods. Do not confuse pure wheat bran with breakfast cereals that have names that sound like they are purely bran. In addition to some wheat bran, these cereals also contain sugar, flavorings, and vitamin supplements. Pure wheat bran looks and tastes like sawdust.

Seitan: A meat substitute made of gluten (wheat protein), with a chewy consistency somewhere between a sponge and a rubber band. The flavor is bland, and it frequently comes packed in soy sauce. This is definitely an acquired taste.

Wheat flakes (rolled wheat): Steamed wheat berries, rolled flat, and is similar to oat, rye, and barley flakes.

Meals: A fine grind of wheat that is used for cereal.
    FARINA: The endosperm of the wheat.
    WHEATINA: The whole grain.
    SEMOLINA: The endosperm of durum wheat.

Flour: The Finest Grind of Wheat

White flour is the ground endosperm. In addition, white flour can be bleached to be more visually appealing. Whole-wheat products are not bleached.

Graham flour: Flour made with the whole-wheat kernel. It has a coarser bran and always includes the germ. Extra germ is sometimes added.

Whole-wheat flour: The name implies that this is the ground whole-wheat kernel. In fact, usually some or all of the germ is removed to prolong shelf life. The term graham flour is often used to describe whole-wheat flour. There are no hard and fast rules about this.

Bread flour: It is usually unbleached and made of high-gluten wheat. As the name indicates, it is best for bread making.

Pastry flour: Flour made from low-gluten wheat that is best for cakes, pastry, and other tender baked goods. It can be made from either white or whole-wheat flour.

Cake flour: Bleached white pastry flour. If substituting for all-purpose flour: 1 cup plus 2 tablespoons cake flour equals 1 cup all-purpose flour.

All-purpose flour: This is the work horse of flours, and is a combination of high- and low-gluten flours. The proportions vary depending on the region where the milling is being done. All-purpose flour can be bleached or unbleached. All-purpose flour can be substituted for cake flour if it is sifted three times before measuring.

Self-rising flour: Flour that has had baking powder and salt added (about 1½ teaspoons baking powder and ½ teaspoon salt per cup). Available as both cake and all-purpose flour.

Semolina flour: Finely ground semolina that is primarily used in pasta making.

Texture and Flavor

The flavor of wheat is pleasing, but difficult to describe. It is mild and pleasant tasting, making it the perfect foil for anything the cook cares to cook or serve in it or with it.

The texture of the cooked whole-wheat berry should be slightly chewy and, for the most part, the berries should swell, but not burst, when they are cooked. The berries usually burst when they are cooked with too much water, and the results will be stickier than desirable. On the other hand, too little water will produce cooked berries that are a little too chewy. Cooked wheat berries should have a pleasant pop when you bite into them, which always reminds me of a whole cherry tomato.

Bulgur, cracked wheat, and couscous cook to a similar texture. They should be fluffy, not soggy or very sticky, and will not have the characteristic pop or chewiness of the cooked whole grain. Cooked cracked wheat is a little heavier and starchier than bulgur. This is because it has not been precooked and still retains its bran layer. Couscous is fluffier and drier than either bulgur or cracked wheat.

The germ is the most flavorful part of the grain. Its flavor is a cross between corn and pignoli nuts, which comes through best in its toasted form, which is also the form most commonly available. The texture is dry and crunchy.

Wheat bran is very dry, feather light, and extremely tasteless.

Wheat flakes cook into a delightful porridge, and can be added, uncooked, to baked goods for a crunchy consistency.

What I call "meals" are better known as hot breakfast cereals. The cooked texture is very soft and creamy. Cereal which has the bran intact will have some crunchy texture along with the characteristic creaminess. Cracked wheat and bulgur can also be cooked into cereal by using additional water and allowing longer cooking times.

The flavor of the different types of wheat flour will vary depending on the amount of processing that it has undergone. Graham flour will be the most flavorful, and white flour the least flavorful. The texture of the finished product in which they are used will, of course, vary depending upon the other ingredients used and the cooking method. The only certainty is that products made with a whole-wheat flour will be heavier than those made with white flour.

Compatible Foods, Herbs, and Spices

All wheat products have universally compatible flavors, and can be used for sweet or savory dishes. Of all the grains, wheat is certainly the most versatile in every way.

Availability

Whole-wheat berries, bulgur, cracked wheat, wheat bran, wheat flakes, wheat germ, and whole-wheat flour can almost always be found in health-food stores and through mail-order grain catalogs (see page 21).

Wheat meals (hot cereals), and sometimes bulgur, cracked wheat, and wheat germ, are carried by supermarkets in the cereals section.

Couscous, and sometimes bulgur and cracked wheat, can be found in the rice, health foods, or international foods sections of the supermarket.

All flours, with the exception of whole-wheat pastry flour and semolina flour, can usually be found at the supermarket with other baking products.

Couscous, semolina, semolina flour, bulgur, and cracked wheat can sometimes, but not always, be found in gourmet or specialty-food stores, and foreign-import stores. Check out Italian and Middle Eastern stores.

Nutritional Content

The more the wheat berry is processed, the more the nutritional qualities go down. Whole-wheat berries and cracked wheat, as well as wheat bran, wheat germ, and whole-wheat flour, are high-fiber foods. Bulgur, couscous, farina, semolina, and white flours have all been denuded of the bran and germ and so have insignificant fiber content.

Wheat germ is a good source of vitamin E, some protein and B vitamins, and fiber. When the germ is discarded, much of the nutritional value of the wheat goes with it.

The bran is the highest source of fiber in the wheat berry. It is also the source of many minerals, notably magnesium and phosphorous, and some B vitamins.

What remains of its nutritional profile once the wheat berry has lost its bran and germ, are starch, and some protein and B vitamins, a mere shadow of the original high-nutrition whole-wheat berry.

Substitutions

Whole-grain Wheat

Any groat or berry (triticale, rye, and oats) can be substituted for wheat berries, but check the other grains for flavor comparisons and cooking times.

Cooked short-grain brown rice: Has a crunchiness similar to the cooked whole-wheat berry.

Barley: Can also be used as a substitute for cooked whole-wheat berries.

Other acceptable substitutes (in order of preference): Job's tears (adjust cooking times).

Bulgur and Cracked Wheat

These two are absolutely interchangeable. Simply adjust cooking times.

Other acceptable substitutes (in order of preference):

Couscous: The perfect substitute for cooked bulgur or cracked wheat, but allowances must be made for the difference in cooking times before using raw couscous in recipes calling for raw bulgur or raw cracked wheat.

Brown rice: A suitable flavor substitute.

Buckwheat and millet: Both are fine texture substitutes, but each has an overpowering flavor that must be taken into consideration before making direct substitutions.

Cooked Couscous

Rizcous, a rice product, is a perfect substitute for couscous. Both cooked bulgur and cracked wheat are excellent substitutions.

Other acceptable substitutes (in order of preference): Millet (cooked by Method I) has a very similar texture, but the flavor will be significantly different. Cooked white rice is suitable, and cooked small pasta shapes are acceptable.

Seitan

Tofu (especially the pressed type) is the only substitute for seitan.

Wheat Flakes

Any grain flake can be interchanged for wheat flakes, but be sure and make flavor comparisons. (Incidentally, I am not referring to breakfast flakes, such as corn flakes.)

Flours

Most recipes for baked goods are a delicate balance between flour, liquid, fat, leavening agents, and sometimes sugar. To randomly substitute one kind of flour for another is simply inviting a baking disaster.

Yeast breads tend to be more forgiving of flour substitutions than delicate cakes and cookies. If you prefer using whole-wheat flour rather than the white flour called for in a recipe, I would suggest finding a similar reliable recipe that has been developed for the use of whole-wheat flour, rather than trying to do a conversion yourself.

Basic Cooking Instructions

Please read *About Cooking Grains* beginning on page 7.

The microwave methods that follow were tested in a 650-watt oven.

Whole-grain Wheat

Please note that salt must always be added *after cooking,* or the whole grain will not absorb the cooking water. Do not cook with broth.

Stove-top method:

> 2½ cups water
> 1 cup whole-grain wheat, rinsed
> ½ teaspoon salt

In a 2-quart saucepan, bring water to a boil over high heat. Stir in wheat and return to boiling. Reduce heat and simmer, covered, for 2 hours, or until almost all of the liquid has been absorbed. Remove from heat and let stand, covered, for 15 minutes. Add salt and fluff with a fork.

MAKES 2¾ CUPS.

Microwave method:

Please note that salt must always be added *after cooking,* or the whole grain will not absorb the water. Do not cook with broth.

> 3 cups water
> 1 cup whole-grain wheat, rinsed
> ½ teaspoon salt

Place water in a 3-quart, microwave-safe bowl. Cover with waxed paper and microwave on high (100% power) for 5 minutes. Stir in wheat. Recover with waxed paper and microwave on high for 5 minutes. Microwave on medium (50% power), still covered with waxed paper, for 1 hour. Let stand 5 minutes. Stir in salt and fluff with a fork.

MAKES 2¼ CUPS.

Medium Bulgur or Cracked Wheat

Stove-top method:

> 2 cups water
> ¾ teaspoon salt
> 1 cup medium bulgur or cracked wheat (do not rinse)

In a 2-quart saucepan, bring the water and salt to a boil over high heat. Stir in bulgur or cracked wheat and return to boiling. Reduce heat and simmer, covered, for 20 minutes, or until almost all the liquid has been absorbed. Remove from heat and let stand, covered, for 5 minutes. Fluff with a fork.

MAKES 3 CUPS.

Microwave method:

> 1¾ cups water
> ¾ teaspoon salt
> 1 cup medium bulgur or cracked wheat (do not rinse)

Place the water and salt in a 3-quart, microwave-safe bowl. Cover with waxed paper and microwave on high (100% power) for 3 minutes. Stir in bulgur or cracked wheat. Recover with waxed paper and microwave on high for 3 minutes. Microwave on medium (50% power), still covered with waxed paper, for 30 minutes. Let stand 2 minutes. Fluff with a fork.

MAKES 3 CUPS.

No-cook method for fine bulgur:

> 1 cup fine bulgur (do not rinse)
> 2 cups boiling water
> ½ teaspoon salt

Place the bulgur in a medium-size bowl. Stir in boiling water and salt. Cover tightly with plastic wrap and let stand for 20 minutes. Fluff with a fork.

MAKES 2½ CUPS.

Stove-top method for fine cracked wheat:

> 2 cups water
> ½ teaspoon salt
> 1 cup fine cracked wheat (do not rinse)

In a 2-quart saucepan, bring the water and salt to a boil over high heat. Stir in cracked wheat and return to boiling. Reduce heat and simmer, covered, for 5 minutes, or until almost all of the liquid has been absorbed. Remove from heat and let stand for 10 minutes. Fluff with a fork.

MAKES 4 CUPS.

No-cook method for couscous:

> 1 cup couscous
> 1¾ cups water
> ½ teaspoon salt

Place couscous in a medium-size bowl. Stir in boiling water and salt and let stand for 5 minutes. Fluff with a fork.

MAKES 2¾ CUPS.

Stove-top method for authentic couscous:

1½ cups couscous
⅔ cup water

Place couscous in a fine strainer. Rinse under cool water until all of the grains have been moistened. Turn into an 8 × 13-inch baking pan. Spread evenly in the pan and let stand for 20 minutes.

In a large saucepan (which should contain the simmering stew that you intend to serve with the couscous), place a steamer, strainer, or colander that fits well into the top of the pot. The bottom of the steamer should be above the stew, not in it.

Line the steamer with a double layer of cheesecloth. If you see steam escaping around the edge of the steamer, tape a doubled length of foil around the side of the pot. Bring the foil up and tuck it into the inside of the steamer, sealing the edges so that the steam is forced through the holes in the steamer and through the couscous.

Sift the couscous through your fingers to break up any lumps and place in the lined steamer. Steam, uncovered, for 20 minutes. Turn the couscous into the baking pan, then gradually stir the water into the couscous. Spread couscous evenly in the pan and let stand for 20 minutes.

Return couscous to the lined steamer and steam for 30 minutes more.

Reheating:

Wheat products can be reheated by lightly steaming or microwaving.

WHEAT RECIPES

(* indicates easy recipes)

———————◇———————

Cheese Straws *
Zucchini Sticks with Honey-Mustard Dipping Sauce
Wheat Berry Scampi *
Coq au Vin with Couscous
Spicy Pork with Lychees
Couscous with Moroccan Lamb Stew
Not Quite Spaghetti and Meat Sauce
Chicken-y Salad with Creamy Garlic Dressing *
Caesar Salad with Seitan Croutons
Tabouli *
Bulgur Tofu Salad *
Fruity Bulgur Salad *
Wheat Berry Tomato Salad *
Bulgur Chili
Broccoli with Wheat Flake Topping *
Kasha and Wheat Berries *
Wheat Berry Veggy Melt *
Couscous with Broiled Vegetables
Whole-Wheat Couscous with Lentils *
Brown Rice and Wheat Berries *
Bulgur Pea-laf *
Fresh Pasta
Fresh Pasta with Egg
Marinara Sauce *
Pesto *
Bolognese Sauce *
Puttanesca Plus Sauce *
Fettucini Alfredo *
The World's Best Pizza
Plain Old White Bread
Whole Wheat Bread
French Bread
Semolina Bread
Cornell Bread
Wheat-Germ Rolls
Delicious Pancakes *
Vanilla Waffles *
Apple Pie Waffles
Maple French Toast *
Whole-Wheat Biscuits *
Basic Muffins *
Pineapple Bran Muffins *
Orange Popovers

37

Basic Sweet Dough
Pecan Coffee Ring
Cream Puffs (Profiteroles)
Puff Pastry (Feuillete)
Puffy Apple Tarts *
Easy Napoleons *
Angel-Food Cake
Whole Wheat Carrot Cake
Sour Cream Apple Cake
Yellow Cake with Vanilla Buttercream Frosting
Decadent Chocolate Cake
Jelly Roll Cake
Mim Jaffe's Butter Cookies *
My Famous Peach Pie

Cheese Straws

These are one of my favorite things to serve with a rich creamy soup. You can also serve them as hors d'oeuvres. If you don't want to make your own puff pastry, you can use prepared frozen puff pastry sheets, thawed. If you are not having a lot of company, you can halve the recipe and freeze the leftover puff pastry.

½ cup grated Parmesan cheese
1 teaspoon paprika
½ teaspoon chili powder
⅛ teaspoon ground red pepper
1 recipe puff pastry (page 81)

Preheat oven to 400°F.

In a medium-size bowl, toss together the Parmesan cheese, paprika, chili powder, and pepper.

Roll half of the pastry into an 8 × 18-inch rectangle. Sprinkle with one quarter of the cheese mixture. Turn over and sprinkle one-quarter of the cheese mixture on the second side of the pastry.

Cut into strips ½-inch wide (by 8-inches long), using a sharp knife or pizza wheel. Place one end of each strip in each hand. Twist in opposite directions to produce a candy-cane effect. Place on ungreased baking sheets. Roll out the second half of the dough and repeat. Bake 12 minutes or until completely puffed. Serve warm or room temperature.

MAKES 4 DOZEN.
CALORIES: 51 CHOLESTEROL: 11 mg SODIUM: 47 mg FIBER: 0 g

Health tip:
Eat just one.

——————— ◇ ———————

Zucchini Sticks with Honey-Mustard Dipping Sauce

The wheat germ makes these extra crunchy. I like to serve them at parties.

Zucchini Sticks:

⅓ cup flour
½ teaspoon salt
¼ teaspoon ground red pepper
2 eggs
1 tablespoon water
⅔ cup wheat germ (regular or honey crunch)
⅓ cup bread crumbs
4 to 5 cups zucchini sticks (3 × ½ × ½-inch)
Oil for frying

Honey-Mustard Dipping Sauce:

¼ cup sour cream
¼ cup plain yogurt
¼ cup mayonnaise
1½ tablespoons honey mustard

On waxed paper, stir together the flour, salt, and pepper.

In a shallow bowl, beat the eggs with the water.

On a separate piece of waxed paper, stir together the wheat germ and bread crumbs.

Dredge the zucchini in the flour mixture, dip in the egg, and then roll in the wheat germ.

Pour enough oil into a skillet to be ½-inch deep. Heat until the oil bubbles as soon as some bread crumbs are dropped in.

Fry the zucchini until golden on both sides. Drain on paper towels.

In a medium-size bowl, stir together the sour cream, yogurt, mayonnaise, and mustard. Serve with fried zucchini sticks.

SERVES 12 (makes 48 zucchini sticks and ¾ cup sauce).
CALORIES: 124   CHOLESTEROL: 40 mg   SODIUM: 178 mg   FIBER: 1 g

Health tip:
Omit the salt; use additional yogurt instead of the sour cream; and use reduced-calorie mayonnaise.
CALORIES: 95   CHOLESTEROL: 36 mg   SODIUM: 89 mg   FIBER: 1 g

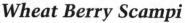

Wheat Berry Scampi

I'm a great garlic lover and this dish is right up my alley. It's an easy dish to prepare and a nice way to introduce people to cooked wheat berries.

½ cup butter
4 cloves garlic, minced
1½ pounds shrimp, peeled and cleaned
¼ cup chopped parsley
1 tablespoon lemon juice
¼ teaspoon pepper
2¾ cups cooked wheat berries

In a large skillet, melt the butter over medium-high heat. Add the garlic and sauté 30 seconds. Add the shrimp and sauté until the shrimp are just cooked through.

Stir in the parsley, lemon juice, and pepper. Stir in the wheat berries and cook, stirring until heated through.

SERVES 4.
CALORIES: 569 mg   CHOLESTEROL: 394 mg   SODIUM: 952 mg   FIBER: 3 g

Health tip:
Use ¼ cup unsalted margarine instead of ½ cup butter; omit the salt from the wheat berries.
CALORIES: 467   CHOLESTEROL: 332 mg   SODIUM: 399 mg   FIBER: 3 g

—————— ◇ ——————

Coq au Vin with Couscous

This is a stew that you can cook the couscous over, if you are using the semi-authentic cooking method; or you can just serve the no-cook couscous on the side.

3½ pound chicken, cut up
¼ cup flour
1 teaspoon salt
1 teaspoon paprika
¼ teaspoon pepper
⅛ teaspoon nutmeg
2 tablespoons butter
2 tablespoons oil
3 tablespoons warm brandy
1½ cups red wine
½ cup water
12 small white onions
1 package (10-ounce) fresh mushrooms, rinsed and bottom ends
    trimmed
2 tablespoons chopped parsley
½ teaspoon rosemary
¼ teaspoon thyme
1 cup couscous (steamed traditionally over the stew or soaked in
    boiling water according to package directions)

Rinse the chicken and pat dry.

On a piece of waxed paper or aluminum foil, stir together the flour, salt, paprika, pepper; and nutmeg. Dredge the chicken in the flour mixture.

In a large saucepan, melt the butter and oil over medium-high heat. Add the chicken and brown on all sides. Pour in the brandy and ignite.

After the flames have extinguished, stir in the wine, water, onions, mushrooms, parsley, rosemary, and thyme. Bring to a boil. Reduce heat and simmer, uncovered, 45 minutes or until the chicken is tender.

Serve over the couscous.

SERVES 4.
CALORIES: 765   CHOLESTEROL: 213 mg   SODIUM: 813 mg   FIBER: 11 g

Health tip:
Cook chicken without skin; omit butter and use only 1 tablespoon oil and cook in nonstick saucepan. Omit salt.
CALORIES: 636   CHOLESTEROL: 169 mg   SODIUM: 201 mg   FIBER: 11 g

——————— ◇ ———————

Spicy Pork with Lychees

This dish is great. I like the combination of exotic and sweet and spicy flavors.

1 pork tenderloin (1½ pound)
1 can (20 ounce) lychees, in heavy syrup, undrained
3 tablespoons soy sauce
2 tablespoons mirin (a sweet rice wine available in Oriental grocery
   stores) or sherry
1 tablespoon cornstarch
1 tablespoon rice vinegar
1 tablespoon sugar
2 cloves garlic, minced
2 teaspoons minced ginger
1 teaspoon chili oil
3 tablespoons oil
1 cup sliced onion
2 cups cooked wheat berries

Thinly slice the tenderloin

Drain lychee nuts, reserving ⅓ cup of syrup. In a small bowl, stir together the soy sauce, mirin, cornstarch, vinegar, sugar, garlic, ginger, chili oil, and lychee syrup; set aside.

In a wok or large skillet, heat the oil over high heat. Add one third of the pork and stir-fry until cooked through. Remove from wok (or skillet) and cook the remaining 2 batches of pork and set aside. Add the onion and cook, stirring, until soft. Stir in the sauce mixture and cook, stirring, until thick. Return the pork to the skillet and add the lychees. Cook, stirring, until heated through. Add the wheat berries and cook, stirring, until heated through.

SERVES 6.
CALORIES: 607   CHOLESTEROL: 109 mg   SODIUM: 848 mg   FIBER: 4 g

Health tip:
Use low-sodium soy sauce and reduce oil to 2 teaspoons and cook in a non-stick skillet. Omit salt when cooking wheat berries.
CALORIES: 559   CHOLESTEROL: 100 mg   SODIUM: 431 mg   FIBER: 4 g

——————— ◇ ———————

Couscous with Moroccan Lamb Stew

This is a stew typical of one that you would cook in the bottom of your couscousinere while you steam the couscous in the top. Follow the instructions for semi-authentic couscous and steam it over this stew.

> 3 tablespoons oil
> 2 cups chopped onion
> 3 cloves garlic, minced
> 1 teaspoon salt
> ½ teaspoon cinnamon
> ½ teaspoon ginger
> ¼ teaspoon clove
> ¼ teaspoon ground red pepper
> 3 cups water
> 2 tablespoons dark-brown sugar
> 2 pounds cubed lamb
> 2 cups cubed rutabaga or turnips
> 2 cups thickly sliced carrots
> 1 can (19 ounce) chick-peas, drained
> ½ cup mini pitted prunes
> ½ cup raisins
> 3 tablespoons lemon juice
> 2 cups cooked couscous

In a large saucepan, heat the oil over medium-high heat. Add the onion and garlic and cook, stirring, until onion is soft. Stir in the salt, cinnamon, ginger, clove, and red pepper until absorbed. Add the water and brown sugar; bring to a boil. Add the lamb and return to a boil. Reduce heat and simmer, covered, 1 hour. Add the rutabaga and carrots. Simmer, uncovered, 30 minutes. Add the chick-peas, prunes, and raisins. Simmer, uncovered, 30 minutes longer. Stir in the lemon juice. Serve over couscous.

SERVES 6.
CALORIES: 899   CHOLESTEROL: 185 mg   SODIUM: 517 mg   FIBER: 11 g

Health tip:
Reduce the oil to 2 teaspoons and cook in a nonstick saucepan; omit salt.
CALORIES: 879 mg   CHOLESTEROL: 185 mg   SODIUM: 178 mg   FIBER: 11 g

---------------◇---------------

Not Quite Spaghetti and Meat Sauce

What a delicious treat! If you didn't mention that there was no meat in the meat sauce, no one would be any the wiser.

1 spaghetti squash (2 pound)
2 tablespoons olive oil
1 cup chopped onion
2 cloves garlic, minced
1 can (14½ ounce) whole peeled tomatoes, undrained
1 can (8 ounce) tomato sauce
1 tablespoon chopped parsley
1 bay leaf
1 teaspoon basil
½ teaspoon oregano
¼ teaspoon sugar
¼ teaspoon salt
⅛ teaspoon pepper
1 cup cooked bulgur

Preheat oven to 375°F.

Cut the squash in half, lengthwise. Scoop out and discard the seeds. Place, cut side down, in a baking dish. Bake 45 to 55 minutes, or until the squash is tender.

While the squash is baking, prepare the sauce. In a 3-quart saucepan, heat the oil over medium-high heat. Add the onion and garlic and cook, stirring, until the onion is soft. Stir in the tomatoes and break up with the back of a spoon. Stir in the tomato sauce, parsley, bay leaf, basil, oregano, sugar, salt, and pepper. Bring to a boil, reduce heat and simmer, uncovered, 20 minutes. Discard the bay leaf. Stir in the bulgur.

Remove the squash from the oven and, using a fork, separate the spaghetti-like strands as you scrape them from the shell. Place in a serving dish and top with sauce.

SERVES 4.
CALORIES: 243   CHOLESTEROL: 0 mg   SODIUM: 837 mg   FIBER: 12 g

Health tip:
Reduce oil to 2 teaspoons and prepare the sauce in a nonstick skillet. Omit the salt.
CALORIES: 204   CHOLESTEROL: 0 mg   SODIUM: 570 mg   FIBER: 12 g

———————◇———————

Chicken-y Salad with Creamy Garlic Dressing

My sister thinks this is really delicious—and I concur.

2 cups cubed cooked chicken
1½ cups cooked wheat berries
1 cup sliced celery
½ cup mayonnaise
3 tablespoons grated Parmesan cheese
1 tablespoon dijon mustard
1 tablespoon lemon juice
1 clove garlic, minced
⅛ teaspoon pepper

In a large bowl, toss together the chicken, wheat berries, and celery.

In a small bowl, stir together the mayonnaise, cheese, mustard, lemon juice, pepper, and garlic. Stir the dressing into the salad.

SERVES 4.
CALORIES: 432   CHOLESTEROL: 159 mg   SODIUM: 309 mg   FIBER: 5 g

Health tip:
Use ¼ cup reduced-calorie mayonnaise and ¼ cup plain yogurt instead of the mayonnaise. Omit salt from wheat berries.
CALORIES: 279   CHOLESTEROL: 66 mg   SODIUM: 237 mg   FIBER: 5 g

———————◇———————

Caesar Salad with Seitan Croutons

The seitan fries up to a soft crouton, but it has a slightly fishy flavor; if you want you can use plain bread croutons.

Oil for frying
½ cup diced seitan, blotted dry with paper towels
3 cloves garlic, divided
3 anchovies
½ teaspoon capers
1 egg yolk
½ teaspoon dry mustard
¼ teaspoon Worcestershire sauce
2 tablespoons olive oil
1 tablespoon lemon juice
1 teaspoon wine vinegar
1 small head romaine lettuce, torn into bite-size pieces
¼ cup grated Parmesan cheese

Pour enough oil into a medium-size skillet to be ½-inch deep. Heat until the oil bubbles as soon as a small piece of seitan is dropped in. Add 2 of the cloves of garlic and then the seitan. Cook the seitan until browned. Drain on paper towels and set aside. Discard garlic.

In a large bowl, mash the anchovies with the capers and the remaining garlic clove, until the mixture is a paste. Stir in the egg yolk, then the mustard and Worcestershire sauce. Stir in the oil, lemon juice, and vinegar.

Add the lettuce to the bowl and toss until coated with the dressing. Top with the seitan croutons and cheese and toss.

SERVES 4.
CALORIES: 99   CHOLESTEROL: 61 mg   SODIUM: 120 mg   FIBER: 1 g

Health tip:
Eat half a portion.
CALORIES: 100   CHOLESTEROL: 30 mg   SODIUM: 60 mg   FIBER: 1 g

––––––––––– ◇ –––––––––––

Tabouli

This is a traditional Middle Eastern salad. You can adjust the amount of mint to your own taste, but it's important that you use fresh, not dried, mint. You can use bulgur if cracked wheat is not available.

2 cups cooked fine-grain cracked wheat, cooled
1 cup chopped cucumber
1 cup chopped tomato
⅓ cup chopped parsley
¼ cup chopped scallion
2 tablespoons chopped mint
1 tablespoon olive oil
1 tablespoon vegetable oil
1 tablespoon lemon juice
½ teaspoon salt
¼ teaspoon pepper

In a large bowl, combine the cracked wheat, cucumber, tomato, parsley, scallion, and mint.

In a small bowl, stir together the oils, lemon juice, salt, and pepper. Pour over salad and toss.

SERVES 6.
CALORIES: 131   CHOLESTEROL: 0 mg   SODIUM: 360 mg   FIBER: 4 g

Health tip:
Use half the dressing and omit the salt.
CALORIES: 111   CHOLESTEROL: 0 mg   SODIUM: 5 mg   FIBER: 4 g

—————— ◊ ——————

Bulgur Tofu Salad

This is a delicious, creamy salad. It complements anything you serve it with—or it can be eaten as a main dish.

1½ cups cooked bulgur
1 cup diced (¼-inch pieces) tofu
½ cup chopped celery
½ cup sliced radish
⅓ cup finely chopped red bell pepper
¼ cup sliced scallion
⅓ cup mayonnaise
3 tablespoons buttermilk
2 tablespoons chopped parsley
1 tablespoons chopped fresh dill
2 teaspoons distilled white vinegar
¼ teaspoon salt
⅛ teaspoon ground red pepper

In a large bowl, toss together the bulgur, tofu, celery, radish, red pepper, and scallion.

In a small bowl, stir together the mayonnaise, buttermilk, parsley, dill, vinegar, salt, and pepper. Pour over the salad and toss until combined.

SERVES 6.
CALORIES: 190   CHOLESTEROL: 7 mg   SODIUM: 313 mg   FIBER: 4 g

Health tip:
Use reduced-calorie mayonnaise; omit salt.
CALORIES: 134   CHOLESTEROL: 4 mg   SODIUM: 90 mg   FIBER: 4 g

—————— ◊ ——————

Fruity Bulgur Salad

I like the fruity taste of the olive oil with the fruits in the salad. The Jerusalem artichoke adds just the right crunch, if you can't find them, use water chestnuts or jicama.

1½ cups bulgur
1 cup diced melon (cantaloupe or honeydew)
½ cup halved grapes
½ cup raspberries
½ cup chopped pecans
½ cup chopped Jerusalem artichoke

2 tablespoons vegetable oil
2 tablespoons olive oil
2 tablespoons lemon juice
1 teaspoon honey mustard
¼ teaspoon salt
⅛ teaspoon pepper

In a large bowl, toss together the bulgur, melon, grapes, raspberries, pecans, and Jerusalem artichoke.

In a small bowl, stir together the oils, lemon juice, mustard, salt, and pepper. Pour over salad and toss.

SERVES 6.

CALORIES: 331   CHOLESTEROL: 0 mg   SODIUM: 105 mg   FIBER: 10 g

Health tip:
Halve the dressing and omit salt.

CALORIES: 290   CHOLESTEROL: 0 mg   SODIUM: 10 mg   FIBER: 10 g

———————— ◇ ————————

Wheat Berry Tomato Salad

This salad is absolutely delicious. Like any salad with onion in it, it's best to make just before serving. If you want to make it in advance, leave out the onion and stir it in at the last minute.

2 cups cooked and cooled wheat berries
2 cups chopped tomatoes
½ cup chopped red onion
¼ cup loosely packed basil leaves
1 tablespoon olive oil
1 tablespoon vegetable oil
1 tablespoon red-wine vinegar
½ clove garlic, minced
½ teaspoon salt
¼ teaspoon pepper

In a large bowl, toss together the wheat berries, tomatoes, and onion.

Put the basil, oils, vinegar, garlic, salt, and pepper into a blender container. Cover and blend until smooth. Pour dressing over salad and toss.

SERVES 6.

CALORIES: 132   CHOLESTEROL: 0 mg   SODIUM: 362 mg   FIBER: 3 g

Health tip:
Omit salt.

CALORIES: 152   CHOLESTEROL: 0   SODIUM: 7 mg   FIBER: 3 g

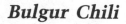

Bulgur Chili

The consistency of the bulgur lends a meat-like consistency to the chili. Serve this with chopped onion, shredded Cheddar, sour cream, sliced olives, or chilies for toppings.

1 cup water
¾ teaspoon salt, divided
½ cup medium or coarse whole-wheat bulgur
2 tablespoons vegetable oil
1 cup chopped onion
1 cup chopped green bell pepper
2 cloves garlic, minced
2½ tablespoons chili powder
2 teaspoons oregano
2 teaspoons paprika
1 teaspoon cumin
2 cans (14½ ounces each) whole peeled tomatoes, undrained
2 cans (16 ounces each) red kidney beans, drained

In a medium-size saucepan, bring the water and ¼ teaspoon of the salt to a boil. Add the bulgur, return to a boil. Reduce the heat and simmer 20 minutes or until the water is absorbed. Remove from heat and set aside.

In a large skillet, heat the oil over medium-high heat. Add onion, green pepper, and garlic and cook, stirring, until onion is soft. Add the chili, oregano, paprika, and cumin and stir until the oil is absorbed. Stir in the tomatoes and break up with the back of a spoon. Stir in the beans, bulgur, and remaining ½ teaspoon salt. Simmer, covered, 20 minutes or until heated through.

SERVES 6.
CALORIES: 272   CHOLESTEROL: 0 mg   SODIUM: 821 mg   FIBER: 18 g

Health tip:
Reduce oil to 2 teaspoons and cook in a nonstick skillet; omit salt.
CALORIES: 246   CHOLESTEROL: 0 mg   SODIUM: 555 mg   FIBER: 18 g

———————◇———————

Broccoli with Wheat Flake Topping

This is a quick and unusual side dish.

2 tablespoons butter
1 cup wheat flakes
¾ cup ready-to-serve chicken or vegetable broth (see page 19)
3 cups broccoli florets
2 tablespoons sunflower seeds

In a large skillet, melt the butter over medium-high heat. Add the wheat flakes, and cook, stirring, until the wheat flakes smell nutty. Remove from skillet and set aside.

Add the broth to the skillet and bring to a boil. Add the broccoli and cook, tossing, until the broccoli is tender-crisp. Add the wheat flakes and sunflower seeds and cook, tossing, 1 minute longer.

SERVES 4.
CALORIES: 174   CHOLESTEROL: 16 mg   SODIUM: 213 mg   FIBER: 5 g

Health tip:
Use 2 teaspoons unsalted margarine instead of the butter and cook in a nonstick skillet. Use low-sodium broth.
CALORIES: 156   CHOLESTEROL: 4 mg   SODIUM: 77 mg   FIBER: 5 g

Kasha and Wheat Berries

I like the fluffy kasha mixed with the crunch of cashews and the chewiness of the wheat berries.

2¼ cups water
½ cup wheat berries (whole grain wheat)
½ cup whole-grain kasha
½ cup chopped cashews
3 tablespoons butter
½ teaspoon salt
⅛ teaspoon pepper

In a 2-quart saucepan bring the water to a boil. Stir in the wheat berries and return to a boil. Reduce heat and simmer 1 hour and 45 minutes. Stir in the kasha and return to a boil. Reduce heat and simmer 12 minutes. Stir in the nuts, butter, salt, and pepper.

SERVES 8.
CALORIES: 165   CHOLESTEROL: 12 mg   SODIUM: 171 mg   FIBER: 3 g

Health tip:
Omit salt and butter.
CALORIES: 127   CHOLESTEROL: 0 mg   SODIUM: 2 mg   FIBER: 3 g

—————◇—————

Wheat Berry Veggy Melt

You can prepare this casserole in advance, and instead of broiling the cheese at the last minute, you can bake the casserole at 375°F until the cheese is melted and the vegetable mixture is heated through.

2 cups cubed peeled butternut squash
1 cup sliced carrots
1 cup sliced yellow squash
2 cups cooked wheat berries
2 tablespoons chopped scallion
1 tablespoon soy sauce
2 cups shredded Monterey Jack cheese

Preheat the broiler.

Place the hubbard squash and carrots in a steamer over boiling water. Cover and steam 10 minutes. Add the yellow squash and steam 5 minutes longer, or until all the vegetables are tender.

In a 2-quart casserole, toss the vegetables with the wheat berries, scallion, and soy sauce. Sprinkle with the cheese and broil 5 minutes, or until the cheese is melted and browned.

SERVES 4.
CALORIES: 388   CHOLESTEROL: 52 mg   SODIUM: 844 mg   FIBER: 4 g

Health tip:
Use low-sodium soy sauce and only half the cheese. Cook wheat berries without salt.
CALORIES: 282   CHOLESTEROL: 26 mg   SODIUM: 355 mg   FIBER: 4 g

––––––––––– ◊ –––––––––––

Couscous with Broiled Vegetables

It's important that the vegetables are well browned in order to bring out their sweetness.

1 medium eggplant
2 medium yellow squash
1 large red onion
3 tablespoons olive oil
2 tablespoons vegetable oil
3 cloves garlic, minced
¼ teaspoon thyme
¼ teaspoon oregano
1¼ cups water
½ teaspoon salt
1 cup couscous
2 tablespoons lemon juice
2 tablespoons chopped parsley

Preheat the broiler.

Cut the eggplant and squash, lengthwise, into ½-inch thick slices. Cut the onion into ¼-inch slices.

In a medium-size bowl, combine the oils, garlic, thyme, and oregano. Place the vegetables in a single layer on baking sheets. Brush with the marinade. Broil until browned or slightly charred. Turn, brush with more marinade and broil until browned on second side. Separate the onion slices into rings. Slice the eggplant and squash into finger-size pieces; set aside.

In a 2-quart saucepan, bring the water and salt to a boil. Stir in the couscous and simmer 2 minutes. Stir in the vegetables and let stand 5 minutes. Stir in the lemon juice and parsley.

SERVES 6.
CALORIES: 244   CHOLESTEROL: 0 mg   SODIUM: 187 mg   FIBER: 11 g

Health tip:
Use only half the oil and brush the vegetables lightly before broiling; omit the salt.
CALORIES: 194   CHOLESTEROL: 0 mg   SODIUM: 9 mg   FIBER: 11 g

———————— ◇ ————————

Whole-Wheat Couscous with Lentils

The cinnamon and currants make this a very unusual dish.

½ stick cinnamon
6 whole cloves
2 tablespoons oil
½ cup chopped onion
1 clove garlic, minced
2¼ cups water
½ teaspoon salt
½ cup lentils
½ cup whole-wheat couscous
½ cup currants
2 tablespoons chopped parsley
2 tablespoons butter

Wrap the cinnamon and cloves in a piece of cheesecloth and tie with a string. Set aside.

In a 2-quart saucepan, heat the oil over medium-high heat. Add the onion and garlic and cook, stirring, until onion is soft. Add the water and salt, and bring to a boil. Add the lentils and spice sack, and return to a boil. Reduce heat and simmer 50 minutes.

Stir in the couscous and simmer 3 minutes. Remove from heat, let stand 5 minutes. Discard packet with spices. Stir in currants, parsley, and butter.

SERVES 4.
CALORIES: 282   CHOLESTEROL: 15 mg   SODIUM: 319 mg   FIBER: 8 g

Health tip:
Omit salt and butter, reduce oil to 2 teaspoons and cook in nonstick saucepan.
CALORIES: 192   CHOLESTEROL: 0 mg   SODIUM: 4 mg   FIBER: 8 g

—————— ◇ ——————

Brown Rice and Wheat Berries

The simplicity of the flavors make this an elegant side dish.

2¼ cups water
⅓ cup wheat berries (whole grain wheat)
⅓ cup long-grain brown rice
1 tablespoon butter
2 tablespoons pignoli
¼ cup chopped scallion
¼ teaspoon salt
⅛ teaspoon pepper

In a 2-quart saucepan, bring the water to a boil over high heat. Add the wheat berries and return to a boil. Reduce heat and simmer, covered, 1 hour.

Stir in the brown rice. Cover and simmer 50 minutes longer.

Melt the butter in a small skillet over medium heat 5 minutes before the rice is cooked. Add the pignoli and cook until lightly toasted. Stir in the scallion, and cook until softened. Stir the pignoli mixture into the rice along with the salt and pepper.

SERVES 4.
CALORIES: 170 CHOLESTEROL: 8 mg SODIUM: 160 mg FIBER: 3 g

Health tip:
Omit the salt and use unsalted margarine instead of butter; omit pignoli.
CALORIES: 130 CHOLESTEROL: 0 mg SODIUM: 6 mg FIBER: 2 g

—————— ◇ ——————

Bulgur Pea-laf

This is a lovely tasting pilaf. I used the pepper to bring out the flavor; you can use less.

2 tablespoons oil
1 cup medium or coarse bulgur
⅓ cup finely chopped onion
1 can (13¾ ounce) ready-to-serve chicken broth or
    1¾ cups vegetable broth (see page 19)
¼ cup water
1 cup frozen peas
2 tablespoons chopped parsley
¼ teaspoon pepper

In a 2-quart saucepan, heat the oil over medium-high heat. Add the bulgur and onion and cook, stirring, until the onion is soft and the bulgur smells nutty.

Add the broth and water, and bring to a boil over high heat. Reduce the heat and simmer, covered, 20 minutes. Stir in the peas, parsley, and pepper. Simmer 5 minutes longer, or until the peas are heated through.

SERVES 6.
CALORIES: 175   CHOLESTEROL: 0 mg   SODIUM: 231 mg   FIBER: 7 g

Health tip:
Use low-sodium broth; reduce oil to 1 tablespoon and cook in a nonstick saucepan.
CALORIES: 155   CHOLESTEROL: 0 mg   SODIUM: 37 mg   FIBER: 7 g

———————— ◇ ————————

Fresh Pasta

These noodles have a very lovely al dente consistency when cooked.

2 cups semolina flour
1½ cups all-purpose flour
1 teaspoon salt
1 cup warm water
2 tablespoons olive oil

In a large bowl, combine the semolina and all-purpose flours, and the salt. Make a well in the center.

Add the water and oil to the well. Using a wooden spoon, start mixing in small circles gradually making larger circles. Incorporate more of the flour as you mix, until you have mixed in as much of the flour as you can and are stirring big circles around the edge of the bowl.

Turn the dough, and any flour that has not been mixed in, onto a board and knead 10 minutes. Lift the dough and lightly flour the surface. Put the ball of dough down, cover with a bowl, and let stand 30 minutes.

Divide the dough into thirds and roll as thin as possible, using a lightly floured rolling pin. (I work on a wooden surface and roll until I can see the wood grain through the dough.) Or put through a hand-cranked pasta machine.

Cut the pasta to the width you desire: fettucini—¼-inch strips, linguini—⅛-inch strips, angel hair pasta—as thin as possible, lasagna—2 inches. (I find a pizza wheel works well for this job.)

Lay the cut pasta on a rack or a large surface to dry for at least one hour before cooking.

MAKES ABOUT 1¼ POUNDS DRIED PASTA.
CALORIES: 272   CHOLESTEROL: 0 mg   SODIUM: 358 mg   FIBER: 2 g

Health tip:
Omit salt.
CALORIES: 272   CHOLESTEROL: 0 mg   SODIUM: 3 mg   FIBER: 2 g

To cook fresh pasta: For each ½ pound of pasta you are cooking, use 4 quarts of boiling water with 1 tablespoon olive oil and 2 teaspoons of salt. Cook until al dente (the time will vary greatly according to how thickly you've cut the pasta and how long you've let it dry). Test the pasta for doneness frequently, by pulling one strand from the water and tasting it, starting about two minutes after you've added it to the water.

———————◇———————

Fresh Pasta with Egg

I'm torn as to whether I truly believe that homemade pasta is worth the time and effort. It is tastier, but I'm not convinced that it's that much tastier than the store-bought fresh pasta currently available. If you want to try your hand at it, the egg pasta is slightly firmer and more distinctive tasting than the pasta without eggs.

1¼ cups semolina flour
1 cup all-purpose flour
1½ teaspoons salt
4 eggs
1 tablespoon olive oil

In a large bowl, combine the semolina and all-purpose flours and the salt. Make a well in the center.

In a medium-size bowl, beat the eggs and olive oil until combined. Pour the egg mixture into the well in the flour.

Using a wooden spoon, start mixing the egg mixture in small circles gradually making larger circles. Incorporate more of the flour as you mix, until you have mixed in as much of the flour as you can and are stirring big circles around the edge of the bowl.

Turn the dough, and any flour that has not been mixed in, onto a board and knead 10 minutes. Lift the dough and lightly flour the surface. Put the ball of dough down, cover with a bowl, and let stand 30 minutes.

Divide the dough into thirds and roll as thin as possible, using a lightly floured rolling pin. (I work on a wooden surface and roll until I can see the wood grain through the dough.) Or put through a hand-cranked pasta machine.

Cut the pasta to the width you desire: fettucini—¼-inch strips, linguini—⅛-inch strips, angel hair pasta—as thin as possible, lasagna—2 inches. (I find a pizza wheel works well for this job.)

Lay the cut pasta on a rack or a large surface to dry for at least one hour before cooking.

MAKES ABOUT 1¼ POUNDS DRIED PASTA.
CALORIES: 219   CHOLESTEROL: 139 mg   SODIUM: 579 mg   FIBER: 1 g

Health tip:
Use the Fresh Pasta recipe without egg; omit salt.
CALORIES: 272   CHOLESTEROL: 0 mg   SODIUM: 3 mg   FIBER: 2 g

---

To cook fresh pasta: For each ½ pound of pasta you are cooking, use 4 quarts of boiling water with 1 tablespoon olive oil and 2 teaspoons of salt. Cook until al dente (the time will vary greatly according to how thickly you've cut the pasta and how long you've let it dry). Test the pasta for doneness frequently, by pulling one strand from the water and tasting it, starting about two minutes after you've added it to the water.

—————— ◇ ——————

Marinara Sauce

This is a very simple sauce that you can serve as is—or you can stir in meat or seafood.

> 2 tablespoons olive oil
> 1 cup chopped onion
> 3 cloves garlic, minced
> 1 can (28 ounce) Italian tomatoes, undrained
> 2 tablespoons tomato paste
> 2 tablespoons fresh chopped parsley
> 2 tablespoons fresh chopped basil or
>   2 teaspoons dried basil
> 1 teaspoon sugar
> ½ teaspoon salt
> ¼ teaspoon pepper
> ⅛ teaspoon thyme

Heat the oil in a 3-quart saucepan, over medium-high heat. Add the onion and garlic and cook, stirring, until the onion is softened. Add the tomatoes with the juice, and break up the tomatoes with the back of a spoon.

Stir in the tomato paste, parsley, basil, sugar, salt, pepper, and thyme. Bring to a boil. Reduce heat and simmer, uncovered, 35 minutes.

SERVES 6.
CALORIES: 86   CHOLESTEROL: 9 mg   SODIUM: 398 mg   FIBER: 2 g

Health tip:
Use 2 teaspoons oil and cook in a nonstick saucepan; omit salt.
CALORIES: 59   CHOLESTEROL: 0 mg   SODIUM: 220 mg   FIBER: 2 g

—————— ◇ ——————

Pesto

I believe that hand-chopped pesto is the best possible version. You have a variety of textures that you lose when you prepare this in a blender. You can put any leftover pesto into an ice cube tray and freeze it, then use the cubes as desired.

> 2 cups packed basil leaves
> ⅔ cup pignoli
> 3 cloves garlic

1 cup grated Parmesan cheese
1 cup olive oil
½ teaspoon salt

Mince the basil, pignoli, and garlic. Put in a bowl and toss with the cheese; gradually stir in the olive oil and salt. Let stand at least one hour, but preferably overnight to mellow.

Food processor method: Put the basil into the processor container fitted with a steel blade. Cover and process until the basil is minced. Empty the basil into a medium-size bowl. Add the pignoli to the processor; cover and process until chopped. Add to the basil. Mince the garlic and toss with the basil. Add the cheese and toss. Gradually stir in the oil, then the salt. Let stand at least one hour.

SERVES 6.
CALORIES: 453   CHOLESTEROL: 10 mg   SODIUM: 438 mg   FIBER: 1 g

Health tip:
Use only half the oil and half the cheese; omit the salt.
CALORIES: 263   CHOLESTEROL: 5 mg   SODIUM: 312 mg   FIBER: 1 g

——————— ◇ ———————

Bolognese Sauce

This is a slightly creamy meat sauce, originating in the Bologna region of Italy. You can use any ground meat that you like or any combination of ground meats.

3 tablespoons olive oil
½ cup finely chopped onion
½ cup finely chopped carrot
½ cup finely chopped celery
1 pound ground meat (you can use beef, pork, or veal)
1 box (35 ounce) Pomi* fresh-strained tomatoes or tomato sauce
1 cup ready-to-serve beef broth
1 cup dry white wine
¼ cup chopped parsley
½ teaspoon salt
⅛ teaspoon nutmeg
½ cup heavy cream

Heat the oil in a 4-quart saucepan over medium-high heat. Add the onion, carrot, and celery and cook, stirring, until the onion is soft. Add the meat and cook until no longer pink. Stir in the —

*Pomi brand is found in supermarkets or gourmet stores.

tomatoes, broth, wine, parsley, salt, and nutmeg. Bring to a boil. Reduce heat and simmer, uncovered, 2 hours. Stir in the cream.

SERVES 12.
CALORIES: 190   CHOLESTEROL: 46 mg   SODIUM: 200 mg   FIBER: 2 g

Health tip:
Reduce oil to 2 teaspoons and cook in a nonstick pot; use half-and-half for heavy cream; omit salt.
CALORIES: 145   CHOLESTEROL: 37 mg   SODIUM: 112 mg   FIBER: 2 g

---

◇

Puttanesca-Plus Sauce

The story goes that this is a quick sauce that the Italian "women of the evening" (puttanseca) would prepare after a night's work. It's an incredibly gutsy sauce, very salty and spicy—like the women it's named after. The plus in the sauce are the sun dried tomatoes. To tone it down, halve the amount of anchovies, garlic, sun-dried tomatoes, and capers.

> 3 tablespoons olive oil
> 6 anchovy fillets
> 3 cloves garlic, minced
> 1 can (14½ ounce) whole peeled tomatoes, undrained
> ⅓ cup water
> 3 tablespoons tomato paste
> Pinch crushed red pepper
> 1 cup chopped black olives
> 3 tablespoons chopped parsley
> 2 tablespoons chopped marinated sun-dried tomatoes
> 1 tablespoon capers

In a 2-quart saucepan, heat the olive oil over medium-high heat. Add the anchovies and cook, stirring, until the anchovies dissolve into a paste. Add the garlic. Stir in the tomatoes, and break up with the back of a spoon. Stir in the water, tomato paste and red pepper. Bring to a boil. Reduce the heat and simmer 15 minutes. Stir in the olives, parsley, sun-dried tomatoes, and capers. Simmer 10 minutes longer.

SERVES 6.
CALORIES: 134   CHOLESTEROL: 7 mg   SODIUM: 335 mg   FIBER: 2 g

Health tip:
Use 1 tablespoon oil and only 2 anchovies.
CALORIES: 89   CHOLESTEROL: 4 mg   SODIUM: 311 mg   FIBER: 2 g

————— ◇ —————

Fettucini Alfredo

I serve small portions of this dish because it is so rich. If you want to dress this up, toss in some proscuitto at the last minute.

1 cup heavy cream
¼ cup butter
Pinch nutmeg
½ pound fettucini, cooked just barely al dente and drained
⅔ cup grated Parmesan cheese
Freshly ground pepper

In a large skillet, bring the cream, butter, and nutmeg to a boil. Cook over high heat 2 minutes. Add the fettucini and toss. Add the cheese and pepper and continue tossing until the pasta is completely coated.

SERVES 4.

CALORIES: 451   CHOLESTEROL: 123 mg   SODIUM: 248 mg   FIBER: 1 g

Health tip:
Eat only a bite.

————— ◇ —————

The World's Best Pizza

In all modesty, I must say that I make the best pizza anywhere. The secret is using simple, basic ingredients that allow each flavor to shine. This recipe makes 4 individual pizzas, since these smaller ones are easier to manage than one large one. I entertain by making one and sharing it while the next one is in the oven.

Crust:

1 cup very warm water (105–115°F)
½ teaspoon sugar
1 package active dry yeast
2 to 2¾ cups all-purpose flour
⅓ cup semolina flour
1 tablespoon salt
1 tablespoon olive oil

Sauce:

> 2 tablespoons olive oil
> 1 cup chopped onion
> 1 can (14½ ounce) whole peeled tomatoes, undrained
> ¼ teaspoon salt

Topping:

> 6 cloves garlic, minced
> 1 or 2 packages (8 or 9 ounce) fresh mozzarella (it's important to the
>   taste that you use the fresh type of mozzarella now available in the
>   refrigerator case of your local supermarket or in gourmet stores),
>   drained and shredded
> 1½ tablespoons olive oil

Optional toppings:

> Partially cooked sausage
> Fresh or dried herbs
> Pepperoni
> Sun-dried tomatoes
> Chopped onion
> Green bell peppers
> Mushrooms

In a glass measuring cup, stir together the warm water and sugar. Stir in yeast and let stand until ¼-inch of bubbly white foam forms on top. (This foaming is called *proofing*, and if it doesn't happen it means that for some reason or other the yeast has not been activated. Discard this batch and try again, double checking the date on the yeast package and the temperature of the water.)

In a large bowl, stir together 1½ cups of the all-purpose flour, the semolina, and salt. Stir in the yeast mixture and oil. Stir in ½ cup more flour to form a soft dough. Turn onto a floured board and knead in as much of the remaining flour as necessary to form a dough that is smooth and elastic (it is very important that the dough be very well kneaded).

Place in a greased bowl and cover with greased plastic wrap. Put in a warm, draft-free spot and let rise until doubled in bulk.

Prepare the sauce by heating the oil in a 2-quart saucepan. Add the onion and cook, stirring, until soft. Add the tomatoes with liquid, and break up the tomatoes with the back of a spoon. Stir in the salt. Bring to a boil, reduce heat and simmer, uncovered, 25 minutes.

Punch down the dough. Divide into fourths.

Remove racks from oven (unless you are using an electric oven, in which case you should leave one rack at the lowest possible rung). Preheat the oven to 450°F.

Place a large baking sheet on the floor of the oven (or the rack in the electric oven), with the rim of the baking sheet in the back of the oven.

On a well-floured surface, pat the one piece of dough as flat as possible. Make a fist and place the flattened dough on it. Then gently lift and spread your fingers to stretch the dough. When you have stretched the dough a little, start using both hands. When the center of the dough is quite thin, hold the dough with both hands, suspended in the air, and rotate the dough as you squeeze the edges, making them thin. You should have an 8-inch circle when you are finished.

Place on a flat baking sheet that has been well dusted with semolina or all-purpose flour.

Sprinkle the dough generously with one quarter of the garlic. Then spread one quarter of the sauce over the dough to within ½ inch of the border (you will be using only a thin layer of sauce). Sprinkle with one quarter of the cheese. (At this point you can add any topping that you like.) Drizzle with oil. (If you put on too much topping or cheese it will run off the edge of the pizza and burn onto the baking sheet—so don't be overly generous.)

Open the oven and transfer the pizza to the preheated baking sheet (you will probably have to use a jerking motion to convince the pizza to slide into the oven). Bake 7 to 10 minutes, or until the crust is browned and the cheese is melted.

To remove the pizza from the oven, slide the baking sheet you used to place the pizza into the oven under the cooked pizza and lift the pizza out (leaving the hot baking sheet in the oven for the next pizza).

Make 3 more pizzas out of the remaining dough, sauce and toppings.

SERVES 4.

CALORIES: 605   CHOLESTEROL: 44 mg   SODIUM: 1826 mg   FIBER: 5 g

Health tip:

Omit the salt and don't drizzle with additional oil; eat only half a pizza.

CALORIES: 281   CHOLESTEROL: 22 mg   SODIUM: 114 mg   FIBER: 3 g

---◇---

Plain Old White Bread

I gave my friend Michele Pigliavento half a loaf to taste. She called to ask what kind of bread it was—she couldn't believe that plain old white bread could taste so good.

½ cup very warm water (105–115°F)
1 teaspoon sugar
2 packages active dry yeast
5 to 5½ cups all-purpose flour, divided
1 tablespoon salt
1 cup milk
¾ cup water

In a glass measuring cup, stir together the warm water and sugar. Stir in the yeast and let stand until about ¼-inch of bubbly white foam forms on top. (This foaming is called *proofing*, and if it doesn't happen it means that for some reason or other the yeast has not been activated. Discard this batch and try again, double checking the date on the yeast package and the temperature of the water.)

In a large bowl, stir together 3 cups of the flour and the salt. Stir in the yeast mixture, milk, and water. Stir in 1½ cups more flour, to form a soft dough.

Turn onto a floured board and knead in enough of the remaining flour to make a dough that is smooth and elastic and no longer sticky. Place in a large greased bowl and cover with greased plastic wrap. Put in a warm, draft-free spot and let rise until doubled in bulk.

Punch down the dough and divide in half. Form into 2 8-inch loaves. Place in greased $8 \times 4½ \times 2¾$-inch loaf pans. Cover with greased plastic wrap and let rise until doubled in bulk.

Preheat oven to 350°F. Bake 50 minutes of until loaf is browned and sounds hollow when tapped on the bottom. Remove from pans and cool on racks.

MAKES 2 LOAVES (14 slices each).
CALORIES: 89   CHOLESTEROL: 1 mg   SODIUM: 233 mg   FIBER: 1 g

Health tip:
Omit salt.
CALORIES: 89   CHOLESTEROL: 1 mg   SODIUM: 5 mg   FIBER: 1 g

——————— ◇ ———————

Whole Wheat Bread

I find this whole wheat bread to be especially good and light.

½ cup very warm water (105–115°F)
3 tablespoons sugar, divided
2 packages active dry yeast
3½ to 4 cups all-purpose flour, divided
3 cups whole-wheat flour
1 tablespoon salt
1½ cups milk
1 cup water
1 egg
3 tablespoons oil

In a glass measuring cup, stir together the warm water and 1 teaspoon of the sugar. Stir in yeast and let stand until about ¼-inch of bubbly white foam forms on top. (This foaming is called *proofing*, and if it doesn't happen it means that for some reason or other the yeast has not been activated. Discard this batch and try again, double checking the date on the yeast package and the temperature of the water.)

In a large bowl, stir together 1½ cups of the all-purpose flour, the whole-wheat flour, salt, and the remaining 2 tablespoons plus 2 teaspoons sugar. Stir in the yeast mixture, milk, water, egg, and oil. Stir in 1½ cups more all-purpose flour to make a soft dough.

Turn onto a floured board and knead in enough of the remaining 1 cup of flour to make a dough that is smooth and elastic and no longer sticky. Place in a large greased bowl and cover with greased plastic wrap. Put in a warm, draft-free spot and let rise until doubled in bulk.

Punch down the dough and divide in half; form into 2 9-inch loaves. Place in two greased 9 × 5 × 3-inch loaf pans.

Preheat the oven to 350°F.

Bake 45 minutes or until loaves are browned and sound hollow when tapped on bottom. Remove from pan and cool on racks.

MAKES 2 LOAVES (18 slices each).
CALORIES: 198   CHOLESTEROL: 13 mg   SODIUM: 367 mg   FIBER: 3 g

Health tip:
Omit salt.
CALORIES: 198   CHOLESTEROL: 13 mg   SODIUM: 12 mg   FIBER: 3 g

———————— ◇ ————————

French Bread

The French make their bread with a flour that is high in gluten—therefore I recommend using bread flour that contains more gluten than all-purpose flour. The typical crispy crust comes from steam in the oven during the first half of the baking. To duplicate this, I suggest tossing ice cubes in the hot oven so they will create steam as they melt.

½ cup very warm water (105–115°F)
1 teaspoon sugar
1 package active dry yeast
2¾ to 3½ cups bread flour, divided
2 teaspoons salt
¾ cup water
1 egg white, optional
6 ice cubes, divided

In a glass measuring cup, stir together the warm water and sugar. Stir in the yeast and let stand until about ¼-inch bubbly white foam forms on top. (This foaming is called *proofing*, and if it doesn't happen it means that for some reason or other the yeast has not been activated. Discard this batch and try again, double checking the date on the yeast package and the temperature of the water.)

In a large bowl, stir together 2 cups of the flour and the salt. Stir in the yeast mixture and the water. Stir in ½ cup more flour to make a dough that is easy to handle.

Turn onto a floured board and knead in enough of the remaining flour to make a dough that is smooth and elastic and no longer sticky. Place in a large greased bowl and cover with greased plastic wrap. Put in a warm, draft-free spot and let rise until doubled in bulk.

Punch down the dough and let rise until doubled in bulk again.

Grease a two-loaf French bread pan or baking sheet.

Punch down the dough and divide in half. Roll each half of the dough into a long thin loaf (about 15 inches long). Place in prepared pan and brush with egg white, if desired. Using a sharp knife, make 3 diagonal slashes. Cover with greased plastic wrap; let rise until doubled in bulk.

Preheat oven to 425°F.

Place pan into the oven and drop 2 ice cubes onto the oven floor (if you have an electric oven you may want to omit the ice cubes). Bake 5 minutes. Open oven and quickly throw in 2 more ice cubes.

Bake 5 minutes longer and add the remaining ice cubes. Continue baking until browned, about 25 minutes total. Cool on racks.

MAKES 2 LOAVES (about 16 slices each).
CALORIES: 88   CHOLESTEROL: 0 mg   SODIUM: 270 mg   FIBER: 1 g

Health tip:
Omit salt.
CALORIES: 88   CHOLESTEROL: 0 mg   SODIUM: 4 mg   FIBER: 1 g

———————◇———————

Semolina Bread

This bread is absolutely fabulous. It has a full flavor and great texture that is dense but not heavy. The secret to making it is to be patient. The first rising can take as long as 2½ hours or more. As long as your yeast has proofed (foamed), the bread will rise eventually.

½ cup very warm water (105–115°F)
½ teaspoon sugar
1 package active dry yeast
2 cups semolina
2 to 2½ cups all-purpose flour
2 teaspoons salt
1 cup milk
2 tablespoons butter, melted
1 egg white, optional
1 tablespoon sesame seeds, optional

In a glass measuring cup, stir together the warm water and sugar. Stir in the yeast and let stand until about ¼-inch bubbly white foam forms on top. (This foaming is called *proofing*, and if it doesn't happen it means that for some reason or other the yeast has not been activated. Discard this batch and try again, double checking the date on the yeast package and the temperature of the water.)

In a large bowl, stir together the semolina flour, ½ cup of the all-purpose flour, and the salt. Stir in the yeast mixture, milk, and butter. Stir in 1 cup more all-purpose flour to make a soft dough.

Turn onto a floured board and knead in enough of the remaining all-purpose flour to make a dough that is elastic and no longer sticky. Place in a large greased bowl and cover with greased plastic wrap. Put in a warm, draft-free spot and let rise until doubled in bulk, about 2 or more hours.

Punch down the dough and form into a round loaf, about 7

inches in diameter. Using a sharp knife, score the top of the bread. Place on a greased baking sheet, cover with greased plastic wrap and let rise until doubled in bulk.

Preheat oven to 375°F.

Beat the egg white lightly and brush on the loaf. Sprinkle with sesame seeds. Bake 40 minutes or until browned and crisp on top and bottom.

SERVES 18.
CALORIES: 112   CHOLESTEROL: 5 mg   SODIUM: 258 mg   FIBER: 1 g

Health tip:
Omit the salt; use unsalted margarine instead of butter.
CALORIES: 112   CHOLESTEROL: 2 mg   SODIUM: 17 mg   FIBER: 1 g

---

———————— ◇ ————————

Cornell Bread

I am including it in this book because, in addition to being delicious, it is very high in protein and healthy. It is my guess that the original formula for this bread was developed at Cornell University.

> ½ cup very warm water (105–115°F)
> 1 teaspoon sugar
> 2 packages dry yeast
> 1½ cups water
> ½ cup whole-wheat flour
> ½ cup nonfat dry milk
> ⅓ cup soy flour
> ¼ cup wheat germ
> 1 egg
> 3 tablespoons honey
> 2 tablespoons oil
> 1 tablespoon salt
> 5 to 6 cups all-purpose flour, divided

In a glass measuring cup, stir together the warm water and the sugar. Stir in the yeast and let stand until about ¼-inch bubbly white foam forms on top. (This foaming is called *proofing,* and if it doesn't happen it means that for some reason or other the yeast has not been activated. Discard this batch and try again, double checking the date on the yeast package and the temperature of the water.)

In a large bowl, beat together the water, whole-wheat flour, milk, soy flour, wheat germ, egg, honey, oil, and salt.

Beat in the yeast mixture, then 2½ cups of the all-purpose flour. Stir in 1½ cups more all-purpose flour. Turn onto a well-floured board and knead in as much of the remaining flour as necessary to make a dough that is no longer sticky.

Place in a large greased bowl and cover with greased plastic wrap. Put in a warm, draft-free spot and let rise until doubled in bulk, about 1 hour.

Punch down the dough and divide in half. Shape each half into a loaf and put into greased 8 × 4½ × 2½-inch loaf pans. Cover with greased plastic wrap and let rise until doubled in bulk.

Preheat the oven to 350°F for 20 minutes. Reduce heat to 325°F and bake 30 minutes longer, or until loaves are browned and sound hollow when thumped on the bottom.

MAKES 2 LOAVES (14 slices each).
CALORIES: 123   CHOLESTEROL: 7 mg   SODIUM: 238 mg   FIBER: 1 g

Health tip:
Omit salt.
CALORIES: 123   CHOLESTEROL: 7 mg   SODIUM: 10 mg   FIBER: 1 g

———————— ◇ ————————

Wheat-Germ Rolls

These rolls are very tasty and have a nice texture. I like to serve them to company at brunch, warm and with giant pats of butter.

½ cup very warm water (105–115°F)
2 teaspoons sugar
2 packages active dry yeast
3 to 4 cups all-purpose flour, divided
1½ teaspoons salt
1 cup water
½ cup Honey Crunch Wheat Germ

In a glass measuring cup, stir together the warm water and sugar. Stir in the yeast and let stand until about ¼-inch bubbly white foam forms on top. (This foaming is called *proofing,* and if it doesn't happen it means that for some reason or other the yeast has not been activated. Discard this batch and try again, double checking the date on the yeast package and the temperature of the water.)

In a large bowl, stir together 2 cups of the flour and the salt. Stir in the water and the yeast mixture. Stir in the wheat germ and ½ cup more flour.

Turn onto a floured board and knead in enough of the remaining flour as necessary to make a dough that is smooth and elastic and not sticky. Place in a large greased bowl and cover with greased plastic wrap. Put in a warm, draft-free spot and let rise until doubled in bulk, about 40 minutes.

Punch down the dough and form into 8 oval rolls. Place on 2 greased cookie sheets. Cover with greased plastic wrap and let rise until doubled in bulk.

Preheat the oven to 350°F. Bake the rolls 35 minutes or until browned and sound hollow when tapped on the bottom.

MAKES 8.
CALORIES: 206   CHOLESTEROL: 0 mg   SODIUM: 402 mg   FIBER: 3 g

Health tip:
Omit salt.
CALORIES: 206   CHOLESTEROL: 0 mg   SODIUM: 2 mg   FIBER: 3 g

———————— ◇ ————————

Delicious Pancakes

These are very thick and light pancakes just like the ones you see in the advertisements, but never seem to be able to make at home.

1½ cups self-rising flour
3 tablespoons sugar
1¼ cups milk
3 tablespoons butter, melted
2 eggs

In a large bowl, stir together the flour and sugar.

In a medium-size bowl, beat the milk, butter, and eggs together until completely combined. Stir the milk mixture into the flour until moistened. The batter will be thick and lumpy.

Heat a griddle or skillet until a drop of water dances across the surface before evaporating. Lightly grease the griddle and drop 2 rounded tablespoons of batter per pancake.

Cook until bubbles break on the surface of the pancake. Because the batter is so thick, you will have to cook on a low heat so that they cook through before they get too dark on the bottom. Turn and cook until browned on the other side.

MAKES 12.
CALORIES: 120   CHOLESTEROL: 46 mg   SODIUM: 217 mg   FIBER: 0 g

Health tip:
Use unsalted margarine instead of butter; scrambled-egg substitute; and 1-percent-fat milk.
CALORIES: 111   CHOLESTEROL: 1 mg   SODIUM: 202 mg   FIBER: 0 g

———————————— ◇ ————————————

Vanilla Waffles

These waffles smell so good as they cook that you'll hardly be able to wait for them to brown. Serve them with maple syrup or, if you feel really indulgent, topped with whipped cream and fresh berries.

    2¼ cups self-rising flour
    ¼ cup sugar
    1¾ cups milk
    ½ cup butter, melted
    2 eggs
    1 teaspoon vanilla extract

Heat the waffle iron.
In a large bowl, stir together the flour and sugar.
In a medium-size bowl, beat together the milk, butter, eggs, and vanilla. Stir the milk mixture into the flour until blended.
Pour about 1 cup of batter onto lightly greased, preheated waffle iron. Bake until golden and crisp.

MAKES 12 4-INCH WAFFLES
CALORIES: 188   CHOLESTEROL: 59 mg   SODIUM: 316 mg   FIBER: 1 g

Health tip:
Use unsalted margarine instead of butter and use scrambled-egg substitute.
CALORIES: 184   CHOLESTEROL: 4 mg   SODIUM: 266 mg   FIBER: 1 g

---◇---

Apple Pie Waffles

These waffles are cinnamon-y and moist—a great candidate for à la mode.

1¼ cup all-purpose flour
1 cup miller's bran (fine grind)
¼ cup sugar
1 tablespoon baking powder
1½ teaspoons cinnamon
1 teaspoon baking soda
¼ teaspoon nutmeg
2 cups buttermilk
½ cup butter, melted
½ cup finely shredded apple
⅓ cup water
3 egg whites
¼ teaspoon salt

Preheat a waffle iron.

In a large bowl, stir together the all-purpose flour, bran, sugar, baking powder, cinnamon, baking soda, and nutmeg.

In a medium-size bowl, beat together the milk, butter, shredded apple, and water; set aside.

In another medium-size bowl, using clean beaters, beat the egg whites with the salt until stiff, but not dry.

Stir the milk mixture into the flour, then fold in the egg whites.

Spread 1¼ cups of batter onto the waffle iron. Bake until golden and crisp.

MAKES 12 4-INCH WAFFLES.
CALORIES: 170   CHOLESTEROL: 22 mg   SODIUM: 316 mg   FIBER: 4 g

Health tip:
Use unsalted margarine instead of butter. Omit salt.
CALORIES: 170   CHOLESTEROL: 1 mg   SODIUM: 236 mg   FIBER: 4 g

---◇---

Maple French Toast

If, by any chance, you have some unsliced white bread left over, this is an ideal way to use it.

4 (1½-inch thick) slices white bread
4 eggs
¾ cup half-and-half
2 tablespoons maple syrup
2 tablespoons sugar
½ teaspoon vanilla extract
⅛ teaspoon salt
¼ cup butter, divided

Remove the crust from the bread. Cut each slice in half diagonally to form triangles.

In a medium-size bowl, beat the eggs, beat in the half-and-half, maple syrup, sugar, vanilla, and salt. Beat until the sugar is dissolved. Dip each piece of bread into egg mixture until soaked.

Melt 2 tablespoons of the butter in a 10-inch skillet, over medium-high heat. Place half of the bread triangles in the skillet. Cook until brown on bottom; turn and cook the second side until browned. Remove the finished pieces to a serving platter (the platter may be placed into the oven to remain warm). Melt remaining butter and cook remaining bread.

SERVES 4.
CALORIES: 359   CHOLESTEROL: 256 mg   SODIUM: 392 mg   FIBER: 0 g

Health tip:
Use milk instead of half-and-half; scrambled-egg substitute; and unsalted margarine instead of butter. Omit salt.
CALORIES: 333   CHOLESTEROL: 17 mg   SODIUM: 278 mg   FIBER: 0 g

―――――――― ◇ ――――――――

Whole Wheat Biscuits

These are the lightest most heavenly biscuits I've ever eaten.

1½ cups all-purpose flour
½ cup whole-wheat flour
2 tablespoons sugar
1 tablespoon baking powder
1 teaspoon salt
1½ cups heavy cream

Preheat the oven to 400°F.

In a large bowl, stir together the all-purpose flour, whole-wheat flour, sugar, baking powder, and salt.

Using a fork, gradually add the cream until a soft dough is formed. Place on a floured board and knead 10 to 12 times. Roll ½-inch thick. Using a 2½-inch biscuit cutter dipped in flour, cut biscuits. Place on ungreased cookie sheets and bake 15 to 18 minutes or until browned.

MAKES 12.
CALORIES: 185   CHOLESTEROL: 41 mg   SODIUM: 272 mg   FIBER: 1 g

Health tip:
Omit salt.
CALORIES: 185   CHOLESTEROL: 41 mg   SODIUM: 94 mg   FIBER: 1 g

―――――――― ◇ ――――――――

Basic Muffins

As the title indicates, these are basic muffins. It's up to you to dress them up. Stir in fresh or dried fruits, spices, nuts, or anything you can think of.

2 cups all-purpose flour
2 tablespoons sugar
1 tablespoon baking powder
½ teaspoon salt
1 cup milk
⅓ cup butter, melted
1 egg

Preheat the oven to 400°F. Grease 12 (2½-inch) muffin cups

In a large bowl, using a whisk, stir together the flour, sugar, baking powder, and salt. Set aside.

In a large bowl, beat together the milk, butter, and egg. Add the milk mixture to the flour all at once. Stir until dry ingredients are just moistened and remain lumpy.

Spoon into prepared baking tins, filling each cup about ⅔ full. Bake 20 to 25 minutes or until browned.

MAKES 12.
CALORIES: 148   CHOLESTEROL: 34 mg   SODIUM: 230 mg   FIBER: 1 g

health tip:
Omit salt; use unsalted margarine instead of butter.
CALORIES: 148   CHOLESTEROL: 20 mg   SODIUM: 104 mg   FIBER: 1 g

———————— ◇ ————————

Pineapple Bran Muffins

I asked a lot of people to taste these muffins for me (since I'm allergic to pineapple and couldn't taste them myself). My neighbors Marie and Bob Riesel said they were good, but just needed a little something. My friend Michele Pigliavento came up with the missing element—brown sugar. This version is very good.

1½ cups miller's bran (fine)
1 cup all-purpose flour
2 teaspoons baking powder
1 teaspoon baking soda
½ teaspoon salt
¾ cup buttermilk
1 can (8¼ ounce) crushed pineapple (syrup packed), undrained
⅓ cup firmly packed dark-brown sugar
¼ cup vegetable oil
2 egg whites

Preheat the oven to 400°F. Grease 12 3-inch muffin cups.

In a large bowl, stir together the bran, flour, baking powder, baking soda, and salt.

In a medium-size bowl, stir together the buttermilk, pineapple with syrup, brown sugar, oil, and egg whites until combined. Add the buttermilk mixture to the dry ingredients. Stir until just moistened.

Spoon into the prepared muffin cups and bake 20 minutes.

SERVES 12.
CALORIES: 135   CHOLESTEROL: 1 mg   SODIUM: 240 mg   FIBER: 2 g

Health tip:
Omit salt; use juice packed pineapple.
CALORIES: 131   CHOLESTEROL: 1 mg   SODIUM: 152 mg   FIBER: 2 g

Orange Popovers

These come out best when made in a popover pan. If you are very fond of popovers, the investment is certainly worthwhile. To make regular popovers, just omit the orange rind and sugar.

1 cup milk
2 eggs
2 teaspoons sugar
1 tablespoon vegetable oil
½ teaspoon salt
1 teaspoon grated orange rind
1 cup sifted flour

Place the milk, eggs, sugar, oil, salt, and orange rind into the blender container (I prefer a blender to a processor for this). Cover and process until just blended. Add the flour, cover and process until smooth. Let stand 1 hour.

Preheat the oven to 425°F.

Place the popover pans in the oven for 5 minutes. (If you don't have popover pans use 6 custard cups—but they have to be deeper than they are wide. Put them onto a baking sheet for easier handling.)

While the pan is heating, process the batter in the blender just a few seconds to stir.

Remove the pans (or cups) from the oven and thoroughly grease each cup. Fill cups a little less than half full. Place in oven and bake 20 minutes, reduce heat to 350°F (don't open the door to peek at any time) and bake 15 minutes longer, or until puffed high.

SERVES 6.
CALORIES: 151   CHOLESTEROL: 75 mg   SODIUM: 220 mg   FIBER: .5 g

Health tip:
Omit salt.
CALORIES: 151   CHOLESTEROL: 75 mg   SODIUM: 43 mg   FIBER: .5 g

———————— ◇ ————————

Basic Sweet Dough

This is a very light and tasty dough. You can make it into raisin bread or monkey bread or any sweet yeast product you want.

1 cup milk
½ cup water
⅓ cup sugar
⅓ cup butter
4½ cups all-purpose flour
1 package active dry yeast
1½ teaspoons salt
2 eggs

In a 1-quart saucepan, over high heat, stir together the milk, water, and sugar. Bring to a boil and continue to boil 3 minutes, reducing the heat if the milk starts to boil over. Remove from the heat and stir in the butter. Let stand 30 minutes.

In a large bowl, stir together 2 cups of the flour, the yeast, and salt. Stir in the cooled milk mixture, then the eggs. Stir in 1¾ cups more of the flour.

Turn onto a floured board and knead in as much of the remaining ½ cups flour as necessary to make a dough that is just slightly sticky, about 7 minutes. (If you find that the dough is too sticky to knead and you've already used all the flour, just dust your hands with flour but don't add more to the dough. A soft dough is essential to a light and delicate crumb.) Place in a large greased bowl and cover with greased plastic wrap. Put in a warm, draft-free spot and let rise until doubled in bulk, about 1½ hours.

Punch down and allow to rise again, about 40 minutes.

Punch down the dough and use in your favorite recipes such as the coffee cake below.

MAKES DOUGH FOR 12 ROLLS OR PASTRIES.
CALORIES: 174   CHOLESTEROL: 34 mg   SODIUM: 219 mg   FIBER: 2 g

Health tip:
Use unsalted margarine instead of butter and omit salt.
CALORIES: 174   CHOLESTEROL: 24 mg   SODIUM: 18 mg   FIBER: 2 g

––––––––– ◇ –––––––––

Pecan Coffee Ring

There's something so homey and wonderful about having a cup of coffee and a slice (or three) of a good homemade coffee cake.

1 recipe sweet dough
3 tablespoons butter, melted
1 cup firmly packed brown sugar (dark or light)
1½ cups chopped pecans
1 teaspoon cinnamon
Icing (optional)
½ cup confectioners' sugar
1 tablespoon milk

Preheat the oven to 350°F. Grease a baking sheet.

On a lightly floured surface roll the dough into a 12 × 20-inch rectangle. Brush with the butter.

In a medium-size bowl, combine the sugar, pecans, and cinnamon. Sprinkle sugar mixture evenly over the dough. Roll into a log, starting at the long edge. Pinch the seams to seal. Bring the two ends together to form a ring and pinch to hold together. Place on prepared baking sheet.

Using a sharp knife or scissors, slice the dough from the outside of the ring ⅔ of the way to the center into 1-inch pieces, making sure that the center remains uncut. Take each 1-inch piece and twist onto its side, exposing the inside spiral. The pieces will lean slightly on each other.

Cover with greased plastic wrap and let rise until doubled in bulk. Bake 25 to 30 minutes or until golden. Remove from baking sheet and cool on rack.

If desired, glaze by stirring together the confectioners' sugar and water and drizzling over the cooled pecan ring.

SERVES 18.
CALORIES: 314   CHOLESTEROL: 39 mg   SODIUM: 241 mg   FIBER: 2 g

Health tip:
Use unsalted margarine instead of butter and have only a sliver. Omit salt from dough.
CALORIES: 314   CHOLESTEROL: 24 mg   SODIUM: 26 mg   FIBER: 2 g

———————◇———————

Cream Puffs (Profiteroles)

You can cut the tops off these little cream puffs and fill with sweet or savory fillings—simplest of all is sweetened whipped cream. This is a recipe for a small batch. If you're entertaining and want to make more, double the recipe.

¼ cup water
2 tablespoons butter
⅛ teaspoon salt
¼ cup flour
1 egg

Preheat the oven to 450°F. Grease a baking sheet.

In a small saucepan, bring the water, butter, and salt to a boil over medium-high heat. Remove from the heat and add flour, all at once, stirring vigorously. Reduce heat to low and cook, stirring constantly, 2 minutes. Cool 5 minutes.

Add the egg and stir until smooth and shiny.

Drop by rounded teaspoonsful at least 1 inch apart onto the prepared baking sheet. Bake 10 mintues. Without opening the oven door, reduce heat to 350°F and bake 15 minutes longer.

Remove puffs to wire rack and cool.

MAKES 12 SMALL PROFITEROLES.
CALORIES: 33   CHOLESTEROL: 22 mg   SODIUM: 43 mg   FIBER: 0 g

Health tip:
Use unsalted margarine instead of butter and omit salt.
CALORIES: 33   CHOLESTEROL: 17 mg   SODIUM: 8 mg   FIBER: 0 g

———————◇———————

Puff Pastry (Feuillete)

This is absolutely the most wonderful pastry ever created. Keeping that in mind may help to overcome the fact that this is a long and involved recipe. Once made, though, puff pastry then becomes the base for very delicious and easy recipes. If you're not up to the challenge of homemade puff pastry, it can be purchased in the freezer department of your local supermarket.

1 cup butter, divided
1½ cups flour
½ cup, minus 1 tablespoon, ice water

Melt ¼ cup of the butter. In a large bowl, stir together the flour, water, and melted butter.

Shape into an 8 × 12-inch rectangle. Wrap in plastic wrap and refrigerate 10 minutes.

Place the remaining butter between 2 pieces of waxed paper. Roll into a 4 × 6-inch rectangle. Fold the butter into thirds and roll into a 4 × 6-inch rectangle again. Repeat this one more time (this process softens the butter to the necessary consistency).

Remove the dough from the refrigerator. Place on a lightly floured board. Place the butter in the center of the dough. Fold the left side of the dough over the butter, then fold the right side over to make a package with the butter enclosed in the center.

Roll, without pressing too hard, into a 8 × 18-inch rectangle. (If butter breaks through the dough, lightly pat the butter with flour until dry.) Fold one third of the dough toward the center (you now have two thirds of the dough in a double layer and one third in a single thickness). Fold the remaining one third of the dough over the double part to form 6 × 8-inch "book."

Roll the dough again into an 8 × 18-inch rectangle, dusting with flour if necessary. Fold into book. Wrap in plastic wrap and place into the refrigerator for 30 minutes. (You have now completed 2 turns.)

Remove the dough from the refrigerator and roll out and fold twice more (2 more turns). Wrap in plastic wrap and chill 30 minutes longer. Repeat once more and let chill at least 45 minutes more.

The dough is now ready to be rolled out for any of your baking needs, or if you prefer, you can freeze it for later use.

Recipe yield depends on what you are making with the pastry
Nutritional count is for the entire recipe. You can divide it into the number of servings according to your use.
CALORIES: 2304   CHOLESTEROL: 497 mg   SODIUM: 1551 mg   FIBER: 5 g

Health tip:
Use unsalted butter. (But it must be butter—no margarine!)
CALORIES: 2304   CHOLESTEROL: 497 mg   SODIUM: 25 mg   FIBER: 5 g

———————— ◇ ————————

Puffy Apple Tarts

These are very delicious and very easy to make (once you've made the pastry).

2 large apples, peeled, cored, and thinly sliced
1 tablespoon lemon juice
½ recipe puff pastry (see page 81) or 1 sheet frozen prepared puff pastry,
  thawed
¼ cup apricot jam, put through a sieve and divided
2 tablespoons sugar, divided
1 cup whipped cream, if desired

Preheat the oven to 400°F.

In a medium-size bowl, toss the apples with the lemon juice. Set aside.

Roll the pastry into a 12 × 12-inch square. Cut into 4 6-inch squares. Place on ungreased baking sheet

Lightly brush each square with some of the apricot jam, to within 1 inch of the borders.

Arrange one quarter of the apple slices evenly over the jam in each square. Brush with remaining jam. Sprinkle each tart, including the pastry, with 1½ teaspoons sugar.

Bake 15 to 20 minutes or until the pastry is puffed and browned.

Cut into triangles and serve with whipped cream, if desired

SERVES 8.
CALORIES: 388 CHOLESTEROL: 51 mg SODIUM: 101 mg FIBER: 0 g

Health tip:
Skip the whipped cream. Have only half a serving.
CALORIES: 165 CHOLESTEROL: 16 mg SODIUM: 52 mg FIBER: 0 g

◇

Easy Napoleons

I had dinner with my friend Holly Garrison one night and she made this exquisite simple dessert—simple if you already have made the puff pastry.

½ recipe puff pastry (see page 81) or 1 sheet frozen prepared puff pastry, thawed
1½ cups heavy cream
2 tablespoons sugar
1 pint fresh berries (if you're using strawberries, hull and halve them)
Confectioners' sugar

Preheat oven to 375°F.

Roll the pastry dough into a 10 × 12-inch rectangle. Cut into 8 3 × 5-inch rectangles. Place on ungreased baking sheets and bake 10 to 15 minutes, or until lightly browned. Cool.

In a large bowl, beat the heavy cream with the sugar until stiff.

Split each piece of pastry in half, horizontal. This will give you a top and a bottom. Spread about ⅓ cup of the heavy cream mixture on the bottom half of each puff pastry. Top with some of the berries. Cover with top half (browned side up). Sprinkle generously with confectioners' sugar.

SERVES 8.

CALORIES: 244   CHOLESTEROL: 61 mg   SODIUM: 102 mg   FIBER: 0 g

Health tip:
Skip the puff pastry and whipped cream—just have fresh berries.

◇

Angel Food Cake

Everyone who knows me, knows that I love white food—vanilla ice cream, milk, marshmallows; and Angel Food Cake is another one that I think is just great. If you are fond of almond flavoring you can add ½ teaspoon when you fold in the vanilla.

1 cup cake flour
1 cup sifted confectioners' sugar
¼ teaspoon salt
12 egg whites, room temperature (about 1¾ cups)
½ teaspoon cream of tartar
¾ cup sugar
1 teaspoon vanilla extract

Preheat the oven to 375°F.

Sift the flour, confectioners' sugar, and salt into a medium-size bowl, or onto a piece of waxed paper.

In a large bowl, beat the egg whites with the cream of tartar until foamy. Beat in the sugar 2 tablespoons at a time until the egg whites are stiff and glossy and all the sugar has been added.

Sift one quarter of the flour mixture over the egg whites and gently fold in, until completely combined. Continue folding in the remaining three quarters of the flour. Fold in the vanilla.

Gently spread the egg mixture into a 10-inch tube pan. Bake 35 minutes, or until browned. Cool upside down at least one hour. Run knife around edges and remove from pan.

Slice with serrated knife.

SERVES 10.
CALORIES: 150   CHOLESTEROL: 0 mg   SODIUM: 114 mg   FIBER: 0 g

Health tip:
Omit salt.
CALORIES: 150   CHOLESTEROL: 0 mg   SODIUM: 61 mg   FIBER: 0 g

———————◇———————

Whole-Wheat Carrot Cake

This is a very moist, yummy, cake. If you want to dress it up you can frost it (try the frosting from the yellow cake, p. 87)

1 cup whole-wheat pastry flour
¾ cup all-purpose flour
2 teaspoons baking powder
1 teaspoon baking soda
1½ teaspoons cinnamon
¼ teaspoon nutmeg
¼ teaspoon salt
⅛ teaspoon clove
¾ cup raisins
½ cup chopped walnuts
⅔ cup corn oil
⅔ cup firmly packed dark-brown sugar
½ cup sugar
1 teaspoon vanilla extract
2 eggs
1½ cups shredded carrot

Preheat the oven to 350°F. Heavily grease and flour a 9 × 5 × 3-inch loaf pan.

In a large bowl, or on waxed paper, using a whisk, stir together the whole-wheat flour, all-purpose flour, baking powder, baking soda, cinnamon, nutmeg, salt, and clove. Add the raisins and nuts and toss.

In a large bowl, beat together the oil, brown sugar, sugar, and vanilla. Beat in the eggs, one at a time. Stir in the carrots, then the flour mixture, stirring until completely combined.

Pour into prepared pan and bake 1 hour, or until a wooden pick inserted in the center comes out clean. Cool in pan 10 minutes, then invert onto rack and cool completely.

SERVES 14.
CALORIES: 239   CHOLESTEROL: 30 mg   SODIUM: 164 mg   FIBER: 3 g

Health tip:
Omit salt.
CALORIES: 239   CHOLESTEROL: 30 mg   SODIUM: 126 mg   FIBER: 3 g

———————— ◇ ————————

Sour Cream Apple Cake

I wrote this recipe some time ago, but it's still my very favorite cake. It's light and moist with an unbelievable flavor.

2½ cups all-purpose flour
½ teaspoon baking powder
½ teaspoon baking soda
¼ teaspoon salt
¼ cup firmly packed light- or dark-brown sugar
½ teaspoon cinnamon
1 cup chopped nuts
1 cup butter, softened
2¼ cups sugar, divided
4 eggs
1 cup sour cream
1 teaspoon vanilla extract
3 cups coarsely chopped peeled apples

Preheat the oven to 350°F. Generously grease and flour a heavy bundt pan (light enamel bundt pans brown the outside of the cake too quickly) or 10-inch tube pan.

In a large bowl, or on a sheet of waxed paper, using a whisk, stir together the flour, baking powder, baking soda, and salt; set aside.

In a medium-size bowl, combine the brown sugar and cinnamon. Stir in the nuts; set aside.

In a large bowl, cream the butter with 2 cups of the sugar until light and fluffy. Beat in the eggs until combined.

Beat the flour mixture into the butter alternately with the sour cream, starting and ending with the flour. Beat in the vanilla.

In a medium-size bowl, toss the apples with the remaining ¼ cup sugar. Fold into the batter. Spoon half of the batter into the prepared pan.

Sprinkle the nut mixture over the batter. Top with the remaining batter and smooth with a spatula.

Bake 1 hour 10 minutes, or until a wooden pick inserted in the center comes out clean. Turn immediately onto a rack to cool.

SERVES 16.

CALORIES: 421   CHOLESTEROL: 89 mg   SODIUM: 194 mg   FIBER: 2 g

Health tip:

Use unsalted margarine instead of butter and omit the salt.

CALORIES: 421   CHOLESTEROL: 58 mg   SODIUM: 77 mg   FIBER: 2 g

—————◇—————

Yellow Cake with Vanilla Buttercream Frosting

This is a very easy cake to make. It's light and delicious with a frosting that's a real bowl licker. It's a perfect birthday, anniversary, or anyday cake.

Cake:

> 2¾ cups all-purpose flour
> 2 teaspoons baking powder
> ½ teaspoon salt
> ¾ cup butter, softened
> 1½ cups sugar
> 3 eggs
> 1 teaspoon vanilla
> 1½ cups milk

Frosting:

> ¾ cup butter, softened
> ½ cup shortening
> 1 pound confectioners' sugar
> 2 tablespoons milk
> 1 tablespoon vanilla

Preheat oven to 350°F. Grease and flour 2 9-inch round cake pans.

In a large bowl, or on waxed paper, using a whisk, stir together the flour, baking powder, and salt.

In a large bowl, cream the butter and sugar until light and fluffy. Beat in the eggs, one at a time, and beat until thoroughly combined. Beat in the vanilla.

Beat in the flour mixture, alternately with the milk, starting and ending with the flour.

Spread into the prepared pans. Bake 40 minutes, or until a wooden pick inserted into the center comes out clean.

Turn onto rack to cool.

In a large bowl, cream the butter and shortening. Beat in 1 cup of the confectioners' sugar. Beat in the milk and then the remaining confectioners' sugar, ½ cup at a time, beating well after each addition. Beat in the vanilla.

Fill and frost the cooled cake with the frosting. If you are making this cake more than 2 or 3 hours before serving, cover and store in refrigerator. Let return to room temperature before serving.

SERVES 12.
CALORIES: 640   CHOLESTEROL: 112 mg   SODIUM: 351 mg   FIBER: .5 g

Health tip:
Use unsalted margarine instead of butter and omit salt.
CALORIES: 640   CHOLESTEROL: 85 mg   SODIUM: 188 mg   FIBER: .5 g

---

◇

Decadent Chocolate Cake

This is a rich dense chocolate-y cake. You can fill and frost it with sweetened whipped cream, if you prefer. Holly Garrison gave me the recipe for this frosting and it is divine indeed.

Cake:

> 6 squares (1 ounce each) unsweetened chocolate
> 2⅔ cups sifted all-purpose flour
> 2 teaspoons baking powder
> 1 cup butter, softened
> 3 cups sugar
> 4 eggs
> 1 teaspoon vanilla extract
> 2 cups milk

Frosting:

> *1 cup sugar*
> *1 cup heavy cream*
> *5 ounces high quality semi-sweet chocolate*
> *½ cup butter, cut into 6 pieces*
> *1 teaspoon vanilla*

Preheat oven to 350°F. Grease and flour 2 9-inch round cake pans.

In the top of a double boiler, over simmering water, melt the chocolate. Remove from heat and set aside.

In a medium-size bowl, or on waxed paper, using a whisk, stir the flour and baking powder together; set aside.

In a large bowl, cream the butter with the sugar until light and fluffy. Beat in the eggs until blended. Beat in the chocolate and vanilla.

Alternately add the flour and milk to the chocolate mixture, beating well after each addition. Pour into prepared pans.

Bake 35 to 45 minutes, or until a wooden pick inserted in the center comes out clean. Cool 10 minutes in the pan, then invert onto racks and cool completely.

Prepare the frosting by combining the sugar and cream in a 2-quart saucepan. Bring to a boil, over medium heat, stirring constantly. Reduce heat and simmer 5 minutes; remove from heat. Add the chocolate and stir until melted. Stir in the butter, 1 piece at a time, then stir in the vanilla. If necessary, chill until spreading consistency

Fill and frost the chocolate layers with the frosting.

SERVES 12.
CALORIES: 676   CHOLESTEROL: 136 mg   SODIUM: 251 mg   FIBER: 2 g

Health tip:
Use unsalted margarine instead of butter. Have only half a piece.
CALORIES: 338   CHOLESTEROL: 51 mg   SODIUM: 75 mg   FIBER: 1 g

Jelly Roll Cake

Jelly rolls are very versatile desserts. Obviously, you can fill them with jelly, but you can also use whipped cream or mousse or butter cream. Any way you serve it, this is a real delight.

6 tablespoons confectioners' sugar, divided
¾ cup all-purpose flour
1 teaspoon baking powder
¼ teaspoon salt
3 eggs
1 cup sugar
⅓ cup milk
1 teaspoon vanilla extract
1 jar (12 ounce) jelly or jam (any flavor you like)

Preheat oven to 375°F. Grease a 15½ × 10½ × 1-inch baking pan (jelly roll pan). Line with waxed paper and grease again.

Place 2 tablespoons of the confectioners' sugar into a strainer. Shake over the surface of a clean kitchen towel; set aside.

In a medium-size bowl, or on waxed paper, using a whisk, stir together the flour, baking powder, and salt; set aside.

In a large bowl, using an electric mixer, beat the eggs on high speed 5 minutes. Add the sugar and beat 3 minutes longer. Beat in the milk and vanilla.

Add the flour all at once and beat on low speed until just smooth. Pour into the prepared pan and spread evenly.

Bake 12 to 15 minutes, or until the cake springs back when gently pressed. Cool 2 minutes in pan, then turn onto prepared towel. Carefully peel off the waxed paper. Trim any uneven edges. Starting at the narrow end, roll up the cake and towel to form a 10-inch long log. Place, seam side down, onto a rack to cool.

Unroll the cake and spread with the jelly to within ½ inch of the edges. Reroll the cake, removing the towel. Place seam side down on a serving platter and sprinkle with the remaining confectioners' sugar.

SERVES 10.
CALORIES: 245   CHOLESTEROL: 63 mg   SODIUM: 114 mg   FIBER: 1 g

Health tip:
Use sugarless preserves and omit salt.
CALORIES: 165   CHOLESTEROL: 63 mg   SODIUM: 94 mg   FIBER: 1 g

Chocolate variation: Use 1 cup sifted flour instead of ¾ cup unsifted and add 3 tablespoons unsweetened cocoa. Stir the cocoa into the flour, baking powder, and salt mixture. Follow directions as in jelly roll recipe.

Sponge Cake: Pour the batter into 2 8-inch round cake pans. Grease pan, line with waxed paper, and regrease. Bake 25 minutes or until the cake springs back when lightly touched. Run knife around the edge, then invert onto racks and peel off paper. Cool.

———————◇———————

Mim Jaffe's Butter Cookies

I told my friend Dori Bernstein that I didn't have a decent recipe for butter cookies. She said that her mother makes the best— and she was right. Here's the recipe.

1 cup butter, softened
½ cup sugar
2 cups plus 2 tablespoons all-purpose flour
1 teaspoon vanilla extract

Preheat oven to 350°F. Grease 2 or 3 baking sheets.
In a large bowl, cream the butter and sugar. Stir in the flour, then the vanilla.
Roll into 1-inch balls and press gently to flatten. Place on prepared baking sheets, about 1½ inches apart. Bake 15 to 20 minutes, until golden. Cool on racks.

MAKES 3 DOZEN.
CALORIES: 82   CHOLESTEROL: 13 mg   SODIUM: 43 mg   FIBER: 0 g

Health tip:
Use unsalted margarine instead of butter.
CALORIES: 82   CHOLESTEROL: 0 mg   SODIUM: 1 mg   FIBER: 0 g

Variations:

Thumb cookies: Press the ball of dough with your thumb to make a well (don't flatten the cookie). Fill the well with jelly or jam. Bake as directed.

Almond cookies: Mix ⅓ cup almond paste into the dough. Press a whole almond into the top of the ball, then flatten slightly. Bake 12 to 15 minutes.

Michelle's favorite: Press chocolate chips onto cookies

———————— ◇ ————————

My Famous Peach Pie

This is one of my most requested dishes. The secret to this outstanding pie is to use very ripe, sweet peaches. If the peaches aren't delicious then the pie won't be either. I love the flavor of all-butter crusts. If you want a little extra flakiness, substitute ¼ vegetable shortening for ¼ cup of the butter.

Crust:

> 2 cups unbleached flour
> ¾ cup butter, cold but not too hard
> 4 to 5 tablespoons ice water

Filling:

> 3 pounds ripe peaches
> 1 tablespoon lemon juice
> ¾ cup firmly packed light- or dark-brown sugar
> 2 tablespoons flour
> ½ teaspoon cinnamon
> ¼ teaspoon salt
> Pinch nutmeg

Preheat oven to 425°F.

Put the flour in a large bowl. Using a pastry cutter or two knives, cut the butter into the flour until the mixture resembles coarse cornmeal.

Sprinkle the water over the flour mixture, one tablespoon at a time, and blend with a fork until the water has been incorporated. Then sprinkle with more water, using just enough to form a dough that will hold together. Divide dough into 2 pieces, one slightly larger than the other; set aside

Using a vegetable peeler, pare the peaches. Cut in half and discard the pits. Slice into medium wedges. Put the peach wedges in a large bowl and toss with the lemon juice. In a medium-size bowl, or on waxed paper, combine the brown sugar, flour, cinnamon, salt, and nutmeg. Add to the peaches and toss until combined; set aside.

Roll out the larger piece of dough, between 2 sheets of waxed paper, until 11 inches in diameter. Place in a 9-inch pie plate. Fill the pie with the peach mixture.

Roll the second piece of dough, between 2 pieces of waxed paper, until 10 inches in diameter. Peel off one sheet of waxed paper and turn the dough over the peaches. Peel off second piece of paper.

Gently press together the edges of the 2 crusts, then fold edges up and crimp.

Bake 45 minutes or until golden. Cool.

SERVES 8.

CALORIES: 414   CHOLESTEROL: 46 mg   SODIUM: 222 mg   FIBER: 4 g

Health tip:

Use unsalted margarine instead of butter; omit salt; and eat only ½ a piece.

CALORIES: 207   CHOLESTEROL: 0 mg   SODIUM: 6 mg   FIBER: 2 g

RICE

(Oryza sativa)

Rice is the staple grain for half of the earth's population, with a staggering number of varieties available worldwide.

Until recently, the population of the United States has been eating just one kind of rice: long-grain white. It has only been within the last few years, maybe as the result of a new health awareness, that long-grain brown rice has gained any acceptance at all. As Americans become more adventuresome in matters of eating and more nutritionally aware, other more exotic rices are also making small gains in popularity. Some of these include the sweet rice that the Japanese use for sushi; basmati, an aromatic rice that is widely used in Indian cooking; and aborio, a short-grain white rice that the Italians use to make risotto.

For the most part, in the cultures and countries where rice is a staple, it is white rice that is valued (brown rice, although nutritionally superior, is still looked upon as food for the have-nots) and is used primarily as an accompaniment for other dishes, not as an ingredient. In Indonesia, for example, the Rijsttafel (which literally translates to mean "rice table") is a banquet at which 30 or more dishes and condiments are served that are intended to be eaten with plain rice.

China and other Asian countries eat greater portions of rice with each meal than the so-called main dish. The preferred rice in Asian cooking is sweet or glutinous rice, which is stickier and sweeter than long-grain rice. (It stands to reason that when using chopsticks, stickier is better.)

In the Orient and India, aging rice is a common practice. At one time, basmati was aged for five to seven years before it was deemed fit for consumption. Of course, at that point the rice was also laden with insects, and the merchant who offered raw rice that was not loaded with weevils would have been accused of trying to gyp his customers.

Rice was introduced to the United States in the mid-1700s. There are various accounts of how rice first arrived in this country, but the most commonly accepted version is that the captain of a ship from Madagascar presented rice to Henry Woodward, one of the founders of South Carolina. No matter what the origins were, the swampy land and free slave labor made rice growing in the U.S. a huge success, which is reflected in the number of southern dishes that are cooked with rice. Today rice is widely grown in Texas and California, as well as many southern states.

94

Types of Rice Available

Long-grain white rice: The hull, bran, and germ of the rice have been removed, leaving the starchy endosperm. The grains are long and thin and usually opaque, although converted rice, which has been specially precooked, has a more transparent quality. The different varieties of white rice are usually similar in shape, but they can range from pale yellow to pure white in color.

Long-grain brown rice: The hulled grain with the germ and bran intact. When buying brown rice, you will usually find green grains mixed in with the brown. Most long-grain brown rice are actually beige in color and fairly opaque. Uncle Ben's brand brown rice, although the box does not clearly state it, is "converted" like their white rice, so the grains are transparent. Aromatic brown rice, those varieties that are bred for specific flavors and other characteristics, come in a vast array of colors, from the standard brown to red and black.

Medium-grain rice: Not readily available in the United States, but if you do happen to find it, it is sold as brown or white rice. The taste and texture fall between those of long- and short-grain rice, and it is not as sticky as short-grain rice nor as fluffy as long-grain rice.

Short-grain white rice: There are two types available in this country. The first is known as glutinous, sweet, sticky, mochi, or pearl rice. It is almost as wide as it is long, and it is very opaque and white in color. It is important to rinse this rice thoroughly before cooking to remove talc and other agents used to enhance the whiteness. As the rice cooks, the grains become very starchy and sticky. This type of rice is also best cooked in a rice cooker or a steamer, rather than the usual method of simmering.

The second type of short-grain white rice is aborio, which is cooked in broth for risotto, and rarely eaten plain.

Short-grain rice is often used for rice cakes and in other dishes where its stickiness is used as a binding agent.

Short-grain brown rice: There are two types currently available and both are almost as wide as they are long. The regular short-grain brown rice has a transparent quality and has some green grains mixed in with the brown. The second type is a glutinous rice that is opaque and the color of unhulled sesame seeds or quinoa. Like glutinous white rice, the brown rice cooks best in a rice cooker or steamer. Neither of these rices are widely used.

Precooked (instant) rice: The rice grains are completely cooked and then dried. The consumer simply has to rehydrate the grains in boiling water and the rice is ready to be eaten. As you might suspect, much of the flavor and chewy texture are lost in this process. Precooked frozen rice is also available.

Rizcous: This product from Lundberg Family Farms is a quick cooking brown rice. It is cut into small pieces and when cooked closely resembles the texture and taste of couscous.

Rice mixes: These are available in many forms. Most are combined with dehydrated broth, vegetables, and herbs. Some are also combined with pasta and wild rice.

Puffed rice: The cooked grains are filled with air to puff them. This product is used as cold breakfast cereal.

Rice flakes: Made by cooking the rice and then rolling it flat. Rice flakes are similar to oat, rye, and barley flakes.

Rice meal: This is ground rice and it is sold as a hot breakfast cereal.

Rice flour: Finely ground rice that can be used for baking and to make rice noodles.

Rice-flour noodles or rice sticks: They come dried (you may be able to obtain fresh noodles in specialized Oriental markets) in varying widths. Rice noodles can be soaked (especially the thinest ones) or simmered. Cooked, they have a delightful chewiness and flavor. Or, you can deep-fry the noodles and watch them almost instantly puff up into an airy crisp nest.

Rice bran: The ground bran of the rice, recently reported to be as effective, (or more so) as oat bran in reducing blood cholesterol.

Texture and Flavor

Because each rice has its own distinctive flavor and texture, I am presenting them individually rather than by making generalizations.

Long-grain white rice: Packaged under familiar brand names, such as Carolina, this is the most common form of rice found in the

American home. The flavor is mild, and the texture is fluffy with a hint of stickiness.

Converted long-grain white rice: The "converted" refers to a process used by Uncle Ben's brand, which supposedly seals in nutrients by a pre-cooking process. The cooked rice has a pleasant chewiness and flavor, and the separate grains that Americans favor, and is less sticky and less fluffy than regular long-grain rice.

Basmati rice (Indian): Very white slender grains with an occasional opaqueness. As this rice cooks, the grains get very long. Cooked basmati is light and primarily fluffy, although individual grains may have a slight stickiness and chewiness. The texture has a fall-apart feeling in the mouth that is faintly similar to instant rice. It has a full flavor that is delicate and sweet, and a noticeably fragrant aroma.

Basmati rice (American): The grains are slightly larger, and the cooked rice a bit more yellow and woodier in flavor than the Indian variety. Both are lighter and fluffier than converted rice.

Jasmine rice: The whitest and, for my taste, the most delicate and delicious rice of all. It has the flavor of Indian basmati rice, but a firmer texture, and is not as fluffy or dry, but has a slight stickiness. I have found this to be the best of all of the white rices.

Aborio: The grains are usually partly transparent and partly opaque. Some brands have no opaqueness on the grains, and I find these less to my liking. Cooked aborio, like all short-grain white rices, is sticky. In risotto, the traditional use for aborio, the stickiness is encouraged by means of constant stirring as the rice cooks. The results are a creamy rice with the grains retaining just a little chewiness, with the rice taking on the flavor of whatever ingredients are cooked with it.

Glutinous rice: This is the stickiest rice of them all: It is used as the rice of choice in many Oriental cultures. The flavor is sweet and the grains have a soft chewiness.

Long-grain brown rice: When they are cooked, these long beige grains are fluffy with a very distinct grainy, and sometimes nutty, flavor. The differences in flavor among the various brown rices are not as noticeable as those in white rices. My own feeling is that long-grain brown rice lacks the pleasant chewiness found in short-grain brown rice. However, if fluffy is the quality you value in rice, and if you've avoided brown rice because you thought it might be heavy, try it and you may be pleasantly surprised.

Wild pecan rice: Given the rather exotic name, you might think that this long-grain brown rice would be exceptionally nutty with a distinct pecan flavor. What I found was a fairly typical, fluffy brown rice, that was not especially pecan flavored.

Waheni rice: A long reddish-brown rice with a texture more similar to wild rice than brown rice. The flavor, however, is more like plain brown rice.

Red rice: Although this is technically a long-grain rice, the grains are fairly short. The color of this rice is similar to waheni, a very reddish-brown, which leaches into the cooking water, but does not fade the color of the cooked rice very much. The texture is fluffy and the flavor is "meaty," rather like a strongly brewed tea with a hint of mushroom.

Black rice (Japonica): The grains of this rice are very long, and the color that leaches into the cooking water is purple, not black. Unlike most long-grain rices, this one is sticky, and the flavor is somewhat grasslike. This rice, which is from Thailand, is traditionally used for desserts, usually combined with coconut.

Short-grain brown rice: It has the grainy, nutty flavor of long-grain brown rice, but a denser, chewier texture. As well as being more pleasing, I find that this texture stands up well to any ingredient with which you choose to serve it.

Short-grain brown glutinous rice: Like its white counterpart, this rice is very sticky. The flavor is sweet and the texture is chewy.

Availability

Long-grain white and brown rices are universally available in supermarkets. Along with the white and brown rices, you will also find rice mixes, and, frequently, wild pecan rice, Texmati (or Calmati), and sometimes basmati rices.

Other rices and rice products can be found in specialty-food stores, Oriental stores, health-food stores, and through mail-order grain catalogs (see page 21).

Nutritional Content

Brown rice is a good source of fiber, B vitamins, vitamin E, iron, phosphorous, calcium, and potassium.

White rice contains considerably less of the vitamins than brown rice. Enrichment returns some of the B vitamins and iron, but not the fiber or vitamin E.

Home Remedy

As my grandmother always said, "Rice is binding." Here, then, is an old-fashioned remedy for diarrhea:

4 cups water
1 cup white rice

Bring water to a boil and stir in rice. Cover and simmer for 20 minutes. Drain the rice, reserving the water. Drink ½ cup of the rice water two times a day until the diarrhea is gone. (Eat the rice, too.)

Substitutions

You can interchange any type of long-grain white rice for another. Although the flavors and textures may vary somewhat, the cooking times are the same and the final results should be comparable. If using converted rice, use a little more water and cook about 5 minutes longer. Similarly, long-grained brown rices are interchangeable with the same comments given for white rice.

You can use short-grain brown rice for long-grain white or brown rice, but the cooking time will have to be longer if you are exchanging for white rice.

Wild rice can be substituted for brown rice, but it will require a little extra cooking time. Cooked wild rice can also be substituted for cooked white rice.

Bulgur can be used for short- or long-grain brown rice, but the cooking time will be shorter. For white rice, the cooking time will be shorter.

Couscous can be used in recipes calling for cooked rice or rizcous.

Cooked berries and groats can always be substituted for cooked rice.

Basic Cooking Instructions

Please read *About Cooking Grains* beginning on page 7.

The microwave methods that follow were tested in a 650-watt oven.

Stove-top method for white rice:

> 2 cups water
> 1 teaspoon salt
> 1 cup white rice

In a 2-quart saucepan, bring water and salt to a boil over high heat. Stir in rice and return to boiling. Reduce heat and simmer, covered, for 20 minutes, or until almost all of the liquid has been absorbed. Remove from heat and let stand, covered, for 5 minutes. Fluff with a fork.

Please note, if cooking short-grain white rice, rinse raw rice thoroughly until water is no longer cloudy and runs clear. Do not rinse enriched long-grain white rice.

MAKES 3 CUPS REGULAR LONG-GRAIN WHITE RICE.
MAKES 3⅔ CUPS INDIAN BASMATI WHITE RICE.
MAKES 4 CUPS TEXMATI WHITE RICE.
MAKES 3 CUPS JASMINE RICE.
MAKES 3 CUPS SHORT-GRAIN WHITE RICE.

Steaming method for short-grain rice:

> 1 cup short-grain rice
> 1½ cups water
> 1 teaspoon salt

Rinse the rice until the water is no longer cloudy. Place rice in a bowl filled with water. Let stand 30 minutes, then drain. Place rice, water, and salt in a 2-quart bowl. Place in a steamer with boiling water in the bottom. Cover the pot, but not the bowl, and steam for 30 minutes, or until the water is absorbed. Fluff with a fork.

MAKES 3 CUPS.

Microwave method for long-grain white rice:

> 2¼ cups water
> 1 teaspoon salt
> 1 cup long-grain white rice

Place the water and salt in a 3-quart, microwave-safe bowl. Cover with waxed paper. Microwave on high (100% power) for 3 minutes, or until water is boiling. Stir in rice. Recover with waxed paper and microwave on high for 4 minutes. Microwave on medium (50% power), still covered with waxed paper, for 15 minutes, rotating dish once, if necessary. Let stand for 2 minutes. Fluff with a fork.

MAKES 3 CUPS.

Stove-top version for converted long-grain white rice:

> 2½ cups water
> 1 teaspoon salt
> 1 cup converted long-grain white rice

In a 2-quart saucepan, bring the water and salt to a boil over high heat. Stir in rice and return to boiling. Reduce heat and simmer, covered, for 20 minutes. Remove from heat and let stand, covered, for 5 minutes. Fluff with a fork.

MAKES 3½ CUPS.

Microwave method for converted long-grain white rice:

Follow directions for regular long-grain white rice, but increase water to 2½ cups.

Stove-top method for brown rice:

> 2¼ cups waters
> 1 teaspoon salt
> 1 cup brown rice

In a 2-quart saucepan, bring the water and salt to a boil over high heat. Stir in rice and return to boiling. Reduce heat and simmer, covered, for 45 minutes. Remove from heat and let stand, covered, for 10 minutes. Fluff with a fork.

MAKES 3½ CUPS.

Microwave method for brown rice:

> 2½ cups water
> 1 teaspoon salt
> 1 cup brown rice

Place water and salt in a 3-quart, microwave-safe bowl. Cover with waxed paper and microwave on high (100% power) for 4 minutes, or until water comes to a boil. Stir in rice. Recover with waxed paper and microwave on high for 4 minutes. Microwave on medium (50% power), still covered with waxed paper, for 35 minutes, rotating dish once, if necessary. Let stand for 3 minutes. Fluff with a fork.

MAKES 3 CUPS.

Stove-top method for black and waheni rice:

Please note that salt must be added *after cooking* or rice will not absorb the cooking water. Do not cook in broth.

> 2 cups water
> 1 cup black or waheni rice
> 1 teaspoon salt

In a 2-quart saucepan, bring the water to a boil over high heat. Stir in rice and return to boiling. Reduce heat and simmer, covered, for 45 minutes. Remove from heat and let stand, covered, for 5 minutes. Stir in salt and fluff with a fork.

MAKES 3½ CUPS.

Stove-top version for red rice:

> 2¼ cups water
> 1 teaspoon salt
> 1 cup red rice

In a 2-quart saucepan, bring water and salt to a boil over high heat. Stir in rice and return to boiling. Reduce heat and simmer, covered, for 35 minutes. Remove from heat and let stand, covered, for 10 minutes. Fluff with a fork.

MAKES 3¾ CUPS.

Reheating

Rice can be reheated by lightly steaming or microwaving.

RICE RECIPES

*(* indicates easy recipes)*

————————◇————————

Stuffed Grape Leaves (Dolmas)
Pork-upines *
Mom's Tomato-Rice Soup *
Sizzling Rice Soup
Red Rice Soup *
Paella
Shrimp and Ham Jambalaya
Arroz con Pollo
Chicken Gumbo
Beef Heaven
Turkey–Brown-Rice Salad*
Chicken-Chutney Salad *
Warm Mexican Salad *
Warm Thai Beef Salad *
Lamb Curry and Rice Salad *
Mozzarella Salad with Sun-Dried Tomato Dressing
Randy's Party Rice Salad
Shredded Root Salad *
Molded Rice Salad *
Lazy Lady's Black Beans and Rice *
Dirty Rice
Hopping John
Fried Rice *
Nasi Goreng (Indonesian Fried Rice) *
Rice Pilau *
Creole Rice and Beans *
Beans, Greens, and Brown Rice *
Chris's Ratatouille Brown Rice
Brown Rice and Spinach '
Orange Rice with Almonds *
Nutty, Nutty Rice *
Basic Risotto
Risotto with Tomato and Basil
Risotto with Porcini Mushrooms
Sushi Rice *
Pecan Waffles
Rice-Bran Pancakes *
Blueberry-Bran Muffins *
Rice Pudding *
Black Rice Pudding

———————— ◇ ————————

Stuffed Grape Leaves (Dolmas)

This traditional Greek dish is a very popular appetizer, it can be eaten warm or cold. You can also serve these as part of an antipasto platter or increase the portion and use as a main course. Grape or vine leaves are available in most gourmet stores.

1 jar (16 ounce) grape or vine leaves, drained
¾ pound ground beef, lamb, or veal
⅓ cup finely chopped onion
¼ cup chopped walnuts
¼ cup uncooked rice
2 tablespoons chopped parsley
2 tablespoons currants
2 cloves garlic, minced
2 teaspoons chopped mint
¼ teaspoon ground cinnamon
¼ teaspoon salt
⅛ teaspoon pepper
1 can (13¾ ounce) ready-to-serve chicken broth
¼ cup fresh lemon juice

Carefully remove the grape leaves from the jar and unfold. Rinse under cold water and pat dry.

In a medium-size bowl, thoroughly combine the meat, onion, walnuts, rice, parsley, currants, garlic, mint, cinnamon, salt, and pepper.

Select the largest untorn leaves. Place one leaf, shiny side down, on the work surface. Place a rounded tablespoon of the filling in the center, near the stem. Fold the outer sides in toward the center, covering the filling. Roll toward the tip end to form a neat packet. Continue until all the filling has been used.

Arrange half of the unused leaves on the bottom of a 4-quart saucepan. Arrange the stuffed grape leaves, seam side down, as close together as possible over the leaves. Top with the remaining leaves. Pour the broth and lemon juice into the pot. Weight the leaves down with a heat-proof plate. Bring to a boil over medium heat. Reduce heat and simmer, covered, 1 hour.

Drain and serve warm, or chill in broth before serving.

SERVES 8.
CALORIES: 192   CHOLESTEROL: 38 mg   SODIUM: 398 mg   FIBER: 2 g

Health tip:
Omit salt and use reduced-sodium broth.
CALORIES: 192 mg   CHOLESTEROL: 38 mg   SODIUM: 55 mg   FIBER: 2 g

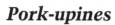

Pork-upines

These make great appetizers at parties.

2 cups water
1¼ teaspoons salt, divided
½ cup short-grain white rice
1 pound ground pork
½ cup minced water chestnuts
3 tablespoons finely chopped scallion
2 tablespoons soy sauce
2 cloves garlic
1 teaspoon sugar
¼ teaspoon five-fragrance powder or ½ teaspoon ginger
⅛ teaspoon pepper

Bring the water and ¾ teaspoon of the salt to a boil in a 1½-quart saucepan over medium-high heat. Add the rice and boil 5 minutes. Drain, rinse with cool water, and separate the grains by sifting them through your fingers. Set aside.

In a large bowl, stir together the pork, waterchestnuts, scallion, soy sauce, garlic, sugar, remaining ½ teaspoon salt, five-fragrance powder, and pepper until thoroughly combined. Form into 24 balls (about 1-inch each).

Roll the balls in the rice (if necessary, separate the grains again). Place the pork-upines about 1 inch apart on a steamer. Place over boiling water and steam, covered, 20 minutes (you may need to make more than one batch).

MAKES 24.
CALORIES: 89   CHOLESTEROL: 19 mg   SODIUM: 421 mg   FIBER: 0 g

Health tip:
Use low-sodium soy sauce. Omit the salt.
CALORIES: 89   CHOLESTEROL: 19 mg   SODIUM: 70 mg   FIBER: 0 g

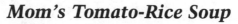

Mom's Tomato-Rice Soup

As you go through this book you will find many of my mother's recipes. This soup is definitely one of the family's favorites. It's a perfect blend of sweet and tart. My mom always stirs the rice into the soup as it cooks, but I find that the rice tends to get too mushy (especially by the second day). I recommend using instant rice, and adding it to the serving bowl just before serving. That way the rice is never overcooked.

2 cans (29 ounces each) tomato puree
4 cups water
1 can (15 ounce) tomato sauce
⅓ cup sugar
¼ teaspoon salt
2 pounds flanken or short ribs
1 large onion, peeled
2 cloves garlic, peeled
Cooked instant or regular long-grain white rice

In an 8-quart sauce pot, stir together the tomato puree, water, tomato sauce, sugar, and salt. Add the flanken, onion and garlic. Bring to a boil. Reduce heat and simmer, uncovered, 2 hours. Discard the onion and garlic. Remove the beef and serve on the side.

Place 2 or 3 tablespoons cooked rice into each serving bowl; pour in hot soup.

SERVES 8.
CALORIES: 209   CHOLESTEROL: 4 mg   SODIUM: 428 mg   FIBER: 5 g

Health tip:
Omit salt.
CALORIES: 209   CHOLESTEROL: 4 mg   SODIUM: 302 mg   FIBER: 5 g

———————◇———————

Sizzling Rice Soup

I love to order this soup in Chinese restaurants. I never thought I'd be able to make it at home. The recipe is not hard, but does require 2 days of cooking: day one to make the rice and the next day to fry the rice and serve the soup (you can make the soup on either day). If you want to make this a vegetarian dish, just omit the shrimp and use vegetable broth. You can make and dry the crusts in advance and then freeze them until needed.

Rice crust:

> 2 cups water
> 1 cup long-grain white rice (not converted)
> 1 teaspoon salt

Soup:

> 2 cans (13¾ ounces each) ready-to-serve chicken broth or
>   3½ cups vegetable broth (see page 19)
> 1 cup + 2 tablespoons water, divided
> 1 tablespoon sherry
> 1 teaspoon soy sauce
> ½ pound medium shrimp, peeled, cleaned, and halved lengthwise.
> ½ cup sliced baby corn
> ⅓ cup straw mushrooms, halved lengthwise
> ¼ cup sliced snow peas
> 2 tablespoons cornstarch
> 2 tablespoons thinly sliced scallion
> Oil for deep-frying

To prepare the rice crust, place the water, rice, and salt in a 10-inch skillet. Bring to a boil over high heat. Reduce heat and simmer, covered, 1 hour and 45 minutes, or until a golden crust forms on the bottom.

Remove skillet from heat and scrape out any loose rice (reserve this rice for some other use), leaving the crust in the skillet. Using a metal spatula gently lift the crust from the pan. Don't worry if the crust breaks into pieces, but try to keep the pieces on the large side. Place the pieces on a baking sheet in a single layer and let them dry, uncovered, overnight.

To prepare the soup, add the broth, 1 cup of the water, sherry and soy sauce to a 3-quart saucepan. Bring to a boil. Add the shrimp, corn, mushrooms, and snow peas. Simmer 5 minutes.

In a small bowl, stir together the remaining 2 tablespoons water and cornstarch. Add to the soup and simmer, stirring until it is slightly thickened. Stir in scallion. Keep warm while you cook the rice crusts.

Pour enough oil for deep-frying into a wok or 2-quart saucepan. Heat until the oil bubbles as soon as a small rice crust is dropped in. Add the rice crusts, a few at a time, until crisp (this only takes a few seconds, you will see that the rice expands right away). Remove to a serving bowl.

Pour the soup into the bowl with the rice crusts and serve immediately.

SERVES 8.
CALORIES: 166   CHOLESTEROL: 10 mg   SODIUM: 747 mg   FIBER: 6 g

Health tip:
Use low-sodium broth; omit soy sauce.
CALORIES: 166   CHOLESTEROL: 10 mg   SODIUM: 423 mg   FIBER: 6 g

———————— ◇ ————————

Red Rice Soup

This is a creamy soup with a chewy texture from the rice.

2 tablespoons butter
½ cup thinly sliced leek (white part only)
2 cans (13¾ ounces each) ready-to-serve chicken broth or
     3½ cups vegetable broth (see page 19)
¾ cup red rice
¼ cup port or marsala wine
1½ cups half and half
¼ teaspoon cinnamon
Sliced scallion, for garnish

In a 3-quart saucepan, melt the butter over medium heat. Add the leeks and sauté until soft. Add the broth and bring to a boil. Stir in the rice. Reduce heat and simmer, uncovered, 40 minutes. Remove from heat.

Using a 1 cup measuring cup, scoop out as much rice as you can and put it into a blender container or food processor fitted with a steel blade. Cover and process until smooth. Stir the pureed rice soup into the remaining soup. Stir in the wine and then the half-and-half and cinnamon.

If necessary, reheat before serving. If desired, sprinkle with scallion before serving.

SERVES 6.
CALORIES: 237   CHOLESTEROL: 33 mg   SODIUM: 467 mg   FIBER: 1 g

Health tip:
Use buttermilk instead of cream and use low-sodium broth.
CALORIES: 179   CHOLESTEROL: 13 mg   SODIUM: 132 mg   FIBER: 1 g

---

◇

Paella

This is a classic Spanish dish. It is authentically prepared with a short-grain rice grown in the Valencia region of Spain. We are using aborio instead. Although paella has come to mean rice dish, its name comes from the shallow pan (paellera) traditionally used to cook it in. If you are feeling truly extravagant, stir in a cut up, cooked lobster when you add the mussels.

3 pound chicken
3 tablespoons olive oil
¼ pound chorizo, sliced
1 cup chopped onion
2 cloves garlic, minced
1½ cups aborio rice
1 can (13¾ ounce) ready-to-serve chicken broth
1½ cups water
½ cup dry white wine
¼ teaspoon saffron
12 clams — NO
¾ pound shrimp, peeled and cleaned
12 mussels — NO
1 cup peas, fresh or frozen
¼ cup chopped pimiento

Rinse the chicken and pat dry. Cut into pieces, separating the leg from the thigh, the wing from the breast, and then cutting the breasts into halves.

In a large saucepan, heat the oil over medium-high heat. Add the chicken and cook until well browned. Remove from pot. Add the chorizo and cook until no longer pink. Remove from skillet. Add the onion and garlic and cook, stirring, until the onion is soft. Add the rice and stir until the grains are coated.

Stir in the chicken broth, water, and wine. Add the saffron and chicken. Cook, covered, 25 minutes. Add the clams, cover, and cook 8 minutes. Add the chorizo, shrimp, mussels, peas, and pimiento and cook 8 minutes longer, or until all the shellfish have opened.

SERVES 6.
CALORIES: 524   CHOLESTEROL: 231 mg   SODIUM: 648 mg   FIBER: 2 g

Health tip:
Omit chorizo; cook the chicken without skin; and use low-sodium broth.
CALORIES: 497   CHOLESTEROL: 201 mg   SODIUM: 300 mg   FIBER: 2 g

———————— ◇ ————————

Shrimp and Ham Jambalaya

The only word I can use to describe this Creole dish is heavenly.

3 tablespoons butter
1 cup chopped onion
½ cup finely chopped celery
¼ cup finely chopped green bell pepper
3 cloves garlic, minced
1 can (14½ ounce) whole peeled tomatoes, undrained
1 can (13¾ ounce) ready-to-serve chicken broth
¼ teaspoon thyme
¼ teaspoon ground red pepper
1 cup long-grain white rice, not converted
1 pound large shrimp, peeled and cleaned
1 cup diced cooked ham
2 tablespoons chopped parsley

Melt the butter in a 3-quart saucepan, over medium-high heat. Add the onion, celery, green pepper, and garlic. Cook, stirring, until the onion is soft. Add the tomatoes and break up with the back of a spoon. Stir in the chicken broth, thyme, and pepper. Bring to a boil. Stir in the rice. Return to a boil, reduce heat and simmer, covered, 15 minutes. Stir in the shrimp, ham, and parsley. Simmer 15 minutes longer, stirring once, or until the shrimp are cooked through.

SERVES 4.
CALORIES: 499   CHOLESTEROL: 261 mg   SODIUM: 1315   FIBER: 3 g

Health tip:
Use 1 tablespoon unsalted margarine instead of the butter and cook in a nonstick skillet; use low-sodium broth and ham.
CALORIES: 422   CHOLESTEROL: 238 mg   SODIUM: 803 mg   FIBER: 3 g

—————— ◇ ——————

Arroz con Pollo

This is a traditional Spanish chicken dish. I like to serve this with a delicious green salad and end the meal with one of my very favorite desserts—flan.

2 tablespoons vegetable oil
1 cup chopped onion
2 cloves garlic, minced
1 can (14½ ounce) whole peeled tomatoes, undrained
2 tablespoons chopped parsley
1 teaspoon oregano
1 teaspoon salt
¼ teaspoon pepper
1 bay leaf
3½ pound chicken, cut up
1¼ cups boiling water
1 cup converted long-grain white rice
½ cup sliced pimento-stuffed olives

In a 4-quart saucepan, heat the oil over medium-high heat. Add the onion and garlic and cook, stirring, until onion is soft. Stir in the tomatoes, parsley, oregano, salt, pepper, and bay leaf, breaking up the tomatoes with the back of a spoon. Add the chicken, bring to a boil. Reduce the heat and simmer, covered, 40 minutes. Add the water and bring to a boil. Stir in the rice, reduce heat and simmer 25 minutes. Stir in the sliced olives.

SERVES 4.
CALORIES: 524   CHOLESTEROL: 197 mg   SODIUM: 1422 mg   FIBER: 4 g

Health tip:
Omit salt. Cook the chicken without the skin. Reduce oil to 2 teaspoons and cook in a nonstick saucepan. Use only half the olives.
CALORIES: 421   CHOLESTEROL: 163 mg   SODIUM: 612 mg   FIBER: 4 g

Chicken Gumbo

This Louisiana specialty is usually thickened with either okra or file powder (ground sassafrass). I've used the okra because it's easier to obtain. Be sure that your roux (cooked flour mixture) is nice and brown before adding the tomatoes.

2 tablespoons butter
2 tablespoons vegetable oil
3 pound chicken; cut into eighths
⅓ cup flour
1 cup chopped onion
½ cup chopped green bell pepper
½ cup chopped celery
2 cloves garlic
1 can (14½ ounce) whole peeled tomatoes, undrained
3 cups water
1 can (13¾ ounce) ready-to-serve chicken broth
1 bay leaf
½ teaspoon Tabasco
2 cups sliced okra or
    1 package (10 ounce) frozen sliced okra
½ cup long-grain white rice (can be converted)
½ teaspoon salt

In a 4-quart saucepan, heat the butter and oil over medium-high heat. Add the chicken and cook until well browned all over.

Remove the chicken from the pot and set aside. Stir in the flour and cook, over low heat, stirring constantly, until well browned. Add the onion, pepper, celery, and garlic and cook, stirring, until the onion is softened. Stir in the tomatoes, and break up with the back of a spoon. Stir in the water and broth and bring to a boil. Return the chicken to the pot and add the bay leaf and Tabasco.

Return to a boil. Reduce heat and simmer, uncovered, 40 minutes. Stir in the okra, rice, and salt and simmer, uncovered, 25 minutes longer.

SERVES 4.
CALORIES: 470   CHOLESTEROL: 95 mg   SODIUM: 498 mg   FIBER: 4 g

Health tip:
Cook the chicken without the skin; omit the butter and cook in a nonstick saucepan; omit the salt; and use low-sodium broth.
CALORIES: 320   CHOLESTEROL: 15 mg   SODIUM: 239 mg   FIBER: 4 g

————— ◇ —————

Beef Heaven

This is a very tasty Thai version of beef jerky. It's sold by street venders and is very popular. I've served it to company many times with very favorable responses.

1¼ pounds London broil
2 tablespoons coriander seeds
¼ cup soy sauce
¼ cup dark-brown sugar
¼ cup molasses
¼ teaspoon black pepper
Cooked glutinous rice

Thinly slice the beef (this may be easier if you freeze the meat until it is firm, not frozen), set aside.

Crush the coriander seeds in a mortar and pestle or put them in a plastic bag and pound with a hammer to break them up. Place in a large bowl. Stir the soy sauce, brown sugar, molasses, and black pepper into the bowl with the seeds. Add the meat and toss to coat completely. Let stand at least ½ hour.

Preheat the broiler. Lay the beef in a single layer (you may have to cook the beef in several batches) on wire racks. Place the racks in a shallow pan; brush the meat with marinade. Broil 3 minutes per side or until glazed.

Serve warm or room temperature with glutinous rice.

SERVES 4.
CALORIES: 312   CHOLESTEROL: 68 mg   SODIUM: 713 mg   FIBER: 1 g

Health tip:
Use low-sodium soy sauce and only half the marinade. Omit salt in rice.
CALORIES: 312   CHOLESTEROL: 68 mg   SODIUM: 466 mg   FIBER: 1 g

———————— ◇ ————————

Turkey–Brown-Rice Salad

Be sure that your rice is al dente so that the salad doesn't turn to mush when you add the dressing.

2 cups cooked and cooled brown rice (preferably short grain)
2 cups diced cooked turkey
1 cup chopped celery
1 cup diced avocado
¾ cup sliced black olives
½ cup chopped red bell pepper
⅓ cup sliced scallion
½ cup mayonnaise
¼ cup salsa (mild or hot)
¼ cup buttermilk
½ teaspoon salt

In a large bowl, toss together the brown rice, turkey, celery, avocado, olives, bell pepper, and scallion.

In a small bowl, stir together the mayonnaise, salsa, buttermilk, and salt. Add to the salad and toss to combine.

SERVES 6.
CALORIES: 390   CHOLESTEROL: 47 mg   SODIUM: 653 mg   FIBER: 6 g

Health tip:
Use reduced-calorie mayonnaise. Omit the salt.
CALORIES: 306   CHOLESTEROL: 41 mg   SODIUM: 294 mg   FIBER: 6 g

———————— ◇ ————————

Chicken-Chutney Salad

I wasn't sure whether to use mango or apple in this recipe, but after it received raves from my sister's co-workers, I decided to leave the mango in.

2 cups cooked and cooled long-grain white rice
(preferably Indian basmati)
1½ cups cooked and cooled diced chicken
1 cup diced mango or nectarine or papaya
½ cup cooked peas
⅓ cup chopped cashews
¼ cup currants
2 tablespoons chopped coriander

⅓ cup unflavored yogurt
¼ cup chopped chutney
¼ cup mayonnaise
1 tablespoon fresh lime juice
¼ teaspoon grated lime rind
¼ teaspoon salt
⅛ teaspoon ground red pepper

In a large bowl, toss together the rice, chicken, mango, peas, cashews, currants, and coriander.

In a small bowl, stir together the yogurt, chutney, mayonnaise, lime juice and rind, salt, and pepper. Pour dressing over salad and toss until combined.

SERVES 4.
CALORIES: 475   CHOLESTEROL: 53 mg   SODIUM: 604 mg   FIBER: 4 g

Health tip:
Omit the salt and use reduced-calorie mayonnaise.
CALORIES: 411   CHOLESTEROL: 49 mg   SODIUM: 201 mg   FIBER: 4 g

————————◇————————

Warm Mexican Salad

This is rather like a shelless taco.

2 tablespoons oil
1 cup chopped onion, divided
3 cloves garlic, minced
½ pound ground beef
2 tablespoons chili powder
½ teaspoon cumin
½ teaspoon salt
1 cup mild salsa or taco sauce
2 cups cooked brown rice
1 cup chopped tomato
1 tablespoon white vinegar
4 cups shredded lettuce

In a large skillet, heat the oil over medium-high heat. Add ½ cup of the onion and the garlic and cook, stirring, until the onion is soft. Add the beef and cook, stirring, until browned. Stir in the chili, cumin, and salt. Stir in the salsa and bring to a boil. Reduce heat and simmer 10 minutes. Remove from heat and stir in the rice, tomato, vinegar, and remaining ½ cup onion. Serve on a bed of lettuce

SERVES 4.
CALORIES: 416   CHOLESTEROL: 51 mg   SODIUM: 674 mg   FIBER: 4 g

Health tip:
Reduce the oil to 2 teaspoons and cook in a nonstick skillet; omit the salt.
CALORIES: 376   CHOLESTEROL: 51 mg   SODIUM: 407 mg   FIBER: 4 g

◇

Warm Thai Beef Salad

This salad is a good example of the Thai cooking principle of balancing sweet and sour, hot and salty flavors.

¼ cup fresh lime juice
1½ tablespoons soy sauce
1 tablespoon vegetable oil
1 tablespoon sugar
2 cloves garlic
½ teaspoon salt
1 pound ground beef
1 teaspoon red pepper flakes
1½ cups cooked and cooled long-grain white rice (preferably jasmine)
½ cup chopped red onion
1 tablespoon fresh chopped coriander
2 cups shredded lettuce
½ cup chopped cucumber
½ cup chopped tomato

Put the lime juice, soy sauce, oil, sugar, garlic, and salt into a blender container. Cover and blend until smooth; set aside.

In a large skillet, cook the beef and pepper flakes until the beef is no longer pink. Stir in the rice, red onion, and coriander. Remove from heat. Pour on the dressing and toss until combined.

Serve on bed of lettuce and top with chopped cucumber and tomato.

SERVES 4.
CALORIES: 457   CHOLESTEROL: 99 mg   SODIUM: 942 mg   FIBER: 1 g

Health tip:
Omit salt.
CALORIES: 457   CHOLESTEROL: 99 mg   SODIUM: 478 mg   FIBER: 1 g

———————— ◇ ————————

Lamb Curry and Rice Salad

This is a delicious and unusual salad. I enjoy it especially in the summertime.

2 tablespoons vegetable oil
1½ cups chopped onion
2 cloves garlic, minced
2 teaspoons ground ginger
2 teaspoons ground coriander
1 teaspoon ground cinnamon
1 teaspoon ground cumin
1 teaspoon ground tumeric
¼ teaspoon salt
⅛ teaspoon ground cloves
⅛ teaspoon ground red pepper
1¼ pounds cubed lamb
1 cup water, divided
2 tablespoons white vinegar
2 cups cooked and cooled long-grain white rice
*   (preferably jasmine or basmati)*
1½ cups chopped tomato
4 cups shredded lettuce
2 tablespoons chopped scallion

In a 3-quart saucepan, heat the oil over medium-high heat. Add the onion and garlic and cook, stirring, until onion is soft. Stir in the ginger, coriander, cinnamon, cumin, tumeric, salt, cloves, and red pepper until absorbed by the oil.

Stir in lamb until coated with the spices. Stir in ½ cup of the water and bring to a boil. Reduce heat and simmer, tightly covered, 1 hour and 45 minutes. If the water seems to cook away, stir in ¼ cup more water at a time, as necessary. Chill.

Remove meat from the pot and shred. Return shredded meat to the pot, stir in the vinegar. Add the rice and tomato; toss until combined.

Line serving plates with lettuce, top with salad, and sprinkle scallion on top.

SERVES 4.
CALORIES: 622   CHOLESTEROL: 139 mg   SODIUM: 492 mg   FIBER: 4 g

Health tip:
Reduce oil to 2 teaspoons and cook in nonstick saucepan; omit salt.
CALORIES: 582   CHOLESTEROL: 139 mg   SODIUM: 97 mg   FIBER: 4 g

———— ◇ ————

Mozzarella Salad with Sun-Dried Tomato Dressing

This salad is a combination of many of my favorite ingredients. Its flavor is rich and has a great depth to it. You might consider serving this salad as an appetizer on plates lined with lettuce. You can omit the proscuitto and make this a vegetarian salad.

⅓ cup wine vinegar
2 tablespoons olive oil
2 tablespoons vegetable oil
4 sun-dried tomato halves (oil packed)
1 clove garlic, minced
½ teaspoon salt
2½ cups cooked and cooled wahini brown rice
8 ounces fresh mozzarella, cut into bite-size pieces
1 jar (6½ ounce) marinated artichoke hearts, drained and chopped into
*   bite-size pieces*
2 ounces thinly sliced proscuitto, chopped
¼ cup grated Parmesan cheese
2 tablespoons chopped fresh basil or
*   ½ teaspoon dried basil*
Freshly ground pepper

Place the vinegar, olive and vegetable oils, tomatoes, garlic, and salt into a blender container (a blender is better than a food processor for this recipe). Cover and blend until smooth; set aside.

In a large bowl, combine the rice, mozzarella, artichoke hearts, and proscuitto. Pour on the dressing and toss. Add the cheese, basil, and pepper; toss again.

SERVES 8.
CALORIES: 238   CHOLESTEROL: 21 mg   SODIUM: 511 mg   FIBER: 2 g

Health tip:
Use half the dressing; omit proscuitto and salt.
CALORIES: 196   CHOLESTEROL: 17 mg   SODIUM: 285 mg   FIBER: 2 g

Randy's Party Rice Salad

Lysa (Randy) Kraft frequently serves this rice at buffets. There is never a grain left over. She suggests this recipe is as good warm as it is cool, and if you like, you can add diced chicken and serve it as a main course salad.

¾ cup olive oil
¼ cup Rose's Lime Juice
¼ cup mayonnaise
1 tablespoon dijon mustard
6 cups cooked and cooled long-grain white rice
2 cups sliced mushrooms
1 cup chopped red bell pepper
1 cup chopped zucchini
⅓ cup sliced scallion
⅓ cup toasted pignoli (place in dry skillet and cook, stirring, over low
    heat until browned)
¼ cup chopped fresh coriander or fresh basil or
    1 tablespoon dried
¼ teaspoon salt
¼ teaspoon pepper

In a small bowl, stir together the oil, lime juice, mayonnaise, and mustard; set aside.

In a large bowl toss together the rice and half of the dressing. Add the mushrooms, red pepper, zucchini, scallion, pignoli, and toss. Let stand ½ hour.

Add the chopped coriander or basil and remaining dressing and toss.

SERVES 12.
CALORIES: 298   CHOLESTEROL: 3 mg   SODIUM: 443 mg   FIBER: 1 g

Health tip:
Use only half the dressing and omit the salt.
CALORIES: 231   CHOLESTEROL: 1 mg   SODIUM: 22 mg   FIBER: 1 g

————— ◇ —————

Shredded Root Salad

I think this salad needs the extra chewiness that short-grain brown rice provides.

> *1½ cups cooked and cooled short-grain brown rice*
> *1 cup shredded carrot*
> *1 cup shredded parsnip*
> *½ cup shredded jicama or daikon radish*
> *2 tablespoons chopped parsley*
> *2 tablespoons vegetable oil*
> *1 tablespoon olive oil*
> *1 tablespoon lemon juice*
> *2 teaspoons cider vinegar*
> *1 teaspoon spicy brown mustard*
> *½ clove garlic, minced*
> *¼ teaspoon salt*
> *⅛ teaspoon pepper*

In a large bowl, combine the rice, carrot, parsnip, jicama, and parsley.

In a small bowl stir together the vegetable and olive oils, lemon juice, vinegar, mustard, garlic, salt, and pepper. Pour the dressing over the salad and toss until combined.

SERVES 6.
CALORIES: 148   CHOLESTEROL: 0 mg   SODIUM: 245 mg   FIBER: 3 g

Health tip:
Omit the salt and use half the dressing.
CALORIES: 117   CHOLESTEROL: 0 mg   SODIUM: 19 mg   FIBER: 3 g

————— ◇ —————

Molded Rice Salad

Molding the rice salad makes a very festive presentation for company, but the salad is equally tasty just served in a bowl as is.

> *2½ cups water*
> *1¼ teaspoons salt*
> *1 cup converted long-grain rice*
> *½ cup slivered almonds*
> *½ cup mayonnaise*
> *⅓ cup sliced pitted ripe olives*

⅓ cup sliced pimiento-stuffed olives
2 tablespoons chopped scallion
2 tablespoons chopped parsley
2 tablespoons fresh lemon juice
1 teaspoon basil
¼ teaspoon pepper

Preheat oven to 350°F. Oil a 4-cup ring mold.

In a 2-quart saucepan, bring the water and salt to a boil over high heat. Add the rice and return to a boil. Reduce heat and simmer, covered, 25 minutes, or until the water is absorbed. Remove from heat.

While the rice is cooking, place the almonds in a baking dish, or on a piece of heavy-duty foil, and bake 10 minutes or until toasted. Remove from oven and cool.

When rice is cooked, stir the almonds, mayonnaise, sliced olives, scallion, parsley, lemon juice, basil, and pepper into the pot with the rice. Spoon into prepared mold and pack slightly. Chill at least 1½ hours.

Invert onto serving plate.

SERVES 6.
CALORIES: 320   CHOLESTEROL: 11 mg   SODIUM: 1177 mg   FIBER: 3 g

Health tip:
Omit the salt and use reduced-calorie mayonnaise. Use only half the olives.
CALORIES: 262   CHOLESTEROL: 5 mg   SODIUM: 729 mg   FIBER: 3 g

---

———————◇———————

Lazy Lady's Black Beans and Rice

Traditionally this soup is made with dried black beans, but I find that this short-cut version, with canned black beans, is just as delicious.

2 tablespoons olive oil
1½ cups chopped onion
1 cup chopped green bell pepper
2 cloves garlic, minced
⅔ cup water
2 bay leaves
½ teaspoon salt
½ teaspoon cumin
½ teaspoon sugar
¼ teaspoon black pepper
2 cans (16 ounces each) black beans, undrained
3 cups cooked long-grain white rice

Heat the oil in a 3-quart saucepan, over medium-high heat. Add the onion, green pepper, and garlic and cook, stirring, until the onion is soft. Stir in the water, bay leaves, salt, cumin, sugar, and pepper. Add the beans, with liquid, and stir. Bring to a boil. Reduce heat and simmer, uncovered, 1 hour. Discard bay leaves. Serve over rice.

SERVES 6.

CALORIES: 220   CHOLESTEROL: 0 mg   SODIUM: 708 mg   FIBER: 7 g

Health tip:
Omit salt; reduce oil to 2 teaspoons and cook in a nonstick saucepan.
CALORIES: 198   CHOLESTEROL: 0 mg   SODIUM: 264 mg   FIBER: 7 g

Dirty Rice

There's nothing pornographic about this rice, but rather, the word dirty refers to the typical brown-grey color from the liver and gizzards. I love the flavor of this dish freshly made, but when reheated, the liver flavor becomes overwhelming. I serve this as a side dish, but it certainly has enough protein in it to be a main course, if you like.

2 cups water
1 can (10½ ounce) double-strength chicken broth
¼ pound chicken gizzards, finely chopped
1 cup long-grain white rice
2 tablespoons vegetable oil or bacon fat
¾ cup finely chopped onion
½ cup finely chopped green bell pepper
½ cup finely chopped celery
½ pound chicken livers
¼ cup chopped parsley
¼ teaspoon salt
¼ teaspoon pepper

In a 3-quart saucepan bring the water and broth to a boil. Add the gizzards, reduce heat and simmer, uncovered, 30 minutes. Stir in the rice, return to a boil. Cover and simmer 15 minutes longer.

While the rice is cooking, heat the oil in a large skillet, over medium-high heat. Add the onion, green pepper, and celery. Cook, stirring, until onion is soft. Add the liver and cook, stirring, until only slightly pink in center. Remove liver from skillet and chop finely.

Stir the sautéed vegetables, liver, parsley, salt, and pepper into the rice. Simmer 5 minutes longer or until the liquid is absorbed.

SERVES 8.
CALORIES: 200   CHOLESTEROL: 206 mg   SODIUM: 335 mg   FIBER: 1 g

Health tip:
Use low-sodium broth; reduce oil to 2 teaspoons and cook in a nonstick skillet; reduce liver to ¼ pound.
CALORIES: 158   CHOLESTEROL: 117 mg   SODIUM: 112 mg   FIBER: 1 g

———————— ◇ ————————

Hopping John

This is a Southern dish traditionally served on New Year's. It always combines pork, black-eyed peas, rice, and onion. The type of pork used varies from person to person. I chose to use salt pork, but you can also use bacon or ham hocks.

1 cup dried black-eyed peas
¼ pound salt pork, blanched
1 cup chopped onion
3 cups water
1 teaspoon salt
Pinch red pepper flakes
1¼ cups long-grain white rice

Cover the beans with water and let stand 8 hours.

Remove and discard the rind from the salt pork and cut into ¼-inch pieces. In a 4-quart saucepan, cook the salt pork over medium-high heat until crisp and browned. Remove from skillet and set aside.

Add the onion to the skillet and cook, stirring, until soft. Add the water, salt, and pepper flakes to the pot. Bring to a boil. Drain the beans and add to the pot along with the reserved salt pork. Cover and simmer 1 hour.

Stir in the rice and simmer 20 minutes longer.

SERVES 8.
CALORIES: 215   CHOLESTEROL: 12 mg   SODIUM: 495 mg   FIBER: 8 g

Health tip:
Use half the salt pork and omit the salt.
CALORIES: 175   CHOLESTEROL: 6 mg   SODIUM: 116 mg   FIBER: 8 g

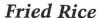

Fried Rice

This recipe is very flexible. You can use any vegetables that you have on hand. If you have broccoli, but no snow peas—no problem. You can also toss in diced cooked chicken, beef, duck, or shrimp and make this a main dish.

3 tablespoons vegetable oil, divided
1 egg, beaten
1½ cups bean sprouts (mung)
½ cup chopped snow peas
½ cup chopped onion
½ cup peas, or peas and carrots
⅓ cup sliced scallion
3 tablespoons soy sauce
2 cups cooked long-grain white rice

In a wok or large skillet, heat 1 tablespoon of the oil over high heat. Add the egg and cook until set (not stirring, as if you were making an omelet). Using a spatula or slotted spoon, lift the egg out of the wok or skillet, chop, and set aside.

Heat the remaining 2 tablespoons of oil in the wok (or skillet). Add the sprouts, snow peas, onion, peas, and scallion and cook, stirring, over high heat until the vegetables are tender-crisp. Stir in the soy sauce.

Add the rice and cook, stirring, until heated through. Stir in the reserved egg.

SERVES 6.
CALORIES: 163   CHOLESTEROL: 34 mg   SODIUM: 542 mg   FIBER: 2 g

Health tip:
Reduce the oil to 1 tablespoon and cook in a nonstick skillet. Use scrambled-egg substitute instead of egg. Used reduced-sodium soy sauce. Omit salt from rice.
CALORIES: 121   CHOLESTEROL: 0 mg   SODIUM: 140 mg   FIBER: 2 g

—————— ◇ ——————

Nasi Goreng (Indonesian fried rice)

You can vary this recipe by stirring in any kind of cooked meat or vegetable when you add the rice. Originally I used a whole jalapeno and liked the result, but I toned it down for the less hearty. If you are feeling strong, use a whole seeded jalapeno. The dried shrimp paste and thick soy sauce are available in Oriental grocery stores.

1½ cups chopped onion, divided
½ fresh jalapeno pepper, seeded or
      ¼ teaspoon ground red pepper
3 cloves garlic
1 teaspoon dried shrimp paste or
      1 anchovy
¼ teaspoon salt
3 tablespoons vegetable oil, divided
1 egg, beaten
3 cups cooked long-grain white rice
1 cup cooked vegetable or meat
3 tablespoons thick soy sauce or
      2 tablespoons soy sauce plus
      1 tablespoon molasses
Sliced tomato
Sliced cucumber

Put ¾ cup of the onion, pepper, garlic, shrimp paste or anchovy, salt, and 1 tablespoon of the oil into a blender container. Cover and blend until the mixture is smooth; set aside.

In a wok or large skillet, heat the remaining 2 tablespoons of oil over high heat. Add the egg and cook until set, stirring occasionally. Remove from skillet and chop; set aside.

Add the remaining ¾ cup onion to the skillet and cook, stirring, until softened. Add the mixture from the blender and cook, stirring, until boiling. Add the rice, vegetables, and chopped egg. Cook, stirring, until heated through. Stir in the soy sauce and cook, stirring, until completely combined.

Serve with sliced tomato and cucumber

SERVES 6.
CALORIES: 218   CHOLESTEROL: 35 mg   SODIUM: 639 mg   FIBER: 3 g

Health tip:
Use low-sodium soy sauce. Omit salt from rice.
CALORIES: 218   CHOLESTEROL: 35 mg   SODIUM: 259 mg   FIBER: 3 g

Rice Pilau

This is a traditional rice pilau, it goes especially well with curry.

2 tablespoons vegetable oil
1 tablespoon butter
1 cup chopped onion
½ cup chopped red bell pepper
1 clove garlic, minced
1 teaspoon salt
6 whole allspice
½ teaspoon curry powder
¼ teaspoon ground cumin
¼ teaspoon ground turmeric
⅛ teaspoon ground cinnamon
⅛ teaspoon ground red pepper
1 cup long-grain white rice (preferably basmati)
2 cups water
½ cup peas, fresh or frozen

In a 2-quart saucepan, heat the oil and butter over medium-high heat until the butter is melted. Add the onion, red pepper, and garlic and cook, stirring, until the onion is soft. Stir in the salt, allspice, curry, cumin, turmeric, cinnamon, and pepper until absorbed. Stir in the rice until coated. Add the water and bring to a boil. Reduce heat and simmer, covered, 15 minutes. Stir in the peas, cover and simmer 7 minutes longer, or until the water is absorbed.

SERVES 4.
CALORIES: 295   CHOLESTEROL: 8 mg   SODIUM: 696 mg   FIBER: 3 g

Health tip:
Omit salt; omit butter and reduce oil to 2 teaspoons, cook in nonstick saucepan.
CALORIES: 229   CHOLESTEROL: 0 mg   SODIUM: 5 mg   FIBER: 3 g

———————— ◇ ————————

Creole Rice and Beans

My friend Leah Weissman assisted me on this dish, and we both agreed it was terrific. The flavor of the vegetables comes through clearly, and the peppery taste wakes up your mouth.

2 tablespoons olive oil
1 cup chopped onion
1 cup chopped red bell pepper
½ cup chopped green bell pepper
½ cup chopped celery
1 can (14½ ounce) whole peeled tomatoes, undrained
1 can (8 ounce) tomato sauce
1 cup water
1 cup converted rice
1 can (16 ounce) pink beans or kidney beans, drained
¼ teaspoon salt
¼ teaspoon black pepper
⅛ teaspoon ground red pepper

In a 3-quart saucepan, heat the olive oil over medium-high heat. Add the onion, red and green peppers, and celery and cook, stirring, until the onion is soft.

Stir in the tomatoes and break up with the back of a spoon. Stir in the tomato sauce and water and bring to a boil. Stir in the rice, return to a boil. Reduce heat and simmer, covered, 20 minutes.

Stir in beans, salt, and black and red pepper. Simmer, covered, 10 minutes longer.

SERVES 12.
CALORIES: 129   CHOLESTEROL: 0 mg   SODIUM: 293 mg   FIBER: 4 g

Health tip:
Omit salt; reduce oil to 2 teaspoons and cook in a nonstick saucepan.
CALORIES: 116   CHOLESTEROL: 0 mg   SODIUM: 250 mg   FIBER: 4 g

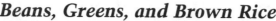

Beans, Greens, and Brown Rice

Christine Koury is one of the most gifted food writers around. She developed this recipe and the next one. For this she suggests that you can experiment with the amount of vinegar you use, and you can substitute spinach or collards for the kale.

5 strips bacon, cut into 1-inch pieces
1 cup chopped onion
1 cup uncooked long-grain brown rice
2½ cups water
½ teaspoon salt
1 package (10 ounce) frozen chopped kale, unthawed
3 tablespoons white vinegar
¼ teaspoon red pepper flakes, crushed
1 can (15½ ounce) kidney beans, drained

In a 4-quart saucepan, cook the bacon over medium heat until browned. Remove the bacon from the pan with slotted spoon and set aside. Add the onion and cook, stirring, over medium-high heat until tender. Add the brown rice and cook, stirring, 1 minute.

Add the water and salt; bring to a boil. Reduce heat and simmer, covered, 30 minutes. Add the greens. Simmer, covered, 20 minutes longer, stirring occasionally until greens are defrosted and heated. Stir in the vinegar and pepper, then the beans. Simmer 5 to 10 minutes, or until beans are heated through, stirring occasionally. Stir in bacon just before serving.

SERVES 8.
CALORIES: 167   CHOLESTEROL: 8 mg   SODIUM: 300 mg   FIBER: 7 g

Health tip:
Reduce bacon to 2 slices and cook in a nonstick saucepan; omit salt.
CALORIES: 153   CHOLESTEROL: 3 mg   SODIUM: 129 mg   FIBER: 7 g

—————◇—————

Chris's Ratatouille Brown Rice

If you want to make this dish a little heartier, you can stir in drained chick-peas or kidney beans. You can also make this into a casserole by putting the cooked rice mixture into a greased baking dish, sprinkling with 1 cup shredded Cheddar cheese, and baking 10 minutes at 350°F, or until heated through.

2 tablespoons vegetable oil
1 cup chopped onion
1 large clove garlic, minced
6 cups cubed eggplant (1¼ pounds eggplant)
4 cups sliced zucchini
¼ cup water
¼ teaspoon rosemary, crushed
½ teaspoon salt
2 cups cooked brown rice
3 cups chopped tomatoes

In a 5-quart saucepan, heat the oil over medium-high heat. Add the onion and garlic and cook, stirring, until the onion is soft. Stir in the eggplant, zucchini, water, and rosemary. Cover and cook over medium-low heat, stirring occasionally, for 30 minutes, adding more water if necessary.

Remove lid and simmer 15 minutes, stirring often or until thickened. Stir in the salt, then the rice and tomatoes. Cook, uncovered, 10 minutes over medium-low heat, or until heated through.

SERVES 8.
CALORIES: 134   CHOLESTEROL: 0 mg   SODIUM: 250 mg   FIBER: 5 g

Health tip:
Reduce oil to 2 teaspoons and cook in nonstick saucepan; omit salt.
CALORIES: 114   CHOLESTEROL: 0 mg   SODIUM: 10 mg   FIBER: 5 g

——————◇——————

Brown Rice and Spinach

This is a very simple and delicious way to prepare brown rice.

2 cups water
1 teaspoon salt
1 cup long-grain brown rice
1 package (10 ounce) frozen chopped spinach, unthawed
2 tablespoons butter
⅛ teaspoon nutmeg
⅛ teaspoon pepper

In a 2-quart saucepan, bring the water and salt to a boil over high heat. Stir in the rice and return to a boil. Reduce the heat and simmer 45 minutes. Add the spinach, butter, nutmeg, and pepper and simmer 10 minutes longer, or until all the liquid has been absorbed and the spinach is heated through. Stir.

SERVES 6.
CALORIES: 158   CHOLESTEROL: 10 mg   SODIUM: 431 mg   FIBER: 2 g

Health tip:
Omit the butter and salt.
CALORIES: 124   CHOLESTEROL: 0 mg   SODIUM: 43 mg   FIBER: 2 g

——————◇——————

Orange Rice with Almonds

I serve this very festive rice dish with game hens and other fancy poultry dishes.

½ cup slivered almonds
2¼ cups water
1 teaspoon salt
1 cup long-grain brown rice
2 tablespoons butter
2 tablespoons chopped scallion
1 tablespoon chopped parsley
1½ teaspoon orange rind

Preheat oven to 350°F. Place almonds in a baking dish or on heavy-duty foil. Bake 10 minutes, or until lightly browned. Set aside.

In a 2-quart saucepan, bring the water and salt to a boil. Stir in the rice and return to a boil. Reduce heat and simmer 45 minutes, or until the liquid is absorbed. Stir in the butter, scallion, parsley, orange rind, and almonds.

SERVES 6.
CALORIES: 212   CHOLESTEROL: 10 mg   SODIUM: 392 mg   FIBER: 2 g

Health tip:
Omit the butter and salt.
CALORIES: 178   CHOLESTEROL: 0 mg   SODIUM: 4 mg   FIBER: 2 g

Nutty, Nutty Rice

Pecan rice is so named because the flavor of that rice is so "nutty." This recipe takes that quality and enhances it by stirring in chopped nuts to further emphasize the flavor. I think it's wonderful and highly recommend it as an easy to make but impressive side dish for company.

> 2 cups water
> 1 teaspoon salt
> 1 cup wild pecan rice or long-grain brown rice
> ½ cup chopped pecans
> ½ cup honey roasted macadamia nuts
> ½ cup chopped cashews
> 2 tablespoons butter

In a 2-quart saucepan, bring the water and salt to a boil over high heat. Stir in the rice and return to a boil. Reduce heat and simmer, covered, 45 minutes, or until all the water has been absorbed. Stir in the nuts and butter.

SERVES 8.
CALORIES: 415   CHOLESTEROL: 8 mg   SODIUM: 299 mg   FIBER: 4 g

Health tip:
Omit the salt and butter.
CALORIES: 390   CHOLESTEROL: 0 mg   SODIUM: 8 mg   FIBER: 4 g

Basic Risotto

It's important that you use aborio rice for risotto. It has a starchiness that is necessary to produce the creamy result associated with risotto. Risotto is a classic Italian dish, and once you have the technique to make a risotto, you can vary it to your heart's delight, stirring in almost any meat, fish, vegetable, or cheese you can think of.

1 can (13¾ ounce) ready-to-serve chicken broth or
    1¾ cups vegetable broth (see page 19)
2¼ cups water
2 tablespoons butter or oil
2 tablespoons finely chopped onion or shallot
1 cup aborio rice
¼ cup grated Parmesan cheese, optional

In a 3-quart saucepan, heat the broth and water until simmering. Keep on low heat so that the liquids stay warm throughout cooking time.

While the broth is heating, melt the butter in a 2-quart saucepan over medium heat. Add the onion or shallots and cook until softened. Add the rice and cook 2 minutes, or until coated with the butter.

Add the broth to the rice mixture, ¼ cup at a time, stirring constantly, until the rice has absorbed the liquid. (You should make the next addition of liquid when you can draw a clear path on the bottom of the pot as you scrape through the rice with a wooden spoon. This will happen rather quickly at first and will take longer as you near the end of the cooking time.)

Stir in the cheese.

SERVES 6.
CALORIES: 172   CHOLESTEROL: 13 mg   SODIUM: 303 mg   FIBER: 1 g

Health tip:
Omit the Parmesan and use low-sodium broth; use 1 tablespoon of oil and cook in a nonstick skillet.
CALORIES: 143   CHOLESTEROL: 0 mg   SODIUM: 12 mg   FIBER: 1 g

———————— ◇ ————————

Risotto with Tomato and Basil

I think, in general, risotto is food of the gods. This risotto is divine. I forgot to peel the tomatoes before chopping, so I was left with little squares of tomato skin in the rice. I thought they added a little something—but you can feel free to peel the tomatoes before chopping.

> 1 can (13¾ ounce) ready-to-serve chicken broth or
>   1¾ cups vegetable broth (see page 19)
> 1¾ cups water
> 2 tablespoons butter
> ¼ cup finely chopped onion
> ½ clove garlic, minced
> 1 cup aborio rice
> 1½ cups chopped, seeded tomato (and peeled, if desired)
> ¼ cup grated Parmesan cheese
> 2 tablespoons chopped fresh basil or
>   1 teaspoon dried basil
> ¼ teaspoon salt
> ⅛ teaspoon pepper

In a 3-quart saucepan, heat the broth and water until simmering. Reduce the heat to low and keep liquid warm.

While the broth is heating, melt the butter in a 2-quart saucepan over medium heat. Add the onion and garlic and cook until the onion is soft. Add the rice and cook 2 minutes, or until coated with butter. Stir in the tomatoes.

Add the broth ¼ cup at a time, stirring constantly, until the rice has absorbed the liquid. (When you can draw a clear path through the rice by drawing a spoon along the bottom of the pot, the rice is ready for the next addition of liquid. This will happen quickly at first and take longer as you near the end of the cooking time.)

Stir in the cheese, basil, salt, and pepper.

SERVES 6.
CALORIES: 186   CHOLESTEROL: 13 mg   SODIUM: 396 mg   FIBER: 1 g

Health tip:
Use 1 tablespoon oil instead of butter and cook in a nonstick saucepan; use low-sodium broth; use only 2 tablespoons cheese; and omit the salt
CALORIES: 165   CHOLESTEROL: 1 mg   SODIUM: 49 mg   FIBER: 1 g

———————◇———————

Risotto with Procini Mushrooms

This is the creamiest, richest rice dish I can ever remember eating (except rice pudding). Serve it to guests and watch them go into ecstasy. For a vegetarian version, use 2 tablespoons of butter or olive oil instead of the pancetta.

¼ cup chopped pancetta (2 ounces) or bacon
2 cups sliced porcini or cremiere mushrooms
⅓ cup heavy cream
2 tablespoons chopped Italian parsley
1 can (13¾ ounce) ready-to-serve chicken broth or
     1¾ cups vegetable broth (see page 19)
2¼ cups water
2 tablespoons butter or oil
2 tablespoons chopped shallots
1 cup aborio rice

In a medium-size skillet, cook the pancetta until crisp. Remove from skillet and drain. Add the mushrooms to the skillet and sauté until soft. Stir in the cream and boil, on high heat, until the cream is slightly thickened, about 3 minutes. Stir in the parsley and set aside.

In a 3-quart saucepan, heat the broth and water until simmering. Reduce heat to keep water just below simmering.

Melt the butter in a 2-quart saucepan, over medium heat. Add the shallots and cook until softened. Add the rice and cook 2 minutes or until coated with the butter.

Add the broth ¼ cup at a time, stirring constantly, until the liquid is absorbed. (When you can draw a spoon along the bottom of the pot and the path remains clear, you are ready for the next addition of liquid. This will happen quickly at first and will take longer as you near the end of the cooking time.)

Stir in the mushroom mixture.

SERVES 6.
CALORIES: 253   CHOLESTEROL: 32 mg   SODIUM: 396 mg   FIBER: 1 g

Health tip:
Use low-sodium broth and omit the cream; use 1 tablespoon oil instead of butter and cook in a nonstick saucepan.
CALORIES: 205   CHOLESTEROL: 8 mg   SODIUM: 165 mg   FIBER: 1 g

—————— ◇ ——————

Sushi Rice

This most popular Japanese dish has gained wide acceptance in the U.S. The basis of sushi is cooked white rice (short- or medium-grain) flavored with vinegar and sugar. This rice is then topped with raw fish, or rolled in seaweed with fish or vegetable fillings. I don't recommend trying to serve raw fish at home, since many fish contain parasites that an untrained cook might not see. Sushi chefs, who are trained for many years, can usually, but not always, detect fish not fit for raw consumption. You can, however, create any kind of vegetable or cooked fish sushi at home. You can find the starred items in oriental grocery stores.

> *2 tablespoons rice vinegar**
> *1 tablespoon sugar*
> *1 tablespoon mirin or sherry**
> *1 cup white sweet or glutinous rice**
> *2 cups water*
> *1 teaspoon salt*

In a small bowl, stir together the vinegar, sugar, and mirin and set aside.

Place the rice in a large bowl. Fill the bowl with cold water, stirring gently. Drain the rice into a strainer. Repeat the rinsing, stirring, and draining 5 more times. The water in the bowl should be fairly clear by the last rinsing. Let stand in strainer 15 minutes before cooking.

Bring the water and salt to a boil in a 2-quart saucepan. Stir in the rice and simmer, covered, 20 minutes. Let stand 5 minutes. Stir in the dressing. Cool to room temperature.

MAKES 3 CUPS. (Serves 6)
CALORIES: 120   CHOLESTEROL: 0 mg   SODIUM: 357 mg   FIBER: .5 g

Health tip:
Omit salt.
CALORIES: 120   CHOLESTEROL: 0 mg   SODIUM: 1 mg   FIBER: .5 g

—————◇—————

Pecan Waffles

The nuts give these waffles a delightful crunch. I served them with fruit syrup, and they were a real hit.

1¼ cups flour
¾ cup rice bran
1 cup finely chopped pecans
1 tablespoon baking powder
½ teaspon salt
1⅓ cups milk
⅓ cup pure maple syrup
⅓ cup vegetable oil
3 egg whites

Preheat the waffle iron.

In a large bowl, stir together the flour, bran, pecans, baking powder, and salt and set aside.

In a medium-size bowl combine the milk, maple syrup, and oil.

In a clean bowl, with clean beaters, beat the egg whites until stiff peaks form.

Stir the maple mixture into the flour until just combined. Fold in the egg whites.

Grease the waffle iron. Pour a generous 1 cup batter onto the waffle iron and spread evenly. Cook until browned, about 5 minutes.

MAKES 12 4-INCH WAFFLES.
CALORIES: 227   CHOLESTEROL: 4 mg   SODIUM: 199 mg   FIBER: 2 g

Health tip:
Omit salt; use 1-percent-fat milk.
CALORIES: 222   CHOLESTEROL: 1 mg   SODIUM: 110 mg   FIBER: 2 g

—————— ◇ ——————

Rice-Bran Pancakes

These pancakes are easy and light. Don't be discouraged by the grayish-brown batter.

1 cup all-purpose flour
½ cup rice bran
2 tablespoons sugar
2 teaspoons baking powder
¼ teaspoon salt
1¼ cup milk
¼ cup butter, melted
2 egg whites

In a large bowl, using a wire whisk, stir together the flour, rice bran, sugar, baking powder, and salt.

In a medium-size bowl, stir together the milk, butter, and egg whites. Add the liquid ingredients to the dry ingredients and stir until combined, but not smooth.

Heat a griddle until a drop of water dances across the surface before evaporating. Drop the batter onto the skillet ¼ cup at a time.

MAKES 12.

CALORIES: 110   CHOLESTEROL: 14 mg   SODIUM: 153 mg   FIBER: 1 g

Health tip:
Omit salt; use unsalted margarine instead of butter; and use 1-percent-fat milk.

CALORIES: 106   CHOLESTEROL: 1 mg   SODIUM: 81 mg   FIBER: 1 g

◇

Blueberry-Bran Muffins

These are very moist muffins, with just a hint of lemon.

1½ cups flour
1 cup rice bran
⅓ cup sugar
2 teaspoons baking powder
1 teaspoon baking soda
½ teaspoon salt
1¼ cups buttermilk
⅓ cup water
¼ cup butter, melted
2 egg whites
1 cup fresh or frozen blueberries, thawed
1½ teaspoons grated lemon rind

Preheat oven to 400°F. Grease 12 3-inch muffin cups.

In a large bowl, stir together the flour, rice bran, sugar, baking powder, baking soda, and salt.

In a medium-size bowl combine the buttermilk, water, butter, and egg whites. Stir in the blueberries and lemon rind. Stir the liquids into the dry ingredients until just combined.

Spoon into the prepared muffin cups and bake 20 minutes, or until browned on top. Remove from pan and cool on rack.

MAKES 12.
CALORIES: 156   CHOLESTEROL: 11 mg   SODIUM: 281 mg   FIBER: 3 g

Health tip:
Use unsalted margarine instead of butter. Omit salt.
CALORIES: 156   CHOLESTEROL: 1 mg   SODIUM: 173 mg   FIBER: 3 g

Rice Pudding

In my quest for the perfect white food, next to roasted marshmallows, rice pudding is one of my greatest passions. I've tried millions (okay maybe not millions) of recipes and none have been as creamy as this. You can stir in raisins before chilling, if desired.

1 cup water
½ cup long-grain white rice, not converted
¼ teaspoon salt
3 cups light cream
½ cup sugar
½ teaspoon vanilla extract
Cinnamon or nutmeg, optional

In a 1½-quart saucepan, bring water, rice, and salt to a boil over medium heat. Reduce heat and simmer, covered, 20 minutes.

Transfer to top of double boiler and stir in the cream and sugar. Cook, uncovered, over simmering water 1 hour, stirring often to separate the grains. (At the end of 1 hour the pudding will be a little liquid, but it will firm as it chills.) Stir in the vanilla. Chill. Sprinkle with cinnamon or nutmeg, if desired.

SERVES 6 (or 2 if you really love it).
CALORIES: 355   CHOLESTEROL: 79 mg   SODIUM: 138 mg   FIBER: 0 g

Health tip:
Use half-and-half instead of light cream, and eat only half a portion. Omit salt.
CALORIES: 139   CHOLESTEROL: 22 mg   SODIUM: 70 mg   FIBER: 0 g

———————— ◇ ————————

Black Rice Pudding

This is a very creamy, rich rice pudding. The black rice cooks up purple, and the finished pudding is a lovely lavender.

2¼ cups water
1 cup black rice
1½ cups half-and-half
¾ cup sweetened cream of coconut
¼ teaspoon rose water or vanilla extract
¼ teaspoon salt
1 cup heavy cream
½ cup chopped pistachios

In a 2-quart saucepan, combine the water and rice and bring to a boil. Reduce heat and simmer, covered, 55 minutes. Stir in the half-and-half and coconut cream. Slowly simmer 1 hour, stirring occasionally. Stir in the rose water or vanilla and salt. Chill completely.

In a large bowl, beat heavy cream until stiff. Fold in the rice and pistachios.

SERVES 12.
CALORIES: 285　CHOLESTEROL: 38 mg　SODIUM: 66 mg　FIBER: 1 g

Health tip:
Omit salt; use 2-percent-fat milk instead of half-and-half and only ½ cup heavy cream.
CALORIES: 216　CHOLESTEROL: 16 mg　SODIUM: 21 mg　FIBER: 1 g

CORN (MAIZE)

(Zea mays)

Originally the word corn was the generic name for all grains. Corn could mean barley, or wheat, or rye, or just any grain. When maize was introduced to the Old World, it was dubbed Indian corn. The settlers in the New World eventually dropped the word Indian and simply used the word corn to mean maize exclusively.

Corn is the only grain that is eaten fresh as a vegetable, and is also one of the few grains native to the Americas. It was corn that the Native Americans taught the settlers to plant that enabled the Colonists to survive during their first few years in the New World.

Types of Corn Available

There are many varieties of corn, each used for a different purpose.

Sweet corn (saccharata): This summertime favorite can be either yellow or white, or a combination of the two, and is eaten fresh.

Dent corn (indentata): So named because it develops a dent in the top as it drys. It is used mostly as animal feed. The small percentage used for human consumption is dried and ground into cornmeal or flour. It can be either yellow or white.

Flint or Indian corn: Because of its brightly colored, hard kernels, this corn is most commonly used for decoration.

Blue corn (Hopi corn): Yellow or white in color, it is used mainly for cornmeal and products made from cornmeal.

Pod corn: Each kernel of this corn has its own little husk. It is probably one of the earliest forms of corn and is not widely available.

Flour corn: This is an especially starchy corn that is favored by Native Americans who grow it for their own use. It is not widely available.

Popcorn: It has a low moisture content and the kernels explode when heated. It can be yellow, white, blue, or multicolored.

142

The varieties of corn are then processed into different grain products:

Frozen and canned corn: Sweet yellow corn, usually removed from the cob, is used almost exclusively for these products.

Cornmeal: Usually made from dent corn that is dried and ground into meal. Yellow and white cornmeal can be used interchangeably. Its most notable uses are for baking, breading, and to make cornmeal mush and polenta. Blue cornmeal is also available, but tends to turn what I consider to be an unappetizing purplish-gray when cooked.

Corn flour: Finely ground cornmeal that is not commonly used. It is available with or without the germ, but is more perishable if the germ is intact.

Hominy: It is also referred to as posole or pozole, or nixtamal, and broken hominy is sometimes called samp. Hominy is dried corn that has been soaked in either slaked lime or lye or wood ash to loosen the hulls. The hull and germ are then removed and the corn is dried. Hominy can be purchased both dried and canned, but neither form is too easily found, except in the South. Canned hominy is sometimes carried by Hispanic markets.

Grits: Dried hominy that has been ground. Grits is available in yellow or white and in coarse, medium, or fine grinds. It is most often used in souffles and baked goods, and as a hot cereal, but its most popular use in the southern part of the United States, where it is eaten as a side dish at nearly every meal with a pat of butter or gravy. Quick-cooking grits are also available.

Masa harina: Finely ground hominy that is used to make tortillas.

Corn bran: The bran of the corn, which is about the same as oat, rice, or miller's wheat bran. It is a good source of soluble fiber.

Corn germ: The germ of the corn can be used the same way as wheat germ, but it is not readily available or commonly used.

Other corn products include: corn starch, corn oil, corn syrup, and corn pasta.

Texture and Flavor

The flavor of fresh corn should be sweet, delicate, and not too starchy. It has long been said that to get the best-tasting corn, the water should be put on to boil before the corn is picked, for all too soon after picking its sugar begins to turn to starch. (It might be worth mentioning here that food engineers are growing corn in which this process has been retarded, thus making the corn stay sweet longer.) If the corn you buy is starchy and tasteless, it's probably because it has been off the stalk for too long. When buying corn, look for bright green husks that are firm and moist, and fresh-looking silk that has not dried out. Next, pull down part of the husk and examine the kernels. They should be plump and luminescent, right down to the tip of the cob. Otherwise the corn is simply too old to eat.

Baked products made with cornmeal will have a coarse and usually crumbly texture and some grittiness. Cooked cornmeal, such as polenta, has a slightly gritty mouth feel and a starchy flavor that may take some getting used to.

Cooked hominy has a very starchy consistency and a strange, faintly sour flavor. It cooks like, and has the texture of, cooked beans. Like cooked cornmeal, it may also be an acquired taste.

Hominy grits are bland, but have a slightly sour aftertaste. Neither hominy or grits tastes like corn. Their flavor is more or less nondescript, except for the sourness. Cooked grits have a grainy, not gritty, texture.

Products made from masa harina, which is also made from hominy, tend to have more of a corn flavor, with no hint of sourness. The texture is very slightly sandy.

Corn bran has only a hint of corn flavor and the consistency of all brans: sawdust.

Compatible Foods, Herbs, and Spices

Sweet corn complements the flavors of the minor and more unusual grains. It goes well with just about any meat or poultry and can be successfully combined with any herb or spice. The starchiness of corn makes it a bit repetitive to use solely with potatoes, rice, or pasta, although certain combinations of these can be wonderful if used as part of a larger recipe, such as corn chowder.

Cornmeal is mild in flavor and can also be used with just about everything. Assuming you like hominy, it also goes well with almost any food or flavor.

Availability

Sweet corn is available nearly all year, but it is always better when purchased during the peak growing months of June through September. Fresh local corn, especially when you buy it from the grower, or raise it yourself, can be quite out of this world. State-of-the-art freezing and canning techniques have made these forms of preserved corn very good and readily available any time of the year.

Yellow or white cornmeal, and quick-cooking or regular hominy grits are available in the cereals section of most supermarkets. Masa harina can often be found with flour and baking supplies. Look for popcorn with the other snacks.

If you have any trouble locating hominy, dried or canned, or masa harina, try a grocery store that caters to Hispanics.

Blue cornmeal and blue popcorn can usually be found in specialty-food stores and health-food stores.

Nutritional Content

Corn is not a great source of vitamins and minerals, although it is the only grain that contains vitamin A, and yellow corn supplies more of it than the white varieties. Corn has some B vitamins, calcium and iron, and protein, but it is low in lysine and needs to be eaten with complementary foods to be of any great nutritional value.

Substitutions

Corn is a very unique grain, and I can't imagine even one suitable substitute for it. However, you can use white, yellow, and blue corn products interchangeably, and frozen or canned corn can almost always be substituted for fresh.

Basic Cooking Instructions

The microwave methods that follow were tested in a 650-watt oven.

There are many methods for boiling sweet corn, but this is the one I happen to like best.

Stove-top method for fresh sweet corn:

> 12 ears fresh corn
> Water
> ½ cup milk
> 1 tablespoon sugar
> Butter, salt, and pepper

Shuck the corn and remove silk. Place in an 8-quart soup pot and cover with water. Stir in milk and sugar. Bring to a boil over high heat and continue to boil for 4 to 6 minutes, or until corn is tender. Drain and serve immediately with butter, salt, and pepper.

Microwave method for fresh sweet corn:

> 2 ears corn
> Butter, salt, and pepper

Peel back husk, but don't remove it. Discard silk. Close husk and microwave on high (100% power) for 3 minutes. Turn corn over and microwave on high for 3 minutes longer. Let stand for 2 minutes. Remove husk and serve immediately with butter, salt, and pepper.

Alternate microwave method for fresh sweet corn:

Shuck corn and remove silk. Place a pat of butter on each ear of corn and wrap in plastic wrap. Microwave following directions above.

For four ears of corn, increase total cooking time to 14 minutes. Let stand for 3 minutes.

Stove-top method for hominy grits:

> 5 cups water
> 1 teaspoon salt
> 1 cup grits

In a 3-quart saucepan, bring the water and salt to a boil over high heat. Gradually stir in grits. Lower heat and simmer, covered, for 20 minutes, stirring frequently until thick.

MAKES 4¼ CUPS.

Microwave method for hominy grits:

2½ cups water
½ teaspoon salt
½ cup grits

Place the water and salt in a 3-quart, microwave-safe bowl. Cover with waxed paper and microwave on high (100% power) for 5 minutes, or until water boils. Gradually stir in grits. Recover with waxed paper and microwave on high for 3 minutes. Microwave on medium (50% power), still covered with waxed paper, for 10 minutes. Let stand for 3 minutes.

MAKES 2½ CUPS.

Stove-top method for quick-cooking grits:

4 cups water
1 teaspoon salt
1 cup grits

In a 3-quart saucepan, bring the water and salt to a boil. Gradually stir in grits. Cook for 5 minutes, stirring, until thick.

MAKES 4 CUPS.

Microwave method for quick-cooking grits:

2 cups water
½ teaspoon salt
½ cup grits

Place the water and salt in a 3-quart, microwave-safe bowl. Cover with waxed paper and microwave on high (100% power) for 5 minutes, or until boiling. Gradually stir in grits. Recover with waxed paper and microwave on high for 2 minutes. Microwave on medium (50% power), still covered with waxed paper, for 2 minutes longer.

MAKES 2 CUPS.

CORN RECIPES

(* indicates easy recipes)

---◇---

Zucchini-Corn Soup *
Best-Ever Cream-of-Corn Soup *
Crab and Corn Chowder
Posole and Shrimp Soup
Fried Catfish
Brunswick Stew
Veal Stew with Corn Wheels
Beef Tamales
Beef and Oriental Vegetables with Hoisin Sauce
Chili-Cheddar Baked Grits
Corn Puppies
Tortillas
Tostada Shell *
Bean Tostada *
Tortilla Chips *
Lite Tortilla Chips *
Fresh Tomato Salsa
Heuvos Rancheros
Nachos *
Puree-of-Pea-Grits Casserole
Polenta
Chicken Cacciatore
Torte di Polenta
Cornmeal Gnocchi with Gorgonzola Sauce
Hush Puppies
New Mexico Corn Salad *
Corn Relish
Succotash *
Better-Than-Canned Creamed Corn *
Skillet Corn *
Johnnycakes *
Can't-Eat-Just-One Corn Fritters
Cornmeal Mush *
Fried Cornmeal Mush *
Spoon Bread
Southern Corn Bread *
Northern Corn Bread *
Cream-of-Corn Bread *
Chestnut Corn-Bread Stuffing
Peppered Blue-Cornmeal Biscuits
Orange Corn-Bran Muffins *
Blue-Cornmeal Pancakes *
Corn-Bran Pancakes *
Indian Pudding
Crunchy Almold-Grits Pound Cake
Cornmeal-Shortbread Cookies

148

◇

Zucchini-Corn Soup

I find this soup rich and delicious. I serve it warm or cold.

2 tablespoons butter
¾ cup thinly sliced leek
2 cups shredded zucchini
1 can (13¾ ounce) ready-to-serve chicken broth or
    1¾ cups vegetable broth (see page 19)
1 can (17 ounce) corn kernels, undrained, divided
½ cup water
½ cup heavy cream

In a 3-quart saucepan, over medium-high heat, melt the butter. Add the leek and cook, stirring, until soft. Stir in the zucchini, broth, and all but ½ cup of the corn and water. Bring to a boil. Reduce heat and simmer, uncovered, 20 minutes.

Put half of the soup into the container of a blender or a food processor fitted with a steel blade. Cover and process until the vegetables are pureed. Pour into a bowl and puree the remaining soup. Return the pureed soup to the saucepan. Stir in the reserved ½ cup corn and the heavy cream. Cook over medium heat until heated through.

SERVES 6.
CALORIES: 176   CHOLESTEROL: 38 mg   SODIUM: 452 mg   FIBER: 2 g

Health tip:
Use buttermilk instead of the heavy cream; use low-sodium broth; and unsalted margarine instead of butter.
CALORIES: 115   CHOLESTEROL: 1 mg   SODIUM: 248 mg   FIBER: 2 g

◇

Best-Ever Cream-of-Corn Soup

My mom always made cream-of-corn soup by stirring milk into canned creamed corn. At the time, I thought that was delicious, but I see now that it doesn't hold a candle to this one. This recipe is based on the same principle of stirring milk into creamed corn.

¼ cup butter
¼ cup flour
1 cup half-and-half
2 cans (15 to 17 ounces each) whole-kernel corn, undrained
½ teaspoon salt
¼ teaspoon pepper
1 cup milk

Melt the butter in a 3-quart saucepan, over medium-high heat. Stir in the flour until absorbed. Gradually stir in the half-and-half. Add the corn with the liquid, salt, and pepper. Cook, stirring, until the mixture comes to a boil. Remove from heat.

Put 1 cup of the creamed corn into a blender container or food processor fitted with a steel blade. Cover and process until pureed. Pour the puree back into the saucepan. Stir in the milk. Cook until heated through.

SERVES 6.
CALORIES: 252   CHOLESTEROL: 41 mg   SODIUM: 637 mg   FIBER: 2 g

Health tip:
Use 1-percent-fat milk instead of the half-and-half and whole milk; omit the salt; use unsalted margarine instead of butter.
CALORIES: 217   CHOLESTEROL: 7 mg   SODIUM: 408 mg   FIBER: 2 g

———————— ◇ ————————

Crab and Corn Chowder

If you're not too fond of crab, or if you can't easily locate it, just leave it out. The soup is excellent even without the crab.

3 slices bacon, cut into 1-inch pieces
1 cup chopped celery
½ cup chopped onion
1 can (10¾ ounce) double-strength chicken broth
1 cup water
½ teaspoon salt
¼ teaspoon pepper
⅛ teaspoon thyme
2 cups peeled and diced new potatoes
2 cups corn kernels, fresh or frozen
6 ounces crab meat, fresh, frozen, or canned
1 cup half-and-half

In a 3-quart saucepan, over medium-high heat, cook the bacon until crisp and remove from pot. Add the celery and onion and cook, stirring, until the onion is soft.

Add the chicken broth, water, salt, pepper, and thyme. Bring to a boil and add the potatoes. Reduce heat and simmer 20 minutes. Stir in the corn, crab, and reserved bacon. Simmer 7 minutes. Stir in the half-and-half and cook until heated.

SERVES 6.
CALORIES: 216   CHOLESTEROL: 43 mg   SODIUM: 529 mg   FIBER: 4 g

Health tip:
Use only 1 slice of bacon for flavoring and cook the chowder in a nonstick saucepan. Use 1 percent-fat milk instead of half-and-half; omit salt; use low-sodium broth.
CALORIES: 168   CHOLESTEROL: 28 mg   SODIUM: 173 mg   FIBER: 4 g

————————— ◇ —————————

Posole and Shrimp Soup

This soup has a very delicate flavor, but you must be a fan of posole to really like it.

8 cups water
1 cup posole
2 tablespoons vegetable oil
1 cup chopped onion
1 cup chopped celery
1 can (14½ ounce) whole peeled tomatoes, undrained
1 bay leaf
1 teaspoon salt
¼ teaspoon ground red pepper
1 pound shrimp, peeled and cleaned

Put the water and posole in a large bowl and let stand, covered with aluminum foil, overnight.

In a 4-quart saucepan, heat the oil over medium-high heat. Add the onion and celery and cook, stirring, until the onions are soft. Add the posole with the soaking water and bring to a boil. Cover and simmer 2 hours. Stir in the tomatoes and break up with the back of a spoon. Add the bay leaf, salt, and pepper. Simmer, uncovered, 30 minutes.

Add the shrimp and simmer 5 to 7 minutes, or until the shrimp are cooked through. Discard the bay leaf.

SERVES 6.
CALORIES: 169   CHOLESTEROL: 115 mg   SODIUM: 435 mg   FIBER: 3 g

Health tip:
Omit the salt.
CALORIES: 169   CHOLESTEROL: 115 mg   SODIUM: 257 mg   FIBER: 3 g

——————— ◇ ———————

Fried Catfish

This recipe for fried catfish keeps the fish moist and delicious inside, and the cornmeal fries up to a very crispy crust. You can use this crust to make fried chicken as well.

4 catfish fillets (about 2 pounds)
¼ cup flour
1½ teaspoons seasoned salt
¼ teaspoon pepper
2 eggs
1 tablespoon water
1 cup cornmeal
Oil for frying

Rinse the fish and pat dry.

On a piece of waxed paper or aluminum foil, stir together the flour, seasoned salt, and pepper.

In a shallow bowl, beat the eggs with the water and set aside.

On a second piece of waxed paper or foil, put the cornmeal.

Dredge the fish in the flour, dip in egg, then coat with cornmeal.

In a large skillet, heat the oil until it bubbles as soon as some cornmeal is sprinkled into the oil.

Fry the fish until golden on both sides.

Drain on paper towels.

SERVES 4.
CALORIES: 548   CHOLESTEROL: 236 mg   SODIUM: 976 mg   FIBER: 3 g

Health tip:
Use an herb salt substitute for the seasoned salt.
CALORIES: 548   CHOLESTEROL: 236 mg   SODIUM: 177 mg   FIBER: 3 g

Brunswick Stew

This stew is thickened at the last minute with a flour wash. If you prefer a thin stew, just omit the flour and water step.

3 slices bacon, cut into 1-inch pieces
2 tablespoons vegetable oil
3½ pound chicken, cut into pieces
1½ cups chopped onion
2 cloves garlic, minced
1 can (14½ ounce) whole peeled tomatoes, undrained
2 cups plus 3 tablespoons water, divided
3 tablespoons chopped parsley
1 teaspoon salt
¼ teaspoon marjoram
1 package (10 ounce) frozen corn, undefrosted
1 package (10 ounce) frozen lima beans, undefrosted
3 tablespoons all-purpose flour

In a large saucepan, over medium heat, fry the bacon until crisp. Remove the bacon from the pot and drain.

Add the oil to the bacon fat in the saucepan. Brown the chicken on all sides. Remove from pot and set aside. (You may have to do this in more than one batch.)

Drain all but 2 tablespoons fat from the saucepan. Add the onion and garlic and cook, stirring, until soft. Stir in the tomatoes, breaking them up with the back of a spoon. Stir in 2 cups of water, parsley, salt, marjoram, and reserved bacon. Bring to a boil. Reduce heat and simmer, uncovered, 30 minutes. Stir in the corn and lima beans. Cook 20 minutes longer.

In a small bowl, stir together the remaining 3 tablespoons water with the flour until smooth. Gradually stir into the stew. Cook until thickened.

SERVES 4.
CALORIES: 613   CHOLESTEROL: 201 mg   SODIUM: 1375 mg   FIBER: 10 g

Health tip:
Discard the chicken skin and omit the step for browning the chicken. Omit the oil; use only 1 slice of bacon for flavor and use 2 teaspoons of the bacon fat to sauté the vegetables; cook in a nonstick saucepot. Omit salt
CALORIES: 440   CHOLESTEROL: 142 mg   SODIUM: 538 mg   FIBER: 10 g

——————— ◇ ———————

Veal Stew with Corn Wheels

I love the way whole chunks of corn on the cob look in a stew, but I must admit that they present a slight eating problem. So, if you prefer, you can use 2 cups of fresh or frozen corn kernels instead of the corn wheels.

2 tablespoons vegetable oil
1½ cups chopped onion
1 pound boneless veal, cubed
2 cups water
2 tablespoons flour
1 cup white wine
1 bay leaf
2 teaspoons sugar
½ teaspoon marjoram
½ teaspoon salt
¼ teaspoon thyme
⅛ teaspoon pepper
1 can (14½ ounce) whole peeled tomatoes, undrained
2 ears corn, cut into 1-inch wheels
2 cups fresh green beans, but into 1-inch pieces
¼ cup chopped parsley

Heat the oil in a 4-quart saucepan, over medium-high heat. Add the onion and cook, stirring, until soft.

Add the veal and brown slightly. Stir the water and flour together until there are no lumps, add to the pot with the wine, bay leaf, sugar, marjoram, salt, thyme, and pepper. Bring to a boil. Reduce heat and simmer 1 hour.

Add the tomatoes and break them up with a spoon, then add the corn and beans and return to a boil. Reduce heat and simmer 7 minutes, or until the corn and beans are cooked through.

SERVES 4.
CALORIES: 464   CHOLESTEROL: 155 mg   SODIUM: 565 mg   FIBER: 5 g

Health tip:
Reduce the oil to 2 teaspoons and cook in a nonstick saucepan; omit salt.
CALORIES: 424   CHOLESTEROL: 155 mg   SODIUM: 298   FIBER: 5 g

—————— ◇ ——————

Beef Tamales

If you don't have corn husks, you can prepare this dish in pieces of aluminum foil instead. Serve it with some Fresh Tomato Salsa (see page 163) on the side. If you cannot find corn husks, wrap the tamales in aluminum foil.

12 to 16 corn husks, fresh or dried (if you're using dried husks, soak them in warm water for 30 minutes)

Filling:

1 tablespoon vegetable oil
¼ cup chopped onion
2 cloves garlic, minced
½ pound ground beef
1 tablespoon masa harina
½ cup taco sauce
¼ teaspoon cumin

Dough:

½ cup lard
2 cups masa harina
1 teaspoon salt
1 cup warm ready-to-serve chicken broth

Wash the husks and remove any cornsilk that may cling to them. Set aside.

In a medium-size skillet, heat the oil over medium-high heat. Add the onion and garlic and sauté until the onion is soft. Add the beef and cook until browned. Stir in the masa harina. Stir in the taco sauce and cumin and set aside.

In a medium-size bowl, beat the lard until fluffy using a mixer on low speed. Add the masa harina and salt and beat, on low speed, until completely combined. Add the broth to make a soft dough.

Spread the husks out on a board (they should be about 5 × 8-inches, if they are smaller, piece 2 or 3 husks together) Spread about 3 tablespoons of the dough onto the center of the husk, spread it to be about 4-inches square.

Spread about 1 rounded tablespoon of the filling in the center of the cornmeal square, leaving about a ½-inch border. Fold the husks in half lengthwise, making sure that the tamale has closed like a book, and press to seal the edges somewhat. Fold the corn husks again lengthwise, folding the part containing the tamale over the husk that is empty. You now have a package that has empty husks on top and bottom with a tamale in the middle. Fold the top and bottom empty husks over the tamale, forming a rectangular package. Tie a string around the package to hold it together.

Place the tamales in a steamer over simmering water. Cover and steam 1 hour. Serve immediately.

SERVES 4. (MAKES 12)
CALORIES: 434   CHOLESTEROL: 74 mg   SODIUM: 536 mg   FIBER: 5 g

Health tip:
Use vegetable shortening instead of lard; use ground chicken or turkey instead of beef; use low-sodium broth.
CALORIES: 373   CHOLESTEROL: 27 mg   SODIUM: 181 mg   FIBER: 5 g

---

Beef and Oriental Vegetables with Hoisin Sauce

I'm not sure if canned baby corn really qualifies as a grain—but just in case it does, I want to cover all bets. Rice wine and hoisin sauce are available in Oriental markets.

¾ pound London broil
2 tablespoons soy sauce
1 tablespoon rice wine or dry sherry
1 tablespoon cornstarch
1 tablespoon hoisin sauce
2 teaspoons sugar
3 tablespoons vegetable oil, divided
2 cloves garlic, minced
1½ cups halved snow peas
1 cup sliced red bell pepper
⅓ cup sliced scallion
1 can (16 ounce) baby corn, drained

Place the steak in the freezer for 15 to 20 minutes so that the beef will be easier to slice. After the beef is chilled, thinly slice against the grain.

In a small bowl, stir together the soy sauce, rice wine (or sherry), cornstarch, hoisin sauce, and sugar. Set aside.

In a wok or large skillet, heat 2 tablespoons of the oil over high heat. Add the steak and cook, stirring, until browned. Remove from skillet.

Add the remaining 1 tablespoon oil to the wok or skillet. Add the garlic, snow peas, red peppers, and scallion. Cook, stirring, until tender-crisp. Return the beef to the skillet and add the baby corn.

Stir the soy sauce mixture and pour into the skillet. Cook, stirring, until the sauce is thickened and the mixture is warm.

SERVES 4.
CALORIES: 474   CHOLESTEROL: 76 mg   SODIUM: 853   FIBER: 3 g

HEALTH TIP:
Reduce oil to 1 tablespoon and cook in nonstick wok or skillet, using 2 teaspoons oil to cook the beef and 1 teaspoon oil for the vegetables; use low-sodium soy suace.
CALORIES: 415   CHOLESTEROL: 76 mg   SODIUM: 403 mg   FIBER: 3 g

———————◇———————

Chili-Cheddar Baked Grits

This is a very substantial dish, I like it as a side dish for brunch, but you can serve it as the main dish as well.

2½ cups water
1 cup milk
¾ cup grits
1 cup shredded sharp Cheddar cheese
¼ cup chopped canned chilies
1 teaspoon salt
½ teaspoon Worcestershire sauce
¼ teaspoon onion powder
¼ teaspoon dry mustard
Dash nutmeg
2 eggs

Preheat oven to 350°F. Grease a 2-quart casserole.

In a 3-quart saucepan, bring water and milk to a boil over high heat. Stir in grits. Cook, stirring, until mixture returns to a boil. Reduce heat and simmer, covered, 30 minutes.

Remove from heat and stir in the cheese until melted. Stir in the chilies, salt, Worcestershire sauce, onion powder, mustard, and nutmeg.

In a medium-size bowl beat the eggs and gradually stir into the grits mixture. Spoon into prepared casserole. Bake 1 hour and 10 minutes, or until baked through.

SERVES 4.
CALORIES: 299   CHOLESTEROL: 142 mg   SODIUM: 777 mg   FIBER: 4 g

Health tip:
Omit salt; use skim milk; use scrambled-egg substitute
CALORIES: 274   CHOLESTEROL: 33 mg   SODIUM: 262 mg   FIBER: 4 g

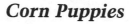
---◇---

Corn Puppies

These are little corn dogs. They make great birthday party fare for your kids. They're easier to make than corn dogs because you don't have to fiddle with the popsicle sticks.

1 package (12 ounce) frankfurters, or cocktail franks
1 cup cornmeal
½ cup flour
1 teaspoon sugar
1 teaspoon baking powder
1 teaspoon salt
⅔ cup milk
2 eggs
Oil for deep-frying

Cut each frankfurter into 6 pieces (if using the whole).

In a medium-size bowl, stir together the cornmeal, flour, sugar, baking powder, and salt. In a separate bowl, beat the milk and egg. Stir the milk mixture into the dry ingredients

In a large saucepan, heat the oil until it bubbles as soon as some batter is dropped in.

Pierce a piece of frankfurter with a fork, dip into the batter until completely coated. Using a second fork, gently push the batter-coated puppy off the first fork and into the oil. Cook until golden on both sides. Drain on paper towel.

MAKES 42 PIECES
CALORIES: 66   CHOLESTEROL: 14 mg   SODIUM: 147 mg   FIBER: .5

Health tip: Eat just one.

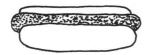

———————◇———————

Tortillas

Tortillas are the base of many Mexican recipes. Most cookbooks call for 2 pieces of equipment for tortilla making: a tortilla press and a comal (a cast-iron tortilla cooker). I will assume that you don't have either piece of equipment (if you do have them you probably already know how to make tortillas). These homemade tortillas seem tougher than store bought, but they are tasty.

2 cups masa harina
1 teaspoon salt
1 cup plus 2 tablespoons warm water

Combine the masa harina and the salt in a large bowl. Make a well in the middle of the "flour" mixture and gradually add the water, mixing it into the flour using a wooden spoon. After you have stirred in the water, continue mixing the dough with your hands until the dough forms a ball. The final dough should be firm and hold together. If it is crumbly, it needs more water; if it is sticky, it needs additional masa harina. Cover with plastic wrap and let rest, at room temperature, 1 hour.

Form into 2-inch balls (you can vary the size of the ball according to how large you want your tortilla to be). If you have a tortilla press, you would flatten the tortillas in it now. If you do not have a tortilla press, place one ball of dough between 2 pieces of waxed paper. Roll into a 7-inch circle. Continue until all the dough has been rolled out.

Heat a heavy skillet (preferably cast iron). Cook the tortillas on the ungreased skillet 1 to 2 minutes per side or until blistery.

Stack the cooked tortillas, wrapped in a cloth or towel to keep them warm and away from the air, which would dry them out.

MAKES 8.
CALORIES: 126   CHOLESTEROL: 0   SODIUM: 267 mg.   FIBER: 3g

Health tip:
Omit the salt.
CALORIES: 126   CHOLESTEROL: 0   SODIUM: 25 mg.   FIBER: 3g

Tostada Shell

Tostadas are open-faced tacos. The tostada shells are easier to make because you don't have to worry about shaping them as they crisp. You can use the same toppings for tostadas as you would use to fill tacos.

Oil for deep-frying
8 tortillas, fresh or frozen and thawed

Heat the oil in a skillet large enough to hold the tortilla. When the oil is hot enough that it bubbles as soon as a small piece of tortilla is thrown in, fry 1 tortilla at a time until crisp. Drain on paper towels.

MAKES 8.
CALORIES: 95   CHOLESTEROL: 0 mg   SODIUM: 1 mg   FIBER: 2 g

Health tip:
Prepare these the same way you would for lite tortilla chips, but don't cut them into wedges (see page 00).
CALORIES: 66   CHOLESTEROL: 0 mg   SODIUM: 0 mg   FIBER: 2 g

Bean Tostada

This is a basic and easy recipe. You can dress it up by serving it with guacamole (you'll find a good recipe for it in the Job's Tears chapter), additional sour cream, salsa, sliced ripe olives, jalapenos, avocado, or anything you can think of.

1 can (16 ounce) refried beans
2 tablespoons sour cream
4 tostada shells (you can use homemade or
    buy them packaged at the supermarket)
1 cup shredded Cheddar cheese
1 cup shredded lettuce
½ cup chopped tomato
¼ cup chopped onion

Preheat the broiler.
In a medium-size bowl, stir together the beans and sour cream. Spoon one quarter of the bean mixture over each of the tostada shells. Sprinkle one quarter of the cheese over each shell. Place on a

baking sheet. Slide under broiler until cheese is melted and bean mixture is warm.

Place 1 tostada on each plate and top with one quarter of the lettuce, tomato, and onion.

SERVES 4.
CALORIES: 317   CHOLESTEROL: 33 mg   SODIUM: 633 mg   FIBER: 12 g

Health tip:
Use yogurt instead of sour cream.
CALORIES: 306   CHOLESTEROL: 30 mg   SODIUM: 633 mg   FIBER: 12 g

———————◇———————

Tortilla Chips

Homemade tortilla chips are totally irresistible. Use them as a snack or eat them with Fresh Tomato Salsa (see page 163).

8 tortillas (homemade or packaged)
Oil for deep-frying
Salt, optional
Chili powder, optional

Cut each tortilla into 8 wedges. Heat the oil until it bubbles as soon as a small piece of tortilla is dropped in. Fry the tortillas, a few at a time, until they are crispy. Drain on paper towels. Sprinkle with salt or chili powder, if desired.

MAKES 64.
CALORIES: 20   CHOLESTEROL: 0 mg   SODIUM: 19 mg   FIBER: 2 g

Health tip:
Make lite tortilla chips (see p. 000).

———————◇———————

Lite Tortilla Chips

These are very tasty. They have a different type of snap from the fried variety.

6 corn tortillas (5-inch), frozen, thawed, or homemade
1 tablespoon vegetable oil
Salt, optional
Chili powder, optional

Preheat oven to 375°F. Lightly brush both sides of each tortilla with oil. Sprinkle with salt. Cut each tortilla into 8 wedges.

Place on an ungreased baking sheet and bake 10 minutes or until crisp. If desired sprinkle with chili powder.

MAKES 48.
CALORIES: 11   CHOLESTEROL: 0 mg   SODIUM: 14 mg   FIBER: 0 g

Health tip:
Omit salt.
CALORIES: 11   CHOLESTEROL: 0 mg   SODIUM: 0 mg   FIBER: 0 g

———◇———

Fresh Tomato Salsa

This is a delicious sauce that you can use as a dip, or as a sauce to top any Mexican dish. It's a little spicy as is, but you can vary that to your own taste.

2 medium tomatoes
¼ small green bell pepper, cut into chunks
¼ small onion, cut into chunks
⅛ lemon with the skin, cut into chunks
¼ teaspoon salt
½ small clove garlic
⅛ teaspoon ground red pepper

Peel the tomatoes by dipping them in boiling water for about 1 minute, then plunging them into ice water. Cool. Lift off skin using a paring knife. (If you have a gas range, you can place the tomato on a fork, hold it in the flame, rotating the tomato until the skin pops and splits in a few places, and lift off the skin.)

Cut half of one of the tomatoes into chunks and put in a blender container or food processor fitted with a steel blade. Add the pepper, onion, and the lemon to the blender or processor. Add the salt, garlic, and red pepper. Cover and process until pureed. Finely chop the remaining 1½ tomatoes and stir into the puree.

MAKES ABOUT 1½ CUPS. (per tablespoon)
CALORIES: 3   CHOLESTEROL: 0 mg   SODIUM: 23 mg   FIBER: 0 g

Health tip:
Omit salt.
CALORIES: 3   CHOLESTEROL: 0 mg   SODIUM: 1 mg   FIBER: 0 g

Huevos Rancheros

This is one of my favorite brunches. Start the meal with a spicy Bloody Mary and end it with Mexican coffee.

8 tortillas (5-inch), homemade or packaged
1 tablespoon vegetable oil
3 tablespoons butter
8 eggs
1 cup salsa (you can use any kind, mild or hot, or you can use
    homemade Fresh Tomato Salsa, see p. 163)
1 small avocado, sliced into 16 wedges

Preheat oven to 350°F.

Brush each tortilla with some of the oil. Place the tortillas in the oven to heat for 7 to 10 minutes, or until crisp.

While the tortillas are in the oven, melt 1½ tablespoons butter in a 10-inch, slope-sided skillet. Add 4 eggs to the skillet and cook until the whites are set, or to desired doneness. Place one egg on each of 4 tortillas and return to oven to keep warm. Melt the remaining 1½ tablespoons of butter in the skillet and cook the remaining eggs. Place one on each of the remaining tortillas.

Top each egg with 2 tablespoons salsa and 2 slices of avocado.

SERVES 4.
CALORIES: 488   CHOLESTEROL: 439 mg   SODIUM: 270 mg   FIBER: 11 g

Health tip:
Use unsalted margarine instead of butter and serve only 1 heuvos rancheros per person.
CALORIES: 244   CHOLESTEROL: 208 mg   SODIUM: 103 mg   FIBER: 11 g

Nachos

Nachos are a favorite appetizer in most Tex-Mex restaurants. You can make them with tortilla chips, but I prefer making it like a pizza on one whole tostada shell, then cutting it into wedges.

1 tostada shell (7-inch)
½ cup shredded Cheddar cheese
¼ cup sliced marinated jalapeno peppers

Preheat oven to 400°F.

Place the tostada shell on a baking sheet. Top with cheese, then sprinkle with pepper slices. Bake 5 minutes, or until the cheese is melted.

Place on serving plate and cut into 8 wedges, using a sharp knife or a pizza wheel.

SERVES 2.
CALORIES: 150   CHOLESTEROL: 30 mg   SODIUM: 425 mg   FIBER: 2 g

Health tip:
Use only ¼ cup Cheddar cheese.
CALORIES: 84   CHOLESTEROL: 15 mg   SODIUM: 337 mg   FIBER: 2 g

—————————◇—————————

Puree-of-Pea-Grits Casserole

The bacon can be omitted and you can make this into a vegetarian dish.

3 slices bacon
½ cup water
1 boullion cube (chicken, beef, or vegetable)
1 package (10 ounce) frozen peas
3 eggs, separated
2 cups cooked grits

Preheat oven to 375°F. Grease a 2-quart casserole.

Cook the bacon in a large skillet, over medium-high heat, until crisp. Remove from skillet and drain on paper towels, crumble, and set aside. Add the water and boullion cube to the skillet and cook, stirring, until the cube dissolves. Add the peas and cook until just heated through.

Place the peas and cooking liquid into a blender container or a food processor fitted with a steel blade. Cover and process until pureed. Place into a large bowl and stir in the egg yolks, and then the grits.

In a clean bowl, using clean beaters, beat the egg whites until stiff. Fold into the grits mixture. Fold in reserved bacon. Spread into the prepared casserole.

Bake 45 minutes or until browned on top.

SERVES 6.
CALORIES: 165   CHOLESTEROL: 109 mg   SODIUM: 230 mg   FIBER: 4 g

Health tip:
Omit the bacon.
CALORIES: 123   CHOLESTEROL: 104 mg   SODIUM: 179 mg   FIBER: 4 g

Polenta

My dog Poppy and I were in the park one day when we ran into my friend Lucia Sciorsci and her dog Topper. We were comparing notes on how awful the previous day had been. For me, no matter what I tried, my polenta had failed. So, here is Lucia's foolproof method for perfect polenta. It's only fair that I warn you that by the time the polenta is finished cooking you will have forearms that look like Popeye's.

8 cups water, divided
2 teaspoons salt
2½ cups yellow cornmeal

In a 4-quart saucepan, bring 5 cups of the water and the salt to a boil over high heat.

While the water is cooking, stir together the remaining 3 cups of water and the cornmeal (Lucia puts them in a jar and shakes it until combined). When the water comes to a boil, add the cornmeal, all at once, and stir like crazy until the cornmeal is completely combined with the water.

Reduce the heat so that the mixture is simmering and cook, stirring constantly, until the polenta pulls away from the side of the pot as it is stirred, about 30 minutes. (At this point, you can stir in any additions that you like, such as butter, cheese, sautéed vegetables, etc.). Pour the polenta into a bowl and let stand 2 minutes. Place a serving plate over the top of the bowl with the polenta and unmold the polenta onto the plate. Cut into wedges to serve (or you can put the cooked polenta into a greased container and chill it 2 or more hours, then slice for broiling, baking, or frying).

SERVES 8.
CALORIES: 157   CHOLESTEROL: 0 mg   SODIUM: 533 mg   FIBER: 3 g

Health tip:
Omit salt.
CALORIES: 157   CHOLESTEROL: 0 mg   SODIUM: 1 mg   FIBER: 3 g

Broiled Polenta: Slice the chilled polenta and place under the broiler until the polenta gets browned; turn and broil second side.

Fried Polenta: Slice the chilled polenta. Cook in a large skillet, with about ¼ inch of hot oil, until browned on both sides.

———————— ◇ ————————

Chicken Cacciatore

Lucia mentioned that her favorite way to eat polenta is with Chicken Cacciatore, so here's my favorite recipe for it.

¼ cup all-purpose flour
½ teaspoon salt, divided
⅛ teaspoon pepper
3½ pound chicken, cut into pieces
2 to 4 tablespoons vegetable oil, divided
1 cup chopped mushrooms
¾ cup chopped onion
2 cloves garlic, minced
1 can (16 ounce) whole peeled tomatoes in puree, undrained
½ cup dry white wine
3 tablespoons chopped parsley
1 teaspoon sugar
1 teaspoon oregano
½ teaspoon basil
¼ teaspoon thyme

On a piece of waxed paper or in a medium-size bowl, combine the flour, ¼ teaspoon of the salt, and the pepper. Dredge the chicken in the flour, shaking off any excess.

In a 4-quart saucepan, heat 2 tablespoons of the oil over medium-high heat. Add the chicken and cook until browned on the bottom. Turn and brown on second side. (You may have to do this in batches and, if necessary, add the remaining oil to the saucepan.) Remove the chicken from the saucepan and set aside.

Add the mushrooms, onion, and garlic to the saucepan and cook, stirring, until the onion is soft. Add the tomatoes with the puree, breaking them up with the back of a spoon. Stir in the wine, parsley, sugar, oregano, basil, thyme, and remaining ¼ teaspoon salt. Return the chicken to the saucepan. Bring to a boil. Reduce heat and simmer, covered, 45 minutes.

SERVES 4.
CALORIES: 505   CHOLESTEROL: 197 mg   SODIUM: 675 mg   FIBER: 2 g

Health tip:
Remove the skin from the chicken before cooking; reduce oil to 1 tablespoon and cook in a nonstick skillet. Omit the salt.
CALORIES: 380   CHOLESTEROL: 141 mg   SODIUM: 346 mg   FIBER: 2 g

Torte di Polenta

This dish is similar to lasagna. If you prefer, you can just prepare the sauce and serve it over freshly cooked polenta, then pass the Parmesan cheese on the side.

Sauce:

> *1 pound ground beef*
> *1 pound Italian sweet sausage*
> *1½ cups chopped onion*
> *1 cup sliced mushroom*
> *3 cloves garlic, minced*
> *1 can (14½ ounce) whole peeled tomatoes, undrained*
> *1 can (8 ounce) tomato sauce*
> *1 can (6 ounce) tomato paste*
> *½ cup water*
> *1 bay leaf*
> *2 teaspoons basil*
> *1 teaspoon sugar*
> *½ teaspoon salt*
> *¼ teaspoon oregano*
> *¼ teaspoon thyme*
> *⅛ teaspoon pepper*
> *1 recipe polenta, chilled in an 8-inch loaf pan*
> *1 cup shredded mozzarella*
> *½ cup grated parmesan, divided*

In a 4-quart saucepan, cook the beef, sausage, onion, mushroom, and garlic until the meats are cooked through and the onion is softened. Stir in the tomatoes, breaking them up with the back of a spoon, then the tomato sauce, tomato paste, water, bay leaf, basil, sugar, salt, oregano, thyme, and pepper. Simmer, uncovered, 40 minutes and set aside. Discard bay leaf.

Preheat oven to 350°F. Grease a 9 × 13 × 2-inch baking pan.

Remove the polenta from the loaf pan and cut into 20 slices. Line the bottom of the prepared pan with 10 slices of the polenta. Spoon the sauce over the polenta and sprinkle with the mozzarella and ¼ cup of the Parmesan. Top with the remaining 10 slices of the polenta; and sprinkle with the remaining ¼ cup of the Parmesan. Bake 40 minutes. Remove from oven and let stand 10 minutes before serving.

SERVES 10.
CALORIES: 492   CHOLESTEROL: 86 mg   SODIUM: 1350 mg   FIBER: 5 g

Health tip:
Drain any excess fat off after cooking beef and sausage; omit salt; use unsalted margarine instead of butter.
CALORIES: 480   CHOLESTEROL: 82 mg   SODIUM: 818 mg   FIBER: 5 g

—————◇—————

Cornmeal Gnocchi with Gorgonzola Sauce

I have read that the Roman's sometimes made their gnocchi of cornmeal, and although I have never seen a recipe for this, it sounded like a great idea. These gnocchi are on the large side. You can make them smaller by cutting them into smaller pieces before you shape them.

2 cups boiling water
1 teaspoon salt
½ cup white cornmeal
½ cup flour
¾ cup half-and-half
⅔ cup firmly packed gorgonzola (8 ounces)
1 tablespoon chopped parsley

In a 3-quart saucepan, bring the water and salt to a racing boil. Gradually stir in the cornmeal, making sure that the water never stops boiling and that the cornmeal doesn't lump. Reduce heat and simmer, stirring constantly, 5 minutes. Remove from heat and stir in flour. Set aside until cool enough to handle.

Divide the dough in half, and on a floured surface roll each half into a 30-inch rope. Cut into one ½ inch pieces. To shape the gnocchi, take one piece of dough and hold it against the floured handle of a wooden spoon (this should give the dough a crescent shape). Using the tines of a fork, score the outside of the crescent (it is easiest to do this while the dough is still on the spoon handle). The final result will be somewhat like a pasta shell.

Prepare the sauce by putting the half-and-half, gorgonzola, and parsley into a 1½-quart saucepan. Cook over medium heat, stirring until the gorgonzola has melted and the sauce has thickened. Keep warm until the gnocchi are cooked.

Bring a large pot of salted water to a boil. Drop the gnocchi into the water. (They will drop to the bottom of the pot. When they rise to the surface, they need just about 20 seconds extra before they are done.) Using a slotted spoon lift the cooked gnocchi out of the pot. Let them drain a few seconds, then put them into the sauce.

SERVES 8.
CALORIES: 210   CHOLESTEROL: 36 mg   SODIUM: 791 mg   FIBER: 2 g

Health tip:
Serve the gnocchi with tomato sauce instead of gorgonzola sauce.
CALORIES: 70   CHOLESTEROL: 0 mg   SODIUM: 186 mg   FIBER: 2 g

—————— ◇ ——————

Hush Puppies

Hush puppies and catfish are a perfect pair. These hush puppies are light and only mildly onion-y. If you like lots of onion flavor just add more.

> 1 cup cornmeal
> 1/3 cup flour
> 2 teaspoons baking powder
> 1 teaspoon salt
> 1 teaspoon sugar
> 3/4 cup milk
> 1 egg
> 1/3 cup finely chopped onion
> Oil for deep-frying

In a medium-size bowl, stir together the cornmeal, flour, baking powder, salt, and sugar.

In a medium-size bowl beat the milk, egg, and onion until completely combined. Stir the liquid mixture into the dry ingredients.

In a medium-size saucepan, heat the oil until bubbles form as soon as a small amount of batter is dropped into the saucepan. Drop the cornmeal batter by tablespoonsful into the hot oil. Fry until browned on both sides and the middle is cooked. Drain on paper towels.

MAKES 24.
CALORIES: 49   CHOLESTEROL: 10 mg   SODIUM: 123 mg   FIBER: 1 g

Health tip:
Omit salt, use 2-percent-fat milk
CALORIES: 48   CHOLESTEROL: 9 mg   SODIUM: 34 mg   FIBER: 1 g

New Mexico Corn Salad

This salad is delicious. The taco sauce adds just a little zip to the dressing. You can jazz it up even more by using hot sauce instead of mild.

1 can (17 ounce) whole-kernel corn, drained
1 can (10 ounce) kidney beans, drained
1 cup sliced celery
½ cup chopped red bell pepper
½ cup chopped green bell pepper
⅓ cup chopped onion
3 tablespoons vegetable oil
3 tablespoons mild taco sauce
1 tablespoon cider vinegar
½ teaspoon chili powder
½ teaspoon salt
¼ teaspoon celery seeds
⅛ teaspoon pepper

In a large bowl, toss the corn, kidney beans, celery, red pepper, green pepper, and onion. In a small bowl, stir together the oil, taco sauce, vinegar, chili powder, salt, celery seeds, and pepper.

Pour the dressing over the salad and toss until combined.

SERVES 8.

CALORIES: 145   CHOLESTEROL: 0 mg   SODIUM: 247 mg   FIBER: 4 g

Health tip:
Use half the dressing and omit the salt.

CALORIES: 121   CHOLESTEROL: 0 mg   SODIUM: 110 mg   FIBER: 4 g

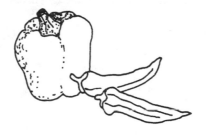

Corn Relish

I made this corn relish fairly plain, but you can add other vegetables to the recipe. Frequently, cabbage, zucchini, and/or green beans are added. If you don't want to spend the time cutting the kernels from the cob, you can use frozen corn.

1 cup cider vinegar
¾ cup sugar
1 teaspoon mustard seeds
½ teaspoon celery seeds
½ teaspoon turmeric
½ teaspoon salt
¼ teaspoon dill seeds
¼ teaspoon coarsely ground pepper
½ cup chopped green bell pepper
½ cup chopped red bell pepper
½ cup chopped celery
⅓ cup chopped onion
3 cups, packed, fresh corn kernels (5 to 6 ears), or frozen

In a 3-quart saucepan, bring the vinegar, sugar, mustard seeds, celery seeds, turmeric, salt, dill seeds, and ground pepper to a boil. Reduce heat and simmer 5 minutes.

Stir in the green and red pepper, celery, and onion. Return to a boil and simmer 10 minutes. Stir in the corn and simmer 10 minutes longer, stirring occasionally. Pack into sterilized jars.

MAKES 3⅓ CUPS. (16 SERVINGS)
CALORIES: 62   CHOLESTEROL: 0 mg   SODIUM: 75 mg   FIBER: 2 g

Health tip:
Omit salt.
CALORIES: 62   CHOLESTEROL: 0 mg   SODIUM: 9 mg   FIBER: 2 g

◇

Succotash

This is a traditional American dish. It can be made with or without the cream, but I think the cream adds something special.

2 tablespoons butter
½ teaspoon sugar
½ teaspoon salt
¼ teaspoon pepper
1 package (10 ounce) frozen corn, unthawed
1 package (10 ounce) frozen lima beams, unthawed
¼ cup heavy cream

In a heavy 10-inch skillet, melt the butter over medium-high heat. Stir in the sugar, salt, and pepper. Add the corn and lima beans. Cook 5 minutes, stirring occasionally. Stir in the cream. Cook, stirring occasionally, until the liquid has almost completely evaporated, about 5 minutes.

SERVES 6.
CALORIES: 155   CHOLESTEROL: 24 mg   SODIUM: 152 mg   FIBER: 6 g

Health tip:
Omit the salt and the cream.
CALORIES: 121   CHOLESTEROL: 12 mg   SODIUM: 60 mg   FIBER: 6 g

◇

Better-Than-Canned Creamed Corn

I find something wonderful about homemade creamed corn, because all the pieces of corn are whole and chewy instead of the canned variety where most of the kernels are mushed. Because canned whole-kernel corn is packed so differently from brand to brand, it's hard to determine how much liquid to expect. You can make this the consistency that you prefer by adding more or less half-and-half.

¼ cup butter
¼ cup flour
1 cup half-and-half, divided
2 cans (15 to 17 ounces) each whole-kernel corn, undrained
½ teaspoon salt
¼ teaspoon pepper

In a 3-quart saucepan, melt the butter over medium-high heat. Stir in the flour until absorbed. Using a wire whisk gradually stir in ½ cup of the half-and-half. Add the corn with the liquid, salt, and pepper. Cook, stirring, until the mixture comes to a boil. Stir in as much of the remaining ½ cup of half-and-half as necessary for your desired consistency. Cook, stirring, one minute longer.

SERVES 6.
CALORIES: 227   CHOLESTEROL: 36 mg   SODIUM: 617 mg   FIBER: 2 g

Health tip:
Use unsalted margarine instead of butter; omit the salt; use 2-percent-fat milk instead of half-and-half.
CALORIES: 195   CHOLESTEROL: 4 mg   SODIUM: 388 mg   FIBER: 2 g

---

◇

Skillet Corn

I absolutely love the way that the hot pepper sneaks up on you after you've started eating this. I think the contrast between the sweet, hot, and salty flavors is outstanding. you can omit the bacon and use 3 tablespoons butter, instead.

3 slices bacon
¼ cup chopped onion
2 cups fresh or frozen corn kernels
2 tablespoons maple syrup
⅛ teaspoon nutmeg
⅛ teaspoon ground red pepper

In a large skillet, cook the bacon until crisp over medium-high heat. Remove the bacon from the skillet and drain on paper towels, then crumble.

Discard all but 2 tablespoons of the bacon fat from the skillet. Add the onion and cook, stirring, until softened. Add the corn, maple syrup, and nutmeg. Cook, stirring, 5 to 7 minutes or until the corn is cooked and any accumulated liquid has evaporated. Remove from heat and stir in the pepper and reserved bacon.

SERVES 4.
CALORIES: 122   CHOLESTEROL: 4 mg   SODIUM: 89 mg   FIBER: 3 g

Health tip:
Use only 1 slice of bacon for flavor (or 2 teaspoons butter) and use a nonstick skillet.
CALORIES: 104   CHOLESTEROL: 1 mg   SODIUM: 38 mg   FIBER: 3 g

––––––––––––⟡––––––––––––

Johnnycakes

Recipes for johnnycakes range from very plain pancakes all the way to corn bread or cake. I've chosen to make them like pancakes. They're easy to make, but they are rather heavy. They taste very much like cereal, and should be served with maple syrup.

1 cup white cornmeal
1 teaspoon sugar
½ teaspoon salt
¾ cup boiling water
⅓ cup milk
1 egg

In a large bowl, stir together the cornmeal, sugar, and salt. Stir in the boiling water. In a medium-size bowl, beat the milk and egg until thoroughly combined. Stir into the cornmeal until blended.

Heat a griddle or slope-sided pan until a drop of water dances across the surface before evaporating. Grease lightly.

Drop by measuring tablespoonsful onto the heated griddle. Cook until browned on the bottom, then turn and cook the second side.

MAKES 32.
CALORIES: 20   CHOLESTEROL: 7mg   SODIUM: 36mg   FIBER: .5g

Health tip:
Omit the salt, use 2-percent-fat milk
CALORIES: 19   CHOLESTEROL: 7mg   SODIUM: 3mg   FIBER: .5g

---◇---

Can't-Eat-Just-One Corn Fritters

These fritters are slightly sweet with plenty of corn. I had a hard time stopping myself from eating the whole batch.

⅔ cup flour
½ cup yellow cornmeal
2 tablespoons sugar
1½ teaspoons baking powder
½ teaspoon salt
1 can (8¾ ounce) cream-style corn
1 egg
3 tablespoons milk
2 tablespoons butter, melted
1 can (8 ounce) whole-kernel corn, drained
Oil for deep-frying

In a large bowl, stir together the flour, cornmeal, sugar, baking powder, and salt.

In a medium-size bowl, beat the creamed corn, egg, milk, and butter until thoroughly blended. Stir in the corn kernels.

Stir the liquid ingredients into the dry.

Heat the oil in a saucepan, until bubbles form as soon as some batter is dropped into the saucepan. Drop the batter by measuring tablespoonsful into the oil. Fry until browned on both sides.

MAKES 24.
CALORIES: 77   CHOLESTEROL: 11mg   SODIUM: 128mg   FIBER: 1g

Health tip:
Omit salt and eat just one.
CALORIES: 77   CHOLESTEROL: 11mg   SODIUM: 84mg   FIBER: 1g

---◇---

Cornmeal Mush

If you've never tried this dish, you will find that it is exactly what the title says. It's very much like cooked farina with a corn flavor. You can serve it for breakfast, but it's really best when chilled and served as fried cornmeal mush.

5 cups water, divided
1 teaspoon salt

1½ cups cornmeal
3 tablespoons butter

Bring 4 cups of the water and the salt to a boil in a 2-quart saucepan.

In a medium-size bowl, stir together the cornmeal and the remaining cup of water. Using a whisk, stir the cornmeal mixture into the boiling water. Cook, stirring, about 10 minutes, until thick and cooked through. Stir in the butter.

SERVES 6.

CALORIES: 176   CHOLESTEROL: 15mg   SODIUM: 404mg   FIBER: 3g

Health tip:
Omit the salt; stir in only 1 tablespoon unsalted margarine instead of butter.
CALORIES: 142   CHOLESTEROL: 0 mg   SODIUM: 2 mg   FIBER: 3 g

———————◇———————

Fried Cornmeal Mush

This fried cornmeal mush has a crispy outside and a smooth and creamy inside. It tastes great with maple syrup.

1 recipe cornmeal mush (see page 176)
¼ cup flour
Oil for frying

Prepare the cornmeal mush according to recipe directions. Pour the warm mush into a greased 9 x 13-inch baking dish. Cover with plastic wrap and chill.

Cut the mush into 24 squares, about 2 inches each. Dredge each square in the flour.

Pour enough oil into a 10-inch slope-sided skillet to be ¼-inch deep. Heat it until the oil bubbles when a little flour is sprinkled into the skillet. Add the cornmeal squares a few at a time and fry on medium-high heat until golden on both sides.

SERVES 24.

CALORIES: 64   CHOLESTEROL: 4mg   SODIUM: 101mg   FIBER: 1g

Health tip:
Prepare the cornmeal mush using the substitutions suggested in the health tip for that recipe.
CALORIES: 55   CHOLESTEROL: 0mg   SODIUM: 0mg   FIBER: 1g

Spoon Bread

Some people like spoon bread with a large pat of butter and plenty of salt and pepper; other people (include me in this group) like to serve it with syrup or powdered sugar.

1 cup yellow cornmeal
1 tablespoon sugar
1 teaspoon salt
2½ cups scalded milk, divided
3 tablespoons butter
3 eggs, separated
2 teaspoons baking powder

Preheat oven to 350°F. Grease a 2-quart casserole.

In a 3-quart saucepan, stir together the cornmeal, sugar, and salt. Gradually stir in 1½ cups of the milk. Cook over low heat, stirring constantly, until the mixture is very thick. Remove from the heat. Stir in the butter until completely melted.

In a medium-size bowl, lightly beat the egg yolks. Gradually beat in the remaining 1 cup of milk and add the baking powder. Stir the yolk mixture into the cornmeal.

In a large bowl, beat the egg whites until soft peaks hold. Stir one quarter of the egg whites into the cornmeal mixture. Fold in the remaining whites. Pour into the prepared dish. Bake 40 minutes, or until browned on top.

10.0 SERVES 6.
CALORIES: 244   CHOLESTEROL: 133mg   SODIUM: 597mg   FIBER: 2g

Health tip:
Use 1-percent-fat milk; omit salt; and use unsalted margarine for butter.
CALORIES: 224   CHOLESTEROL: 108mg   SODIUM: 201mg   FIBER: 2g

———————◇———————

Southern Corn Bread

Traditionally, when Southerners prepare corn bread, it has little or no sugar. You can dress this corn bread up by stirring 1 to 2 teaspoons of your favorite dried herb into the batter, or stir in 1 cup shredded Cheddar and 1 can (3 ounce) chopped chilies, drained.

1¼ *cups yellow cornmeal*
¾ *cup flour*
1 *tablespoon baking powder*
2 *teaspoons sugar*
1 *teaspoon salt*
1¼ *cups half-and-half*
3 *eggs*
⅓ *cup butter, melted*

Preheat oven to 400°F. Grease a 9 × 9 × 2-inch baking pan.

In a large bowl, stir together the cornmeal, flour, baking powder, sugar, and salt.

In a medium-size bowl, beat the half-and-half, eggs, and butter until thoroughly combined.

Stir the liquid ingredients into the cornmeal mixture until completely combined. Pour into the prepared pan.

Bake 25 minutes, or until a wooden pick inserted in the center comes out clean. Cut into 12 squares.

SERVES 12.
CALORIES: 181   CHOLESTEROL: 75mg   SODIUM: 330mg   FIBER: 1g

Health tip:
Use milk instead of half-and-half; omit salt; use unsalted margarine instead of butter.
CALORIES: 157   CHOLESTEROL: 4mg   SODIUM: 126mg   FIBER: 1g

—————— ◇ ——————

Northern Corn Bread

I like my corn bread sweet and moist—and this one is both.

1 cup all-purpose flour
1 cup yellow cornmeal
½ cup sugar
1 tablespoon baking powder
½ teaspoon salt
1 cup milk
2 eggs
⅓ cup butter, melted

Preheat oven to 400°F. Grease an 8 × 8 × 2-inch baking pan.

In a large bowl, stir together the all-purpose flour, cornmeal, sugar, baking powder and salt.

In a medium-size bowl, beat together the milk, eggs, and butter. Stir the liquid ingredients into the dry ingredients until just blended. Pour into prepared pan. Bake 25 to 30 minutes, or until top is golden. Cut into 12 pieces.

SERVES 12.
CALORIES: 183   CHOLESTEROL: 51mg   SODIUM: 235mg   FIBER: 1g

Health tip:
Use unsalted margarine instead of butter; use scrambled-egg substitute; omit salt.
CALORIES: 178   CHOLESTEROL: 3mg   SODIUM: 3mg   FIBER: 1g

Variations:

Corn Muffins: Place the batter for Northern Corn Bread into 12 greased 2½-inch muffin cups, filling each ⅔ full. Bake 15 to 20 minutes (in 400°F oven).
You can stir blueberries or apples into the batter before making the muffins, if desired.

MAKES 12.

Corn Sticks: Grease cast-iron corn-stick pan. Place in hot oven (400°F) as you prepare batter. Fill each corn-stick form ⅔ full. Bake 10 to 12 minutes, or until golden.

MAKES 24.

———————◇———————

Cream-of-Corn Bread

I served this bread at Thanksgiving and it was a great hit. It bakes up to be very dense and moist.

1⅓ cups yellow cornmeal
1⅓ cups all-purpose flour
½ cup sugar
1 tablespoon baking powder
1 teaspoon salt
3 eggs
1 can (15 or 16 ounce) cream-style corn
1 cup milk
⅓ cup butter, melted

Preheat oven to 400°F. Grease a 9 × 9 × 2-inch baking pan.

In a large bowl, stir together the cornmeal, flour, sugar, baking powder, and salt.

In a medium-size bowl, beat the eggs, stir in the cream-style corn, milk, and butter until completely combined.

Stir the liquid ingredients into the dry ingredients until just blended. Pour into the prepared pan.

Bake 40 to 50 minutes, or until the top is golden and a wooden pick inserted in center comes out clean.

Cut into 12 pieces.

SERVES 12.
CALORIES: 241 CHOLESTEROL: 68mg SODIUM: 431mg FIBER: 2g

Health tip:
Reduce sugar to ¼ cup; use scrambled-egg substitute; use 1-percent-fat milk; omit salt; use unsalted margarine instead of butter.
CALORIES: 214 CHOLESTEROL: 34mg SODIUM: 225mg FIBER: 2g

———————— ◇ ————————

Chestnut Corn-Bread Stuffing

This recipe makes enough stuffing to fill a 6-pound roasting chicken. You can double the recipe for a turkey.

¼ cup butter
½ cup finely chopped celery
⅓ cup finely chopped onion
2 tablespoons chopped parsley
½ teaspoon poultry seasoning
¼ teaspoon sage
¼ teaspoon salt
¼ teaspoon pepper
⅛ teaspoon thyme
3 cups coarsely crumbled corn bread
3 slices white bread, cubed (I like the squishy type)
1 cup cooked and peeled chestnuts, chopped
1 egg
¾ cup chicken or vegetable broth (see page 19)

In a large skillet, melt the butter over medium-high heat. Add the celery and onion, and cook until the vegetables are softened. Stir in the parsley, poultry seasoning, sage, salt, pepper, and thyme. Stir in the corn bread, bread cubes, and chestnuts.

In a small bowl, beat the egg and broth until combined. Gradually pour the broth mixture over the corn-bread mixture, tossing constantly until the stuffing has absorbed the liquid.

Use this stuffing to fill the cavity of a roasting chicken, capon, or turkey.

SERVES 8 (makes 4 cups).
CALORIES: 229   CHOLESTEROL: 56mg   SODIUM: 365mg   FIBER: 5g

Health tip:
Use unsalted margarine instead of butter; omit salt.
CALORIES: 229   CHOLESTEROL: 41mg   SODIUM: 265mg   FIBER: 5g

————————— ◇ —————————

Peppered Blue-Cornmeal Biscuits

Use white or yellow cornmeal if you can't get blue, or if you find that purplish food is unappealing. These biscuits are light and delicious, with an extra snap from the pepper.

1½ cups flour
½ cup blue cornmeal
2 teaspoons baking powder
1 teaspoon baking soda
1½ teaspoons medium-grind pepper
1 teaspoon salt
½ cup shortening
¾ cup buttermilk

Preheat oven to 425°F.

In a large bowl, stir together the flour, cornmeal, baking powder, baking soda, pepper, and salt.

Using a pastry cutter or two knives, cut the shortening into the flour mixture until it resembles coarse cornmeal.

Stir in the buttermilk until a soft dough is formed. Turn onto a floured board and knead 10 to 12 times. Pat ½-inch thick and cut with floured 2½-inch biscuit cutter. Place the biscuits on an ungreased baking sheet. Bake 12 minutes, or until lightly browned.

MAKES 12.
CALORIES: 123   CHOLESTEROL: 1mg   SODIUM: 317mg   FIBER: 1g

Health tip:
Omit the salt.
CALORIES: 123   CHOLESTEROL: 1mg   SODIUM: 140mg   FIBER: 1g

——————— ◇ ———————

Orange Corn-Bran Muffins

I like these muffins because the flavor is so subtle and delicate. The hint of orange is a perfect complement to the corn, and the amount of sweetness is just right.

1¼ cups all-purpose flour
¾ cup corn bran
½ cup cornmeal
2 teaspoons baking powder
1 teaspoon baking soda
½ teaspoon salt
¾ cup buttermilk
½ cup orange juice
⅓ cup firmly packed dark-brown sugar
¼ cup oil
2 egg whites
2 teaspoons grated orange rind
½ teaspoon vanilla extract

Preheat oven to 400°F. Grease 12 3-inch muffin cups.

In a large bowl, stir together the flour, corn bran, cornmeal, baking powder, baking soda, and salt.

In a medium-size bowl, stir together the buttermilk, orange juice, brown sugar, oil, egg whites, orange rind, and vanilla. Add the orange mixture to the dry ingredients and stir until just moistened.

Spoon into prepared cups and bake 20 minutes.

MAKES 12.
CALORIES: 158   CHOLESTEROL: 1mg   SODIUM: 241mg   FIBER: 2g

Health tip:
Omit the salt.
CALORIES: 158   CHOLESTEROL: 1mg   SODIUM: 152mg   FIBER: 2g

———————— ◇ ————————

Blue-Cornmeal Pancakes

These pancakes have a lovely flavor and a bit more consistency than traditional pancakes. You can use white or yellow cornmeal, if you prefer.

1 cup blue cornmeal
3 tablespoons sugar
½ teaspoon salt
¾ cup boiling water
½ cup milk
2 eggs
3 tablespoons butter, melted
¾ cup flour
1½ teaspoons baking powder

In a large bowl, stir together the cornmeal, sugar, and salt. Stir in the boiling water until all the cornmeal is moistened.

In a medium-size bowl, beat together the milk, eggs, and butter. Stir into the cornmeal mixture.

On a piece of waxed paper or in a medium-size bowl, stir together the flour and baking powder. Stir into the cornmeal mixture.

Heat a griddle or slope-sided skillet until a drop of water dances across the surface before evaporating. Drop about 2 tablespoons of the batter at a time to make 3-inch pancakes. Cook until bubbles on top start to burst. Turn and cook on second side.

MAKES 18.
CALORIES: 85   CHOLESTEROL: 29mg   SODIUM: 114mg   FIBER: 1g

Health tip:
Omit salt; Use 1-percent-fat milk and unsalted margarine.
CALORIES: 83   CHOLESTEROL: 23mg   SODIUM: 41mg   FIBER: 1g

————— ◇ —————

Corn-Bran Pancakes

Here's a great change from plain pancakes. These pancakes have the grittiness of the corn and the sweetness of maple syrup.

1 cup flour
¾ cup cornmeal
¾ cup corn bran
1 tablespoon baking powder
½ teaspoon salt
1⅓ cups milk
⅓ cup maple syrup
⅓ cup corn oil
2 egg whites

In a large bowl, stir together the flour, cornmeal, corn bran, baking powder, and salt.

In a medium-size bowl, beat the milk, maple syrup, oil, and egg whites until combined. Stir the liquid ingredients into the corn-bran mixture, until just moistened.

Heat a skillet until a drop of water dances across the surface before evaporating. Drop about ¼ cup batter per pancake. Cook, over medium heat, until bubbles burst on the surface. Turn and cook second side until browned.

MAKES 18.
CALORIES: 119   CHOLESTEROL: 2mg   SODIUM: 130mg   FIBER: 1g

Health tip:
Omit salt.
CALORIES: 119   CHOLESTEROL: 2mg   SODIUM: 71mg   FIBER: 1g

———————— ◇ ————————

Indian Pudding

This pudding is slightly gritty and pretty sweet. I like it best warm with lots of vanilla ice cream or whipped cream.

1 cup milk
½ cup cornmeal
3 cups scalded milk
2 tablespoons butter
3 eggs
½ cup molasses
¼ cup firmly packed light- or dark-brown sugar
1 teaspoon cinnamon
½ teaspoon ginger
½ teaspoon salt
½ cup light cream

Preheat oven to 325°F. Grease a 2-quart casserole.

In a 2-quart saucepan, stir together the milk and cornmeal. Stir in the scalded milk. Place over medium-high heat and cook, stirring frequently, until the mixture comes to a boil. Reduce heat and simmer until the mixture is thickened. Remove from heat and stir in the butter until completely melted.

In a medium-size bowl, beat the eggs. Beat in the molasses, brown sugar, cinnamon, ginger, and salt. Stir the egg mixture into the cornmeal mixture until completely combined.

Pour into the prepared casserole. Pour light cream on top, but do not mix in. Bake 1 hour to 1 hour and 15 minutes, or until a knife inserted in the center comes out clean. Let stand at least 15 minutes before serving. Serve warm or cool.

SERVES 8.
CALORIES: 258   CHOLESTEROL: 112mg   SODIUM: 255mg   FIBER: 1g

Health tip:
Use 2-percent-fat milk; use scrambled-egg substitute; omit the light cream; omit the salt.
CALORIES: 187   CHOLESTEROL: 99mg   SODIUM: 116mg   FIBER: 1g

——————— ◇ ———————

Crunchy Almond-Grits Pound Cake

This is an absolutely perfect cake to have with a cup of coffee. It's dense and sweet with a crusty almond coating.

Almond crunch crust:

> ½ cup butter, softened
> 1 cup firmly packed light- or dark-brown sugar
> 1½ cups flour
> 1½ cups finely chopped almonds

Cake:

> ½ cup water
> ½ cup milk
> 3 tablespoons quick grits
> 1 cup butter, softened
> 2¼ cups sugar
> 6 eggs
> 1 teaspoon vanilla extract
> ½ teaspoon grated lemon rind
> 3 cups flour
> 1 teaspoon baking powder
> 1 teaspoon baking soda
> ½ teaspoon salt
> ½ cup sour cream

Preheat oven to 350°F. Grease a 10-inch tube.

Prepare the crust by creaming the butter and the brown sugar until light and fluffy. Add the flour and beat until crumbly. Stir in the almonds. Pat this mixture into the bottom and three-quarters of the way up the outer wall of the tube pan. Set aside.

In a 1½-quart saucepan, bring the water and milk to a boil. Gradually add the grits to the water, stirring constantly. Reduce heat and simmer 2 minutes. Remove from heat and set aside to cool.

In a large bowl, beat the butter with the sugar until light and fluffy. Beat in the eggs, one at a time, beating thoroughly after each. Beat in the vanilla and lemon rind.

Place the flour, baking powder, baking soda, and salt in a medium-size bowl, or on waxed paper, and stir with a whisk until completely combined. Set aside.

Stir the sour cream into the grits.

Add the dry ingredients to the butter, alternating with the grits, beating until smooth.

Spoon the batter into the prepared cake pan and bake 1 hour and 20 minutes, or until a wooden pick inserted in the center comes out clean. Cool on rack 5 minutes. Run knife around edges of the inner and outer tube, and turn onto rack to cool.

SERVES 16.
CALORIES: 567   CHOLESTEROL: 129mg   SODIUM: 325mg   FIBER: 3g

Health tip:
Use unsalted margarine instead of butter; omit salt.
CALORIES: 567   CHOLESTEROL: 71mg   SODIUM: 92mg   FIBER: 3g

◇

Cornmeal-Shortbread Cookies

These buttery cookies just melt in your mouth. The cornmeal gives them a little extra flavor and slightly gritty texture. Everyone who tasted them loved them.

1½ cups flour
¾ cup white cornmeal
¾ cup superfine sugar
1 cup butter

Preheat oven to 325°F.

In a large bowl, stir together the flour, cornmeal, and sugar. Using a pastry cutter, or two knives, cut the butter into the flour until the mixture resembles coarse sand.

Using your hands, sift the mixture through your fingers, pressing the dough slightly so that each time you lift some of the dough, it starts to form larger and larger clumps. When the clumps start to hold together, turn onto a board and knead until the dough holds together and cracks when pressed down.

On a lightly floured board, roll the dough ¼-inch thick.

Cut into 1½-inch squares and place ½ inch apart, on ungreased baking sheets. If desired, press a design into each cookie using the dull edge of a cookie or aspic cutter.

Bake 12 minutes, or until the cookies are barely colored around the edges. Cool on racks.

MAKES 48.

CALORIES: 68   CHOLESTEROL: 10mg   SODIUM: 32mg   FIBER: .5g

Health tip:
Use unsalted margarine instead of butter.

CALORIES: 68   CHOLESTEROL: 0mg   SODIUM: 5mg   FIBER: .5g

PART

III

◇

THE MINOR GRAINS:
FOR MAN OR BEAST?

◇

Barley
Buckwheat/Kasha
Millet
Oats
Rye
Wild Rice

The grains in this section are considered "minor" only in the sense that they constitute a small portion of the diet of mainstream America. In larger matters, such as world hunger, many of them are very major players.

Nutritionally, the so-called minor grains have it all over those in the major-grains category (wheat, rice, and corn), since they are almost always higher in protein, vitamins, and fiber than their more popular counterparts. The unrefined versions of the major grains rank about as high in nutrition as the minor grains, but it's rare when a whole major grain ever makes it to the American dining table. Usually by the time they get that far they've been hulled (bye-bye fiber), ground, and often bleached. Even rice is denuded of many of its finer nutritional properties before it hits the supermarket shelves.

Although the minor grains are known, albeit vaguely, to most Americans, their use has been largely stereotyped: Oats are for breakfast, and sometimes for cookies. Barley is for soup. Rye is for bread. Millet is for health nuts. Wild rice is for special occasions. Buckwheat had something to do with "Our Gang." Often they are even better known for their uss other than human consumption. Barley is used to make malt for beer. Millet is bird seed. Rye is used to make whiskey. Oats are for horses.

I think that many of the reasons these grains are neglected are understandable. Their flavors tend to be strong and require some getting used to. Barley is musky, millet is bitter, rye is a little sour, oats have a starchy consistency, buckwheat is overwhelming to some palates, and, although wild rice is wonderful, it's too expensive to eat very often.

Another reason these grains are ignored is that most of them take a long time to cook. For today's lifestyles, faster is better. Corn, for instance, heats or cooks in just moments, and white rice takes a mere 20 minutes from package to table. This is a far cry from any whole grain that can take from 1 to 2 hours to cook properly. Even when using a microwave oven, cooking times are still discouragingly long.

After reviewing the downsides of the minor grains, you may be inclined to wonder, why bother? The nutritional aspects alone, especially the dietary fiber in these unrefined or less-refined grains, should be motivation enough for moving away from preconceived notions, and at least *trying* them.

Most of us have heard about the blood cholesterol-lowering effects of oat bran, and wheat bran, it is now thought, reduces the risk of colon cancer. The claims that fiber will lessen your chances

193

of a confrontation with heart disease, cancer, diverticulitis, hemorrhoids, and obesity, and will lead to an overall improvement in health, are well documented. Quite simply, unrefined and less-refined grains are excellent sources of crude dietary fiber, and that is reason enough to eat them.

On a less practical and more creative side, introducing new uses for grains into your diet offers a wide range of possibilities that are bound to enliven everyday meals. (Remember that it wasn't too long ago that the thought of eating cold pasta would have elicited a wide round of yucks.) The recipes that follow in this and Part IV offer many opportunities for interesting and sometimes even exciting alternatives to meat and potatoes.

BARLEY

(Horeium sativum vulgare)

Except for an occasional appearance in soups and stews, barley is sadly neglected. Its major uses are for animal feed and to make malt for beer.

The barley with which most of us are familiar is pearl or pearled barley (whole barley with the hull and bran removed), which is easily obtained in the supermarket.

Types of Barley Available

Unhulled barley: This is not particularly recommended, since it takes forever to cook and never does completely lose its toughness.

Pot or hulled or scotch barley: All of the hull (outer husk) and some of the bran has been removed by polishing (grinding off the tough hull). Pot barley is darker in color than pearl barley.

Hulless barley: New to the consumer market, this barley is cultivated so that its hull comes off more easily than pot or scotch barley, and so does not require polishing. It is a rich brown color and not quite as rounded in shape as pot or pearl barley.

Pearl or pearled barley: All of the hull, most of the bran, and some of the germ has been polished away, leaving a small rounded nugget that looks a lot like a seed pearl. (The pearl barley sold at the supermarket seems to me to be slightly lighter in color and slightly smaller than the pearl barley that I've found in health-food stores. The health-food-store variety also requires 5 to 10 minutes longer to cook.)

Barley grits: Toasted pot barley, broken into five or six pieces. Grits cook in less time than pot or pearl barley, and end up as a sort of sticky mixture that will remind you of cooked oatmeal and can be used the same way.

Barley flakes: Pearl barley that has been toasted and rolled into flakes, similar to the process that is used to produce rolled oats. Use barley flakes the same way that you would use rolled oats (baked goods, meatloaves, etc.). When cooked in water, barley flakes make a tasty hot cereal.

195

Barley flour: It can be substituted for up to 25 percent of the whole-wheat flour called for in recipes for baked goods. However, because barley flour is low in gluten, the finished product will have a slightly heavy consistency. If you have the proper equipment (a home grain mill, available in stores that carry highly specialized kitchen equipment), you can grind your own flour from toasted barley.

Barley malt: A sweet syrup, similar to molasses, that can be found in health-food stores. Unsulphured molasses may be substituted.

Texture and Flavor

Barley is usually found in recipes that are titled "hearty," such as "hearty" soups and "hearty" stews, or in so-called "winter" recipes. It has a pleasant earthy flavor. You can compare barley with beans for its ability to make the eater feel well fed. Its "toothiness" and the feeling of satiety that barley provides makes it the perfect grain for those who are looking for meat substitutes.

The texture of pearl barley will vary according to the amount of water in which it's cooked. It can range from a soft starchy porridge to a chewy separate grain that is similar to al dente–cooked pasta.

Pot and hulless barleys will be more chewy and take longer to cook than pearl barley.

Compatible Foods, Herbs, and Spices

Because of its distinct flavor, barley is compatible with meats that are also earthy and substantial, such as beef, pork, liver, lamb, and dark-meat fowl, such as duck or goose. Vegetables, beans, and nuts are also good cooked with barley. Barley's assertive taste can sometimes overwhelm the more subtle flavors of light-meat fowl (chicken and turkey), fish, and dairy products. Although barley would certainly be a suitable side dish for these foods, it is usually better if it is not actually cooked *with* them.

Barley can be enhanced by parsley, chives (or anything in the onion family, for that matter), bay leaf, fennel, garlic, anise, basil, caraway, cloves, pepper, rosemary, and thyme.

The thickening properties of barley are desirable for enriching soups and stews, and can be used to advantage in molded salads.

Availability

Pearl barley is available in supermarkets (look for it in the dried-bean section) and health-food stores, as well as through mail-order grain catalogs (see page 21). Pot barley, hulless barley, barley grits, barley flakes, and barley flour are available in health-food stores and mail-order catalogs.

Nutritional Content

Pot barley is a good source of fiber, niacin, thiamin, potassium, iron, phosphorous, and calcium. Pearl barley has less fiber than pot barley, and contains somewhat lower amounts of the other nutrients.

———— ◇ ————

Home Remedy

Barley water, a liquid made from barley, lemon juice, and water, is frequently used as treatment for diarrhea, ulcers, and for the stimulation of breast milk.

3 cups water
2 tablespoons pearl barley
2 tablespoons lemon juice (optional)
2 tablespoons sugar (optional)

In a medium-size saucepan, boil the water and barley until reduced to 1½ cups. Strain through a sieve, discarding barley. If desired, stir lemon juice and sugar into barley water and simmer for 20 minutes.

Substitutions

Oat groats: They are similarly chewy with a flavor that is comparable to cooked barley, and have a slightly better nutritional profile. Use cooked oat groats in place of barley in salads or other dishes that call for already-cooked barley. However, the extreme starchiness of this grain does not make it the ideal choice for recipes in which the barley is cooked.

Brown rice: Either the short- or long-grain varieties may be substituted for barley, although I prefer to use the short-grain rice. This grain has a texture that is much like barley, but the flavor is more neutral. Substitute brown rice in recipes calling for either cooked or raw barley, but cook the rice about 5 minutes longer.

Wheat and triticale berries: Both of these grains have flavors that are comparable to barley, but take significantly longer to cook. I would not suggest substituting these berries in recipes calling for raw barley, but they do work well in recipes that call for cooked barley.

Other acceptable substitutes (in order of preference): Job's tears (allow longer cooking time); rye berries (same restrictions as wheat and triticale berries); white rice (allow shorter cooking time).

Basic Cooking Instructions

Please read *About Cooking Grains* beginning on page 7. *Note that all recipes in this section, unless otherwise noted, were tested with pearl barley from the supermarket.* If you like, you can substitute cooked pot or hulless barley for pearl barley in equal amounts. However, in recipes calling for uncooked barley, increase the liquid content by ½ cup and cook about 10 minutes longer.

I prefer to use the microwave oven for cooking plain barley, since it makes the cooked barley less sticky. The microwave methods that follow for cooking barley were tested in a 650-watt oven.

———————— ◇ ————————

Pot and Hulless Barley

Stove-top method:

> 2½ cups water
> 1 teaspoon salt
> 1 cup pot or hulless barley, rinsed

In a 2-quart saucepan, bring the water and salt to a boil over high heat. Stir in barley and return to boiling. Reduce heat, cover, and simmer for 1 hour and 20 minutes, or until almost all of the liquid has been absorbed. Remove from heat and let stand, covered, for 10 minutes. Fluff with fork.

MAKES 3¼ CUPS POT BARLEY.
      4¼ CUPS HULLESS BARLEY.

Microwave method:

> 3 cups water
> 1 teaspoon salt
> 1 cup pot or hulless barley, rinsed

Place the water and salt in a 3-quart, microwave-safe bowl; cover with waxed paper. Microwave on high (100% power) for 5 minutes, or until boiling. Stir in barley. Recover with waxed paper and microwave on high for 5 minutes. Microwave on medium (50% power), still covered with waxed paper, for 40 minutes, rotating dish once, if necessary. Let stand 5 minutes. Fluff with a fork.

MAKES 3 CUPS POT BARLEY.
        3½ CUPS HULLESS BARLEY.

——————◇——————

Pearl Barley

Stove-top method:

2⅔ cups water
1 teaspoon salt
1 cup pearl barley, rinsed

In a 2-quart saucepan, bring the water and salt to a boil over high heat. Stir in barley and return to boiling. Reduce heat, cover, and simmer for 40 minutes. (If you are using barley from a health-food store, you may need to add 5 to 10 minutes of cooking time for a total of 45 to 50 minutes.) Remove from heat and let stand, covered, for 10 minutes. Fluff with a fork.

MAKES 3½ TO 3⅔ CUPS.

Microwave method:

2½ cups water
1 teaspoon salt
1 cup pearl barley, rinsed

Place the water and salt in a 3-quart, microwave-safe bowl. Cover with waxed paper. Microwave on high (100% power) for 5 minutes, or until boiling. Stir in barley. Recover with waxed paper and continue to microwave on high for 5 minutes. Microwave on medium (50% power), still covered with waxed paper, for 30 minutes, rotating dish once, if necessary. (If you are using barley from a health-food store, you may need to add 5 minutes of cooking for a total of 35 minutes.) Let stand 5 minutes. Fluff with a fork.

MAKES 3½ CUPS.

Reheating

Barley gets slightly dense when chilled, so it's best to steam it or reheat it in the microwave oven to restore its softer texture.

BARLEY RECIPES

*(*indicates easy recipes)*

————————◇————————

Mom's Mushroom-Barley Soup
Cock-a-Leekie
A Very Rich Lamb-and-Barley Soup
Lima-bean-and-Barley Stew
Basil-Split-Pea-Soup
Barley-and-Chick-pea Soup *
Beef-and-Barley Bourguignon
Chicken Livers and Barley *
Cholent
Duck Ragout
Zesty Meatloaf *
Veal, Sausage, and Barley Stew *
Stuffed Veal-Shoulder Roast
Clubhouse Barley-and-Ham Salad *
Progresso Salad *
Barley-Beet Salad with Honey-Mustard Dressing *
New-Fangled Mushrooms and Barley *
Good Old-Fashioned Mushrooms and Barley *
Winter-Vegetable-and-Barley Bake *
Leeks, Lentils, and Barley *
Barley and Bows *
Nancy Jane's Simple Barley Recipe *
Fiesta Barley and Beans *
Barley and Peas *
Crisp Vegetables and Barley
Barley Green *
Sweet Barley Bread
Barley-Potato Doughnut Holes
Yummy Barley-Date Bars
Spiced Barley-Raisin Cookies *

Mom's Mushroom-Barley Soup

My mom makes the best soups in the world. This is one of them, and one of my favorites. Try to find dried Polish mushrooms, because they have an incredible intense flavor that adds much to the finished soup. If you can't find them, or are hesitant to buy them because of the price, substitute dried shiitake mushrooms.

1 ounce dried imported mushrooms (Polish mushrooms are best)
1 cup boiling water
4 quarts cold water
2½ pounds marrow bones
3 cups chopped carrot
2 cups chopped celery
1½ cups chopped onion
1 cup chopped parsnip
1 cup chopped celery root (also called celeriac)
¾ cup barley, rinsed
2 teaspoons salt
⅛ teaspoon pepper
1 bunch Italian parsley
1 bunch dill

Rinse the mushrooms under cold running water to remove any soil. Place in a medium-size bowl and pour boiling water over them. Let stand for 10 minutes, or until mushrooms are softened.

Reserve the soaking water, then finely chop mushrooms and place in an 8-quart soup pot, along with reserved soaking water. Add cold water, bones, carrot, celery, onion, parsnip, celery root, barley, salt, and pepper. Bring to a boil over high heat, then lower heat and cook at a slow boil, uncovered, for 2 hours. Add parsley and dill. Simmer 30 minutes longer. Discard bones. (Better yet, dig the mushy marrow out of the bones and spread it on fresh bread. Sprinkle with salt and enjoy, but don't tell your cardiologist that you did it.) You can discard the parsley and dill, but you may enjoy them, as I do, served as a side dish with the rest of the meal. Skim fat from the surface of the soup before serving.

SERVES 10.
CALORIES: 135   CHOLESTEROL: 3mg   SODIUM: 465 mg   FIBER: 10 g

Health tip:
Use only bones without marrow (soup-bone knuckles, for instance), since marrow adds lots of fat to the soup; omit salt.
CALORIES: 100   CHOLESTEROL: 2 mg   SODIUM: 32 mg   FIBER: 10 g

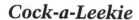

Cock-a-Leekie

I've tried many recipes for this traditional Scottish soup (also called *cockie leekie*). Some are made with leeks and a cock (an old rooster). Some include veal, some prunes; some use barley, some use oats, and some don't use any grain at all. In my version, I prefer to cook the soup with the prunes, then serve the soup without them.

> 3-pound broiler-fryer chicken (*It's unlikely that you will be able to obtain an old rooster, but if you can find a fowl, which is actually an old laying hen, you can use that, if you want to. You will have to cook the soup much longer in that case, and you may also have to adjust the amount of water, but you will also get a more intensely chicken-flavored soup.*)
> 3 medium-size leeks, cut into 1-inch pieces (both white and green parts)
> 8 sprigs parsley
> 1 bay leaf
> 1 teaspoon salt
> ¼ teaspoon crumbled thyme
> ⅛ teaspoon pepper
> 6 cups water
> 2 tablespoons barley, rinsed
> ¼ cup sliced leek (white part only)
> 8 prunes

Place the chicken, white and green slices of leek, parsley, bay leaf, salt, thyme, and pepper in a 4-quart saucepan. Add water and bring to a boil. Reduce heat and simmer, uncovered, for 1 hour.

Remove chicken from the pan. Strain the liquid into a 3-quart saucepan, discarding vegetables. Skim off fat. Stir barley, white slices of leek, and prunes into the broth. Simmer for 40 minutes. Pull skin from chicken and cut meat into large chunks. Add to broth and cook until heated through. Remove prunes before serving.

SERVES 6.
CALORIES: 255   CHOLESTEROL: 113 mg   SODIUM: 187 mg   FIBER: .5 g

Health tip:
Cook chicken without skin; omit salt.
CALORIES: 200   CHOLESTEROL: 50 mg   SODIUM: 120 mg   FIBER: .5 g

—————— ◇ ——————

A Very Rich Lamb-and-Barley Soup

To borrow a phrase from an advertising jingle, this is "a soup that eats like a meal," especially when it's served with bread (whole-grain, of course) and a side salad. The lamb-neck base gives the soup its incredible richness.

9 cups water, divided
2 pounds lamb necks
2½ tablespoons barley, rinsed
1½ cups chopped onion
1½ cups chopped celery
1 cup chopped carrot
2 parsnips, peeled
1 bunch Italian parsley
1 bunch dill
¾ teaspoon salt
⅛ teaspoon pepper

Place 6 cups of the water and lamb necks in a large soup pot. Bring to a boil over high heat. Lower heat and simmer, covered, for 45 minutes. Add remaining 3 cups water and barley. Bring to a boil, then lower heat and simmer, covered, for 15 minutes longer. Add onion, celery, carrot, and parsnips. Simmer, covered, for 45 minutes more. Add parsley and dill and continue to simmer, covered, for 30 minutes longer.

Remove pot from heat. Discard parsley and dill (or, better yet, set these aside to serve as a side dish with the soup) and remove lamb. Pull meat from the bones and return it to the pot, discarding bones. (Or, if you prefer, serve the lamb for dinner, along with the parsley and dill, and serve the soup meatless.) Add salt and pepper and stir the soup hard so that the parsnips break up and completely combine with the soup.

SERVES 6.
CALORIES: 302   CHOLESTEROL: 93 mg   SODIUM: 365 mg   FIBER: 4 g

Health tip:
Omit salt.
CALORIES: 302   CHOLESTEROL: 93 mg   SODIUM: 99 mg   FIBER: 4 g

——————— ◇ ———————

Lima-Bean-and-Barley Stew

This is definitely one of those hearty-type recipes frequently associated with barley. If you prefer a more "soupy" consistency, simply stir in boiling water as suggested. In either case, serve this very-filling dish with some of the beef in each portion.

12 cups water
1½ pounds oxtails or beef soup bones
1 cup dried baby lima beans, rinsed and picked over
2 cups chopped onion
1½ cups chopped celery
1 cup chopped turnip
½ cup barley, rinsed
1½ teaspoon salt
1 bay leaf
¼ teaspoon crumbled thyme
¼ teaspoon pepper
1 can (14½ ounce) whole peeled tomatoes, undrained
1 can (8 ounce) tomato sauce

Bring water to a boil in a large soup pot. Add oxtails and simmer, uncovered, for 45 minutes. Add lima beans and continue to simmer, uncovered, for 45 minutes longer. Stir in onion, celery, turnip, barley, salt, bay leaf, thyme, and pepper. Simmer, uncovered, 1 hour longer. As the stew cooks, stir in as much as 4 cups of *boiling* water if you want a more souplike dish. Stir in tomatoes and tomato sauce. Simmer for 15 minutes more. Remove bay leaf before serving.

SERVES 6.
CALORIES: 466   CHOLESTEROL: 68 mg   SODIUM: 928 mg   FIBER: 8 g

Health tip:
Omit salt.
CALORIES: 466   CHOLESTEROL: 68 mg   SODIUM: 395 mg   FIBER: 8 g

Basil-Split-Pea Soup

Fresh chopped basil, stirred into this soup at the last minute, gives the soup an unusual touch of flavor. If you don't fancy basil, then leave it out. The soup will still be good. And, if you *must* have smoked ham in your pea soup, add a ham bone or a couple of smoked hocks right at the beginning, or a little chopped cooked ham at the end.

14 cups water
1 package (16 ounce) dry split peas, rinsed and picked over
4 carrots, peeled
2 large parsnips, peeled
2 celery ribs
1 large onion, peeled
2 parsley roots (save tops for some other use)
½ cup barley, rinsed
¼ cup chopped celery leaves
1½ teaspoons celery salt
1 teaspoon salt
¼ cup chopped fresh basil (optional)

In a large soup pot, bring the water to a boil. Add split peas, carrots, parsnips, celery, onion, parsley roots, barley, celery leaves, celery salt, and salt. Reduce heat and simmer, uncovered, stirring occasionally, for 1¾ hours, or until peas have disintegrated. Discard vegetables, or chop them coarsely and serve as a side dish with the soup. Stir in basil just before serving.

SERVES 8.
CALORIES: 304   CHOLESTEROL: 0 mg   SODIUM: 717 mg   FIBER: 13g

Health tip:
Omit celery salt and salt.
CALORIES: 304   CHOLESTEROL: 0 mg   SODIUM: 33 mg   FIBER: 13 g

———————— ◇ ————————

Barley-and-Chick-Pea Soup

I usually prefer to make my soups from scratch. However, in some cases, this being one of them, a soup mix works beautifully to bring slow-simmered goodness to a quick and easy, meatless soup.

5 cups water
1 package (1.4 ounce) vegetable soup and recipe mix (Knorr)
1 can (10½ ounce) chick-peas (garbanzo beans), undrained
⅓ cup barley, rinsed

In a 3-quart saucepan, bring the water to a boil. Stir in soup mix, then beans and barley. Simmer 55 minutes.

SERVES 6.
CALORIES: 133   CHOLESTEROL: 0 mg   SODIUM: 431 mg   FIBER: 5 g

Health tip:
This is as healthy as it gets.

———————— ◇ ————————

Beef-and-Barley Bourguignon

This is an excellent version of a classic French recipe, and you don't have to follow it too exactly, either. For instance, you can use more or fewer mushrooms or onions, according to taste, or depending on how much or many of anything you happen to have on hand. Serve with bread and a green salad.

3 slices bacon, cut into 1-inch pieces
1 cup chopped onion
2 cloves garlic, minced
1 pound stewing beef, cut into 1-inch cubes
2–3 cups water
1 can (13¾ ounce) ready-to-serve beef broth
1 cup dry red wine
1 bay leaf
¼ teaspoon crumbled thyme
1 cup barley, rinsed
10 ounces small mushrooms, rinsed and left whole (or larger
*   mushrooms, cut into quarters)*
12 small white onions, peeled
¼ cup chopped parsley

In a large heavy saucepan or 4-quart Dutch oven, cook the bacon over medium-high heat until crisp. Remove bacon and drain on paper towels.

Add the chopped onion and garlic to bacon fat remaining in pot. Cook over medium-high heat until softened. Add beef cubes and cook, turning frequently, until richly browned on the outside. Add 2 cups of the water, broth, wine, bay leaf, and thyme. Bring to a boil. Reduce heat and simmer, uncovered, for 1 hour. Stir in barley and continue to simmer, covered, for 20 minutes. Add mushrooms, small onions, and parsley. Continue to simmer, uncovered, for 35 minutes longer. (If you want a more "saucy" consistency in the stew, add some or all of the remaining 1 cup water during the last 35 minutes of cooking time.) Remove bay leaf and stir in reserved bacon just before serving.

SERVES 4.
CALORIES: 487   CHOLESTEROL: 94 mg   SODIUM: 726 mg   FIBER: 10 g

Health tip:
Omit bacon; use a nonstick saucepan. Or use a nonstick skillet for softening onion and garlic and browning the beef, then transfer to the larger pan to finish cooking; use low-sodium beef broth.
CALORIES: 453 mg   CHOLESTEROL: 83 mg   SODIUM: 170 mg   FIBER: 10 g

———————————— ◇ ————————————

Chicken Livers and Barley

I automatically feel healthier when I eat liver, even though I know it's loaded with cholesterol. But liver also contains rich amounts of iron, vitamin A, phosphorous, potassium, and niacin, not to mention protein. For me, this is a delicious nutritious meal. Just add a salad.

3 tablespoons vegetable oil
1 cup chopped onion
1 pound chicken livers, rinsed and tough membranes removed
2 teaspoons white-wine Worcestershire sauce
1/2 teaspoon salt
1/4 teaspoon pepper
1/8 teaspoon crumbled thyme
2 cups cooked barley
1/4 cup chopped parsley

In a large skillet, heat the oil over medium-high heat. Add onion and cook, stirring occasionally, until softened. Add livers and cook, stirring and tossing, just until the centers are pale pink. Stir in Worcestershire sauce, salt, pepper, and thyme. Stir in barley and parsley. Cook, stirring occasionally, until heated through.

SERVES 4.
CALORIES: 369   CHOLESTEROL: 558 mg   SODIUM: 776 mg   FIBER: 3 g

Health tip:
If you are watching your cholesterol, perhaps you'd better skip this. Sodium watchers should omit salt.
CALORIES: 369   CHOLESTEROL: 558 mg   SODIUM: 73 mg   FIBER 3 g

———————— ◇ ————————

Cholent

In the Jewish religion you are not supposed to work on the Sabbath, so the ingredients for cholent are put together on Friday before Sabbath begins. Then the pot is covered tightly and put into the oven to bake for 24 hours at a low heat. Then, the moment that Sabbath ends, instant dinner! In earlier times, before people had ovens in their homes, the women would take their filled pots to the village baker on Friday evening and bring home the cooked meal on Saturday evening. This recipe assumes that most people would rather not bake overnight, and so I have shortened the process.

8 cups water
2 pounds beef flanken or lean short ribs
1 large onion, peeled and left whole
2 teaspoons salt
⅛ teaspoon pepper
1 cup dried beans, rinsed and picked over (I use navy beans, but it's not
    uncommon to find kidney beans or lima beans in this dish)
1 cup barley, rinsed
6 medium (about ¾ pound) red potatoes, scrubbed

Preheat oven to 325° F.

In a large, ovenproof soup pot or Dutch oven, place the water, beef, onion, salt, and pepper. Bring to a boil over high heat. Stir in beans, barley, and potatoes. Cover tightly and bake for 4 hours without stirring—or peeking.

SERVES 6.
CALORIES: 706   CHOLESTEROL: 84 mg   SODIUM: 776 mg   FIBER: 10 g

Health tip:
Omit salt.
CALORIES: 706   CHOLESTEROL: 84 mg   SODIUM: 73 mg   FIBER: 10 g

Duck Ragout

Because it is a very rich dish, the ragout needs only a tart green salad to make it a complete meal.

4 slices bacon, cut into 1-inch pieces
4½-pound duck, cut into 8 pieces, visible fat removed
1½ cups chopped onion
½ cup chopped carrot
1 clove garlic, minced
½ cup dry red wine
1 cup water
¼ cup chopped parsley
1 bay leaf
¼ teaspoon salt
¼ teaspoon crumbled rosemary
⅛ teaspoon crumbled thyme
⅛ teaspoon pepper
1 package (10 ounce) frozen lima beans
½ cup barley, rinsed

In a large heavy saucepan or 4-quart Dutch oven, cook the bacon over medium-high heat until crisp. Remove bacon and drain on paper towels. Add duck to bacon fat in pan and cook over medium-high heat until browned on all sides. (You will probably be able to brown only three or four pieces of duck at a time.)

Remove duck from pan and discard all but 2 tablespoons of the fat. Add onion, carrot, and garlic to fat remaining in pan and cook over high heat, stirring until vegetables are softened. Stir in wine, scraping up any browned bits that cling to the bottom and side of the pan. Stir in water, parsley, bay leaf, salt, rosemary, thyme, and pepper. Return duck to pot. Cover and simmer for 45 minutes. Stir in lima beans and barley. Cover and simmer for 35 minutes longer. Stir in reserved bacon and simmer, covered, for 10 minutes longer, or until barley and duck are tender. Discard bay leaf and skim fat from surface before serving.

SERVES 4.
CALORIES: 1361 mg   CHOLESTEROL: 248 mg   SODIUM: 383 mg   FIBER: 9 g

Health tips:
This will never be a low-calorie dish, but you can cut down a little on the fat and salt content. Remove as much skin and fat as possible from the duck. Omit bacon and brown duck in 1 tablespoon oil in a nonstick skillet; omit salt.
CALORIES: 901   CHOLESTEROL: 124 mg   SODIUM: 60 mg   FIBER: 9 g

Zesty Meatloaf

If you're not too fond of barbecue sauce, you can use plain or spicy catsup as a substitute. I serve this with salad and a baked potato and it's always a hit.

Loaf:

>   1 pound ground veal or beef
>   1 pound ground pork
>   1 cup chopped onion
>   ¾ cup thick spicy barbecue sauce
>   ½ cup chopped green bell pepper
>   ½ cup barley flakes
>   1 egg
>   ½ teaspoon salt

Topping:

>   ¼ cup apricot jam
>   2 tablespoons thick spicy barbecue sauce
>   1 tablespoon steak sauce (A-1)
>   ½ teaspoon dry mustard

Preheat oven to 350°F.

In a large bowl, lightly and thoroughly combine the veal, pork, onion, barbecue sauce, bell pepper, barley flakes, egg, and salt. Shape meat mixture into a loaf measuring about 8 × 5 inches and set the loaf on a rack in a baking pan.

Stir together jam, barbecue sauce, steak sauce, and dry mustard in a small bowl. Spread over top and sides of meatloaf.

Bake for 1 hour and 15 minutes.

SERVES 6.

CALORIES: 472   CHOLESTEROL: 205 mg   SODIUM: 765 mg   FIBER: .5 g

Health tip:

Use 2 pounds ground veal and omit ground pork; omit salt and topping.

CALORIES: 400   CHOLESTEROL: 205 mg   SODIUM: 367 mg   FIBER: .5 g

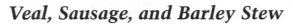

Veal, Sausage, and Barley Stew

Tender veal, spicy sausage, and the chewy texture of barley are a wonderful combination.

1 tablespoon vegetable oil
1 cup chopped onion
½ pound Italian sausage, cut into 1-inch pieces
1 pound stewing veal, cut into 1-inch pieces
4 cups water
¾ cup barley, rinsed
1 large green bell pepper, cut into strips
½ teaspoon salt
⅛ teaspoon pepper

In a 4-quart saucepan, heat the oil over medium-high heat. Add onion and cook, stirring, until softened. Add sausage and cook, stirring occasionally, until no longer pink in the center. Stir in veal and water. Cover and simmer over medium heat for 45 minutes, stirring occasionally. Stir in barley, pepper strips, salt, and pepper. Cook, uncovered, for 40 minutes, or until veal and barley are tender.

SERVES 4.
CALORIES: 602   CHOLESTEROL: 148 mg   SODIUM: 709 mg   FIBER: 1 g

Health tip:
Omit sausage (but keep in mind that by doing so you will also be sacrificing a lot of flavor) and salt.
CALORIES: 365   CHOLESTEROL: 109 mg   SODIUM: 62 mg   FIBER: 1 g

———————— ◇ ————————

Stuffed Veal-Shoulder Roast

Veal shoulder has a lot of flavor, and when it's boned and stuffed can be quite out of this world. I often serve this roast for company, set on a big platter, surrounded by steamed baby vegetables. The pan juices have an exquisite flavor with not many calories, so be sure to pour the cooking juice into a sauce bowl and serve it on the side.

¾ cup cooked barley
⅓ cup finely chopped celery
¼ cup finely chopped onion
2 tablespoons chopped parsley
1 tablespoon snipped dill or
*   1 teaspoon dried dill weed*
¼ teaspoon crumbled tarragon
3-pound boneless veal shoulder
1 medium onion, sliced
1 cup sliced celery
1 cup sliced carrot
½ cup white wine or chicken broth
¼ teaspoon salt

Preheat oven to 325°F.

In a medium-size bowl, combine the barley, chopped celery, chopped onion, parsley, dill, and tarragon.

Cut veal shoulder, lengthwise, going almost all the way through the meat. Open the cut meat (like a book) and pound it to flatten. (Or, better yet, have the butcher do this for you.) Place barley mixture in the center of the flattened meat. Roll meat to enclose stuffing and tie in several places with string. (It's easiest to tie by starting in the center of the roll and working your way out to the ends. You can also use a few wooden picks to help keep the roll closed and the stuffing inside while you work.)

Place roast in a baking pan. Arrange sliced vegetables around roast. Pour wine over roast and sprinkle with salt. Cover tightly with foil and bake for 2 hours. Remove foil and continue baking for 1 hour longer.

Slice roast and serve with the vegetables and pan juices.

SERVES 8.

CALORIES: 506   CHOLESTEROL: 218 mg   SODIUM: 281 mg   FIBER: 1 g

Health tip:
Omit salt.

CALORIES: 506   CHOLESTEROL: 218 mg   SODIUM: 139 mg   FIBER: 1 g

―――――◇―――――

Clubhouse Barley-and-Ham Salad

I'm always so pleased with the way this salad tastes. The ingredients are just right and work so well together.

1½ cups cooked barley
1 cup ½-inch cubes cooked ham
1 cup cooked peas (thawed, if using frozen)
¼ cup chopped red bell pepper
¼ cup finely chopped pecans
2 tablespoons finely chopped scallion
1 tablespoon snipped fresh dill or
   1 teaspoon dried dill weed
⅛ teaspoon pepper
¼ cup mayonnaise

In a large bowl, toss the barley, ham, peas, bell pepper, pecans, scallion, dill, and pepper. Lightly mix in mayonnaise until thoroughly combined. Chill until serving time.

SERVES 6.
CALORIES: 259   CHOLESTEROL: 37 mg   SODIUM: 665 mg   FIBER: 3 g

Health tip:
Substitute chicken for ham; use reduced-calorie mayonnaise. Omit salt from barley.
CALORIES: 179   CHOLESTEROL: 4 mg   SODIUM: 100 mg   FIBER: 3 g

◇

Progresso Salad

This salad is based on two excellent Progresso brand products: marinated olive salad and caponata. The olive salad is very vinegary, but if you enjoy food with a sharp flavor, add the olive salad without draining off the liquid in the jar.

2 cups cooked barley
1 jar (9¾ ounce) marinated olive salad, drained (see above)
1 can (4½ ounce) caponata
⅓ cup pignoli (pine nuts)
2 tablespoons mayonnaise
2 tablespoons sour cream
Lettuce, optional

In a large bowl, lightly toss the barley, olive salad, caponata, pignoli, mayonnaise, and sour cream until thoroughly combined. Chill until serving time. Serve on lettuce leaves, if you like.

SERVES 8. (Nutrition information not available for the Progresso appetizers.)
Health tip:
Use ¼ cup reduced-calorie mayonnaise instead of regular mayonnaise and sour cream. Sodium watchers: Beware!

◇

Barley-Beet Salad with Honey-Mustard Dressing

Toss this salad shortly before serving time so that each vegetable retains its own pretty color, rather than turning a bright beet pink.

4 medium-size beets
1 cup cooked barley
½ cup sliced radish
12 snow peas, blanched in boiling water, rinsed in cold water, and cut in half widthwise
¼ cup sliced scallion, both white and green parts
2 tablespoons olive oil
2 tablespoons orange juice
1 tablespoon cider vinegar
2 teaspoons honey mustard
¼ teaspoon salt
Boston-lettuce leaves

Cook the beets until tender in boiling water, then peel and cut into julienne strips (you should have about 2 cups). Chill separately until ready to mix salad.

Combine the barley, radish, snow peas, and scallion. Chill until ready to mix salad.

In a small bowl, combine oil, orange juice, vinegar, honey mustard, and salt. Chill until ready to mix salad.

Just before serving, lightly toss beets and vegetables with dressing. Serve on lettuce leaves.

SERVES 4.
CALORIES: 146   CHOLESTEROL: 0 mg   SODIUM: 350 mg   FIBER: 4 g

Health tip:
Omit salt.
CALORIES: 146   CHOLESTEROL: 0 mg   SODIUM: 65 mg   FIBER: 4 g

---

———————◇———————

New-Fangled Mushrooms and Barley

This is my updated version of an old family recipe. For those who are more inclined toward the old ways, I've also included the old-fashioned recipe, which follows. Both go well as side dishes with roast chicken, or could be used as a main dish when served with a salad of watercress, endive, or arugula, dressed with a creamy vinaigrette.

¼ cup butter, divided
1 cup barley, rinsed
¼ cup finely chopped shallot or the white part of a scallion
1 cup (3 ounces) sliced shiitaki mushrooms
1 cup (3 ounces) sliced crimini or porcini mushrooms
1 cup (3 ounces) sliced white button mushrooms
1 can (13¾ ounce) ready-to-serve chicken broth or
*   1¾ cups vegetable broth (see page 19)*
1½ cups water
¼ teaspoon pepper
⅛ teaspoon salt
½ cup chopped pecans

Melt 2 tablespoons of the butter in a 3-quart saucepan over medium heat. Add barley and cook, stirring frequently, until barley is lightly browned, 5 to 7 minutes. Remove from pan and set aside. Add the remaining 2 tablespoons butter to pan. Melt over medium heat. Add shallot and cook, stirring, until softened. Add all three types of mushrooms and continue to cook, stirring, until softened. Stir in broth, water, pepper, and salt. Cover and bring to a boil. Stir in barley and simmer for 45 minutes, or until liquid has been absorbed and barley is tender. Stir in pecans.

SERVES 6.

CALORIES: 268   CHOLESTEROL: 21 mg   SODIUM: 318 mg   FIBER: 7 g

Health tip:
Use oil instead of butter; substitute water for broth; omit salt.
CALORIES: 270   CHOLESTEROL: 0 mg   SODIUM: 102 mg   FIBER: 7 g

---

◇

Good Old-Fashioned Mushrooms and Barley

This is one of the few uses for barley with which most people are familiar. It is also one of the easiest, and goes well with roasted anything, a nice change from potatoes and other starches.

> 2 tablespoons vegetable oil
> 1 cup chopped onion
> ½ cup chopped green bell pepper
> 2 cups sliced mushrooms
> 2⅔ cups water
> 1 cup barley, rinsed
> 1 teaspoon salt
> ¼ teaspoon pepper

Heat the oil in a 2-quart saucepan. Add the onion and green pepper and cook, stirring, over medium-high heat until softened. Add mushrooms and continue to cook, stirring, until softened. Stir in water and bring to a boil over high heat. Add barley, salt, and pepper. Return to boiling. Cover and simmer for 45 minutes longer, or until liquid has been absorbed.

SERVES 6.

CALORIES: 174   CHOLESTEROL: 0 mg   SODIUM: 358 mg   FIBER: 6 g

Health tip:
Use a nonstick saucepan and reduce oil to 1 tablespoon; omit salt.
CALORIES: 154   CHOLESTEROL: 0 mg   SODIUM: 10 mg   FIBER: 6 g

Winter-Vegetable-and-Barley Bake

I like this particular combination of winter vegetables. Each one has a natural sweetness that goes well with the other, and the sherry adds a nippy little taste surprise.

½ cup barley, rinsed
2 cups 1-inch cubes butternut squash
2 cups julienned carrot
1 cup julienned parsnip
1¼ cups boiling water
¼ cup dry or medium-dry sherry
2 tablespoons light- or dark-brown sugar
¾ teaspoon salt
⅛ teaspoon ground nutmeg
2 tablespoons butter

Preheat oven to 350° F.

Place the barley in a 2-quart casserole. Arrange squash, carrot, and parsnip over barley. Drizzle water and sherry over vegetables. Sprinkle evenly with brown sugar, salt, and nutmeg. Dot with butter.

Cover and bake for 1 hour, or until barley and vegetables are tender. Stir to combine vegetables with barley just before serving.

SERVES 6.
CALORIES: 159   CHOLESTEROL: 7 mg   SODIUM: 300 mg   FIBER: 7 g

Health tip·
Omit salt and butter.
CALORIES: 135   CHOLESTEROL: 0 mg   SODIUM: 10 mg   FIBER: 7 g

——————— ◇ ———————

Leeks, Lentils, and Barley

If you're fortunate enough to have leftovers of this delightful mixture, chill them and then toss with fresh chopped vegetables and your favorite Italian dressing to create a terrific salad.

2 tablespoons vegetable oil
3 cups thinly sliced leeks (white and light-green portions only)
1 can (13¾ ounce) ready-to-serve beef broth or
*   1¾ cups vegetable broth (see page 19)*
1 cup water
¾ cup lentils, rinsed and picked over
½ cup barley, rinsed
1 bay leaf
¼ teaspoon salt
¼ teaspoon pepper

Heat the oil in a large saucepan over medium-high heat. Add the leeks and cook, stirring, until softened. Add broth and water and bring to a boil. Stir in lentils, barley, and bay leaf. Cover and simmer for 40 minutes, or until liquid has been absorbed. Stir in salt and pepper. Remove bay leaf before serving.

SERVES 6.
CALORIES: 144   CHOLESTEROL: 1 mg   SODIUM: 312 mg   FIBER: 4 g

Health tip:
Use a nonstick skillet and reduce oil to 1 tablespoon. Use low-sodium broth; omit salt.
CALORIES: 144   CHOLESTEROL: 1 mg   SODIUM: 223 mg   FIBER: 4 g

——————— ◇ ———————

Barley and Bows

This wonderful combination of vegetables, pasta, and barley is based on an old German recipe called *kraut flekerl*. It is pleasantly peppery tasting and is usually served as a side dish. However, if it's sprinkled with confectioners' sugar it can also be served as dessert (believe me).

2 tablespoons vegetable oil
1 cup chopped onion
4 cups ¼-inch diced cabbage
1 tablespoon butter

1 cup cooked barley
½ cup cooked small bow ties or other small pasta
¾ teaspoon salt
½ teaspoon pepper

In a large skillet, heat the oil over medium-high heat. Add the onion and cook, stirring, until golden. Add cabbage and continue to cook, stirring, until wilted. Add butter, then stir in barley, bow ties, salt, and pepper. Cook stirring, until barley and bow ties are heated through.

SERVES 4.
CALORIES: 188   CHOLESTEROL: 1 mg   SODIUM: 437 mg   FIBER: 4 g

Health tip:
Use a nonstick skillet and reduce oil to 1 tablespoon; omit butter and salt.
CALORIES: 132   CHOLESTEROL: 0 mg   SODIUM: 14 mg   FIBER: 4 g

———————◇———————

Nancy Jane's Simple Barley Recipe

I got this recipe from my friend, Nancy Jane Goldstein, who is an excellent cook and hostess. She serves this as a side dish at many of her company dinners.

2¾ cups vegetable broth (see page 19) or
canned chicken broth
1 cup barley, rinsed
½ cup toasted almonds (place almonds on a baking sheet and toast in a
350°F oven for 10 minutes, stirring occasionally)
⅓ cup chopped parsley
⅛ teaspoon pepper

Bring the broth to a boil in a medium-size saucepan. Stir in barley and cook for 50 minutes, or until liquid has been absorbed. Toss with almonds, parsley, and pepper.

SERVES 6.
CALORIES: 169   CHOLESTEROL: 0 mg   SODIUM: 343 mg   FIBER: 6 g

Health tip:
Use low-sodium broth.
CALORIES: 169   CHOLESTEROL: 0 mg   SODIUM: 139 mg   FIBER: 6 g

———————◇———————

Fiesta Barley and Beans

You can vary this recipe to suit your own taste by choosing the kind of sauce you use. If you are wildly adventurous, try tomato-jalapeno pepper sauce. Those of a more conservative nature can use a mild taco sauce

2 tablespoons vegetable oil
½ cup chopped onion
½ cup chopped red or yellow bell pepper
½ cup chopped green bell pepper (or you can use 1 cup chopped green
    pepper and omit the red and yellow varieties altogether)
1⅓ cups water
1 cup tomato-jalapeno pepper sauce or mild taco sauce
¼ teaspoon ground cumin
⅛ teaspoon crumbled oregano
½ cup barley, rinsed
1 can (16 ounce) pinto or kidney beans, undrained

Heat the oil in a 2-quart saucepan. Add onion and bell peppers and cook, stirring, until softened. Stir in the water, sauce, cumin, and oregano and bring to a boil. Stir in barley and return to boiling. Cover and simmer for 40 minutes, stirring once or twice as barley approaches doneness. Stir in undrained beans. Simmer 5 minutes longer, or until beans are heated through.

SERVES 6.
CALORIES: 184   CHOLESTEROL: 0 mg   SODIUM: 302 mg   FIBER: 9 g

Health tip:
Use a nonstick saucepan and reduce oil to 1 tablesppon.
CALORIES: 164   CHOLESTEROL: 0 mg   SODIUM: 302 mg   FIBER: 9 g

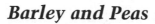

Barley and Peas

I love peas with starchy food. This is a simple, yet flavorfully impressive, side dish that goes well with almost anything, although I often find it extremely satisfying, just by itself, when I'm dining alone and too lazy or tired to fix anything more complicated.

1⅓ cups water
½ teaspoon salt
½ cup barley, rinsed
1 cup frozen peas
2 tablespoons finely chopped scallion
1 tablespoon butter

In a 1-quart saucepan, bring the water and salt to a boil. Stir in barley and return to boiling. Cover, reduce heat, and simmer for 40 minutes. Stir in peas, scallion, and butter. Cover and simmer for 5 minutes more, or until peas are heated through.

SERVES 4.
CALORIES: 129   CHOLESTEROL: 8 mg   SODIUM: 293 mg   FIBER: 6 g

Health tip:
Omit salt and butter.
CALORIES: 103   CHOLESTEROL: 0 mg   SODIUM: 21 mg   FIBER: 6 g

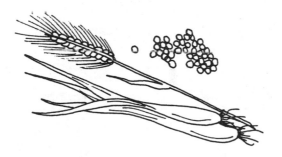

Crisp Vegetables and Barley

Stirring the vegetables in during the last 15 minutes of cooking time keeps them bright and flavorful. This is a side dish that looks pretty and tastes good with roast chicken or other poultry.

3 tablespoons vegetable oil
1 cup barley, rinsed
2 cups chopped onion
1 can (13¾ ounce) ready-to-serve chicken broth or
*   1¾ cups vegetable broth (see page 19)*
¾ cup white wine
1 cup frozen peas
½ cup chopped zucchini
½ cup chopped yellow squash
2 tablespoons chopped roasted red peppers or pimiento
2 tablespoons chopped parsley
¼ teaspoon salt
¼ teaspoon pepper

In a 3-quart saucepan, heat the oil over medium-high heat. Add barley and cook over medium heat, stirring, until lightly browned, about 5 minutes. Stir in the onion and cook until soft. Stir in broth and wine. Lower heat and simmer, covered, for 30 minutes. Stir in peas, zucchini, yellow squash, red pepper, parsley, salt, and pepper. Cover and simmer for 15 minutes longer, or until liquid has been absorbed.

SERVES 8.
CALORIES: 191   CHOLESTEROL: 1 mg   SODIUM: 242 mg   FIBER: 6 g

Health tip:
Use a nonstick saucepan and reduce oil to 1 tablespoon; use low-sodium broth; omit salt.
CALORIES: 133   CHOLESTEROL: 1 mg   SODIUM: 21 mg   FIBER: 6 g

Barley Green

You can use vegetables other than asparagus in this recipe, if you like. Try green beans, lima beans, or even chopped spinach.

1 can (10½ ounce) concentrated French onion soup or
    1¼ cups vegetable broth (see page 19)
1½ cups water or additional vegetable broth
1 cup barley, rinsed
½ pound fresh asparagus, cut into 1-inch pieces
¼ cup chopped parsley
¼ teaspoon pepper

In a 2-quart saucepan, bring the soup and water to a boil. Stir in barley, and simmer, covered, for 35 minutes, or until most of the liquid has been absorbed. Stir in asparagus, parsley, and pepper. Continue to simmer for 10 minutes more. Remove from heat and let stand for 5 minutes, or until remaining liquid has been absorbed.

SERVES 4.
CALORIES: 223   CHOLESTEROL: 2 mg   SODIUM: 644 mg   FIBER: 5 g

Health tip:
Substitute low-sodium beef broth for onion soup.
CALORIES: 223   CHOLESTEROL: 2 mg   SODIUM: 50 mg   FIBER: 5 g

Sweet Barley Bread

Spread this slightly sweet bread with jam or butter (or both!) and enjoy it at coffee or tea time.

1¼ cups hot (105–115° F) water, divided
1 package dry yeast
2 cups all-purpose flour, divided
¾ cup barley flour
⅓ cup sugar
1½ teaspoons salt
¼ teaspoon anise seed or
    1½ teaspoons ground cinnamon
3 tablespoons barley malt or unsulphured molasses
2 tablespoons butter, softened
½ cup raisins

Grease a 9-inch-round layer-cake pan and set aside.

Place ½ cup of the water in a glass measuring cup, then stir in yeast (and a pinch of sugar, if you like, to encourage the yeast to activate). Let stand until about ¼ inch of white bubbly foam forms on top. (This foaming is called *proofing*, and if it doesn't happen it means that for some reason or other the yeast has not been activated. Discard this batch and try again, double checking the date on the yeast package and the temperature of the water.)

In a large bowl, stir together 1¼ cups of the all-purpose flour, barley flour, sugar, salt, and anise seed.

Combine proofed-yeast mixture and remaining ¾ cup water with barley malt. Stir into flour mixture, along with butter. Beat with an electric mixer at high speed for 5 minutes. Stir in ½ cup of the remaining all-purpose flour. Cover with greased plastic wrap and let rise in a warm spot, out of drafts, for 1 hour and 15 minutes.

Stir in the remaining ¼ cup all-purpose flour and raisins. Turn dough into prepared pan. With floured hands, pat dough into an even layer in the pan.

Cover with greased plastic wrap and let rise until dough reaches top of pan, about 1 hour and 15 minutes.

Preheat oven to 350°F.

Bake for 40 to 50 minutes, or until golden brown. Turn bread out of pan and cool on a wire rack. Cut into wedges to serve.

MAKES 1 LOAF (16 wedges).
CALORIES: 125   CHOLESTEROL: 4 mg   SODIUM: 213 mg   FIBER: 1 g

Health tip:
Omit salt; substitute unsalted margarine for butter.
CALORIES: 125   CHOLESTEROL: 0 mg   SODIUM: 37 mg   FIBER: 1 g

———————— ◇ ————————

Barley-Potato Doughnut Holes

If you like doughnuts, you'll really enjoy these. They are light, tasty, and have a slightly unusual flavor. Like most doughnuts, these are best when freshly made.

1 cup all-purpose flour
1 cup barley flour
1 tablespoon baking powder
½ teaspoon salt
½ teaspoon ground nutmeg
¼ teaspoon ground cinnamon
2 eggs
⅔ cup sugar
⅓ cup cold mashed potatoes (can be made from instant)
¼ cup butter, melted
1 teaspoon vanilla extract
½ cup milk
Oil, for frying
Granulated sugar, for coating doughnuts

In a medium-size bowl, combine the all-purpose flour, barley flour, baking powder, salt, nutmeg, and cinnamon. Stir with a whisk so that the flour mixture is light and well blended.

In a large bowl, beat eggs and sugar until light and fluffy, about 5 minutes. Beat in potatoes, then butter and vanilla. Mix dry ingredients into potato mixture, alternating with milk, until well blended.

Pour enough oil into a deep-fryer or large saucepan to measure about 2 inches deep. Heat oil to 375° F. Drop by rounded teaspoons into oil and fry until brown on each side. Drain on paper towels. Roll in granulated sugar to coat. Serve as soon after frying as possible.

MAKES ABOUT 4 DOZEN DOUGHNUTS.
CALORIES: 56   CHOLESTEROL: 14 mg   SODIUM: 120 mg   FIBER: .5 g

Health tip:
Use unsalted margarine instead of butter—and eat just one!
CALORIES: 56   CHOLESTEROL: 9 mg   SODIUM: 40 mg   FIBER: .5 g

———————— ◇ ————————

Yummy Barley-Date Bars

I often take these bars to food-photography sessions and every-one loves them, which I find flattering, since all of the people I work with are food professionals.

1 cup water
2 packages (8 ounces each) pitted dates
1 tablespoon lemon juice
1½ cups all-purpose flour
¾ cup firmly packed dark-brown sugar (light-brown sugar is okay, too, if
    that's what you have on hand)
¼ teaspoon salt
¾ cup butter
1½ cups barley flakes

Preheat oven to 350°F.
Grease a 13 × 9 × 2-inch baking pan.
In a 2-quart saucepan, combine the water, dates, and lemon juice. Bring to a boil over high heat. Reduce heat and simmer for 10 minutes, stirring occasionally, or until nearly all of the liquid has been absorbed. Stir hard with a wooden spoon until the dates are a fairly smooth paste.
    In a large bowl, stir together the flour, sugar, and salt. With a pastry blender or two knives, cut butter into flour mixture until it resembles coarse cornmeal. Stir in barley flakes.
    Press two-thirds of the barley-crumb mixture into the prepared pan, pressing down with the back of a measuring cup to make the layer firm and even. Spread the date mixture evenly over the crumb mixture. (This is a little tricky, since it is sticky and tends to lift some of the crumb mixture. To avoid this, spread with a rubber spatula, pressing down lightly. Spread in one direction at a time, and be careful each time you lift the spatula.) Sprinkle remaining barley-crumb mixture over date mixture.
    Bake for 45 to 50 minutes, or until topping is lightly browned. Cool on a wire rack. Cut into 32 bars.

MAKES 32 BARS.
CALORIES: 109   CHOLESTEROL: 12 mg   SODIUM: 56 mg   FIBER: 1 g

Health tip:
Omit salt; use unsalted margarine instead of butter.
CALORIES: 109   CHOLESTEROL: 0 mg   SODIUM: 8 mg   FIBER: 1 g

————————◇————————

Spiced Barley-Raisin Cookies

These are cakelike cookies. They have a nice flavor-snap from the spices, and raisins give them a chewy sweetness.

¾ cup all-purpose flour
⅓ cup barley flour
1 teaspoon ground cinnamon
1 teaspoon baking soda
½ teaspoon salt
¼ teaspoon ground nutmeg
¼ teaspoon ground cloves
½ cup butter, softened
⅓ cup sugar
⅓ cup firmly packed light-brown sugar (dark-brown sugar is okay, too)
½ teaspoon vanilla extract
2 eggs
½ cup barley flakes
1 cup raisins

Preheat oven to 375°F.

Grease one or two cookie sheets and set aside.

In a small bowl, stir together the all-purpose flour, barley flour, cinnamon, baking soda, salt, nutmeg, and cloves.

In a large bowl, beat together the butter, sugar, brown sugar, and vanilla until creamy. Beat in eggs, then flour mixture. Stir in barley flakes and raisins. Drop by measuring tablespoonful onto prepared cookie sheets.

Bake for 9 to 11 minutes, or until lightly browned. Remove from cookie sheets and cool completely on wire racks.

MAKES 2 DOZEN COOKIES.
CALORIES: 110   CHOLESTEROL: 28 mg   SODIUM: 119 mg   FIBER: 1 g

Health tip:
Omit salt; use unsalted margarine instead of butter.
CALORIES: 110   CHOLESTEROL: 17 mg   SODIUM: 45 mg   FIBER: 1 g

BUCKWHEAT
(Fagopyrum esculentum)

Buckwheat is not a grain (which is technically a grass seed), but rather the fruit of a plant related to rhubarb. But so many of its properties are similar to those of a true grain that I've gone ahead and included it, and referred to it as a grain, in this book.

When most people think of buckwheat, it is not the raw product that usually comes to mind. The so-called buckwheat with which most of us are familiar, and which is most readily available, is actually kasha, raw buckwheat that has been roasted. In its raw state, buckwheat is rather difficult to find. The reddish-brown grain you see in buckwheat bins is really kasha, and most recipes that call for buckwheat are actually calling for kasha.

Types of Buckwheat/Kasha Available

Whole buckwheat seed (raw): Dark brown in color; not recommended for eating, but very good for sprouting and making into flour.

Hulled buckwheat (raw): Greenish-khaki color; can be used in any recipe calling for kasha.

Whole kasha: Hulled buckwheat that has been roasted. It is especially suitable for salads, stews, or any recipe that would be best with distinct separate grains.

Coarse kasha: Similar to whole kasha, except that the grain has been cracked into a few pieces. The cooked pieces will not be quite as separate as whole kasha.

Medium kasha: Cracked into smaller pieces than coarse kasha, but can be used the same way.

Fine kasha: The smallest of the cracked kashas. The cooked consistency is stickier than the larger-cracked forms.

Buckwheat flour: Available as light or dark flour, the darker having a stronger buckwheat flavor. It is mainly used for making blini and other pancakes. Since buckwheat flour does tend to remain grainy with an unpleasant sandy mouth feel, I don't recommend it as a substitute for white or whole-wheat flours in breads and other baked goods.

Soda: Noodles made from buckwheat flour.

Texture and Flavor

Raw, unroasted buckwheat is shaped something like a round-cut diamond. It has a distinctive flowery flavor that will remind you of a blend of rosemary and green tea.

Kasha is probably one of the only grains from which you can get a sense of the flavor by smelling it before it's cooked. That's because the roasting has already brought out its aroma. It tastes slightly nutty, almost scorched, when it's warm, but loses this slightly burnt taste when it cools.

The consistency of cooked kasha is rather soft and fluffy, with an occasional piece of hull that will cling to the roof of your mouth like popcorn hull. The texture is especially nice when mixed with chewy foods.

When cooked with too much water, kasha becomes soggy and clumpy. Otherwise, it has a light mouth feel, and the feeling of satiety that it provides makes it a good choice for a meat substitute.

Compatible Foods, Herbs, and Spices

Because it has a strong taste, kasha works best in recipes with bland flavors that allow it to dominate. Most meats, game, and vegetables go well with kasha, and starchy foods, such as pasta and potatoes, are especially suitable companions.

Ginger, pepper, allspice, nutmeg, and other spices that hold their flavor tend to be more compatible with kasha than more delicate herbs.

Availability

Kasha is available in most supermarkets. (Try the foreign or gourmet food sections. Sometimes you can locate it with the rice, and other times with the cereal.)

Raw buckwheat, on the other hand, can only be found in some well-stocked health-food stores and from mail-order grain catalogs (see page 21).

Nutritional Content

Buckwheat is high in lysine, an amino acid that is found in very low amounts in true grains. But like true grains, buckwheat is high in B vitamins, protein, iron, and calcium.

Substitutions

The assertive flavor of kasha precludes a simple substitution with any other grain. However, you can substitute each form of kasha for another (fine kasha for whole kasha, etc.).

Whole-wheat flour can be substituted for buckwheat flour.

Basic Cooking Instructions

Please read *About Cooking Grains* beginning on page 7. *Note that all recipes in this section, unless otherwise noted, were tested with kasha, not buckwheat.*

When cooking kasha, always remember to remove it from the heat just as soon as most of the water has been absorbed and holes appear on the surface. Tilt the pan to determine that there is very little water left, then remove from the heat. The small amount of water that remains will be absorbed during a few minutes of standing time. (This vigilance will also prevent a difficult clean-up job, as the kasha and pot seem to be inseparable if the kasha is cooked until every last drop of water has been absorbed.)

Kasha cooks perfectly in a microwave oven, which also gives it a fluffier texture than the stove-top method. The microwave method that follows for cooking kasha was tested in a 650-watt oven.

Another method for cooking kasha involves coating the grains with egg and then drying them in a pot or skillet before adding liquid. Cooking the kasha this way will keep the grains fluffier and more separate than simple boiling.

The finer the grind of the kasha, the more like cereal the cooked product will be. For use in salads, whole or coarse kasha is a better choice than medium or fine grinds. But the finer grinds are good choices in recipes in which you want the kasha evenly distributed.

Stove-top method I:

> 2 cups water
> 1 teaspoon salt
> 1 cup whole kasha or buckwheat

In a 2-quart saucepan, bring the water and salt to a boil over high heat. Stir in kasha. Cover and simmer for 12 minutes, or until almost all of the water has been absorbed. Remove from heat and let stand for 7 minutes, or until all of the water has been absorbed. Fluff with a fork.

MAKES 3½ TO 3¾ CUPS.

Stove-top method II:

> *1 egg*
> *1 cup whole kasha or buckwheat*
> *2 cups boiling water*
> *1 teaspoon salt*

Beat the egg in a medium-size bowl. Add kasha and stir until all of the grains are coated with egg. Place coated kasha in a 2-quart saucepan and cook, stirring, until egg has dried. Stir in boiling water and salt. When water has returned to a boil, reduce heat, cover, and simmer for 10 minutes. Remove from heat and let stand 5 minutes. Fluff with a fork.

MAKES 3½ CUPS.

Microwave method:

> *1¾ cups hot tap water*
> *1 teaspoon salt*
> *1 cup whole kasha or buckwheat*

Place the water and salt in a 2-quart, microwave-safe bowl. Cover with waxed paper. Cook on high (100% power) for 3 to 5 minutes, or until boiling. Stir in kasha. Recover with waxed paper and cook for 15 minutes on medium (50% power), or until water has been absorbed. Let stand 5 minutes. Fluff with a fork.

MAKES 3¼ CUPS.

Reheating

Kasha remains soft after refrigeration and does not have to be reheated to be used in salads or other recipes. Should you want to reheat kasha, it can be microwaved, steamed, or baked.

BUCKWHEAT/KASHA RECIPES

*(*indicates easy recipe.)*

———————◇———————

Blini
Piroshki (miniature turnovers)
Delicious Knishes
Winter Lamb Stew *
Very Chicken-y Croquettes
Kasha-Potato Salad *
Waldorf-ish Buckwheat Salad *
Kasha Varniskas *
Kasha-Vegetable Strudel
Mushrooms Paprikash *
Kasha with Leeks and Endive *
Kasha with Brussels Sprouts and Bacon *
Boiled Soba
Zaru Soba (noodles in a basket)
Soba Noodles with Peanut Sauce
Buckwheat and Wild Rice Dressing *
Buckwheat Griddlecakes *
Low-cholesterol Buckwheat-and-Bran Muffins *
Buckwheat-Currant Brown Bread
Sweet Cheese Squares (kroopyenik) *

———————— ◇ ————————

Blini

These small buckwheat pancakes are a traditional Russian treat that is almost always eaten before Lent. The warm blini are first brushed with melted butter and then topped with such luxurious goodies as sour cream, caviar, red salmon roe, smoked sturgeon, smoked salmon, and pickled herring. Russian cooks figure on about 15 pancakes per person—unless someone is really hungry. (Don't forget a bottle of icy vodka!)

⅓ cup very warm water (105–115°F.)
1 package quick-rise yeast
3 tablespoons plus 1 teaspoon sugar, divided
1 cup all-purpose flour
1 cup buckwheat flour
½ teaspoon salt
⅓ cup butter
1⅔ cups milk, scalded (bubbles form around edge of the pot, but the
*   milk should not actually boil)*
3 eggs, separated
Melted butter
Sour cream
Caviar (the best you can afford)

Place the warm water in a glass measuring cup, then stir in yeast and 1 teaspoon of the sugar. Let stand until ¼ inch of white bubbly foam forms on top. (This foaming is called *proofing,* and if it doesn't happen it means that for some reason or other the yeast has not been activated. Discard this batch and try again, double checking the date on the yeast package and the temperature of the water.)

While the yeast is proofing, stir together both kinds of flour, salt, and remaining 3 tablespoons sugar in a large bowl.

Stir butter into scalded milk until nearly melted. Stir the milk mixture and the proofed-yeast mixture into the flour mixture. Beat in egg yolks. Cover and let rise in a warm spot, out of drafts, until doubled in bulk.

In a clean, grease-free, medium-size bowl, beat egg whites with clean beaters until stiff peaks form when beaters are lifted. Fold beaten egg whites into the risen batter. Cover with greased plastic wrap and let rise for an additional 30 minutes.

Heat a griddle or a large skillet until a few drops of water sprinkled on the hot griddle bounce about before evaporating. Butter the griddle *lightly.* (This is important, for if there is too much butter, the blini will have a somewhat unattractive gray appearance.) Drop batter by ¼ cupsful onto the griddle. Cook until bubbles on top have broken. Turn and cook until second side is browned.

Brush cooked pancakes with melted butter and top with sour cream and caviar.

MAKES 16 BLINI.
CALORIES: 66   CHOLESTEROL: 28 mg   SODIUM: 66 mg   FIBER: .5 g

Health tip:
Omit salt; substitute unsalted margarine for butter; use 2-percent-fat milk.
CALORIES: 63   CHOLESTEROL: 26 mg   SODIUM: 31 mg   FIBER: .5 g

---

————————— ◇ —————————

Piroshki (miniature turnovers)

Like blini, piroshki is Russian in origin. You can fill them with almost anything you like. My grandmother used to favor chopped lung as a filling, but that's no longer available, so you'll have to settle for beef, poultry, or cheese mixtures, for instance, or the following vegetarian filling that I like very much.

Pastry Dough:

> ¾ cup sour cream
> ½ teaspoon baking soda
> 2½ cups all-purpose flour
> 1 teaspoon salt
> ½ teaspoon baking powder
> ½ cup butter, chilled
> 2 eggs, beaten

Filling:

> 2 tablespoons butter
> 1 cup finely chopped cabbage
> ⅓ cup finely chopped onion
> 1 cup cooked kasha
> ⅓ cup sour cream
> ½ teaspoon salt
> ¼ teaspoon pepper
> 1 egg, for glaze (optional)

Grease and flour two or three baking sheets and set aside.

To make the pastry dough, stir together sour cream and baking soda in a medium-size bowl. Set aside.

In a large bowl, stir together flour, salt, and baking powder. With a pastry cutter or two knives, cut in butter until mixture resembles coarse cornmeal.

Beat eggs into sour-cream mixture. Stir into flour mixture until completely combined. Turn onto a floured surface. Knead for 1 or 2 minutes, or until the dough is smooth and pliable. Form into a ball. Wrap in foil or plastic wrap and chill for 30 minutes while making filling.

To make filling, melt the butter in a large skillet over medium-high heat. Add cabbage and onion and cook, stirring, until vegetables are softened. Remove from heat and stir in cooked kasha, sour cream, salt, and pepper. Set aside.

Preheat oven to 400°F.

Roll dough into a rectangle measuring about 18 × 14 inches. Cut out 24 3-inch circles with a biscuit or cookie cutter. Or, if it's easier, cut the dough into 24 2½-inch squares. Brush around the edge of each circle, or square, with beaten egg. Place a level tablespoon of the filling in the center of each circle. Fold in half to form half moons (or triangles, if using squares of dough), then press the coated edges together with the tines of a fork to seal the pastries and make a decorative edge, as well. Prick the top with fork tines to vent steam.

Brush tops of dough with beaten egg; place on prepared baking sheets.

Bake for about 20 minutes, or until golden.

MAKES 24 PIROSHKI.

CALORIES: 121 CHOLESTEROL: 32 mg SODIUM: 201 mg FIBER: 1 g

Health tip:
Use unsalted margarine for butter.
CALORIES: 121 CHOLESTEROL: 22 mg SODIUM: 40 mg FIBER: 1 g

————————— ◇ —————————

Delicious Knishes

Knishes are traditionally made with a mashed-potato or kasha filling. In my grandmother's house, large knishes were served for lunch or as a light meal with soup or a salad. Sometimes my mom makes "mini-knishes" and offers them as an appetizer when company comes.

Dough:

> ½ cup cottage cheese
> ½ cup butter, softened
> 1 cup all-purpose flour
> 1 egg, beaten, for glaze (optional)

Filling:

> ¼ cup butter
> ½ cup finely chopped onion
> 1½ cups cooked fine or medium kasha
> 1 cup mashed potatoes (can be made from instant)
> 1 egg, beaten
> ¼ teaspoon pepper
> ⅛ teaspoon salt

Grease and flour two or three baking sheets and set aside.

To make te dough, push cottage cheese through a fine strainer with the back of a spoon into a small bowl. Add butter and stir to combine. Stir in flour and chill for 15 minutes.

To make the filling, melt butter in a large skillet over medium-high heat. Add onion and cook, stirring, until softened. Remove from heat. Stir in kasha and mashed potatoes. Allow mixture to cool slightly. Stir in egg, pepper, and salt.

Preheat oven to 350 F.

Turned chilled dough out onto a floured surface. Roll dough into a rectangle measuring about 18 × 12 inches. (The dough will be very thin, so you may periodically have to lift it and add more flour to the work surface.)

To make 6 lunch-size knishes: Cut the dough into 6 squares measuring 6 × 6 inches. Place ⅓ cup of the kasha mixture in the center of each square. Brush around edges with beaten egg. Lift the four points of each square to meet over filling. Pinch the top together, then the seams, to secure the dough and seal the seams. Place on prepared baking sheets in one of two ways: seam-side up, or seam-side down for a more conventional looking knish. Brush with beaten egg. Cut tiny vents in the dough with the tip of a knife, or prick with a fork to vent steam.

Bake for about 40 minutes, or until golden.

Makes 6 lunch-size knishes.
CALORIES: 395   CHOLESTEROL: 98 mg   SODIUM: 494 mg   FIBER: 3 g

Health tip:
Substitute unsalted margarine for butter; omit salt; substitute water for beaten egg used for sealing and glazing dough.
CALORIES: 395   CHOLESTEROL: 36 mg   SODIUM: 214 mg   FIBER: 3 g

---

To make 12 appetizer knishes: Cut dough into 12 4-inch squares (you'll have a little dough left over). Place 2 rounded tablespoonsful of filling in the center of each square. Follow directions above for folding and baking, reducing baking time slightly.

CALORIES: 190   CHOLESTEROL: 50 mg   SODIUM: 260 mg   FIBER: 1 g

Health tip:
Same as for lunch-size knishes.
CALORIES: 190   CHOLESTEROL: 18 mg   SODIUM: 107 mg   FIBER: 1 g

---

———————— ◇ ————————

Winter Lamb Stew

Although I enjoy this stew any time of the year, I like it the best on cold, blustery nights when I am joined for supper by two or three good friends. Serve the stew accompanied by chunks of crusty whole-grain bread in front of a cozy fire. A warm pie for dessert is all you need for an easy and memorable meal.

1 pound cubed stewing lamb
3 tablespoons all-purpose flour
3 tablespoons vegetable oil
2 cups water
1½ cups sliced celery
1 cup chopped onion
1 can (8 ounce) tomato sauce
½ teaspoon salt
⅛ teaspoon pepper
1 package (10 ounce) frozen cut green beans
2 cups cooked kasha (method II)

Dredge the lamb in flour. Heat oil in a 3-quart saucepan over medium-high heat. Add lamb and cook, turning, until browned on all sides. Add water, celery, onion, tomato sauce, salt, and pepper. Bring to a boil, then lower heat and simmer, uncovered, for 1 hour and 15 minutes. Stir in green beans and simmer for 45 minutes longer. (If you like your beans crisp, simmer the stew for 1 hour and 35 minutes, then stir in the beans and cook until heated through, 5 to 10 minutes.)

Serve stew over kasha.

SERVES 4.
CALORIES: 522   CHOLESTEROL: 104 mg   SODIUM: 133 mg   FIBER: 7 g

Health tip:
Reduce oil to 2 teaspoons and cook in a nonstick saucepan. Or, brown lamb in a nonstick skillet, transferring to the larger pan to finish cooking. Omit salt.
CALORIES: 453   CHOLESTEROL 104 mg   SODIUM: 467 mg   FIBER: 7 g

––––––––––––◇––––––––––––

Very Chicken-y Croquettes

I developed the recipe for these croquettes with my mother in mind, because they are one of her favorite foods. Mine, too

¼ cup butter
½ cup finely chopped celery
¼ cup finely chopped onion
¼ cup all-purpose flour
¾ cup chicken broth
2 tablespoons chopped parsley
1 teaspoon white vinegar
¼ teaspoon dry mustard
¼ teaspoon poultry seasoning
¼ teaspoon salt
¼ teaspoon pepper
1½ cups finely chopped cooked chicken
1 cup cooked fine kasha
¼ cup unflavored dry bread crumbs
¼ cup finely chopped pecans
Additional bread crumbs, for coating
Oil, for frying

Melt the butter in a 2-quart saucepan over medium-high heat. Add celery and onion and cook, stirring, until softened. Stir in flour until completely absorbed. Using a whisk, gradually stir in the broth. Cook, stirring constantly, until mixture comes to a boil. Stir in parsley, vinegar, mustard, poultry seasoning, salt, and pepper until well combined. Remove from heat. Stir in chicken, kasha, bread crumbs, and pecans. Place saucepan in the refrigerator until mixture is cold and slightly stiffened.

Form chilled croquette mixture into 8 patties. Roll patties in bread crumbs to coat.

Pour enough oil into a large skillet so that it measures about ¼-inch deep. Heat until oil bubbles when a few bread crumbs are sprinkled on the surface. Cook patties on both sides until appetizingly browned.

MAKES 8 CROQUETTES.
CALORIES: 227   CHOLESTEROL: 37 mg   SODIUM: 295 mg   FIBER: 1 g

Health tip:
Use low-sodium broth; substitute unsalted margarine for butter. Omit salt from kasha.
CALORIES: 227   CHOLESTEROL: 22 mg   SODIUM: 20 mg   FIBER: 1 g

◇

Kasha-Potato Salad

This is an absolutely yummy potato salad. The texture of the kasha contrasts so nicely with the crunchiness of the chopped vegetables and the chewiness of the potatoes. For a heartier salad, you can stir in a couple of chopped hard-cooked eggs.

1 pound (6 to 8) small waxy new potatoes
1 cup cooked whole or coarse kasha
½ cup finely chopped green bell pepper
2 tablespoons minced onion
⅓ cup mayonnaise
1 tablespoon water
2 teaspoons spicy brown mustard
1 teaspoon cider vinegar
½ teaspoon salt
¼ teaspoon pepper

Cook the potatoes in boiling water for 20 minutes, or until just tender when pierced with the tip of a knife. Drain and cool. Peel potatoes (or not) then slice into a large bowl. Add kasha, green pepper, and onion. Toss gently to combine.

In a small bowl, stir together the mayonnaise, water, mustard, vinegar, salt, and pepper. Gently toss salad with dressing until well combined.

SERVES 6.
CALORIES: 183   CHOLESTEROL: 7 mg   SODIUM: 369 mg   FIBER: 2 g

Health tip:
Use reduced-calorie mayonnaise; omit salt.
CALORIES: 178   CHOLESTEROL: 7 mg   SODIUM: 134 mg   FIBER: 2 g

———— ◇ ————

Waldorf-ish Buckwheat Salad

My version of a Waldorf Salad makes a complete light meal, and you can make it even heartier by stirring in chunks of cooked chicken.

3 cups cooked and cooled Kasha
1½ cups cored and chopped apple
1 cup seedless grapes, cut in half
⅓ cup raisins
½ cup radishes, sliced
½ cup diced celery
¼ cup pignoli (pine nuts)
¼ cup finely chopped scallion
½ cup plain yogurt
⅓ cup mayonnaise
1 tablespoon honey
½ teaspoon ground cinnamon

In a large bowl, toss together the kasha, apples, grapes, raisins, radishes, celery, pignoli, and scallion.

In a small bowl, stir together the yogurt, mayonnaise, honey, and cinnamon. Gently toss dressing and salad mixture until well combined.

SERVES 6.
CALORIES: 309   CHOLESTEROL: 12 mg   SODIUM: 270 mg   FIBER: 5g

Health tip:
Omit salt when cooking kasha; substitute reduced-calorie mayonnaise for regular mayonnaise, omit pignoli.
CALORIES: 205   CHOLESTEROL: 6 mg   SODIUM: 31 mg   FIBER: 5g

Kasha Varniskas

This is the buckwheat dish with which I am most familiar. It's a very traditional Eastern European side dish that is good served with any kind of meat.

1 egg, beaten
¾ cup whole kasha
2 tablespoons vegetable oil
1 cup chopped onion
1½ cups boiling chicken broth or vegetable broth (see page 000)
¼ teaspoon pepper
1 cup uncooked bow-tie pasta

Stir the egg and kasha together in a small bowl. Heat a large skillet and cook the kasha mixture, stirring constantly, in the *dry* skillet until the egg has dried and the grains are separate. Remove from heat.

In a 2-quart saucepan, heat oil over medium-high heat. Add onion and cook, stirring frequently, until softened. Stir in the kasha mixture, broth, and pepper and bring to a boil. Simmer, covered, for 15 minutes.

While kasha is cooking, cook bow ties in boiling water for about 8 minutes, or until tender, and drain. Stir bow ties into kasha.

SERVES 8.
CALORIES: 159   CHOLESTEROL: 26 mg   SODIUM: 156 mg   FIBER: 2 g

Health tip:
Use low-sodium broth. Reduce oil to 2 teaspoons and use a nonstick saucepan. Or, cook onion in a nonstick skillet, transferring to the larger pan to finish cooking.
CALORIES: 159   CHOLESTEROL: 26 mg   SODIUM: 14 mg   FIBER: 2 g

————————◇————————

Kasha-Vegetable Strudel

Like all strudels, this one is rich and filling. Serve thin slices for a first course or side dish, or make the portions larger and accompany the strudel with a salad for a light meal.

¼ cup butter, divided
1 cup coarsely shredded zucchini
¾ cup coarsely shredded carrot
½ cup chopped onion
1½ cups cooked kasha (any type)
1 cup shredded Monterey Jack or Cheddar cheese
½ cup cottage cheese
1 tablespoon chopped parsley
½ teaspoon dried dill weed
¼ teaspoon salt
¼ teaspoon pepper
4 phyllo-dough sheets (17 × 12 inches), thawed as package directs
3 tablespoons dry unflavored bread crumbs

Preheat oven to 375°F.

In a large skillet, melt the butter over medium-high heat. Pour 2 tablespoons of the melted butter into a small bowl and set aside. Add zucchini, carrot, and onion to butter remaining in skillet and cook, stirring, until vegetables are softened. Remove from heat. Stir in kasha, cheeses, parsley, dill weed, salt, and pepper.

Remove thawed phyllo sheets from package (reseal package tightly so that remaining sheets won't dry out). Place one sheet on a work surface with a long side facing you. (Cover remaining two sheets of phyllo with a damp towel or plastic wrap to keep them from drying out.) Brush sheet lightly with reserved melted butter, then sprinkle with about 2 teaspoons bread crumbs. Place another phyllo sheet on top of the first. Brush with butter and sprinkle with bread crumbs as before. Repeat with remaining sheet of phyllo.

Spoon filling onto the stack of phyllo, 2 inches in from the long edge nearest you, leaving a 2-inch border at each side. (What you will have is a "log" of filling about 2 inches wide and 15 inches long.) Fold the two side edges in over the ends of the filling. Fold the 2-inch long edge near you over the log of filling. Start rolling the phyllo and filling away from you to the end of the dough, enclosing the filling in a neat, loglike package.

Place strudel on a baking sheet and brush top with any remaining butter.

Bake for 30 minutes, or until golden. Cut into slices to serve.

MAKES 4 MAIN-DISH SERVINGS.
CALORIES: 320   CHOLESTEROL: 61 mg   SODIUM: 721 mg   FIBER: 3 g

Health tip:
Use unsalted margarine instead of butter; omit salt.
CALORIES: 316   CHOLESTEROL: 27 mg   SODIUM: 513 mg   FIBER: 3g

—————— ◇ ——————

Mushrooms Paprikash

Paprikash is a Hungarian term and it means that the dish is flavored with paprika, usually lots of it, and cream. You can find real Hungarian paprika in specialty food stores. It is worth seeking out, for it has a lovely intense flavor, much more interesting than our domestic paprikas. The recipe that follows is an excellent side dish for plain roasted poultry or meat.

3 tablespoons vegetable oil
12 ounces mushrooms, rinsed, patted dry, and coarsely chopped
1 cup chopped onion
1 clove garlic, minced
2 tablespoons Hungarian or domestic paprika
¾ teaspoon salt
¼ teaspoon pepper
1 cup chicken broth or vegetable broth (see page 19)
¾ cup water
1 cup kasha
½ cup sour cream
2 tablespoons chopped parsley

In a 3-quart saucepan, heat the oil over medium-high heat. Add mushrooms, onion, and garlic. Cook, stirring, until vegetables are softened. Stir in paprika, salt, and pepper. Add broth and water and bring to a boil. Stir in kasha and return to boiling. Lower heat and simmer, covered, for 12 minutes. Remove from heat and let stand 5 minutes. Stir in sour cream and parsley.

SERVES 6.
CALORIES: 177   CHOLESTEROL: 6 mg   SODIUM: 308 mg   FIBER: 4 g

Health tip:
Reduce oil to 2 teaspoons and use a nonstick saucepan. Or, cook vegetables in a nonstick skillet, transferring to the larger pan to finish cooking. Use low-sodium broth; substitute plain lowfat yogurt for sour cream.
CALORIES: 102   CHOLESTEROL: 6 mg   SODIUM: 60 mg   FIBER: 4 g

Kasha with Leeks and Endive

Leeks and endive (not the lettuce, but rather those small oval heads that are light green in color and are often called "Belgian" endive, although much of it is grown in France), are both greatly under-utilized vgetables in this country. Leeks are part of the onion family, and look like a giant green onion. When cooked they are sweet and mellow. Endive has a slightly bitter, but nevertheless pleasing, taste, and they're both sure enough of themselves to stand up to the bold flavor of kasha.

1 can (13¾ ounce) ready-to-serve chicken broth or
    1¾ cups vegetable broth (see page 19)
¼ cup water
1 egg
1 cup kasha
⅛ teaspoon pepper
2 tablespoons butter
1½ cups thinly sliced leeks, both white and green parts
1 head endive, cut into 1-inch pieces

Combine chicken broth and water in a 2-quart saucepan and bring to a boil. Set aside.

Beat egg in a medium-size bowl. Stir in kasha to completely coat with egg. Cook the kasha in a *dry* 2-quart saucepan over medium-high heat, stirring, until egg is dried and grains are separate. Stir in hot chicken broth and water and pepper and bring to a boil. Reduce heat and simmer for 20 minutes. Remove from heat and let stand for 5 minutes. Turn into a serving bowl.

Melt the butter over medium-high heat in the same saucepan used to cook the kasha. Add leeks and cook, stirring often, until softened. Add endive and continue to cook, stirring, until wilted. Spoon leek-and-endive mixture on top of kasha to serve.

SERVES 8.

CALORIES: 129   CHOLESTEROL: 34 mg   SODIUM: 193 mg   FIBER: 3 g

Health tip:
Use low-sodium broth; substitute unsalted margarine for butter.
CALORIES: 128   CHOLESTEROL: 26 mg   SODIUM: 30 mg   FIBER: 3 g

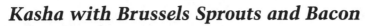

Kasha with Brussels Sprouts and Bacon

You can use frozen Brussels sprouts, if fresh are not available. Omit the bacon and use 2 tablespoons butter for a vegetarian dish.

2 slices bacon, cut into 1-inch pieces
1 cup chopped onion
1 pint Brussels sprouts, cut in half
½ cup chicken broth or vegetable broth (see page 19)
1 cup cooked coarse or medium kasha
1 teaspoon sugar
½ teaspoon white vinegar
¼ teaspoon salt
¼ teaspoon pepper

In a large skillet, cook the bacon until crisp. Remove bacon and drain on paper towels.

Discard all but 2 tablespoons of fat in skillet. Stir onion and Brussels sprouts into hot fat and cook over medium-high heat, stirring, until onions are softened. Stir in broth. Cover and cook for 5 minutes, or until sprouts are tender. Stir in kasha, sugar, vinegar, salt, and pepper and cook, stirring, until heated through.

SERVES 6.
CALORIES: 91   CHOLESTEROL: 24 mg   SODIUM: 301 mg   FIBER: 5 g

Health tip:
Use only 1 slice bacon and 1 tablespoon bacon fat. Use low-sodium broth; omit salt
CALORIES: 86   CHOLESTEROL: 12 mg   SODIUM: 46 mg   FIBER: 5 g

Boiled Soba

The term soba in Japanese means buckwheat. The word also refers to a special type of Japanese noodle that is generally made of buckwheat. Although it's possible to make soba noodles at home, the process is very complicated. So, if you'd like to use the noodle recipes that follow, I suggest that you buy dried soba noodles, which you can find in Oriental grocery stores, and sometimes in health-food stores. However, if challenges excite you, you will find a recipe for homemade soba in "The Book of Soba," by James Udesky. The recipe that follows is the proper way to cook dried soba noodles, which, like other pastas, should be cooked al dente.

3 quarts water
1 package (8 ounce) dried soba noodles
1½ cups cold water, divided

Use a pot that is large enough to make sure that the noodles will not stick together as they cook. Bring 3 quarts of water to a fast boil. Stir in noodles so that the water continues to boil to some degree as you do so.

As the noodles cook, the water will start to bubble up, foam, and some scum will accumulate. At this point, stir in ½ cup cold water and reduce heat to medium. When the water bubbles up again, add another ½ cup cold water. Repeat this procedure once more, using the final ½ cup cold water. When the water boils for the fourth time, take out one noodle and test for doneness by biting into it to determine that it is still firm, but not uncooked, in the center. If noodles are not done, continue to boil, testing a strand every 30 seconds or so.

Drain noodles in a colander. Refill the cooking pot with cool water and add the cooked drained noodles. Swish the noodles around in the cool water, then drain again. The noodles are now ready to serve. If you are planning to use the noodles in a warm dish, place them in a strainer and dip them into boiling water for a minute or so just before serving to warm them. Drain again.

SERVES 4.

CALORIES: 209   CHOLESTEROL: 0 mg   SODIUM: 1 mg   FIBER: 2 g

Health tip:
None.

———————◇———————

Zaru Soba (noodles in a basket)

Soba noodles are traditionally eaten in a hot broth, or cold with a dipping sauce. Both the dipping sauce and the hot-broth variation that follow use the following recipes for flavor base and the dashi (dipping sauce). (By the way, don't plan to whip this up just before the company arrives, because the flavor base needs at least 4 hours, preferably a day or two, for the flavors to develop.) Both of these recipes are standard for soba, but many variations exist. To learn more about soba, consult a Japanese cookbook.

This dish is so named because it is traditionally served in bamboo baskets (zaru). The Japanese products called for may be found in Oriental food stores.

Flavor Base:

> ⅓ cup Japanese soy sauce (Chinese soy sauce is too dark and salty)
> 1 tablespoon mirin (sweet rice wine)
> 2½ teaspoons sugar

Dashi:

> 2¼ cups water, divided
> 2 pieces giant kelp (kombu)
> 1 cup dried bonito flakes (hana-katsuo)
> 1 package (8 ounce) dried soba noodles,
>   cooked according to previous recipe
> 1 sheet nori (dried laver seaweed), optional
> 2 green onions (or to taste) thinly sliced on the diagonal
> 2 tablespoons (or to taste) grated daikon radish
> ½ teaspoon (or to taste) wasabi (green horseradish paste)

To make the flavor base, stir together the soy sauce and mirin in a small saucepan. Cook over medium heat until mixture is scalded (bubbles form around edge of pot). Reduce heat to low and gradually stir in sugar. Stir continuously until sugar is completely dissolved. Cook until mixture is scalded once again. Immediately remove from heat. Pour into a small bowl and let stand for at least 4 hours, or up to 2 days, to allow the flavors to develop. (Note: It is important that at no time is water allowed to come into contact with this mixture. Be sure that all utensils you use are dry, and if you choose to cover the sauce while it stands, use brown paper, cheesecloth, or some other porous material so that no condensation forms.)

To make dashi, place 2 cups of the water and kelp in a medium-size saucepan. Cook over medium heat until water shows the first signs of boiling, but does not actually boil. Remove from heat and pour in remaining ¼ cup water. Discard kelp. Stir in bonito flakes. Return to heat and bring to a boil. As soon as mixture boils, remove from heat and allow flakes to settle to the bottom of the pan. Strain mixture through cheesecloth and discard flakes. Stir base mixture into dashi and chill.

Place some of the chilled cooked noodles in a bamboo basket or serving plate for each person.

Toast the nori under the broiler until crisp, then crumble over noodles.

Stir as much of the scallion, radish, and wasabi as desired into the dashi. Divide sauce among 4 individual bowls, placing one on each basket or plate.

Eat by picking up some of the noodles with chopsticks and dipping into sauce.

SERVES 4.
CALORIES: 244   CHOLESTEROL: 0 mg   SODIUM: 1566 mg   FIBER: 6 g

Health tip:
Like so many Oriental dishes, this is low in fat and calories, but high in sodium, so you may want to use low-sodium Japanese soy sauce.
CALORIES: 244   CHOLESTEROL: 0 mg   SODIUM: 1358 mg   FIBER: 6 g

---

◇

Hot Soba Noodles in Broth

Here is another traditional recipe for preparing soba noodles.

One recipe for flavor base (see page 247)
Double recipe for dashi (see page 247)
1 package (8 ounce) dried soba noodles, cooked and reheated according
    to previous recipe
1 scallion, thinly sliced on the diagonal
2 teaspoons grated fresh ginger

Make the flavor base and stir it into the dashi. Heat until almost boiling.

Place warm noodles in four bowls. Pour broth over noodles and top each with a sprinkling of scallion and ginger.

SERVES 4.
CALORIES: 244   CHOLESTEROL: 0 mg   SODIUM: mg   FIBER: 6 g

Health tip:
Use low-sodium Japanese soy sauce.
CALORIES: 244   CHOLESTEROL: 0 mg   SODIUM: 1358 mg   FIBER: 6g

—————— ◇ ——————

Soba Noodles with Peanut Sauce

This is really a Chinese recipe for noodles, but it's one that I like very much, and it seems to work just as well with the Japanese noodles.

1 package (8 ounce) dried soba noodles,
*   cooked according to previous recipe*
¼ cup chopped scallion
¼ cup smooth peanut butter
3 tablespoons dark Chinese soy sauce
1½ tablespoons Chinese red vinegar (available in Oriental grocery
*   stores) or cider vinegar*
1 tablespoon hot chili oil or Oriental sesame oil (both available in
*   Oriental grocery stores)*
1½ teaspoons sugar

In a large bowl, toss together the noodles and scallion.

Place peanut butter, soy sauce, vinegar, chili oil, and sugar in the container of an electric blender. Cover and blend until completely combined. Pour over noodles and toss.

SERVES 4.
CALORIES: 326   CHOLESTEROL: 0 mg   SODIUM: 775 mg   FIBER: 3 g

Health tip:
Use low-sodium Chinese soy sauce.
CALORIES: 258   CHOLESTEROL: 0 mg   SODIUM: 38 mg   FIBER: 3 g

————————◇————————

Buckwheat and Wild Rice Dressing

Try this instead of your traditional dressing at holiday time, or serve it as a side dish whenever you feel like something special and a little different.

4 slices bacon, cut into 1-inch pieces
1 tablespoon butter
1 cup chopped onion
1 cup sliced mushrooms
½ finely chopped celery
½ cup finely chopped green bell pepper
2 cups cooked wild rice
1¾ cups cooked kasha
1 can (8 ounce) water chestnuts, drained and chopped
¼ cup chopped parsley
¼ teaspoon ground sage
¼ teaspoon pepper

In a large skillet, cook the bacon until crisp. Remove bacon and drain on paper towels.

Discard all but 2 tablespoons of fat in the skillet. Add butter to fat and melt over medium-high heat. Add onion, mushrooms, celery, and green pepper and cook, stirring frequently, until vegetables are softened. Stir in wild rice, kasha, water chestnuts, parsley, sage, pepper, and reserved bacon. Cook, stirring, until heated through.

SERVES 12.
CALORIES: 59   CHOLESTEROL: 2 mg   SODIUM: 409 mg   FIBER: 2g

Health tip:
Use only 2 slices bacon and omit butter. Omit salt when cooking kasha.
CALORIES: 47   CHOLESTEROL: 1 mg   SODIUM: 128 mg   FIBER: 2 g

———————◇———————

Buckwheat Griddlecakes

These light, but substantial, pancakes are sweet before you even add syrup. Try them for breakfast or brunch on a leisurely morning sometime soon.

1⅓ cups milk
⅓ cup butter, melted
2 eggs
½ teaspoon vanilla extract
1 cup all-purpose flour
⅓ cup buckwheat flour
3 tablespoons sugar
1 tablespoon baking powder
1 teaspoon baking soda
¾ teaspoon salt
Additional melted butter, for brushing skillet.

In a medium-size bowl, beat the milk, butter, eggs, and vanilla with a wire whisk until thoroughly combined.

In another medium-size bowl, stir both flours, sugar, baking powder, baking soda, and salt together until blended. Add milk mixture to flour mixture and stir just until blended. Do not over-mix. The batter should be lumpy. Let stand 5 minutes.

Heat a large skillet or griddle over medium heat until a few drops of water sprinkled in the hot skillet bounce about before evaporating. Brush skillet with a thin coating of melted butter. Immediately pour ¼ cup of the batter into the skillet for each pancake. (You should be able to make 3 or 4 pancakes at once in a large skillet. If you are particularly well coordinated, you may want to have more than one skillet going at a time.) Cook until bubbles break on top of cakes. Turn with a wide spatula and cook the second side until lightly browned.

MAKES 12 TO 14 PANCAKES.
CALORIES: 143   CHOLESTEROL: 55 mg   SODIUM: 360 mg   FIBER: 1 g

Health tip:
Use unsalted margarine instead of butter; substitute scrambled-egg substitute for eggs; omit salt.
CALORIES: 136   CHOLESTEROL: 0 mg   SODIUM: 180 mg   FIBER: 1 g

Low-Cholesterol Buckwheat-and-Bran Muffins

These muffins are moist and mouthwatering, but small, so you may want to eat a second one, and that's okay, because they're so good for you. Just don't forget to count the extra calories. (No food in the world is *that* perfect!)

¾ cup apple juice
½ cup plain nonfat yogurt
½ cup applesauce
1 cup morsels of wheat bran cereal (Kellogg's Bran Buds)
2 egg whites
1 cup all-purpose flour
⅓ cup buckwheat flour
¼ cup sugar
1 tablespoon baking powder
1 teaspoon baking soda
1½ teaspoons ground cinnamon
¼ teaspoon ground nutmeg

Preheat oven to 400°F.
Place paper liners in 16 muffin cups and set aside.
In a medium-size bowl, stir together the apple juice, yogurt, and applesauce. Stir in cereal. Set aside for 5 minutes. Stir in egg whites.
In a large bowl, stir together both flours, sugar, baking powder, baking soda, cinnamon, and nutmeg. Stir liquid mixture into flour mixture just until blended. Don't overmix. The batter should be lumpy. Divide batter evenly among muffin cups.
Bake for 15 to 18 minutes, or until a wooden pick inserted in the center of a few of the muffins comes out clean. Turn muffins out of pan to cool on wire racks.

MAKES 16 MUFFINS.
CALORIES: 85   CHOLESTEROL: 0 mg   SODIUM: 157 mg   FIBER: 2 g

Health tip:
None. These muffins are perfect just the way they are.

———————— ◇ ————————

Buckwheat-Currant Brown Bread

This bread will remind you of raisin-pumpernickel, but the texture is lighter. To serve, cut into thick slices, and cut the slices into halves or quarters. If you can afford the calories, spread generously with butter or cream cheese. Thinner slices may be lightly toasted.

½ cup very warm water (105–115°F)
2 packages dry yeast
½ teaspoon sugar
1 cup buckwheat flour
2 tablespoons unsweetened cocoa powder
1 tablespoon caraway seeds (optional)
2 teaspoons salt
1 teaspoon instant coffee granules
1 cup buttermilk
½ cup unsulphured molasses
2 tablespoons vegetable oil
½ cup dried currants
3 cups all-purpose flour, divided

Grease a 9 × 5 × 3-inch loaf pan and set aside.

Place warm water in a glass measuring cup, then stir in yeast and sugar. Let stand until ¼ inch of white bubbly foam forms on top. (This foaming is called *proofing*, and if it doesn't happen it means that for some reason or other the yeast has not been activated. Discard this batch and try again, double checking the date on the yeast package and the temperature of the water.)

While yeast is proofing, in a large bowl, stir together buckwheat flour, cocoa, caraway seeds, salt and coffee. Stir in buttermilk, molasses, oil, and proofed-yeast mixture. Stir until completely combined. Stir in currants, then 2¼ cups of the all-purpose flour.

Turn dough onto a heavily floured surface. Knead for about 7 minutes, using as much of the remaining flour as necessary to form a smooth, elastic dough that is still slightly sticky.

Place dough in a greased bowl. Cover with greased plastic wrap and let rise in a warm spot, out of drafts, until doubled in bulk. Punch down and knead again for 1 minute.

Shape dough into a loaf and place in prepared pan. Cover with greased plastic wrap and let rise until doubled in bulk.

Preheat oven to 350°F.

Bake for 50 minutes, or until top and bottom are browned. Turn loaf out of pan to cool on a wire rack.

MAKES 1 LOAF (20 servings).
CALORIES: 129   CHOLESTEROL: 0 mg   SODIUM: 228 mg   FIBER: 2 g

Health tip:
Omit salt.
CALORIES: 129   CHOLESTEROL: 0 mg   SODIUM: 15 mg   FIBER: 2 g

---

————————◇————————

Sweet Cheese Squares (kroopyenik)

You'll probably think of noodle pudding when you eat this traditional Russian dish that may be served as a side dish or dessert.

1 container (8 ounce) cottage cheese
1 package (3 ounce) cream cheese, softened
½ cup sugar
½ teaspoon grated lemon rind
3 eggs, separated
2 cups cooked whole kasha
½ cup golden raisins
¼ teaspoon salt

Preheat oven to 375°F.
Grease an 8-inch-square baking pan and set aside.
In a large bowl, beat the cottage cheese, cream cheese, sugar, and lemon rind until well combined. Beat in egg yolks. Stir in kasha and raisins.
In a grease-free, medium-size bowl, with clean beaters, beat egg whites with salt until stiff peaks form when beaters are lifted. Stir about one-quarter of the beaten whites into the cheese mixture. Fold in remaining whites. Spread batter into prepared pan.
Bake for 30 minutes, or until top is browned and a knife inserted in the center comes out clean. Cut into squares to serve.

MAKES 16 SQUARES.
CALORIES: 106   CHOLESTEROL: 47 mg   SODIUM: 190 mg   FIBER: 1 g

Health tip:
Omit salt.
CALORIES: 106   CHOLESTEROL: 45 mg   SODIUM: 157 mg   FIBER: 1 g

MILLET
(Panicum miliaceum)

It can safely be said that millet is "for the birds," since bird feed—(and cattle feed)—is its primary use in the United States. But in many parts of the world, mainly Africa, China, and India, millet is a dietary staple.

Millet is a sturdy grain, capable of flourishing in dry and underfertilized soil. The seed can even manage to survive in times of severe drought, only to sprout anew when the lightest rain falls.

Frankly, millet has its drawbacks. Because of a definite bitter taste and an odd starchiness when it is improperly cooked and served, millet is deliberately avoided in this country—even by grain lovers and health faddists. However, it can be absolutely delicious *when it is cooked properly with compatible foods.* Even if you've tried millet in the past and decided you didn't like it, you owe it to yourself to try it again—my way.

Not to be overlooked, of course, is millet's enviable nutritional profile and great versatility. Inexpensive millet can be used to extend or replace meat dishes, thereby cutting down on fat and calories, and its dense, moist texture adds a satisfying element to salads and vegetable dishes.

Types of Millet Available

Whole millet: The whole grain with the hull removed.

Millet meal: Whole millet, coarsely ground. It looks a lot like small hulled sesame seeds. Use it in breads and for cereal.

Millet flour: The whole grain, finely ground. Millet flour has no gluten, so it must be used in conjunction with gluten-containing flours when making yeast-baked goods. You can substitute millet flour for part of the whole-wheat flour (up to 25%) in baking, but the texture of the finished product will be heavier. Millet flour is sometimes referred to as *teff,* and is used to make *injera,* the national bread of Ethiopia.

Puffed millet: The whole grain, cooked and processed. Use as a breakfast cereal.

Texture and Flavor

Millet is small, round, and golden-yellow in color with a beady appearance that will remind you of mustard seeds. As it cooks, the grains swell and explode (like popcorn), exposing the starchy inside of the grain that has burst out of the tough bran layer.

Cooked millet has a consistency similar to cornmeal mush (dense and heavy), the difference being that you will occasionally find an undercooked grain (that will be slightly crunchy, but not unpleasantly so) and there will always be some empty bran left. The only way to eliminate the uncooked grains is to increase the amount of water and the cooking time. However, this will produce a sticky porridge that I would not recommend for the recipes in this chapter.

The bitterness of cooked millet can be mostly eliminated by sautéing the uncooked millet in oil or butter before adding boiling water (method I). Or it can simply be toasted in a dry skillet before cooking. I prefer the sauté method. Both of these procedures will also help to keep the grains separate as they cook.

Boiling millet (method II) will produce a sticky mixture that is excellent for holding together croquettes, or in other recipes where its binding properties are desirable.

Cooking millet in stewing liquid or soups, I have found, gives the finished dish a strange sort of starchiness. I found this undesirable, so most of the recipes that follow start with cooked millet. The preferred cooking method for the millet is included in each recipe.

Compatible Foods, Herbs, and Spices

Because of its inherent bitterness, it is best to use millet in dishes with strong flavors that are either compatible with, or will mask, this undesirable trait. Recipes that use any of the four basic flavor sensations; sweet, spicy, salty, or sour work well with millet. Subtle flavorings, such as delicate herbs, are not good choices. Most meats, fruits, and vegetables are fine served with millet.

Availability

There are many varieties of millet grown worldwide, but only one is available in the United States: pearl millet. The packages are labeled "whole millet," even though the grain has been hulled.

Millet is widely available in health-food stores and can be purchased through mail-order grain catalogs (see page 21). At this writing, I have not been able to find millet in any supermarket.

Nutritional Content

Although the millet is hulled (meaning the outer layer has been removed), the bran, with its fiber and vitamin content, remains.

Millet has a high nutritional profile when compared to other non-meat sources, in both the amount of protein and the amino-acid balance, which is pretty close to complete. It is also a good source of B vitamins, potassium, magnesium, phosphorous, and iron. Millet is naturally alkaline, which makes it good for the digestive tract, and it is touted to be the grain most likely to be tolerated by people who are allergic to other grains.

Substitutions

Because millet is not easily available, and because of the bitter aftertaste, to which some palates are more sensitive than others, you may want to substitute other grains for the millet in the recipes that follow.

Couscous: Cooked, it's texture is similar to cooked millet, and makes an excellent substitute. Couscous is available in most supermarkets.

Rizcous: A brown rice product is an excellent substitute. It can be found in gourmet stores.

Quinoa: The flavors and nutritional profile are similar, but the textures are not, so quinoa is not a suitable substitute for recipes in which the sticky consistency of millet is required (making croquettes, etc.). It has the same drawback as millet of only being available in health-food stores.

Brown rice: I prefer the short-grain variety because it has enough "toothiness" and flavor to work well in millet recipes. But because of textural differences, it is not possible to substitute brown rice—or any rice—when millet is used as a binding agent.

Cooked cornmeal: This is an excellent substitute for use in recipes where millet is used as a binding agent.

Other acceptable substitutes (in order of preference): White rice, bulgur, barley, and wild rice.

Basic Cooking Instructions

Please read *About Cooking Grains* beginning on page 7. The microwave methods that follow for cooking millet were tested in a 650-watt oven.

Stove-top method I:

> 1 tablespoon vegetable oil or butter
> 1 cup millet, rinsed
> 2 cups boiling water
> ½ teaspoon salt

Heat oil in a 2-quart saucepan. Add millet and cook over medium heat, stirring, until it is milky in appearance and some of the grains have browned. (The millet will make lots of crackling sounds at this point.) Stir in boiling water and salt. (Stand away from the pot because it will be giving off lots of steam.) Return to boiling, then cover and simmer for 30 minutes, or until all of the water has been absorbed. Remove from heat and let stand 5 minutes. Fluff with a fork.

MAKES 4 CUPS.

Stove-top method II:

> 2 cups water
> ½ teaspoon salt
> 1 cup millet, rinsed

Bring the water and salt to a boil in a 2-quart covered saucepan. Stir in millet and return to boiling. Reduce heat and simmer, covered, for 30 minutes, or until all of the liquid has been absorbed. Remove from heat and let stand 5 minutes. Fluff with a fork.

MAKES 3 CUPS.

Microwave method I:

> 1 tablespoon oil or butter
> 1 cup millet, rinsed
> 1¾ cups hot tap water
> ½ teaspoon salt

In a 3-quart, microwave-safe casserole, stir together the oil and millet. Microwave on high (100% power), uncovered, for 2 minutes. Stir, then continue to microwave on high, uncovered, for 2 minutes longer. Stir in hot water and salt. Cover with waxed paper and microwave on high for 5 minutes. Microwave on medium (50% power), still covered with waxed paper, for 20 minutes. Let stand 4 minutes. Fluff with a fork.

MAKES 3½ CUPS.

Microwave method II:

> 1¾ cups water
> 1 cup millet, rinsed

Place the water in a 3-quart, microwave-safe casserole. Cover with waxed paper. Microwave on high (100% power), for 3 minutes. Stir in millet, recover with waxed paper, and microwave on high for 5 minutes. Microwave on medium, still covered with waxed paper, for 20 minutes. Let stand 4 minutes. Fluff with a fork.

MAKES 3¼ CUPS.

Reheating

Many of the recipes given here call for cooked millet. As long as you use freshly cooked millet, you will have moist, separate, fluffy (if cooked by method I) grains. If you have cooked the millet in advance and chilled it, you'll find that the grains are hard, dry, and clumpy. You can remedy this by microwaving or steaming the millet slightly to return it to its just-cooked consistency.

MILLET RECIPES
*(*indicates easy recipe.)*

———————◇———————

Codfish Cakes *
Sweet-and-Sour Milletballs *
Groundnut Stew *
Southwestern Beef Stew with Millet
Lamb Biriani with Onion Relish
California Salad *
Oriental Millet Salad *
Lightly Curried Millet Salad *
Italian Bean-and-Millet Salad *
Cheddar-Bacon Millet *
Autumn Casserole *
Eggplant-and-Chick-Pea Curry with Millet
Fried Corn Cakes
Bruncheon Spoon Bread
Orange-Flavored Millet-Meal Bread

——————— ◇ ———————

Codfish Cakes

I like these tasty little fish cakes for lunch or a light supper, served with tartar sauce and coleslaw.

1 cup cooked millet (method II)
1 cup cooked flaked cod
¼ cup chopped scallion, both white and green parts
2 tablespoons grated onion
2 tablespoons minced green bell pepper
1 egg
½ teaspoon salt
¼ teaspoon pepper
¼ cup dry unflavored bread crumbs
Oil, for frying

In a large bowl, thoroughly combine millet, cod, green onion, shredded onion, green pepper, egg, salt, and pepper. Shape into 8 patties.

Scatter bread crumbs on a piece of waxed paper. Carefully roll each patty in crumbs.

Pour enough oil into a large skillet so that it measures ⅛-inch deep. Heat over medium-high heat until a few crumbs brown quickly when sprinkled on the oil. Place 4 patties in skillet and cook until browned on one side. Turn and brown second side. Repeat with remaining patties.

MAKES 8 FISH CAKES.
CALORIES: 107   CHOLESTEROL: 34 mg   SODIUM: 192 mg   FIBER: 1g

Health tip:
Omit salt. Instead of frying cakes, bake on a greased baking sheet until appetizingly browned.
CALORIES: 61   CHOLESTEROL: 34 mg   SODIUM: 27 mg   FIBER: 1 g

—————— ◇ ——————

Sweet-and-Sour Milletballs

I use millet in this recipe as a meat extender. Serve these little balls plain as a hot appetizer, or as a main course served over additional millet or pasta.

1 pound lean ground beef (I use ground round)
1 cup cooked millet (any method)
2 cloves garlic, minced
¼ teaspoon salt
1 tablespoon oil
½ cup finely chopped onion
½ cup water
½ cup catsup
½ cup orange juice
⅓ cup firmly packed light or dark-brown sugar
2 tablespoons lemon juice
1 tablespoon white vinegar
2 teaspoons thick steak sauce (A-1)
3 gingersnaps
1 can crushed pineapple, drained

In a medium-size bowl, combine the ground beef, millet, garlic, and salt. Shape into 16 balls.

In a 3-quart saucepan, heat the oil over medium-high heat. Add onion and cook, stirring frequently, until softened. Stir in water, catsup, orange juice, brown sugar, lemon juice, vinegar, steak sauce, and gingersnaps. Simmer for 10 minutes. Stir in milletballs and simmer for 10 minutes longer, or until balls are cooked through. Gently stir in pineapple, and cook until heated.

MAKES 16 MILLETBALLS.
CALORIES: 124   CHOLESTEROL: 27 mg   SODIUM: 155 mg   FIBER: 1 g

Health tip:
Omit salt; use low-sodium catsup.
CALORIES: 124   CHOLESTEROL: 27 mg   SODIUM: 105 mg   FIBER: 1g

—————— ◇ ——————

Groundnut Stew

My friend, Paula Rudolph, served in the Peace Corps in Ethiopia. She said she frequently ate millet while she lived there, but didn't have a specific recipe to give me. So, in her honor, I've made up a probably-not-too-authentic African stew to serve with millet.

2 tablespoons vegetable oil
3½-pound chicken, cut into parts
¾ cup finely chopped onion
1¼ cups chopped tomato
1 can (13¾ ounce) ready-to-serve chicken broth
⅓ cup tomato paste
¼ cup peanut butter
¼ teaspoon crumbled thyme
¼ teaspoon salt
¼ teaspoon ground red pepper
2 cups cooked millet (method I)

In a large heavy saucepan or Dutch oven, heat the oil over medium-high heat. Add chicken and cook, turning, until browned. Remove chicken from pan. Add onion and cook, stirring frequently, until softened. Add tomato and cook, stirring frequently, until softened.

In a medium-size bowl, combine broth, tomato paste, peanut butter, thyme, salt, and red pepper and whisk until smooth. Stir this mixture into the onion mixture in the saucepan. (You may be tempted to taste the sauce at this point, but restrain yourself. It doesn't taste very good until it's fully cooked and mellowed. Then it's delicious.) Bring to a boil and return chicken to pan. Cover and simmer for 40 minutes, or until chicken is cooked through. Serve over millet.

SERVES 4.
CALORIES: 600   CHOLESTEROL: 198 mg   SODIUM: 813 mg   FIBER: 5 g

Health tip:
Omit salt and use low-sodium broth, cook chicken without skin.
CALORIES: 556   CHOLESTEROL: 164 mg   SODIUM: 221 mg   FIBER: 5 g

—————— ◇ ——————

Southwestern Beef Stew with Millet

I like the complex flavors of this dish, mainly spicy with a hint of sweetness. Serve the stew with a salad, and maybe some cornbread or biscuits, for a complete meal.

2 tablespoons vegetable oil
1 cup chopped onion
¾ cup chopped green bell pepper
2 cloves garlic, minced
1½ pounds stewing beef, cubed
1 can (14½ ounce) whole peeled tomatoes
1 can (8 ounce) tomato sauce
1 can (4 ounce) chopped mild green chilies, drained
2 tablespoons dark-brown sugar
2 teaspoons red-wine vinegar
1½ teaspoons ground coriander
1 teaspoon chili powder
½ teaspoon ground cumin
¼ teaspoon crumbled oregano
¼ teaspoon salt
3 cups cooked millet (method I)

In a large saucepan or Dutch oven, heat the oil over medium-high heat. Add onion, green pepper, and garlic and cook, stirring frequently, until vegetables are softened. Stir in beef, tomatoes, tomato sauce, chopped chilies, brown sugar, vinegar, coriander, chili powder, cumin, oregano, and salt. Bring to a boil. Reduce heat and simmer, covered, for 1 hour and 15 minutes. Uncover and cook for 30 minutes longer. (If the mixture starts to look too thick, or if it begins to stick to the bottom of the pot, stir in some extra water.) Serve over millet.

SERVES 6.
CALORIES: 388   CHOLESTEROL: 92 mg   SODIUM: 479 mg   FIBER: 4 g

Health tip:
Reduce oil to 2 teaspoons and cook in a nonstick saucepan. Or, cook onion, green pepper, and garlic in a nonstick skillet, transferring to the large saucepan to finish cooking. Use low-sodium tomato sauce and omit salt.
CALORIES: 362   CHOLESTEROL: 92 mg   SODIUM: 390 mg   FIBER 4 g

———————— ◇ ————————

Lamb Biriani with Onion Relish

Curry is THE flavor that was made for millet. This dish is a real show-stopper and makes wonderful party food. There are a lot of ingredients, but the dish actually goes together very quickly once you have everything assembled.

Stew:

> *3 tablespoons ghee (clarified butter) or vegetable oil*
> *1½ cups chopped onion*
> *3 cloves garlic, minced*
> *1 tablespoon minced fresh ginger or 2 teaspoons ground ginger*
> *2 tablespoons curry powder*
> *2 teaspoons ground coriander*
> *1¼ teaspoons salt*
> *1 teaspoon turmeric*
> *½ teaspoon ground cinnamon*
> *1½ pounds boneless lamb, cubed*
> *2 cups chopped tomato*
> *¾ cup water*
> *2 tablespoons chopped fresh mint or 2 teaspoons dried mint flakes*

Relish:

> *1 cup chopped onion*
> *1 teaspoon salt*
> *2 tablespoons water*
> *1½ teaspoons tomato paste*
> *1 teaspoon white vinegar*
> *1 teaspoon paprika*
> *1 teaspoon lemon juice*
> *½ teaspoon sugar*
> *¼ teaspoon ground ginger*
> *⅛ teaspoon ground cumin*
> *⅛ teaspoon ground red pepper*
> *2 cups cooked millet (method I)*

To make a stew, heat ghee in a large heavy saucepan or Dutch oven over medium-high heat. Add onion, garlic, and ginger and cook, stirring frequently, until onion is softened. Stir in curry, coriander, salt, turmeric, and cinnamon. Cook over low heat, stirring, for 1 minute. Add lamb and stir until coated with spice mixture. Stir in tomato, water, and mint and bring to a boil. Reduce heat and simmer, covered, for 1 hour. Uncover and simmer for 20 minutes more, or until lamb is tender.

While stew is cooking, make relish. Toss onion with salt in a medium-size bowl. Let stand 30 minutes. Transfer onion to a colander and rinse well. Drain thoroughly and turn back into bowl. Stir in water, tomato paste, vinegar, paprika, lemon juice, sugar, ginger, cumin, and red pepper.

Serve stew with millet and relish.

SERVES 6.
CALORIES: 538   CHOLESTEROL: 156 mg   SODIUM: 892 mg   FIBER: 4g

Health tip:
Use 2 teaspoons oil instead of ghee and cook in a nonstick saucepan. Or, cook onion, garlic, and ginger in a nonstick skillet, transferring to the larger pan to finish cooking. Omit salt.
CALORIES: 521   CHOLESTEROL: 139 mg   SODIUM: 92 mg   FIBER: 4g

---

◇

California Salad

If you like avocado, you'll enjoy this summery salad that combines the creamy sweetness of avocado and corn with the tartness of lime juice, and the nubbiness of cooked millet.

> 1½ cups cooked millet (method II)
> 1 can (7 ounce) whole-kernel corn, drained
> 1 cup chopped celery
> 1 small avocado, diced (1 cup)
> ½ cup chopped red bell pepper
> 1 tablespoon finely chopped scallion, both white and green parts
> 2½ tablespoons fresh lime juice
> 1 tablespoon olive oil
> 1 tablespoon vegetable oil
> ¼ teaspoon grated lime rind
> ¼ teaspoon celery seed
> ¼ teaspoon salt
> ⅛ teaspoon ground red pepper

In a large bowl, gently toss the millet, corn, celery, avocado, red bell pepper, and scallion until well combined.

In a small bowl, stir together the lime juice, olive oil, lime rind, vegetable oil, celery seed, salt, and ground red pepper. Pour over millet mixture and toss gently until completely combined.

SERVES 8.
CALORIES: 105   CHOLESTEROL: 0 mg   SODIUM: 140 mg   FIBER: 3 g

Health tip:
Omit salt.
CALORIES: 105   CHOLESTEROL: 0 mg   SODIUM: 73 mg   FIBER: 3 g

---

Oriental Millet Salad

I like spicy food, and this recipe is mildly so. Experiment with the amount of chili oil or hot sesame oil. If you're not crazy about spicy food, use plain Oriental sesame oil. (All of these oils, and the rice vinegar, by the way, can be found in Oriental grocery stores.)

2 cups cooked and cooled millet (Method I)
1 cup mung bean sprouts
½ cup coarsely chopped snow peas (about 16)
½ cup chopped canned water chestnuts
¼ cup chopped green onion, both white and green parts
2 tablespoons vegetable oil
1½ tablespoons soy sauce
1 tablespoon smooth peanut butter
1 tablespoon rice vinegar or white vinegar
½ teaspoon (or to taste) chili oil or hot
*   sesame oil (plain Oriental sesame oil may be substituted)*
1 clove garlic, minced

In a medium-size bowl, toss together the millet, sprouts, snow peas, water chestnuts, and scallion.

In a small bowl, combine the oil, soy sauce, peanut butter, rice vinegar, chili oil, and garlic. Pour dressing over millet mixture and toss until completely combined.

SERVES 6.
CALORIES: 115   CHOLESTEROL: 0 mg   SODIUM. 350 mg   FIBER: 2 g

Health tip:
Use low-sodium soy sauce. Omit salt from millet.CALORIES: 115   CHOLESTEROL: 0 mg   SODIUM: 98 mg   FIBER: 2 g

_____◇_____

Lightly Curried Millet Salad

I was thrilled with the way this exciting blend of vegetables and spicy curry dressing tasted after I prefected it.

2 cups cooked millet (method I)
1 cup chopped tomato
½ cup chopped cucumber
½ cup chopped green bell pepper
¼ cup sliced scallion, both white and green parts
2 tablespoons vegetable oil
1 tablespoon cider vinegar
1 teaspoon curry powder
¼ teaspoon ground cinnamon
¼ teaspoon ground coriander
¼ teaspoon paprika
⅛ teaspoon salt
⅛ teaspoon ground red pepper, or black pepper for a milder taste

In a large bowl, toss together the millet, tomato, cucumber, green pepper, and green onion.

In a small bowl, stir together the oil, vinegar, curry powder, cinnamon, coriander, paprika, salt, and pepper. Toss with millet mixture until completely combined.

SERVES 6.
CALORIES: 98   CHOLESTEROL: 0 mg   SODIUM: 136 mg   FIBER: 2 g

Health tip:
Omit salt.
CALORIES: 98   CHOLESTEROL: 0 mg   SODIUM: 4 mg   FIBER: 2 g

_____◇_____

Italian Bean-and-Millet Salad

Beans and millet together make this a very satisfying salad, so that it can also be served as a meal by itself, as well as a side dish.

2 cups cooked and cooled millet (method I)
1 can (10½ ounce) cannellini (white kidney beans)
    or red kidney beans, drained
½ cup chopped red onion
½ cup sliced black olives

¼ cup chopped parsley
1 tablespoon chopped cilantro (fresh coriander)
3 tablespoons lemon juice
1 tablespoon vegetable oil
1 tablespoon olive oil

In a large bowl, gently toss together the millet, beans, onion, olives, parsley, and cilantro.

In a small bowl, stir together the lemon juice, vegetable oil, and olive oil. Toss with millet mixture until completely combined.

SERVES 6 (as a side dish).
CALORIES: 152   CHOLESTEROL: 0 mg   SODIUM: 285 mg   FIBER: 6 g

Health tip:
Omit olives; rinse canned beans, which will remove excess sodium.
CALORIES: 129   CHOLESTEROL: 0 mg   SODIUM: 45 mg   FIBER: 6 g

———————◇———————

Cheddar-Bacon Millet

The texture of this dish—dense, sticky, and cheesy—makes it a good choice to serve with eggs. A nice change from fried potatoes or grits.

3 slices bacon, cut into 1-inch pieces
½ cup millet
1 cup boiling water
2 cups shredded Cheddar cheese
¼ cup chopped scallion, both white and green parts

In a 2-quart saucepan, cook the bacon until crisp. Remove bacon and drain on paper towels.

Remove all but 1 tablespoon of the fat in the pan. Add millet and cook, stirring, until browned and making crackling noises. Stir in boiling water. Bring to a boil, reduce heat, and simmer for 30 minutes. Stir in cheese, scallion, and reserved bacon. Cook, stirring, until cheese is melted.

SERVES 4.
CALORIES: 381   CHOLESTEROL: 69 mg   SODIUM: 562 mg   FIBER: 4 g

Health tip:
This dish is hopeless. Try another side dish.

◇

Autumn Casserole

Try this sweet blend of millet, squash, nuts, and cranberries with the holiday turkey or ham.

1 cup cooked millet (method I)
1 cup ½-inch-diced butternut squash
½ cup chopped walnuts
½ cup apple juice or cider
¼ cup cranberries
2 tablespoons honey
2 tablespoons dark-brown sugar
1 teaspoon ground cinnamon

Preheat oven to 350° F.

Combine the millet, squash, walnuts, apple juice, cranberries, honey, brown sugar, and cinnamon in a 1½-quart casserole. Cover and bake for 35 to 40 minutes, or until squash is soft.

SERVES 6.

CALORIES: 147   CHOLESTEROL: 0 mg   SODIUM: 49 mg   FIBER: 2 g

Health tip:

Use half the amounts of honey and sugar. Cook millet without salt.

CALORIES: 128   CHOLESTEROL: 0 mg   SODIUM: 4 mg   FIBER: 2 g

———————— ◇ ————————

Eggplant-and-Chick-Pea Curry with Millet

Although I find this spicy curry delightful, if it's too hot for your taste, omit the ground red pepper.

3 tablespoons ghee (clarified butter) or vegetable oil
1½ cups chopped onion
2 large cloves garlic, minced
1½ tablespoons curry powder
1 teaspoon salt
½ teaspoon ground ginger
½ teaspoon ground turmeric
½ teaspoon ground cumin
½ teaspoon ground coriander
¼ teaspoon ground red pepper
1 large (about 1½ pounds) eggplant, unpeeled and cut into cubes
1 can (10½ ounce) chick-peas, undrained
2 medium tomatoes, diced
¾ cup water
¼ cup chutney, chopped
3 cups cooked millet (method I)

In a large heavy saucepan or Dutch oven, heat ghee over medium-high heat. Add onion and garlic and cook, stirring frequently, until softened. Stir in curry powder, salt, ginger, turmeric, cumin, coriander, and red pepper. Cook over low heat, stirring constantly, for 1 minute. Add eggplant, undrained chick-peas, and tomatoes, stirring until vegetables are coated with spices. Stir in water and bring to a boil. Lower heat and simmer for 40 minutes. Stir in chutney. Serve over millet.

SERVES 6.
CALORIES: 263   CHOLESTEROL: 17 mg   SODIUM: 501 mg   FIBER: 10 g

Health tip:
Use oil instead of ghee; omit salt.
CALORIES: 263   CHOLESTEROL: 0 mg   SODIUM: 14 mg   FIBER: 10 g

Fried Corn Cakes

Crunchy on the outside, creamy on the inside, these little cakes go nicely with a pot roast.

1 cup cooked millet (method II)
1 can (8¾ ounce) cream-style corn
1 egg, beaten
3 tablespoons flour
1 tablespoon sugar
¼ teaspoon salt
Oil, for frying

In a medium-size bowl, stir together the millet, corn, egg, flour, sugar, and salt until thoroughly combined.

Pour oil into a large skillet until it measures about ¼-inch deep. Heat the oil over medium-high heat until bubbles form when a drop of batter is put into the oil. Drop batter by heaping table-spoonsful into the hot oil. (These cakes spatter a lot while they're frying, so if you have a spatter shield, use it. Otherwise, be careful and stand back while you're frying.) Fry until browned on both sides. Drain on paper towels.

MAKES 12 CORN CAKES.
CALORIES: 81   CHOLESTEROL: 17 mg   SODIUM: 131 mg   FIBER: .5 g

Health tip:
Use scrambled-egg substitute instead of egg; omit salt.
CALORIES: 70   CHOLESTEROL: 0 mg   SODIUM: 67 mg   FIBER: .5 g

——————— ◇ ———————

Bruncheon Spoon Bread

I often serve this versatile casserole as a main dish for brunch or lunch with a salad. Other times I use it as an accompaniment for eggs. And I don't see why it couldn't be used as a replacement for a traditional turkey stuffing at Thanksgiving.

½ pound bulk breakfast sausage
¼ cup finely chopped onion
½ cup millet
1 cup boiling water
3 eggs, separated
1 cup shredded Vermont Cheddar cheese
1 can (4 ounce) chopped mild green chilies, drained
1 teaspoon baking powder

Preheat oven to 375°F.
Grease a 1½- or 2-quart casserole and set aside.
In a medium-size saucepan, cook the sausage over medium-high heat, stirring frequently, until it is no longer pink. Remove from skillet to a large bowl.
Pour off all but 2 tablespoons fat in the skillet. Add onion and millet and cook over medium-high heat until millet is browned and onion is softened. Add water and bring to a boil. Lower heat and simmer, covered, for 30 minutes, or until liquid is absorbed. Remove from heat.
In a medium-size bowl, beat egg yolks slightly. Beat in ½ cup of the millet mixture. Stir egg-yolk mixture back into pan with remaining millet mixture.
Add millet-and-egg mixture to cooked sausage, along with cheese and chilies. Stir until well combined. Stir in baking powder.
Beat egg whites in a clean, grease-free bowl with clean beaters until stiff peaks form when beaters are lifted. Stir one-quarter of the beaten egg whites into the sausage mixture. Fold in remaining egg whites. Spoon into prepared casserole.
Bake for about 45 minutes, or until top is golden. Serve immediately.

SERVES 6.
CALORIES: 291   CHOLESTEROL: 153 mg   SODIUM: 558 mg   FIBER: 3 g

Health tip:
Regular cornbread (see page 000) would probably be more healthful than this.

Orange-Flavored Millet-Meal Bread

This bakes up into a large, impressive loaf. If you'd like to try the bread with a grain other than millet, substitute uncooked fine couscous, or even teff.

½ cup softened butter, divided
½ cup millet meal
3 cup all-purpose flour
1 teaspoon baking powder
1 teaspoon baking soda
1 teaspoon salt
1 cup sugar
2 eggs
½ cup orange juice
1 tablespoon grated orange rind
1 teaspoon vanilla extract
¾ cup milk

Preheat oven to 350°F.
Grease and flour a 9 × 5 × 3-inch loaf pan and set aside.
Melt 1 tablespoon of the butter in a medium-size skillet over medium-high heat. Add millet and cook, stirring, until lightly browned. Set aside.
In a medium-size bowl, stir together the flour, baking powder, baking soda, and salt and set aside.
In a large bowl, cream the remaining butter with sugar until light and fluffy. Beat in eggs, then orange juice, orange rind, and vanilla. Alternately beat in reserved flour mixture with milk until blended. Fold in reserved millet. Spoon into prepared loaf pan.
Bake for 1 hour, or until a wooden pick inserted in the center comes out clean. Cool on a wire rack before slicing.

MAKES 1 LOAF (16 slices).
CALORIES: 204   CHOLESTEROL: 43 mg   SODIUM: 276 mg   FIBER: 1 g

Health tip:
Substitute unsalted margarine for butter; omit salt.
CALORIES: 208   CHOLESTEROL: 27 mg   SODIUM: 93 mg   FIBER: 1 g

OATS
(Avena)

Oats are the only one of the so-called minor grains that are generally incorporated into everyday eating patterns in the American home. But, popular as oats may be for breakfast and for cookies, the bulk of the crop still goes to feed horses and other livestock.

Oats thrive in harsher climates, so it's not surprising that they are a staple in Ireland and Scotland. They are valued for their high nutrition profile and their filling and warming qualities.

Although this grain has always been a great favorite in the United States, what we know today about the health benefits derived from eating oat bran makes oats more popular than ever.

Types of Oats Available

Oat groats: The whole oat grain with the husk removed. It is suitable for use in salads, stews, and baked products, and is similar in size and shape to long-grain rice.

Irish or Scottish oats: Oat groats, sometimes toasted, that have been cut with steel blades into small pieces, and are often called steel-cut oats. Like rolled oats, they are used to make porridge (better known as oatmeal), but take longer to cook.

Rolled oats: The Quaker Oats Company has been calling this product "old-fashioned oats" for so many years, that the term is practically generic. Rolled oats are groats that have been steamed and rolled flat.

Quick-cooking rolled oats: Oat groats that have been steamed, rolled and then cut into pieces. They take less time to cook than the regular variety.

Oat flakes: Rolled oats, which have been steamed and then put through rollers to flatten them. They are similar to rolled oats, but the flakes are slightly thicker and require a longer cooking time, though not as long as Irish or Scottish oats.

Instant oatmeal: Oats that have been partially cooked and dried before being rolled. This cereal product does not require cooking, but is hydrated by letting it stand in boiling water until it is brought to the familiar oatmeal consistency. Flavored instant oatmeal is also available. In my opinion, instant oatmeal is not a satisfactory recipe ingredient.

Oat bran: This is the highly touted outer covering of the hulled oat that is credited with being able to lower blood-cholesterol levels. (All oat products, except some oat flour, contain *some* oat bran.)

Oat flour: The whole oat or just the endosperm that has been ground. Although this product is readily available in health-food stores, it is also very simple to make at home. For each cup of oat flour, place 1¼ cups oatmeal (either regular or quick-cooking, but not instant since this contains ingredients other than just oats) in the container of an electric blender or food processor. Cover and process until all the large pieces have been reduced to flour. This flour will be slightly coarser than the flour you can buy, but it will be very fresh and you can make just what you need. *All the recipes in this chapter calling for oat flour were made with homemade flour, according to the directions above.*

Texture and Flavor

Oats come in many different forms, and each will give you a slightly different texture. Cooked oat groats (whole-grain oats with only the husk removed) are similar in size and shape to pignoli (pine nuts). Its color is a pale, yellow-beige.

Cooked groats are chewy, with individual grains that have a slightly starchy mouth feel. Although expected and pleasant in hot cereal, this starchiness is not desirable in salads, and can be removed by rinsing the cooked grains before they are mixed with other ingredients. But remember that in doing so you will also be sacrificing some of the B vitamins, which are water soluble.

The flavor of the oat groat is very delicate and mild, bordering on naturally sweet and definitely pleasant. The flavor is not at all "oatmealy." In fact, blindfolded, you might guess that you were eating brown rice, especially if the oats were rinsed.

If you like oatmeal, you will undoubtedly be thrilled with the Irish or Scottish variety, which is sometimes toasted before it is packaged, and cooks into a lovely thick porridge with a robust flavor.

All forms of oatmeal and oat flakes are basically grey-white in color and are thinly rolled. Oat flakes are somewhat thicker than oatmeal, and regular oatmeal is less broken up than the quick-cooking or instant varieties. Instant oatmeal often has salt (sodium-watchers beware) and wheat germ added. Flavored instant oatmeal also contains sugar, salt, and a variety of other flavoring agents. Check the list of ingredients on the package.

Irish oatmeal, oat flakes, and various other oatmeals have a distinctly starchy texture and a soft consistency. They all have a nutty delicate flavor.

Compatible Foods, Herbs, and Spices

The mild flavor of the oat groat makes this a grain that is compatible with any flavor. It goes well with all kinds of meat, vegetables, nuts, dairy products, and virtually any seasoning.

In America, oatmeal is traditionally used in sweetened dishes—especially cookies and streusel toppings—and is frequently coupled with milk.

Availability

Oat groats and oat flakes are available in health-food stores and through mail-order grain catalogs (see page 21).

Regular rolled oats, quick-cooking rolled oats and instant oatmeal are all available at the supermarket in the breakfast-cereals section.

Irish steel-cut oats are now in some supermarkets, and always in health-food stores, gourmet stores, and through mail-order grain catalogs.

You can find oat bran in some supermarkets, health-food stores, and grain catalogs.

Oat flour is available in health-food stores and through catalogs, and can also be easily made at home in a blender or food processor (see under Types of Oats Available).

Nutritional Content

The most exceptional nutritional advantage of oats has to do with the current findings that oat bran can lower LDL blood-cholesterol of levels. There are at least two kinds of cholesterol: high-density lipoprotein (HDL cholesterol), which is the good kind and acts like a magnet to prevent cholesterol from sticking to the walls of the arteries; and low-density lipoprotein (LDL cholesterol), which is the kind that sticks to your arteries and causes trouble.

More good news is that ALL oat products contain some bran. Oats are one of the few grains from which the bran and germ are not removed during processing. Naturally, you will need less pure oat bran (about ⅔ cup cooked oat bran per day) than oatmeal (about 2 cups cooked oatmeal per day) to achieve any significant cholesterol-lowering effects. And, of course, a healthier cardiovascular system will also depend upon your other eating habits (less saturated fat, the kind that is found in eggs, dairy products, meat, and many prepared foods) and regular exercise.

Lately oat bran is being incorporated into many commercial products, such as cookies, muffins, breakfast cereals, and breads. However, always read the ingredient list of every packaged food you buy to make sure that cholesterol-raising ingredients, such as hydrogenated or tropical (palm and coconut) oils are not also present, or only in limited amounts. (Ingredients, you know, must be listed in the order of their importance.)

Warning: Before you hasten into the kitchen, remember that introducing large portions of oat bran into your diet all at once can lead to severe digestive-tract disturbances, and although they are far from life threatening, can be very uncomfortable. Start your oat bran intake gradually, so that your body can become accustomed to it.

With the exception of the newly introduced super-grains, such as quinoa and amaranth, oatmeal is the grain leader in protein content. It also has good quantities of B vitamins, vitamin E, iron, calcium, and phosphorous.

Home Remedy

Uncooked oatmeal is an excellent remedy for acid indigestion. Start with a teaspoonful or so, and chew it slowly.

Substitutions

You can always used regular rolled oats and quick-cooking rolled oats interchangeably.

Brown rice: Its flavor and consistency make this a very satisfactory substitute in any recipe calling for cooked groats.

Bulgur: The flavor is comparable to oat groats, but the consistency is less chewy, and cooking times will vary greatly. Used cooked bulgur when cooked oats are called for, but not in recipes calling for uncooked groats.

Barley: The texture is similar to oat groats, but the flavor is slightly stronger.

Whole-wheat flour: May be substituted for oat flour.

Wheat, corn or rice bran: Can be substituted for oat bran, but remember that wheat bran does not have the beneficial cholesterol-lowering qualities of oat bran.

Other acceptable substitutes (in order of preference): Wild rice, white rice, wheat berries, triticale berries, and rye berries.

Basic Cooking Instructions

Please read *About Cooking Grains* beginning on page 7. For a richer-tasting cereal but not groats, substitute half of the water with milk.

The microwave methods that follow for cooking oats were tested in a 650-watt oven.

⸻⸻⸻ ◇ ⸻⸻⸻

Oat Groats

Stove-top method:

> 2 cups water
> ½ teaspoon salt
> 1 cup oat groats, rinsed

In a 2-quart saucepan, bring the water and salt to a boil over high heat. Stir in groats and return to boiling. Reduce heat and simmer, covered, for 1 hour, or until almost all of the liquid has been absorbed. Remove from heat and let stand for 10 minutes. Fluff with a fork.

MAKES 2½ CUPS.

NOTE: You can reduce the water to 1¾ cups and the cooking time to 55 minutes for a chewier, less starchy grain.

Microwave method:

> 3 cups water
> 1 cup oat groats, rinsed
> ½ teaspoon salt

Place the water in a 3-quart, microwave-safe bowl Cover with waxed paper and microwave on high (100% power) for 5 minutes. Stir in groats. Recover with waxed paper and microwave on high for 4 minutes. Microwave on medium (50% power), still covered with waxed paper, for 1 hour, rotating dish once, if necessary. Let stand 5 minutes. Stir in salt and fluff with a fork.

MAKES 2¾ CUPS.

Irish Oatmeal

Stove-top method:

> *3 cups water*
> *½ teaspoon salt*
> *1 cup Irish oatmeal*

In a 2-quart saucepan, bring the water and salt to a boil over high heat. Stir in oatmeal and return to boiling. Reduce heat and simmer, uncovered, for 1½ hours.

MAKES 3 CUPS.

Microwave method:

> *3½ cups water*
> *1 teaspoon salt*
> *1 cup Irish oatmeal*

Place the water and salt in a 3-quart, microwave-safe bowl. Cover with waxed paper and microwave on high (100% power) for 5 minutes. Stir in oats. Recover with waxed paper and microwave on high for 4 minutes. Microwave on medium (50% power), still covered with waxed paper, for 20 minutes. Stir and let stand for 3 minutes.

MAKES 3½ CUPS.

---◇---

Oat Flakes

Stove-top method:

>2 cups water
>¼ teaspoon salt
>1 cup oat flakes

In a 1½-quart saucepan, bring the water and salt to a boil. Stir in oat flakes and return to boiling. Reduce heat and simmer, covered, for 15 minutes. Remove from heat and let stand 5 minutes.

MAKES 2½ CUPS.

Microwave method:

>1¾ cups water
>¼ teaspoon salt
>1 cup oat flakes

Place the water in a 3-quart, microwave-safe bowl. Cover with waxed paper and microwave on high (100% power) for 4 minutes. Stir in salt and oat flakes. Recover with waxed paper and microwave on high for 3 minutes. Microwave on medium (50% power), still covered with waxed paper, for 8 minutes. Let stand 4 minutes. Stir well.

MAKES 2¼ CUPS.

---◇---

Regular Rolled Oats

Stove-top method:

>2¼ cups water
>¼ teaspoon salt
>1 cup old-fashioned rolled oats

In a 1½-quart saucepan, bring the water and salt to a boil. Stir in oats and return to boiling. Reduce heat and simmer, uncovered, for 7 minutes, stirring occasionally.

MAKES 1½ CUPS.

Microwave method:

> 2 cups water
> ¼ teaspoon salt
> 1 cup old-fashioned rolled oats

Place water in a 3-quart, microwave-safe bowl. Cover with waxed paper and microwave on high (100% power) for 3 minutes. Stir in salt and oats. Recover with waxed paper and microwave on medium (50% power) for 5 minutes.

MAKES 1¼ CUPS.

Quick-cooking Rolled Oats

Stove-top method:

> 2 cups water
> ¼ teaspoon salt
> 1 cup quick-cooking rolled oats

In a 1½-quart saucepan, bring water and salt to a boil. Stir in oats and return to boiling. Reduce heat and simmer, uncovered, for 2 minutes, stirring almost constantly.

MAKES 1¼ CUPS.

Microwave method:

> 2 cups water
> ¼ teaspoon salt
> 1 cup quick-cooking rolled oats

Place water in a 2-quart, microwave-safe bowl. Cover with waxed paper and microwave on high (100% power) for 3 minutes. Stir in salt and oatmeal. Recover with waxed paper and microwave on high for 1 minute.

MAKES 1¼ CUPS.

Reheating

Oats do not have to be reheated for use in salads and other recipes calling for cooked oats. They can be reheated by microwaving or steaming, if desired.

OATS RECIPES

(Indicates easy recipe.)*

———————◇———————

Oatsy Stuffed Mushrooms *
Creamy Cauliflower-and-Oats Soup *
Oats-Lentil-and-Chicken Soup
Roast and Groats
Veal, Chicken, or Turkey-Oats Schnitzel *
Oats and Kielbasa *
Spinach, Oats, and Turkey Loaf *
Spicy Oven-Baked Chicken *
Oats-and-Sardine Salad *
Crunchy Sprouts Salad *
Groats and Kidney Beans *
Pignoli-Oats Salad *
West Coast Pear-Watercress-and-Oats Salad *
Zucchini and Oat Groats *
Oats and Black Beans *
The World's Most Perfect Oatmeal *
Homemade Granola *
Extra-Good Oatmeal Pancakes *
Gingerbread Waffles
Bannocks *
Oatcakes *
Honey-Topped Biscuits *
Oat-Bran Muffins *
Betty-the-Baker's Oat-Bran Bread
Winter-Squash Bread
Irish-Oatmeal Soda Bread
Oatmeal Toasting Bread
Crunchy Irish-Oats Bread
Apple-Pear-Cranberry Crumble *
Bernice's Garbage
Oatmeal Brownies *
Prune-Filled Bar Cookies *
Giant Raisin-Oatmeal Cookies *
Plum Crumb Cake *

Oatsy Stuffed Mushrooms

These are a nice accompaniment for broiled steaks or chops. And they are wonderful as a hot appetizer.

18 medium mushrooms (about 12 ounces)
2 tablespoons butter
1 tablespoon minced shallot or the white part of scallion
1 tablespoon chopped parsley
⅛ teaspoon crumbled thyme
⅛ teaspoon salt
⅛ teaspoon pepper
1 tablespoon quick-cooking rolled oats
1 tablespoon oat bran

Preheat broiler.

Rinse the mushrooms briefly and pat dry on paper towels. Remove stems from caps. Chop stems and set aside.

Melt 1 tablespoon of the butter in a medium-size skillet and use to lightly brush mushroom caps. Set aside.

Add remaining 1 tablespoon butter to skillet. Add shallot and cook over medium-high heat, stirring, until softened. Add reserved chopped stems and cook over high heat, stirring and tossing, until soft. Remove from heat and stir in parsley, thyme, salt, and pepper. Stir in oats and oat bran.

Fill each mushroom cap with oats mixture. Place on broiler pan. Broil mushrooms for about 5 minutes, or until browned. Serve immediately.

MAKES 18 STUFFED CAPS.
CALORIES: 18   CHOLESTEROL: 3 mg   SODIUM: 26 mg   FIBER: 1 g

Health tip:
Use unsalted margarine instead of butter; omit salt.
CALORIES: 18   CHOLESTEROL: 0 mg   SODIUM: 2 mg   FIBER: 1 g

—————— ◇ ——————

Creamy Cauliflower-and-Oats Soup

I could eat this soup every day and never tire of it. It tastes very rich, but actually it's not, since it's pureed cauliflower and oats that give the soup its delightful creamy consistency.

1 tablespoon butter
1 cup sliced leek, both white and green parts
2 cups water
1 can (13¾ ounce) ready-to-serve chicken broth or
     1¾ cups vegetable broth (see page 19)
4 cups cauliflower florets
⅓ cup quick-cooking rolled oats
½ teaspoon salt
⅛ teaspoon ground red pepper
½ cup buttermilk

In a large saucepan, melt the butter over medium-high heat. Add leek and cook, stirring, until tender. Stir in water and chicken broth. Bring to a boil. Add florets, oatmeal, salt, and red pepper and return to boiling. Lower heat and simmer, covered, for 45 minutes. Remove from heat and set aside to cool slightly.

Measure 2 cups of the soup mixture into the container of a blender or food processor. Cover and process until smooth. Transfer to a large bowl. Continue processing, 2 cups at a time, until all of the mixture is pureed. Add the buttermilk. Reheat soup and serve immediately. Or chill the soup and serve it cold, but in that case you may have to add a little more salt, and possibly more red pepper, since chilling dulls flavors.

SERVES 6.
CALORIES: 80   CHOLESTEROL: 6 mg   SODIUM: 434 mg   FIBER: 2 g

Health tip:
Use low-sodium broth or water; omit salt.
CALORIES: 80   CHOLESTEROL: 6 mg   SODIUM: 50 mg   FIBER: 2 g

————————◇————————

Oats-Lentil-and-Chicken Soup

If you serve this soup with the chicken in it, it becomes a whole meal. Or serve the soup as a first course and the chicken as part of the main course. Either way, this is a thick soup, so you may want to add a little more water, especially if you reheat any leftovers. By the way, turnip adds incredibly good flavor to a soup or stew, so don't be tempted to leave it out if you don't happen to have one or two in the crisper.

12 cups water, divided
3½ pound chicken, cut into quarters
2 cups shredded cabbage
1 cup chopped onion
1 cup diced carrot
1 cup diced turnip
1 cup lentils, rinsed and picked over
1 cup oat groats
¼ cup chopped parsley
1 teaspoon dried dill weed
1 teaspoon salt
⅛ teaspoon pepper

Place 10 cups of the water and chicken in a large soup pot. Bring to a boil over high heat. Reduce heat and simmer, uncovered, for 1 hour. Add cabbage, onion, carrot, turnip, lentils, and groats. Simmer, uncovered, for 45 minutes longer.

Remove chicken from pot and set aside. Stir in the remaining 2 cups water, parsley, dill, salt, and pepper. Simmer, uncovered, for 40 minutes. Reheat chicken in the soup, or remove it and serve as part of the main course.

SERVES 8.
CALORIES: 296   CHOLESTEROL: 43 mg   SODIUM: 327 mg   FIBER: 6 g

Health tip:
Remove skin before cooking chicken; omit salt.
CALORIES: 230   CHOLESTEROL: 23 mg   SODIUM: 238 mg   FIBER: 6 g

Roast and Groats

After the groats have cooked in this stew they are so full of flavor that they could convert a so-called grain-hater after the first bite. If you like, you can drain the extra liquid from the groats and serve it on the side like gravy.

1 tablespoon vegetable oil
1 cup chopped onion
1 can (14½ ounce) whole peeled tomatoes, undrained
1 can (12 ounce) beer
½ cup water
1 bay leaf
¼ teaspoon salt
⅛ teaspoon pepper
2½ to 2¾ pounds top round or chuck pot roast
1 cup oat groats

Heat oil in a large heavy saucepan or Dutch oven over medium-high heat. Add onion and cook, stirring, until softened. Stir in tomatoes, beer, water, bay leaf, salt, and pepper. Place beef in pot, spooning tomato mixture over top. Cover and simmer for 1½ hours. Add groats and continue to simmer, covered, for 1 hour longer. Discard bay leaf before serving.

SERVES 4.
CALORIES: 418   CHOLESTEROL: 91 mg   SODIUM: 573 mg   FIBER: 3 g

Health tip:
Omit salt.
CALORIES: 418   CHOLESTEROL: 91 mg   SODIUM: 229 mg   FIBER 3 g

––––––––––– ◇ –––––––––––

Veal, Chicken, or Turkey Schnitzel

Oat bran gives extra crunchiness to the breading on this schnitzel. Do the breading in advance, if that's more convenient, and refrigerate until cooking time. You can turn this into a veal, chicken, or turkey Parmesan by topping cooked schnitzels with tomato sauce and mozzarella cheese, and then baking in a 350°F. oven for 10 to 15 minutes, or until cheese has melted.

⅔ cup dry unflavored bread crumbs
⅓ cup oat bran
⅓ cup all-purpose flour
½ teaspoon salt
⅛ teaspoon pepper
3 egg whites
1¼ pounds veal, chicken, or turkey scallops, pounded thin
Oil, for frying

Combine the bread crumbs and oat bran on a piece of waxed paper. On another piece of waxed paper, combine flour, salt, and pepper.

Beat egg whites slightly in a wide shallow dish or pie plate. Dip both sides of each scallop into flour mixture, then into egg whites, then into crumb mixture, patting the crumbs on gently to help them adhere. Chill for 15 minutes, which helps to keep the coating in place.

Add enough oil to a large skillet to measure about ⅛-inch. Heat over medium-high heat until oil bubbles when some of the bread crumbs are sprinkled on it. Reduce heat slightly and cook scallops until browned on both sides.

SERVES 4. (nutritional values for veal)
CALORIES: 448   CHOLESTEROL: 195 mg   SODIUM: 415 mg   FIBER: 3 g

Health tip:
Omit salt.
CALORIES: 448   CHOLESTEROL: 195 mg   SODIUM: 281 mg   FIBER: 3 g

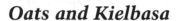

Oats and Kielbasa

This is one of those rare oats recipes not recommended for those who are concerned with lowering either their cholesterol or blood pressure. But it's good!

1 tablespoon vegetable oil
½ pound kielbasa (Polish sausage), chopped
¾ cup chopped onion
¾ cup chopped green bell pepper
¼ teaspoon crumbled thyme
2 cups cooked oat groats

In a large skillet, heat oil over medium-high heat. Add kielbasa, onion, bell pepper, and thyme. Cook, stirring frequently, until vegetables are softened. Add oats and cook, stirring, until heated through.

SERVES 4.
CALORIES: 263   CHOLESTEROL: 37 mg   SODIUM: 720 mg   FIBER: 3 g

Health tip:
Unfortunately, this is about as healthy as this recipe gets.

Spinach, Oats, and Turkey Loaf

It's the pesto sauce (that wonderful blend of fresh basil, pine nuts, oil, and garlic) that gives this loaf its fine flavor and moistness. You can make you own pesto (following the recipe on page 60) or you can buy it in the tomato-sauce section or refrigerator case at the supermarket. In order to keep the cholesterol count low, make sure that the ground turkey that you buy is low in fat, or grind your own in the food processor.

1 pound ground turkey
1 package (10 ounce) frozen chopped spinach, thawed and squeezed dry
⅓ cup quick-cooking rolled oats
¼ cup pesto sauce
2 tablespoons water
2 tablespoons oat bran
½ teaspoon salt
¼ teaspoon pepper

Preheat oven to 350°F.

In a medium-size bowl, combine the turkey, spinach, oats, pesto sauce, water, oat bran, salt, and pepper.

Shape turkey mixture into a loaf measuring about 8 × 4 inches in a baking pan. Or press into an 8 × 4-inch loaf pan. Bake for 1 hour, or until cooked through.

SERVES 4.
CALORIES: 305   CHOLESTEROL: 87 mg   SODIUM: 408 mg   FIBER: 3 g

Health tip:
Omit salt.
CALORIES: 305   CHOLESTEROL: 87 mg   SODIUM: 142 mg   FIBER: 3 g

———————◇———————

Spicy Oven-Baked Chicken

I like those little cheese-flavored fish-shaped crackers in my chicken coating, but you can use any cracker you happen to have around. This is a particularly nice work-day company dish. Prepare the chicken early in the day and then refrigerate it until baking time. Serve with a salad and maybe bread or rolls, an easy dessert, and that's it.

¼ cup sour cream
¼ cup mayonnaise
1 tablespoon liquid red pepper
1 tablespoon Worcestershire (Tabasco) sauce
½ teaspoon ground cumin
1 clove garlic, minced
1⅓ cups Cheddar-flavored fish-shaped crackers
½ cup oat bran
¼ teaspoon ground red pepper (optional)
3-pound chicken, cut into 8 parts, skinned

Preheat oven to 400°F.

Lightly grease a shallow baking pan that is just large enough to hold the chicken comfortably and set aside.

In a small bowl, stir together the sour cream, mayonnaise, liquid red pepper, Worcestershire sauce, cumin, and garlic. Set aside.

Place crackers in a 1-gallon plastic bag and finely crush with a rolling pin. Add oat bran and red pepper, if using, to bag. Shake until completely combined.

Liberally brush the chicken with sour-cream mixture. Place chicken pieces, one or two at a time, in the bag with the crumb mixture. Shake to coat completely. Place chicken pieces in prepared pan.

Bake for 40 to 45 minutes (a little longer if chicken has been refrigerated), or until browned and cooked through.

SERVES 4.
CALORIES: 680   CHOLESTEROL: 48 mg   SODIUM: 743 mg   FIBER: 2 g

Health tip:
Substitute plain yogurt for sour cream; use reduced-calorie mayonnaise.
CALORIES: 650   CHOLESTEROL: 40 mg   SODIUM: 743 mg   FIBER: 2 g

---

—————◇—————

Oats-and-Sardine Salad

Truthfully, I'm not all that wild about sardines, but I do like this salad—especially when I think how good it is for me. In addition to the well-known health benefits of oat groats, the sardines contain huge amounts of calcium (if you eat the tender little bones), and Omega-3 fatty acids that are now believed to protect against heart disease.

1 cup cooked oat groats, rinsed to remove any starchiness
½ cup chopped tomato
⅓ cup chopped cucumber
3 tablespoons chopped red onion
1½ tablespoons vegetable oil
1 tablespoon lemon juice
Lettuce leaves
1 can (3½ ounce) whole Maine or Norwegian sardines, drained

In a medium-size bowl, toss together the oats, tomato, cucumber, onion, oil, and lemon juice.

Line two luncheon plates with lettuce leaves. Top each with half of the oats mixture, then half of the sardines.

SERVES 2.
CALORIES: 301   CHOLESTEROL: 66 mg   SODIUM: 366 mg   FIBER: 3 g

Health tip:
Use sardines packed in water. Omit salt from oats.
CALORIES: 270   CHOLESTEROL: 60 mg   SODIUM: 215 mg   FIBER: 3 g

——————— ◇ ———————

Crunchy Sprouts Salad

Crunchy sprouts are simply beans that are sprouted, a combination of lentil sprouts, azuki-bean sprouts, and sweet-pea sprouts. You can find them in the produce section of a health-food store and sometimes at the supermarket. Other sprouts may be substituted.

1½ cups cooked oat groats, rinsed to remove any starchiness
1 package (3½ ounce) crunchy sprouts
½ cup chopped red bell pepper
½ cup chopped celery
¼ cup chopped scallion, both white and green parts
2 tablespoon chopped parsley
2 tablespoons vegetable oil
1½ tablespoon cider vinegar
¼ teaspoon salt
⅛ teaspoon pepper

In a medium-size bowl, gently toss the oats, sprouts, red bell pepper, celery, scallion, and parsley.

In a small bowl, stir together the oil, vinegar, salt, and pepper. Pour over salad ingredients and toss gently until well combined.

SERVES 6.
CALORIES: 154   CHOLESTEROL: 0 mg   SODIUM: 206 mg   FIBER: 2 g

Health tip:
Omit salt and use half the oil and half the vinegar in the dressing.
CALORIES: 144   CHOLESTEROL: 0 mg   SODIUM: 11 mg   FIBER: 2 g

——————— ◇ ———————

Groats and Kidney Beans

Because it contains oat groats, kidney beans, and cheese, this salad is packed with nutrition. (Vegetarians who do not eat cheese should simply leave it out.)

1 can (10½ ounce) kidney beans, drained
1 cup cooked oat groats, rinsed to remove any starchiness
½ cup diced Monterey Jack cheese
¼ cup sliced scallion, both white and green parts
¼ cup chopped mild green chilies (from a 4-ounce can)
3 tablespoons oil

1 tablespoon red-wine vinegar
½ clove garlic, minced
¼ teaspoon crumbled oregano

In a large bowl, gently toss together the kidney beans, oats, cheese, scallion, and chilies.

In a small bowl, stir together the oil, vinegar, garlic, and oregano. Pour over salad ingredients and toss gently until well combined.

SERVES 4.
CALORIES: 301 CHOLESTEROL: 26 mg SODIUM: 698 mg FIBER: 8 g

Health tip:
Omit cheese and cut dressing ingredients in half.
CALORIES: 195 CHOLESTEROL: 0 mg SODIUM: 371 mg FIBER: 8 g

◇

Pignoli-Oats Salad

Pignoli in case you're wondering, means pine nuts in Italian. Despite the ease of preparation, this salad draws raves in any language. The pine nuts look so much like cooked oat groats that you wouldn't know they were in the salad until you bit into one. Nice surprise.

2 cups cooked oat groats, rinsed to remove any starchiness
1½ cups chopped tomato
¼ cup sliced scallion, both white and green parts
¼ cup pignoli, raw or toasted (cook in a dry skillet, stirring, until they
    smell toasted)
2 tablespoons chopped parsley
1 tablespoon olive oil
1 tablespoon vegetable oil
1 tablespoon white-wine vinegar with shallots (or without shallots)

In a large bowl, toss together the oats, tomato, scallion, pignoli, and parsley.

In a small bowl, stir together the olive oil, vegetable oil, and vinegar. Pour over salad ingredients and toss until well combined.

SERVES 6.
CALORIES: 165 CHOLESTEROL: 0 mg SODIUM: 74 mg FIBER: 2 g

Health tip:
Use half the dressing ingredients.
CALORIES: 145 CHOLESTEROL: 0 mg SODIUM: 3 mg FIBER: 2 g

—————— ◇ ——————

West Coast Pear-Watercress-and-Oats Salad

In true California style, this salad is a delightful mixture of fruits, nuts, vegetables, and, of course, grain—all good for you.

1½ cups cooked oat groats, rinsed to remove any starchiness
1 cup chopped fresh or canned pear
½ cup chopped walnuts
¼ cup chopped red onion
¼ cup orange juice
2 tablespoons olive oil
1 tablespoon balsamic vinegar
1 tablespoon lemon juice
2 teaspoons honey mustard
¼ teaspoon salt
⅛ teaspoon pepper
2 cups watercress (remove any tough stems)
1 head Belgian endive, cut into 1-inch pieces

In a large bowl, gently toss together the oats, pear, walnuts, and onion.

In a small bowl, stir together the orange juice, oil, vinegar, lemon juice, honey mustard, salt, and pepper until thoroughly mixed. Pour over oats mixture and gently toss until well combined.

Combine watercress and endive on a serving platter. Top with salad mixture.

SERVES 4.
CALORIES: 229   CHOLESTEROL: 0 mg   SODIUM: 339 mg   FIBER: 4g

Health tip:
Omit salt.
CALORIES: 229   CHOLESTEROL: 0 mg   SODIUM: 46 mg   FIBER: 4 g

—————— ◇ ——————

Zucchini and Oat Groats

Substitute yellow squash for all or part of the zucchini, if you like.

2 tablespoons vegetable oil
½ cup chopped onion
1 can (13¾ ounce) ready-to-serve chicken broth or
*   1¾ cups vegetable broth (see page 19)*
1 cup oat groats
2 cups chopped zucchini
¼ cup chopped parsley
¼ teaspoon pepper

In a 2-quart saucepan, heat the oil over medium-high heat. Add onion and cook, stirring frequently, until softened. Stir in broth and bring to a boil. Stir in oats. Cover and simmer for 45 minutes. Stir in zucchini, parsley, and pepper. Cover and simmer for 7 minutes longer, or until zucchini is tender-crisp.

SERVES 6.
CALORIES: 147   CHOLESTEROL: 0 mg   SODIUM: 208 mg   FIBER: 2 g

Health tip:
Use water or low-sodium broth.
CALORIES: 147   CHOLESTEROL: 0 mg   SODIUM: 20 mg   FIBER: 2 g

———————— ◇ ————————

Oats and Black Beans

This is a variation of a popular dish served throughout Latin America. Rice, not oat groats, is the usual grain combined with the beans, but because the oats have a consistency similar to rice, and a greater nutritional value, I tried substituting oat groats in this recipe and it worked beautifully.

¾ cup water
½ cup oat groats
1 can (15 ounce) Cuban black bean soup (Goya brand)
1 clove garlic, minced
1 bay leaf
½ teaspoon ground cumin
½ teaspoon salt
¼ teaspoon crumbled oregano
⅛ teaspoon ground red pepper
½ cup chopped onion
¼ cup chopped parsley

In a 1½–2-quart saucepan, bring the water to a boil. Stir in oats and return to boiling. Reduce heat, cover, and simmer for 30 minutes. Stir in bean soup, garlic, bay leaf, cumin, salt, oregano, and red pepper. Cover and simmer 20 to 25 minutes longer, or until most of the liquid has been absorbed. Remove bay leaf.

In a small bowl, stir together onion and parsley. Serve over oats and beans, to be stirred in just before eating.

SERVES 6.
CALORIES: 94   CHOLESTEROL: 0 mg   SODIUM: 545 mg   FIBER: 2 g

Health tip:
Omit salt.
CALORIES: 94   CHOLESTEROL: 0 mg   SODIUM: 367 mg   FIBER: 2 g

———————— ◇ ————————

The World's Most Perfect Oatmeal

To me (and a lot of other people, I suppose) this means that rich creamy cereal that Mother would prepare when I was feeling ill. If you like a firmer oatmeal, reduce the water by ¼ cup.

1½ cups water
1½ cups milk
1 teaspoon salt
1⅓ cups regular rolled oats
2 tablespoons butter
½ cup half-and-half

In a medium-size saucepan, stir together water, milk, and salt. Stir in oats. Set over medium heat and bring to a boil, stirring occasionally. Reduce heat and simmer for 3 minutes. Remove from heat and let stand for 3 minutes.

At this point you have some choices. You can stir in the butter and half-and-half, or you can serve the cereal topped with butter and half-and-half.

SERVES 4.
CALORIES: 250   CHOLESTEROL: 39 mg   SODIUM: 639 mg   FIBER: 3 g

Health tip:
Omit salt, butter, and half-and-half—but then the oatmeal is not so perfect anymore.
CALORIES: 225   CHOLESTEROL: 13 mg   SODIUM: 67 mg   FIBER: 3 g

Homemade Granola

This homemade version of granola is every bit as good (and probably better) than any you can buy, even in a health-food store. Vary the recipe to suit your own taste. For instance: Use any nut instead of almonds; replace sunflower seeds with pumpkin seeds; omit sesame seeds; stir in as much or as many varieties of chopped dried fruit as you like.

1/4 cup butter
3 tablespoons dark-brown sugar
2 tablespoons honey
2 cups regular rolled oats
1/2 cup chopped almonds
1/2 cup sunflower seeds
2 tablespoons sesame seeds
1/2 cup wheat germ
1/2 cup chopped dates

Preheat oven to 350°F.

Place butter in a 9 × 13-inch baking dish. Place baking dish in oven for 5 minutes to melt butter. Stir in brown sugar and honey until well mixed. Stir in oats, almonds, sunflower seeds, and sesame seeds. Bake for 15 minutes, stirring twice. Stir in wheat germ. Bake for 10 minutes longer, stirring once. Remove from oven and stir in dates. Cool and store in an air-tight container.

SERVES 12.
CALORIES: 238   CHOLESTEROL: 10 mg   SODIUM: 37 mg   FIBER: 5 g

Health tip:
Use unsalted margarine for butter.
CALORIES: 231   CHOLESTEROL: 0 mg   SODIUM: 8 mg   FIBER: 5 g

Extra-Good Oatmeal Pancakes

These pancakes are just about perfect: moist and satisfying with just the right combination of sweetness and saltiness. If you feel like boosting their dietary-fiber content, stir a little oat bran into the batter.

1 cup oat flour
1 cup all-purpose flour
3 tablespoons sugar
1 tablespoon baking powder
1 teaspoon salt
2 eggs
1¾ cups milk
⅓ cup butter, melted
Additional butter

In a large bowl, stir together both kinds of flour, sugar, baking powder, and salt.

In a medium-size bowl, beat the eggs. Beat in milk and butter. Stir egg mixture into flour mixture just until blended. Do not overbeat. The batter should be slightly lumpy.

Heat a large skillet over medium-high heat until a few drops of water sprinkled in the hot skillet bounce about before evaporating. Brush skillet lightly with melted butter. Pour ¼ cup batter for each pancake onto skillet. Cook until bubbles break on top of pancakes. Turn with a wide spatula and cook until second side is browned.

SERVES 6 TO 8.
CALORIES: 249 CHOLESTEROL: 91 mg SODIUM: 569 mg FIBER: 2 g

Health tip:
Omit salt; substitute scrambled-egg substitute for eggs; use 1-percent milk instead of whole milk; use unsalted margarine instead of butter.
CALORIES: 230 CHOLESTEROL: 26 mg SODIUM: 275 mg FIBER: 2 g

—————◇—————

Gingerbread Waffles

One of these crisp little waffles for breakfast is filling enough to keep you going till lunch. They also freeze well and can be reheated in a toaster or microwave oven.

> 1 cup all-purpose flour
> ¾ cup oat flour
> ⅓ cup oat bran
> ⅓ cup sugar
> 1 tablespoon baking powder
> 2 teaspoons ground ginger
> 1 teaspoon ground cinnamon
> ½ teaspoon ground cloves
> ½ teaspoon salt
> 1⅓ cups milk
> ⅓ cup vegetable oil
> 3 egg whites

Preheat and grease a waffle iron as manufacturer directs.

In a large bowl, stir together both kinds of flour, oat bran, sugar, baking powder, ginger, cinnamon, cloves, and salt. Add milk and oil and stir just until blended. Do not overmix. The batter should be slightly lumpy.

In a clean, grease-free, medium-size bowl, beat egg whites with clean beaters until stiff peaks form when beaters are lifted. Fold egg whites into batter.

Spread half the batter into the prepared waffle iron. Bake until the steaming stops, about 5 minutes, or until browned. Repeat with remaining batter.

SERVES 8.

CALORIES: 250   CHOLESTEROL: 5 mg   SODIUM: 298 mg   FIBER: 2 g

Health tip:

Omit salt; use 1-percent milk.

CALORIES: 242   CHOLESTEROL: 2 mg   SODIUM: 165 mg   FIBER: 2 g

———————◇———————

Bannocks

Strange as it may sound, these griddle cakes were originally used for communion bread. They can be made with either oatmeal flour or barley flour, or some combination thereof. Serve these anytime you need a plain cracker that is a bit unusual.

¾ cup oat flour
3 tablespoons hot water
1 tablespoon butter, softened
Pinch salt

In a large bowl, stir together the oat flour, water, butter, and salt. Knead on a floured surface until thoroughly combined. Roll out to a 6-inch circle. Cut into 8 wedges.

Heat a large skillet or griddle until a few drops of water sprinkled in the hot skillet bounce about before evaporating. Lightly grease skillet. Place bannocks in skillet and cook until lightly browned on each side. Cool on a wire rack.

MAKES 8.
CALORIES: 27   CHOLESTEROL: 4 mg   SODIUM: 12 mg   FIBER: 1 g

Health tip:
Use unsalted margarine instead of butter; omit salt.
CALORIES: 27   CHOLESTEROL: 0 mg   SODIUM: 0 mg   FIBER: 1 g

———————◇———————

Oatcakes

These are not actually cakes, but crackers, which grow on you as you eat them. They make a healthy snack and are good with cheese and other spreads.

¼ cup oat flour
1 teaspoon baking powder
1 teaspoon sugar
½ teaspoon salt
2 tablespoons butter
1½ cups quick-cooking rolled oats
⅓ cup milk

Preheat oven to 375°F.
Grease two baking sheets and set aside.

In a medium-size bowl, stir together the oat flour, baking powder, sugar, and salt. Using a pastry cutter or two knives, cut butter into flour mixture until it resembles coarse cornmeal. Cut in rolled oats until the mixture forms balls. Then using a fork stir in milk.

On a lightly floured surfaced, roll dough out into a 10-inch circle. Cut into 2¼- or 2½-inch circles using a biscuit or cookie cutter. (If you don't have these, or can't find them, cut the dough into squares.) Place on prepared baking sheets.

Bake for 20 minutes, or until lightly browned.

MAKES 15 OATCAKES.
CALORIES: 54   CHOLESTEROL: 5 mg   SODIUM: 109 mg   FIBER: 1 g

Health tip:
Use unsalted margarine instead of butter. However, if the salt is omitted, the flavor of these cakes will suffer terribly. So sodium watchers would do better to skip this recipe.
CALORIES: 54   CHOLESTEROL: 1 mg   SODIUM: 27 mg   FIBER: 1 g

---

◇

Honey-Topped Biscuits

Every cook should have a good recipe for biscuits on hand. While most biscuits are simply a combination of all-purpose flour, shortening, and milk, these biscuits, made with generous amounts of oatmeal flour and oat bran, are as good for you and they are good to eat.

> 1 cup all-purpose flour
> 1 cup oat flour
> ¼ cup oat bran
> 1 tablespoon baking powder
> 1 teaspoon salt
> ⅓ cup butter
> ⅔ cup plus 2 tablespoons milk
> 2 tablespoons honey

Preheat oven to 425°F.
Grease a large baking sheet and set aside.
In a medium-size bowl, stir together both kinds of flour, bran, baking powder, and salt. Using a pastry cutter or two knives, cut butter into flour mixture until it resembles coarse cornmeal. Gradually stir in ⅔ cup of the milk to make a dough that is soft, but not

sticky. If necessary, stir in as much of the remaining 2 tablespoons of the milk as needed.

Turn dough onto a lightly floured surface and knead 12 times. Roll out to a ½-inch thickness and cut into circles with 2- or 3-inch cookie cutters.

Bake for 12 to 15 minutes, or until lightly browned. Remove from oven and brush with honey.

MAKES ABOUT 12 BISCUITS.
CALORIES: 142   CHOLESTEROL: 16 mg   SODIUM: 312 mg   FIBER: 2 g

Health tip:
Omit salt; substitute unsalted margarine for butter.
CALORIES: 142   CHOLESTEROL: 2 mg   SODIUM: 97 mg   FIBER: 2 g

———————— ◇ ————————

Oat-Bran Muffins

If you're trying to lower your cholesterol, or even if you're not, one or two of these muffins make a great stick-to-the-ribs breakfast. They also freeze well and reheat nicely in a toaster oven or microwave.

1 cup all-purpose flour
¾ cup oat flour
½ cup oat bran
¼ cup sugar
2 teaspoons baking powder
1½ teaspoons ground cinnamon
1 teaspoon baking soda
¼ teaspoon ground nutmeg
¼ teaspoon salt
2 egg whites
½ cup buttermilk
½ cup milk
¼ cup butter, melted

Preheat oven to 400° F.

Grease 18 2½-inch muffin cups and set aside.

In a large bowl, stir together both kinds of flour, bran, sugar, baking powder, cinnamon, baking soda, nutmeg, and salt.

In a small bowl, beat the egg whites, buttermilk, milk, and butter just until blended. Stir egg mixture into flour mixture just until blended. Do not overmix. Batter should be lumpy. Spoon batter into muffin cups, filling two-thirds full.

Bake for 25 minutes, or until browned. Remove muffins from pan and cool on wire racks.

MAKES 18 MUFFINS.
CALORIES: 91   CHOLESTEROL: 8 mg   SODIUM: 150 mg   FIBER: 1 g

Health tip
Omit salt; use unsalted margarine instead of butter.
CALORIES: 91   CHOLESTEROL: 1 mg   SODIUM: 102 mg   FIBER: 1 g

─────── ◇ ───────

Betty-the-Baker's Oat-Bran Bread

My friend, Betty Boldt, owns a bakery in New York, and she sells a *lot* of this bread.

> 2 cups all-purpose flour
> 1 cup oat bran
> 1 cup quick-cooking rolled oats
> 2 teaspoons baking soda
> 2 teaspoons baking powder
> 1 teaspoon ground cinnamon
> 1 cup butter
> 1 cup buttermilk
> ½ cup honey
> 1 cup finely chopped apple or the fruit of your choice (Betty often uses drained crushed pineapple, for instance)

Preheat oven to 325°F.
Heavily grease and flour a 9 × 5 × 3-inch loaf pan and set aside.
In a large bowl, stir together the flour, bran, oats, baking soda, baking powder, and cinnamon. Using a pastry cutter or two knives, cut butter into flour mixture until it resembles coarse cornmeal. Add the buttermilk and honey and stir just until blended. Do not overmix. Batter should be lumpy. Stir in apples. Turn batter into prepared pan.
Bake 60 to 70 minutes, or until a wooden pick inserted in the center comes out clean. Turn bread onto a wire rack to cool.

MAKES 1 LOAF (16 slices.)
CALORIES: 229   CHOLESTEROL: 32 mg   SODIUM: 259 mg   FIBER: 2 g

Health tip
Use unsalted margarine instead of butter.
CALORIES: 229   CHOLESTEROL: 1 mg   SODIUM: 96 mg   FIBER: 2 g

——————— ◇ ———————

Winter-Squash Bread

This is a moist, delicious bread that's good for breakfast, for a snack, or even dessert. Slice, wrap, and freeze any leftovers. Like most sweet breads, this one cuts best if you use a serrated knife.

Topping:

> 1½ tablespoons all-purpose flour
> 1½ tablespoons sugar
> ⅓ cup regular rolled oats
> 1 tablespoon butter

Bread:

> 2 cups ½-inch-cubes of peeled butternut squash, buttercup squash, or fresh pumpkin (You can also use 1 cup canned pureed pumpkin and skip the cooking, draining, and mashing. But since pumpkin is not as sweet as squash, you may want to add an extra tablespoon or two of sugar.)
> 1 cup sugar
> ½ cup vegetable oil
> ⅓ cup apple juice
> 2 eggs
> 1 cup all-purpose flour
> ½ cup oat flour
> ¼ cup oat bran
> 2 teaspoons baking soda
> ½ teaspoon baking powder
> ½ teaspoon salt
> ½ teaspoon ground cinnamon
> ½ cup chopped pecans

Preheat oven to 325°F.

Grease and flour a 9 × 5 × 3-inch loaf pan and set aside.

Prepare topping by mixing the flour, sugar, oats, and butter in a medium-size bowl until crumbly (I use my fingertips to do this) and set aside.

To make the bread, cook squash in a medium-size saucepan in boiling water until soft, about 12 minutes. Drain well. Turn into a large bowl and mash until smooth. Add sugar, oil, apple juice, and eggs. Beat until completely combined. Add both kinds of flour, bran, baking soda, baking powder salt, and cinnamon. Stir until well combined. Stir in pecans. Turn batter into prepared pan.

Bake for 1 hour, or until a wooden pick inserted in the center comes out clean. Turn bread onto a wire rack to cool.

MAKES 1 LOAF (16 slices).
CALORIES: 215   CHOLESTEROL: 28 mg   SODIUM: 185 mg   FIBER: 2 g

Health tip:
Use unsalted margarine instead of butter. Omit salt.
CALORIES: 212   CHOLESTEROL: 12 mg   SODIUM: 118 mg   FIBER: 2 g

---

Irish-Oatmeal Soda Bread

It's oatmeal that gives this almost-traditional soda bread extra moistness and a good dense consistency. If you like your soda bread a little on the sweet side, add 3 tablespoons of sugar when you stir the dry ingredients together.

1½ cups oat flour
1½ cups all-purpose flour
1 tablespoon caraway seeds
1½ teaspoons salt
1½ teaspoons baking soda
1½ teaspoons baking powder
½ cup raisins
1½ cups buttermilk

Preheat oven to 350°F.
Grease a baking sheet and set aside.
In a large bowl, stir together both kinds of flour, caraway seeds, salt, baking soda, and baking powder. Toss in raisins. Stir in buttermilk just until blended. Turn out onto a floured surface and knead for about 1 minute. Form into a 6-inch-round loaf. Place on prepared baking sheet.
Bake for 35 to 40 minutes, or until browned.

MAKES 1 LOAF (12 servings).
CALORIES: 141   CHOLESTEROL: 1 mg   SODIUM: 444 mg   FIBER: 2 g

Health tip:
Omit salt.
CALORIES: 141   CHOLESTEROL: 1 mg   SODIUM: 177 mg   FIBER: 2 g

———————◇———————

Oatmeal Toasting Bread

When this bread is freshly baked, it is dense, chewy, and utterly delicious, but I like it even better when it's toasted and spread with a little sweet butter and jam.

1 cup boiling water
¾ cup quick-cooking rolled oats
½ cup water
½ cup milk
1 cup whole-wheat flour
½ cup oat bran
2 tablespoons sugar
2 teaspoons salt
1 egg
1 package yeast
2 to 3 cups bread flour or all-purpose flour

Grease two 8½ × 4½ × 2¾-inch loaf pans and set aside.

In a large bowl, stir together boiling water and oatmeal. Let stand 1 minute. Stir in the water and milk. Stir in whole-wheat flour, bran, sugar, and salt. Beat in egg, then yeast. Stir in 2 cups of the bread flour. Turn out onto a heavily floured surface and knead for 7 minutes, or until smooth and elastic, using only as much of the remaining 1 cup flour as necessary to make a smooth dough that is only slightly sticky.

Place dough in a greased bowl and cover with greased plastic wrap. Let rise in a warm spot, free from drafts, until doubled in bulk, about 1 hour. Punch dough down.

Form dough into two loaves and place in prepared pans. Cover with greased plastic wrap and let rise until doubled in bulk.

Preheat oven to 375°F.

Bake for 40 minutes, or until browned. Turn bread out onto wire racks to cool.

YIELD: 2 LOAVES (14 slices each).
CALORIES: 72   CHOLESTEROL: 8 mg   SODIUM: 138 mg   FIBER: 2 g

Health tip:
Omit salt.
CALORIES: 72   CHOLESTEROL: 8 mg   SODIUM: 6 mg   FIBER: 2 g

———————— ◇ ————————

Crunchy Irish-Oats Bread

It gives me a lot of satisfaction when I notice my dinner guests guiltlessly indulging in two or even three slices of my bread because they know it's good for them. This bread is particularly nice to serve when you are having a simple meal, such as a hearty soup, stew, or salad.

> 2 cups boiling water
> ¾ cup Irish or Scottish oats
> 1 package dry yeast
> 1 tablespoon sugar
> 3½ cups all-purpose flour, divided
> 1 cup oat flour
> 1 egg
> 2 tablespoons vegetable oil
> 2 tablespoons unsulphured molasses
> 2 teaspoons salt

In a large bowl, stir together boiling water and Irish oats. Let stand until the mixture cools to very warm (105–115°F). This can take as long as 15 or 20 minutes, so don't rush it. Stir in yeast and sugar. Let stand for about 10 minutes, or until foamy. Stir in ½ cup of the all-purpose flour. Place plastic wrap loosely over top of bowl. Let stand in a warm spot, out of drafts, for 8 to 12 hours or overnight.

Grease two 8½ × 4¼ × 2¾-inch loaf pans and set aside.

Stir oat flour, egg, oil, molasses, and salt into yeast mixture. Stir in 2 cups of the remaining all-purpose flour, then stir in as much of the remaining 1 cup flour as necessary to make a dough that is not too sticky to handle.

Turn dough onto a heavily floured surface. Knead for 10 minutes, using as much of the remaining flour as necessary to make a dough that is smooth and elastic. Place in a large greased bowl and cover with greased plastic wrap. Let stand in a warm spot, out of drafts, until doubled in bulk, about 2 hours.

Punch dough down. Form into two loaves and place in prepared pans. Cover with greased plastic wrap and let stand until doubled in bulk, 1 to 1½ hours.

Preheat oven to 350°F.

Bake for 35 to 45 minutes, or until top is brown and bottom is golden. Turn out of pans to cool on wire racks.

MAKES 2 LOAVES (16 slices each).
CALORIES: 84   CHOLESTEROL: 6 mg   SODIUM: 136 mg   FIBER: 1 g

Health tip:
Omit egg and salt.
CALORIES: 82   CHOLESTEROL: 0 mg   SODIUM: 1 mg   FIBER: 1 g

—————— ◇ ——————

Apple-Pear-Cranberry Crumble

A scoop of vanilla ice cream on top of this warm crumble is absolutely heavenly. (By the way did you know that you can almost always buy out-of-season cranberries frozen? You can also freeze them yourself. Just throw a bag or two of cranberries into the freezer to use like fresh all year.)

2 cups peeled cubed apple
2 cups peeled cubed pear
½ cup chopped fresh or frozen cranberries
½ cup sugar, divided
½ cup all-purpose flour, divided
1 tablespoon lemon juice
⅛ teaspoon ground nutmeg
3 tablespoons butter, divided
½ cup regular rolled oats

Preheat oven to 400°F.
In a 1½- to 2-quart casserole, toss together apples, pears, cranberries, ¼ cup of the sugar, 2 tablespoons of the all-purpose flour, lemon juice, and nutmeg until thoroughly combined.
In a small saucepan, melt 2 tablespoons of the butter. Add the oats and cook over medium heat, stirring constantly, until lightly browned. Stir in remaining 1 tablespoon butter until melted. Stir in remaining ¼ cup sugar, and remaining ¼ cup plus 2 tablespoons all-purpose flour until mixture is crumbly. Sprinkle over fruit mixture.
Bake for 30 minutes, or until hot and bubbly and topping is browned. Serve warm, cool, or chilled.

SERVES 6.
CALORIES: 238   CHOLESTEROL: 15 mg   SODIUM: 50 mg   FIBER: 4 g

Health tip:
Use unsalted margarine instead of butter.
CALORIES: 238   CHOLESTEROL: 0 mg   SODIUM: 9 mg   FIBER: 4 g

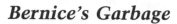

Bernice's Garbage

My mother's friend, Bernice Gurtman, is a *great* baker. One day she came over to our house with some terrific cookies she'd just baked. When we asked what they were she said, "Oh, just some garbage I made." So they've been known as "garbage cookies" ever since. Of course, Bern's cookies didn't have any oats in them. That's *my* addition.

½ cup oat flour
½ cup all-purpose flour, divided
½ cup sugar, divided
¼ teaspoon baking soda
½ cup butter
1 egg, separated
⅓ cup quick-cooking rolled oats
½ cup apricot butter
½ cup chopped nuts

Preheat oven to 350°F.

In a large bowl, stir together both kinds of flour, ¼ cup of the sugar, and baking soda. Using a pastry cutter or two knives, cut butter into flour mixture until it resembles coarse cornmeal. Stir in egg yolk, then oats. Press into a 9×9-inch baking pan. Gently spread apricot butter to within ¼ inch of the edge.

In a clean, grease-free, medium-size bowl, beat egg white with clean beaters until foamy. Gradually beat in remaining ¼ cup sugar. Continue beating until white forms stiff peaks when beaters are lifted. Spread over apricot butter. Sprinkle with nuts.

Bake for 40 minutes, or until lightly browned. Cool on a wire rack and cut into squares.

MAKES 16 COOKIES.
CALORIES: 135   CHOLESTEROL: 14 mg   SODIUM: 69 mg   FIBER: 1 g

Health tip:
Omit salt; use unsalted margarine instead of butter.
CALORIES: 135   CHOLESTEROL: 2 mg   SODIUM: 28 mg   FIBER: 1 g

———————— ◇ ————————

Oatmeal Brownies

This is not actually an attempt to "healthy-up" brownies, but rather a recipe for people who cannot easily tolerate wheat products. However, the brownies are also a tribute to a true friend, Lonnie Sterling, who sat through more than one multi-grain-course dinner while I was testing the recipes for this book. Lonnie, whose taste runs more to steak and fries, definitely appreciated these brownies I whipped up for dessert on one of these occasions, even though they do contain some oat flour.

2 squares unsweetened chocolate
½ cup butter
1 cup sugar
2 eggs
½ teaspoon vanilla extract
¾ cup oat flour
½ cup chopped walnuts

Preheat oven to 350°F.

Grease and flour (you can use oatmeal flour) an 8-inch-square baking pan and set aside.

Melt chocolate and butter in a medium saucepan over very low heat and set aside.

In a large bowl, beat the sugar and eggs until light and fluffy, about 5 minutes. Beat in reserved chocolate mixture and vanilla. Stir in flour and nuts until well combined. Turn into prepared pan.

Bake for 35 minutes. Place in refrigerator to cool. Cut into squares.

MAKES 16 BROWNIES.
CALORIES: 168   CHOLESTEROL: 41 mg   SODIUM: 58 mg   FIBER: 1 g

Health tip:
Use unsalted margarine instead of butter.
CALORIES: 168   CHOLESTEROL: 13 mg   SODIUM: 14 mg   FIBER: 1 g

———————◇———————

Prune-Filled Bar Cookies

You'll love the cakey bottom, crumbly topping, and moist, chewy centers.

¾ cup water
¼ cup sugar, divided
1 cup firmly packed pitted prunes
2 teaspoons lemon juice
¾ cup all-purpose flour
¼ cup firmly packed brown sugar
6 tablespoons butter
¾ cup quick-cooking rolled oats
⅓ cup chopped almonds

Preheat oven to 350°F.
Grease an 8-inch-square baking pan and set aside.
In a medium-size saucepan, combine water and 2 tablespoons of the sugar. Stir in prunes. Bring to a boil over high heat. Reduce heat and simmer for about 20 minutes, stirring occasionally, until almost all of the water has been absorbed. Stir in lemon juice.
Place prune mixture in the container of an electric blender or food processor. Cover and process until smooth and set aside.
In a large bowl, stir together the flour, brown sugar, and remaining 2 tablespoons sugar. Using a pastry blender or two knives, cut butter into flour mixture until it resembles coarse cornmeal. Stir in oats.
Press 1¾ cups of the oats mixture into prepared pan. Spread prune puree over oats mixture in pan. Stir almonds into the remaining oats mixture. Sprinkle over puree.
Bake for 45 minutes, or until topping is lightly browned. Cool on a wire rack. Cut into 12 bars.

MAKES 12 BAR COOKIES.
CALORIES: 188   CHOLESTEROL: 15 mg   SODIUM: 52 mg   FIBER: 3 g

Health tip:
Use unsalted margarine instead of butter.
CALORIES: 188   CHOLESTEROL: 0 mg   SODIUM: 5 mg   FIBER: 3 g

——————— ◇ ———————

Plum Crumb Cake

Besides being simple to make, you can also change this recipe to suit your mood or the season by substituting other fruits, such as peaches, apples, nectarines, etc. for the plums.

Cake:

> ½ cup butter
> ¾ cup sugar
> 3 eggs
> 1½ cups all-purpose flour
> 1 teaspoon baking powder
> ½ cup milk
> 1½ cups chopped ripe plums
> 1 teaspoon vanilla extract

Topping:

> ⅓ cup all-purpose flour
> ¼ cup sugar
> ¼ teaspoon ground cinnamon
> 2 tablespoons butter, melted
> ⅓ cup regular rolled oats

Preheat oven to 375°F.

Grease and flour an 8-inch-square baking pan and set aside.

To make the cake, cream butter and sugar in a large bowl until light and fluffy, about 5 minutes. Beat in eggs one at a time.

Stir together flour and baking powder. Add to butter mixture, alternately with milk, beating well after each addition. Stir in plums and vanilla. Pour into prepared pan.

To make topping, stir together flour, sugar, and cinnamon. Stir in butter until mixture makes fine crumbs. Stir in oats. Sprinkle over plums.

Bake for 50 minutes, or until a wooden pick inserted in the center comes out clean. Cool on a wire rack. Cut into 12 squares.

MAKES 12 CAKE SQUARES.

CALORIES: 276   CHOLESTEROL: 95 mg   SODIUM: 179 mg   FIBER: 2 g

Health tip:

Substitute unsalted margarine for butter; use scrambled-egg substitute for eggs.

CALORIES: 276   CHOLESTEROL: 34 mg   SODIUM: 104 mg   FIBER: 2 g

———————— ◇ ————————

Giant Raisin-Oatmeal Cookies

These cookies are very crisp and sweet. If you think they may be too sweet, reduce the granulated sugar to ¼ cup.

⅓ cup all-purpose flour
¼ cup oat bran
½ teaspoon baking soda
½ teaspoon salt
1 cup raisins
½ cup butter
⅓ cup firmly packed brown sugar
⅓ cup sugar
2 tablespoons milk
1 teaspoon vanilla extract
1½ cups regular rolled oats

Preheat oven to 350°F.

Grease two baking sheets and set aside.

In a medium-size bowl, stir together the flour, bran, baking soda, and salt. Stir in raisins until well coated and set aside.

In another medium-size bowl, cream butter, brown sugar, and granulated sugar until light and fluffy, about 5 minutes. Beat in milk and vanilla. Beat in reserved flour mixture, then stir in oats. Shape dough into 1½-inch balls and place two inches apart on prepared baking sheets. Flatten slightly with the back of a spoon.

Bake 12 to 14 minutes, or until light golden. Allow cookies to cool on baking sheets for 5 minutes. Using a spatula, remove cookies from baking sheets to cool on wire racks.

MAKES 15 COOKIES.
CALORIES: 168   CHOLESTEROL: 17 mg   SODIUM: 155 mg   FIBER: 2 g

Health tip:
Omit salt; use unsalted margarine instead of butter.
CALORIES: 168   CHOLESTEROL: 0 mg   SODIUM: 41 mg   FIBER: 2 g

---

Chewy Oatmeal Cookie Variation:

Increase flour to ½ cup
Increase milk to ¼ cup

Follow instructions for crispy cookies, but decrease baking time by 2 minutes.

CALORIES: 175   CHOLESTEROL: 17 mg   SODIUM: 156 mg   FIBER: 2 g

Health tip:

Omit salt; use unsalted margarine instead of butter.

CALORIES: 175   CHOLESTEROL: 0 mg   SODIUM: 41 mg   FIBER: 2 g

RYE
(Secale cereale)

Rye is a grain that flourishes in cold, damp climates. For that reason it has become a staple in Russia, Scandinavia, and Eastern Europe, where it is valued more as flour rather than as whole grain.

Rye bread and pumpernickel are the most common uses of rye flour in this country. However, the rye breads that we are accustomed to eating are actually made with some combination of rye and wheat flours, since rye flour alone has very little gluten and bakes up into a loaf that is too dense, chewy, and strong flavored for the taste of most Americans.

Types of Rye Available

Whole-grain rye: The rye berry with just the outer hull removed.

Rye grits: Whole rye that has been cracked into pieces. Can be used as a cereal.

Rye flakes: Rye berries that have been steamed and then flattened between steel rollers. Suitable for cereal or to add to baked goods or meat loaves, or as a topping for casseroles. May be used the same way as barley flakes, oat flakes, or wheat flakes.

Rye flour: There is a choice of dark flour, medium flour, and light flour. The difference is that the dark flour is made from the whole grain, and the medium and light flours are made from rye that has had the bran and/or the germ removed.

Texture and Flavor

Rye flour and undercooked rye groats have a strong sour aftertaste, but the flavor of rye itself is rather elusive. The flavor that comes to mind when most people think of rye bread is actually the flavor of caraway seeds that are baked in the bread. Properly cooked, rye berries are plump and chewy with a slight starchiness that can be rinsed off after cooking, but there will still be a faint sour aftertaste.

Compatible Foods, Herbs, and Spices

The flavor of rye is compatible with just about any meat, cheese, herb, or spice.

316

Dill and caraway seeds are most often used with rye, but other seeds are also acceptable. Parsley and dill are the herbs of choice, but any other herb that you like would undoubtedly work well, too.

All vegetables, especially root vegetables, and all of the onion family, go well with rye.

Apple is the most suitable fruit to pair with rye, and although the orange flavor in Swedish limpa bread seems to be a good match, on the whole, the sour taste of rye does not lend itself to fruity or sweet dishes.

Nuts, like fruit, are not very compatible with rye in most cases.

Availability

Whole-grain rye, rye grits, and rye flakes are available in health-food stores and from mail-order grain catalogs (see page 21). Rye flour is more commonly available and can usually be found at the supermarket.

Nutritional Content

Like most grains, rye is a good source of B vitamins. It also contains iron, calcium, phosphorous, potassium, and fiber.

Substitutions

Triticale: Since triticale is a hybrid of wheat and rye, it is the best substitute in any recipe. But it is not as flavorful as rye and less sour. Cooking time is about the same. Triticale flour is an acceptable substitute for rye flour, but it can be hard to find and has less flavor character than rye flour.

Wheat: Wheat berries are similar to rye berries, but have a sweeter flavor. The cooking times are similar. Whole-wheat flour can be used instead of rye flour when making bread, but the loaves will not have the characteristic sourness and denseness that is such an important part of rye bread.

Oat groats: A fine substitute for rye in salads, but oat groats are a bit too starchy for cooking purposes.

Brown rice: It can be used as a substitute, but cooking times will vary greatly.

Other substitutes (in order of preference): White rice and cracked wheat.

Basic Cooking Instructions

Please read *About Cooking Grains* beginning on page 7.

The microwave methods that follow for cooking rye were tested in a 650-watt oven.

─────── ◇ ───────

Whole-grain Rye (rye berries)

Stove-top method:

> 2½ cups water
> 1 cup whole-grain rye
> ½ teaspoon salt

Bring the water to a boil in a 3-quart saucepan over high heat. Stir in rye and salt and return to boiling. Reduce heat and simmer, covered, for 2 hours and 15 minutes, or until most of the liquid has been absorbed. Remove from heat and let stand for 10 minutes.

MAKES 3⅓ CUPS.

Microwave method:

> 3 cups water
> 1½ teaspoons salt
> 1 cup whole-grain rye

Place the water and salt in a 3-quart, microwave-safe bowl. Cover with waxed paper and microwave on high (100% power) for 5 minutes. Stir in rye. Recover with waxed paper and microwave on high for 5 minutes. Microwave on medium (50% power), still covered with waxed paper, for 1 hour. Stir and let stand for 5 minutes.

MAKES 2¼ CUPS.

Rye Grits

Stove-top method:

> 2⅓ cups water
> 1 cup rye grits
> ½ teaspoon salt

In a 3-quart saucepan, bring the water to a boil over high heat. Stir in rye grits and salt and return to boiling. Reduce heat and simmer, covered, for 35 minutes, or until all of the liquid has been absorbed.

MAKES 2 CUPS.

Microwave method:

> 2 cups water
> 1 cup rye grits
> ½ teaspoon salt

Place the water in a 3-quart, microwave-safe bowl. Cover with waxed paper and microwave on high (100% power) for 4 minutes. Stir in grits and salt. Recover with waxed paper and microwave on high for 4 minutes. Microwave on medium (50% power), still covered with waxed paper, for 20 minutes, rotating dish once, if necessary. Let stand 5 minutes.

MAKES 1¾ CUPS.

Rye Flakes

Stove-top method

> 2 cups water
> 1 cup rye flakes
> ½ teaspoon salt

In a 3-quart saucepan, bring the water to a boil over high heat. Stir in rye flakes and salt and return to boiling. Reduce heat and simmer, covered, for 30 minutes, or until the mixture is a thick porridge.

MAKES 2½ CUPS.

Microwave method:

> *1¾ cups water*
> *1 cup rye flakes*
> *½ teaspoon salt*

Place the water in a 3-quart, microwave-safe bowl. Cover with waxed paper and microwave on high (100% power) for 3 minutes. Stir in rye flakes and salt. Recover with waxed paper and microwave on high for 4 minutes. Microwave on medium (50% power), still covered with waxed paper, for 10 minutes, rotating dish once, if necessary. Let stand 4 minutes.

MAKES 2½ CUPS.

Reheating

Whole-grain rye does get tough when refrigerated, and gentle steaming or microwaving will restore tenderness. Otherwise, plan to use the rye shortly after cooking while the grain is still fresh and soft.

For use in salads, cool the cooked rye only to room temperature before adding to the other ingredients.

RYE RECIPES

(*indicates easy recipe.)

—————— ◇ ——————

Mom's Chopped Liver *
Franks, Rye, and Beans *
More-or-Less Stuffed Cabbage *
Eggs-in-a-Nest *
Savory Rye-Bread Pudding *
Open-Faced Reuben Sandwich *
Best-Ever Chicken Salad *
Tuna-and-Rye-Berry Salad *
Celeriac-Rye Salad *
Club Salad *
Ham-and-Cheese on "Rye" *
Rye and Mushrooms *
Classic Rye Bread
Pumpernickel Bread
Miami-Style Rye Bread
Raisin-Pumpernickel Bread *
Rye English Muffins
Crunchy Rye Bread
Dilled Rye-Beer Bread
Swedish Limpa Bread
Mini Rye-Soda Breads *
Garlic-Rye Crackers *
Rye Waffles

Mom's Chopped Liver

I managed to get the ingredients for my mother's chopped-liver recipe into cups and teaspoons (she uses handfuls of this and pinches of that) for my friend Holly Garrison's book, *Comfort Food*, because it is certainly one of my favorite comfort foods. I'm including it here because this really is the best chopped liver to be found anywhere. I like it on untoasted rye bread with a little extra "mayo" "schmeared" on the bread, and lots of iceberg lettuce. It tastes good, too, with garlic-rye crackers (see page 343).

¼ cup vegetable oil
2 cups chopped onion
*1 pound chicken livers, rinsed and any fat or tough membranes
    removed*
4 hard-cooked eggs, cut into quarters
⅓ cup mayonnaise
1½ teaspoons kosher (coarse) salt, or to taste
¼ teaspoon pepper

Heat the oil in a large skillet over medium-high heat. Add onion and cook, stirring frequently, until golden. Add livers and cook until they are no longer pink in the center, about 7 minutes. Remove from heat and let cool completely.

Place liver mixture and eggs in a food processor (or you can put it through a meat grinder). Process until liver and eggs are fairly smooth.

Scrape into a medium-size bowl. Stir in mayonnaise, salt, and pepper. Adjust seasonings to taste. Refrigerate until ready to serve.

SERVES 8 (2½ to 3 cups).
CALORIES: 265   CHOLESTEROL: 467 mg   SODIUM: 856 mg   FIBER: 0 g

Health tip:
Cholesterol watchers should not even *think* about this recipe. Sodium watchers should omit salt.
CALORIES: 265   CHOLESTERAL: 467 mg   SODIUM: 115 mg   FIBER: 0 g

————————— ◇ —————————

Franks, Rye, and Beans

I had to think twice about including a recipe for franks-and-beans in a grains cookbook. But the truth of it is that I love this combination, and I think most other people do, too. Adding rye berries (first simmered in beer) to this old favorite turned out to be truly inspired. If you like, you can serve the rye-and-beans, without the franks, as a side dish.

1 cup beer
¼ cup water
½ cup whole-grain rye, rinsed and drained
1 can (16 ounce) baked beans (vegetarian beans, pork-and-beans, or
  oven-baked beans)
1 tablespoon mustard
1 package (8 ounce) frankfurters, sliced

In a 1½-quart saucepan, bring the beer and water to a boil. Add rye berries and return to boiling. Reduce heat, cover, and simmer for 1 hour, or until the liquid has been absorbed. Stir in baked beans and mustard, then sliced frankfurters. Simmer, stirring occasionally, for 15 minutes.

SERVES 4.
CALORIES: 396   CHOLESTEROL: 35 mg   SODIUM: 1132 mg   FIBER: 10 g

Health tip:
Omit frankfurters.
CALORIES: 213   CHOLESTEROL: 8 mg   SODIUM: 552 mg   FIBER: 10 g

————————— ◇ —————————

More-or-Less Stuffed Cabbage

My sister invented this clever way to make a version of stuffed cabbage without the bother of separating the cabbage leaves and rolling them up with the filling. Her method is quick and easy, and you get the same wonderful flavors as you do when you make it the old-fashioned way.

1 pound lean ground beef
⅓ cup rye flakes
1 egg
¾ teaspoon salt, divided
½ teaspoon pepper, divided
2 tablespoons vegetable oil
1 cup chopped onion
1 large clove garlic, minced
3 cups coarsely shredded cabbage
1 can (14½ ounce) diced peeled tomatoes
1 can (8 ounce) tomato sauce
1 cup sauerkraut, well drained and firmly packed
⅓ cup firmly packed brown sugar

In a medium-size bowl, combine the beef, rye flakes, egg, ½ teaspoon of the salt and ¼ teaspoon of the pepper. Form into 16 balls measuring about 1½ inches. Set aside.

In a large heavy saucepan or Dutch oven, heat the oil over medium-high heat. Add onion and garlic and cook, stirring, until softened. Stir in cabbage and cook, stirring frequently, until wilted. Stir in the tomatoes, tomato sauce, sauerkraut, brown sugar, and remaining ¼ teaspoon salt and ¼ teaspoon pepper. Bring to a boil over high heat. Lower heat and add meatballs. Return to boiling, then reduce heat. Cover and simmer for 20 minutes.

SERVES 4.
CALORIES: 428   CHOLESTEROL: 151 mg   SODIUM: 1438 mg   FIBER: 6 g

Health tip:
Omit salt; rinse sauerkraut, decrease oil to 2 teaspoons and cook in a nonstick saucepan. Or, cook onion and garlic in a nonstick skillet, transferring to the larger pan to finish cooking. Reduce sugar to taste.
CALORIES: 386   CHOLESTEROL: 151 mg   SODIUM: 1038 mg   FIBER: 6 g

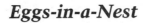

Eggs-in-a-Nest

I think this is the kind of breakfast that kids really like, and it's easy and fun to serve: a whole meal in one course. The amount of ingredients in this recipe will serve two, but you can make as many of these as you need. The leftover cutouts of rye bread can be dried out and used for bread crumbs.

2 slices rye bread, lightly toasted
2 tablespoons butter, softened
2 eggs
Salt, to taste
Pepper, to taste

Using a 3-inch biscuit cutter, cut a hole in the center of each slice of toast. Butter the toast on both sides, using about 1 teaspoon butter per side.

Heat a 10-inch skillet over medium heat. Turn toast over. Divide remaining butter in half and melt in the cut-out circles of the toast. Break an egg into the cut-out circle of each slice of toast. Sprinkle eggs with salt and pepper to taste. Cook until eggs are done as you like them.

SERVES 2.
CALORIES: 241   CHOLESTEROL: 239 mg   SODIUM: 726 mg   FIBER: 2 g

Health tip:
This breakfast is not a good choice for cholesterol watchers. Sodium watchers should omit salt and use unsalted butter.
CALORIES: 241   CHOLESTEROL: 239 mg   SODIUM: 244 mg   FIBER: 2 g

——————◇——————

Savory Rye-Bread Pudding

Not long ago, I served this for lunch to a few friends and *everyone* asked for the recipe.

¼ cup butter
6 slices rye bread, cubed
½ cup shredded Cheddar cheese
3 eggs
¼ cup grated Parmesan cheese
½ teaspoon salt
½ teaspoon Worcestershire sauce
⅛ teaspoon pepper
2 cups milk, scalded (bubbles form around the edge of the pot, but the milk does not actually boil)

Preheat oven to 350°F.

Place the butter in a 2-quart soufflé dish. Place dish in preheated oven (or microwave) until butter melts. Swirl melted butter around dish to coat side and bottom. Add bread cubes and Cheddar cheese to soufflé dish and toss until well combined.

In a medium-size bowl, beat together egg, Parmesan cheese, salt, Worcestershire sauce, and pepper. Gradually beat in milk. Pour over bread mixture in soufflé dish.

Bake for 45 minutes. Serve immediately.

SERVES 4.

CALORIES: 410   CHOLESTEROL: 222 mg   SODIUM: 918 mg   FIBER: 3 g

Health tip:

Use unsalted margarine instead of butter; omit salt.

CALORIES: 410   CHOLESTEROL: 191 mg   SODIUM: 568 mg   FIBER: 3 g

———◇———

Open-Faced Reuben Sandwich

I've always wondered who thought of this sort of strange combination of ingredients for a sandwich. After researching the matter, I discovered that it was an entry—in fact, the winner—of the first sandwich contest, sponsored by the Wheat Flour Institute.

2 slices rye bread
2 tablespoons Russian dressing, divided
¼ pound sliced corned beef, divided
½ cup sauerkraut, well drained
2 slices Swiss cheese, divided

Preheat broiler.

Place the bread on a baking sheet. Spread each slice with 1 tablespoon Russian dressing. Top each slice with half the corned beef, then half the sauerkraut, and, finally, one slice of cheese.

Place under broiler for about 2 minutes, or until cheese is melted and flecked with brown. Serve with sour pickles and potato chips.

SERVES 2.
CALORIES: 741   CHOLESTEROL: 143 mg   SODIUM: 3009 mg   FIBER: 6 g

Health tip:
Have a turkey sandwich instead!

———————◇———————

Best-Ever Chicken Salad

I wouldn't feel that I had satisfactorily completed the rye section of this cookbook if I neglected the most familiar use for this grain, which is bread for sandwiches. After all, how would you serve corned beef if there was no rye? My mother makes great sandwiches on rye bread. She serves this salad on rye toast with lettuce and Russian dressing.

2 cups diced cooked chicken
½ cup chopped celery
⅓ cup mayonnaise
1 teaspoon grated onion
1 teaspoon white vinegar
¼ teaspoon salt
⅛ teaspoon pepper, or to taste

In a medium-size bowl, toss the chicken with celery.

In a small bowl, stir together mayonnaise, onion, vinegar, salt, and pepper. Pour mayonnaise mixture over chicken and celery and mix gently until well combined.

SERVES 4 (enough salad to make 2 huge sandwiches, 3 generous sandwiches, or 4 regular sandwiches).
CALORIES: 258   CHOLESTEROL: 69 mg   SODIUM: 300 mg   FIBER: 0 g

Health tip:
Use reduced-calorie mayonnaise; omit salt.
CALORIES: 174   CHOLESTEROL: 63 mg   SODIUM: 162 mg   FIBER: 0 g

—————— ◇ ——————

Tuna-and-Rye-Berry Salad

This salad is a nice alternative to a plain old tuna-salad sandwich, and the whole-grain rye (rye berries) stretch the tuna so that one can is enough for 2 or 3 generous-size servings.

1 cup cooked and cooled whole-grain rye
1 can (6¾ ounce) solid-white tuna, packed in oil and drained
½ cup chopped celery
¼ cup chopped red onion
1 tablespoon vegetable oil
1 tablespoon mayonnaise
1 tablespoon lemon juice

In a small bowl, place the rye, tuna, celery, and onion. Toss gently until well mixed.

Mix the oil, mayonnaise, and lemon juice in a cup. Pour over tuna mixture and toss until completely combined.

SERVES 3.
CALORIES: 265   CHOLESTEROL: 37 mg   SODIUM: 370 mg   FIBER: 2 g

Health tip:
Use low-sodium, water-packed tuna; substitute reduced-calorie mayonnaise for regular mayonnaise.
CALORIES: 172   CHOLESTEROL: 14 mg   SODIUM: 271 mg   FIBER: 2 g

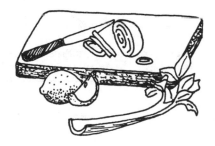

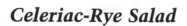

Celeriac-Rye Salad

Don't be put off by the appearance of celeriac (also known as celery root and knob celery), as it is a rather unattractive root vegetable. Its white flesh, which tastes sort of like a turnip, is covered by brown knobby skin that is peeled away before it is cooked. (An honest produce man will tell you that if the root is any larger than his fist, it's not worth buying.) If you have never tried celeriac, this salad is a good place to start. It's important to use a good brand of extra-virgin olive oil in the preparation of the dressing. (I like the Colavita brand the best.)

1½ cups cooked and cooled whole-grain rye
1 cup cooked julienned celeriac
1 cup sliced celery
¼ cup sliced scallion, both white and green parts
2 tablespoons extra-virgin olive oil
2 teaspoons white-wine vinegar
1 teaspoon Dijon mustard
¼ teaspoon celery salt
¼ teaspoon celery seed
⅛ teaspoon pepper

In a large bowl, toss together the rye, celeriac, celery, and scallion.

In a small bowl, stir together the oil, vinegar, mustard, celery salt, celery seed, and pepper. Pour over salad ingredients and toss until thoroughly combined.

SERVES 4.
CALORIES: 186   CHOLESTEROL: 0 mg   SODIUM: 322 mg   FIBER: 4 g

Health tip:
Omit celery salt and reduce dressing ingredients by half.
CALORIES: 161   CHOLESTEROL: 0 mg   SODIUM: 155 mg   FIBER: 4 g

Club Salad

Like ham-and-cheese on rye, this salad is based on a sandwich that is almost always served on rye bread. The results are superb! (Needless to say, this salad is one terrific way to dispose of some of the remnants of the holiday bird.)

1½ cups cooked and cooled rye berries
1 cup diced turkey
1 cup chopped tomato
¼ cup chopped scallion, both white and green parts
3 slices bacon, cooked crisp and crumbled
¼ cup mayonnaise
1 tablespoon catsup
1 tablespoon India relish
1 tablespoon chopped parsley
¼ teaspoon salt
¼ teaspoon pepper

In a medium-size bowl, toss together the rye, turkey, tomato, scallion, and bacon.

In a small bowl, stir together the mayonnaise, catsup, relish, parsley, salt, and pepper. Spoon dressing over salad ingredients and toss until completely combined.

SERVES 4.
CALORIES: 262   CHOLESTEROL: 39 mg   SODIUM: 460 mg   FIBER: 2 g

Health tip
Substitute reduced-caloric mayonnaise for regular mayonnaise; omit bacon and salt.
CALORIES: 160   CHOLESTEROL: 31 mg   SODIUM: 220 mg   FIBER: 2 g

———————◇———————

Ham-and-Cheese on "Rye"

I couldn't resist developing this recipe because I liked the name so much. As it turns out, it tastes good, too.

1½ cups cooked and cooled whole-grain rye
3 tablespoons mayonnaise
1 tablespoon Dijon mustard
1 tablespoon snipped dill
¼ teaspoon pepper
1 cup ¼-inch-diced Muenster cheese with or without caraway seeds
1 package (5 ounce) ham, diced

In a medium-size bowl, combine the rye, mayonnaise, mustard, dill, and pepper. Top with cheese and ham.

SERVES 4.
CALORIES: 355   CHOLESTEROL: 57 mg   SODIUM: 817 mg   FIBER: 2 g

Health tip:
Use reduced-calorie mayonnaise.
CALORIES: 307   CHOLESTEROL: 54 mg   SODIUM: 814 mg   FIBER: 2 g

———————◇———————

Rye and Mushrooms

The combination of whole-grain rye and mushrooms is an excellent one, because their consistencies are so compatible. This is a very good side dish for hamburgers, roasts, and chops.

2 tablespoons butter
1 cup sliced white button mushrooms
1 cup sliced shiitake mushrooms
2 cloves garlic, minced
1 cup whole-grain rye, rinsed
1¾ cups water
½ cup grated Parmesan cheese
½ teaspoon salt
¼ teaspoon pepper

In a 2-quart saucepan, melt the butter. Stir in both kinds of mushrooms and garlic. Cook over medium heat, stirring, until softened. Add water and bring to a boil. Stir in rye. Cover and simmer for 1 hour. Stir in Parmesan cheese, salt, and pepper.

SERVES 6.
CALORIES: 196   CHOLESTEROL: 16 mg   SODIUM: 338 mg   FIBER: 6 g

Health tip:
Use unsalted margarine instead of butter; omit Parmesan cheese and salt.
CALORIES: 165   CHOLESTEROL: 0 mg   SODIUM: 7 mg   FIBER: 6 g

———————— ◇ ————————

Classic Rye Bread

This is it! And better than you can buy at any bakery.

½ cup very warm water (105–115°F)
½ teaspoon sugar
1 package dry yeast
2 cups rye flour
1½ to 2 cups all-purpose flour
1 tablespoon caraway seeds (optional)
2 teaspoons salt
1 cup water

Grease an 8½ × 4½ × 2¾-inch loaf pan and set aside.

In a glass measuring cup, stir together the warm water and sugar. Stir in yeast and let stand until ¼ inch of white bubbly foam forms on top. (This foaming is called *proofing*, and if it doesn't happen it means that for some reason or other the yeast has not yet been activated. Discard this batch and try again, double checking the date on the yeast package and the temperature of the water.)

In a large bowl, stir together the rye flour, ½ cup of the all-purpose flour, caraway seeds, if using, and salt. Stir in yeast mixture and water. Stir in ⅔ cup more of the all-purpose flour to make a dough that is easy to handle.

Turn dough out onto a floured surface and knead in enough of the remaining all-purpose flour to make a dough that is smooth, elastic, and no longer sticky. Place dough in a large greased bowl and cover with greased plastic wrap. Set in a warm spot, out of drafts, until doubled in bulk, about 1 hour.

Punch dough down and form into an 8-inch loaf. Place in prepared pan. Cover with greased plastic wrap and let rise until doubled in bulk.

Preheat oven to 350°F.

Bake for 50 to 60 minutes, or until loaf is browned on top and bottom. Remove from pan and cool on a wire rack.

MAKES 1 LOAF (14 slices).
CALORIES: 102   CHOLESTEROL: 0 mg   SODIUM: 267 mg   FIBER: 3 g

Health tip:
Omit salt.
CALORIES: 102   CHOLESTEROL: 0 mg   SODIUM: 0 mg   FIBER: 3 g

Rye Bread Sticks

Use the above recipe for the dough, but omit caraway seeds. After the first rise, cut dough into 12 equal pieces. Roll into sticks about 12 inches long on a floured surface. Brush each stick with melted butter and roll in your choice of: coarse salt, dehydrated onion, caraway seeds, poppy seeds, or sesame seeds. Place on greased baking sheets, leaving 1½ inches around each bread stick. Cover with greased plastic wrap and let rise until doubled in bulk.
Bake for about 18 minutes, or until golden.

MAKES 12 BREAD STICKS.

Rye Pretzels

Shape bread sticks into pretzel shapes after rolling in the topping of your choice. Bake as directed for bread sticks.

MAKES 12 PRETZELS.

—————— ◇ ——————

Pumpernickel Bread

When I think of pumpernickel bread, a dark-brown loaf comes to mind, which is similar to rye bread, but that is actually a Russian black bread. True pumpernickel was supposedly developed by a German gentleman named Pumper Nickel. It is light in color with a dense chewy texture. This bread involves many steps (none of them very difficult), so it pays to make several loaves at once. (Extra loaves may be tightly wrapped and frozen.) Now, get out a BIG, BIG bowl to allow the dough plenty of room to rise.

3 cups water
¾ cup cormeal
2 tablespoons butter
2 tablespoons sugar

1 tablespoon salt
1 tablespoon caraway seeds
2 packages dry yeast
½ cup very warm water (105–115°F)
2 cups mashed potatoes (can be made from instant)
4 cups rye flour
2 cups whole-wheat flour
2 to 3 cups all-purpose flour

Grease four 8½ × 4½ × 2¾-inch loaf pans (or three 9-inch layer-cake pans) and set aside.

In a medium-size saucepan, stir together the water and cornmeal. Cook over medium heat, stirring constantly, until mixture is thick. Remove from heat. Stir in butter, sugar, salt, and caraway seeds. Let stand for about 40 minutes, or until lukewarm.

When cornmeal mixture has cooled to lukewarm, stir the yeast into warm water. Let stand until ¼ inch of white bubbly foam forms on top. (This foaming is called *proofing*, and if it doesn't happen it means that for some reason or other the yeast has not been activated. Discard this batch and try again, double checking the date on the yeast package and the temperature of the water.)

Stir potatoes into cornmeal mixture, then stir in proofed yeast. Stir in rye flour and whole-wheat flour. Stir in 1 cup of the all-purpose flour to form a dough that is stiff enough to handle.

Turn dough onto a well-floured surface. Knead in enough of the remaining 2 cups all-purpose flour to form a dough that is only very slightly sticky (or until you're too exhausted to continue kneading any longer).

Place dough in a very large greased bowl and cover with greased plastic wrap. Let stand in a warm spot, out of drafts, until doubled in bulk, about 1 hour.

Shape dough into four loaves and place in prepared loaf pans. (Or, if you want to make three round loaves, knead in a little extra flour, shape into rounds, and place in prepared layer-cake pans.) Cover with greased plastic wrap and let rise until doubled in bulk.

Preheat oven to 375°F.

Bake for 45 to 50 minutes, or until browned on top and bottom. Remove from pans and cool on wire racks.

MAKES 4 LOAVES (14 slices each) OR 3 ROUND LOAVES.
CALORIES: 113   CHOLESTEROL: 2 mg   SODIUM: 186 mg   FIBER: 2 g

Health tip:
Omit salt.
CALORIES: 113   CHOLESTEROL: 2 mg   SODIUM: 57 mg   FIBER: 2 g

———————— ◇ ————————

Miami-Style Rye Bread

"Miami-style" means that golden-fried onions are tucked inside the loaf of rye bread before it is baked, adding their own special sweetness and flavor.

¾ cup very warm water (105–115°F)
½ teaspoon sugar
1 package dry yeast
1 cup rye flour
2 teaspoons caraway seeds
1 teaspoon salt
1 to 1½ cups all-purpose flour
2 tablespoons butter
½ cup finely chopped onion
1 teaspoon poppy seeds
1 egg white, for glaze (optional)
Additional poppy seeds (optional)

Grease an 8½ × 4½ × 2¾-inch loaf pan and set aside.

In a glass measuring cup, stir together the water and sugar. Add yeast and let stand until ¼ inch of white bubbly foam forms on top. (This foaming is called *proofing,* and if it doesn't happen it means that for some reason or other the yeast has not been activated. Discard this batch and try again, double checking the date on the yeast package and the temperature of the water.)

In a large bowl, stir together rye flour, caraway seeds, salt, and ¾ cup of the all-purpose flour. Stir in proofed-yeast mixture. Stir in ½ cup flour. Turn dough onto a floured surface and knead for 10 minutes using as much of remaining flour as necessary to form a dough that is no longer sticky. Place in a large greased bowl. Cover with greased plastic wrap. Set in a warm spot, out of drafts, until doubled in bulk, about 1 hour.

Melt the butter in a small skillet over medium-high heat. Add onion and cook, stirring, until golden brown. Stir in poppy seeds and set aside.

Punch dough down. Roll into an 8-inch square. Spread onion mixture over one side of the square to within 1 inch of the edges. Starting on the onion-side of the bread, roll dough into a log so that onion is tucked into the center of the bread. Pinch the seam and the ends to seal. Place seam side down on prepared baking sheet. Cover lightly with greased plastic wrap and let rise until doubled in bulk. (This will be a small loaf, so don't expect it to rise to the top of the pan.) Brush with egg white and sprinkle with poppy seeds, if you like.

Preheat oven to 375°F.

Bake for 40 minutes, or until browned. Remove from baking sheet and cool on a wire rack.

MAKES 1 LOAF (10 slices).
CALORIES: 117   CHOLESTEROL: 6 mg   SODIUM: 239 mg   FIBER: 3 g

Health tip:
Omit salt; substitute unsalted margarine for butter.
CALORIES: 116   CHOLESTEROL: 0 mg   SODIUM: 9 mg   FIBER: 3 g

─────── ◇ ───────

Raisin-Pumpernickel Bread
(Russian Black Bread)

This is the dark-brown loaf that most people think of as being pumpernickel, but it's really a Russian black bread. If you prefer your bread plain, leave out the raisins.

½ cup very warm water (105–115°F)
½ teaspoon sugar
2 packages dry yeast
3 cups rye flour
1 cup whole wheat flour
1 cup morsels of wheat bran cereal (Kellogg's Bran Buds)
¼ cup unsweetened cocoa powder
2 tablespoons caraway seeds
1 teaspoon fennel or anise seeds (optional)
1 tablespoon salt
1½ cups water
⅔ cup unsulphured molasses
¼ cup butter, melted
2 teaspoons instant-coffee powder or granules
1 teaspoon white vinegar
1½ cups dark raisins
2 to 3 cups bread flour or all-purpose flour

Grease a baking sheet and set aside.

In a glass measuring cup, stir together the warm water and sugar. Stir in yeast and let stand until ¼ inch of white foam forms on top. (This foaming is called *proofing*, and if it doesn't happen it means that for some reason or other the yeast has not been activated. Discard this batch and try again, double checking the date on the yeast package and the temperature of the water.)

While yeast is proofing, in a large bowl, stir together rye and whole-wheat flours. Stir in cereal, cocoa, caraway seeds, fennel seeds, if using, and salt. Add water, molasses, melted butter, instant-coffee powder, vinegar, and proofed-yeast mixture. Stir in raisins and 1 cup of the bread flour. Turn dough onto a floured surface and knead in as much of the remaining bread flour as necessary to form a dough that is no longer sticky. Place in a large greased bowl. Cover with greased plastic wrap. Set in a warm spot, out of drafts, until doubled in bulk, about 2 hours. (As a point of interest, the last time I made this bread the dough didn't rise much at all, but just enough to assure me that the yeast was active. So, after two hours, I just proceeded with the recipe and the results were fine.)

Punch dough down and form into a round loaf. Place on prepared baking sheet. Cover lightly with greased plastic wrap. Let rise until doubled in bulk, about 1 hour. (Here again, the dough may not really double in bulk, but it will rise.)

Preheat oven to 350°F.

Bake for 1 hour, or until loaf sounds hollow when tapped, and the bottom is nicely browned. Remove from baking sheet to cool on a wire rack.

MAKES 1 LOAF (24 servings).
CALORIES: 183   CHOLESTEROL: 7 mg   SODIUM: 313 mg   FIBER: 6 g

Health tip:
Omit salt; use unsalted margarine instead of butter.
CALORIES: 183   CHOLESTEROL: 0 mg   SODIUM: 28 mg   FIBER: 6 g

---

———————◇———————

Rye English Muffins

Sixteen-year-old Jesse Weissman was my primary taster for these muffins. He loved them, but had a very legitimate criticism. He found (as did I) that the 3-inch muffin is just a little too small to remove easily from an ordinary toaster. If you can find a 4-inch-round cookie or biscuit cutter, use that, or toast the muffins in a toaster oven or under the broiler in your regular oven

> 1 package dry yeast
> ½ cup very warm water (105–115°F)
> 3 cups rye flour
> 1 tablespoon sugar
> 1 tablespoon caraway seeds

1½ teaspoons salt
1½ cups milk
¼ cup butter, melted
2 to 2½ cups all-purpose flour
Cornmeal

In a glass measuring cup, stir the yeast into water. Let stand until ¼ inch bubbly foam forms on top. (This foaming is called *proofing,* and if it doesn't happen it means that for some reason or other the yeast has not been activated. Discard this batch and try again, double checking the date on the yeast package and the temperature of the water.)

While yeast is proofing, in a large bowl, stir together the rye flour, sugar, caraway seeds, and salt. Stir in milk and melted butter. Stir in 1½ cups of the all-purpose flour. Turn dough onto a floured surface. Knead in as much of the remaining 1 cup all-purpose flour as necessary to form a dough that is fairly stiff and only barely sticky. Place dough in a greased bowl. Cover with greased plastic wrap. Set in a warm spot, out of drafts, until doubled in bulk. Punch dough down.

Generously sprinkle a work surface with cornmeal. Turn dough onto cornmeal and pat into a 12-inch circle. Using a 3-inch biscuit or cookie cutter, cut into 16 to 18 muffins. (Pat scraps together for an extra muffin, if you like.) Place muffins on aluminum foil or waxed paper, leaving 2 inches around each one. Cover lightly with greased plastic wrap and let rise until doubled in bulk.

Heat a large skillet or griddle until it is moderately hot and grease it lightly. Cook muffins a few at a time over medium heat until browned on both sides, about 7 minutes per side. (If your muffins seem to be browning much faster than this, reduce heat.) Cool muffins on wire racks, then split with a fork. The muffins are now ready to be toasted and enjoyed, or you may freeze them. No need to defrost before toasting.

MAKES 18 MUFFINS.
CALORIES: 151   CHOLESTEROL: 10 mg   SODIUM: 210 mg   FIBER: 3 g

Health tip:
Omit salt; use unsalted margarine instead of butter.
CALORIES: 151   CHOLESTEROL: 3 mg   SODIUM: 14 mg   FIBER: 3 g

———————— ◇ ————————

Crunchy Rye Bread

This bread is very dense and slightly sweet, with a hint of honey flavor. The combination of different flours and milk powder also makes it especially healthful.

> *½ cup very warm water (105–115°F)*
> *½ teaspoon sugar*
> *2 packages dry yeast*
> *2 to 2½ cups all-purpose flour*
> *1½ cups rye flour*
> *½ cup cornmeal*
> *½ cup soy flour*
> *½ cup rye flakes*
> *⅓ cup dry-milk powder*
> *2 teaspoons salt*
> *1 cup water*
> *½ cup honey*

Grease a baking sheet and set aside.

In a glass measuring cup, stir together the water and sugar. Stir in yeast and let stand until ¼ inch of white bubbly foam forms on top. (This foaming is called *proofing,* and if it doesn't happen it means that for one reason or other the yeast has not been activated. Discard this batch and try again, double checking the date on the yeast package and the temperature of the water.)

While yeast is proofing, in a large bowl, stir together ¾ cup of the all-purpose flour, rye flour, cornmeal, soy flour, rye flakes, milk powder, and salt. Stir in proofed-yeast mixture, water, and honey. Stir in 1 more cup all-purpose flour. Turn out onto a floured surface and knead in as much of the remaining all-purpose flour as necessary to make a dough that is no longer sticky. Place in a large greased bowl. Cover with greased plastic wrap. Set in a warm spot, out of drafts, until doubled in bulk, about 1½ hours.

Punch dough down and form into a round loaf. Place on prepared baking sheet. Cover lightly with greased plastic wrap and let rise until doubled in bulk.

Preheat oven to 350°F.

Bake for 40 minutes, or until loaf is browned on top and bottom. Remove from baking sheet and cool on a wire rack.

MAKES 1 LOAF (20 slices).
CALORIES: 124   CHOLESTEROL: 0 mg   SODIUM: 219 mg   FIBER: 3 g

Health tip:
Omit salt.
CALORIES: 124   CHOLESTEROL: 0 mg   SODIUM: 6 mg   FIBER: 3 g

———————— ◇ ————————

Dilled Rye-Beer Bread

Dill is the favorite herb of many people, me included, so I'm especially fond of this light delicious bread. It's wonderful spread with butter or for sandwiches.

½ cup very warm water (105–115°F)
½ teaspoon sugar
1 package dry yeast
3 cups rye flour
2 to 2¼ cups all-purpose flour
1 tablespoon dried dill weed
1 tablespoon salt
1 teaspoon dill seed (optional)
1 can (12 ounce) beer, room temperature

Grease a 9 × 5 × 3-inch loaf pan and set aside.

In a glass measuring cup, stir together the water and sugar. Stir in yeast and let stand until ¼ inch of white bubbly foam forms on top. (This foaming is called *proofing*, and if it doesn't happen it means that for one reason or other the yeast has not been activated. Discard this batch and try again, double checking the date on the yeast package and the temperature of the water.)

While yeast is proofing, in a large bowl, stir together rye flour, 1 cup of the all-purpose flour, dill weed, salt, and dill seed, if using. Stir in proofed-yeast mixture and beer. Stir in ½ cup more of the all-purpose flour.

Turn dough onto a floured surface and knead in as much of the remaining ¾ cup all-purpose flour as necessary to make a dough that is no longer sticky. Place in a large greased bowl and cover with greased plastic wrap. Set in a warm spot, out of drafts, until doubled in bulk, about 1½ hours.

Punch dough down and form into a 9-inch loaf. Place in prepared pan. Cover lightly with greased plastic wrap and let rise until doubled in bulk, about 40 minutes.

Preheat oven to 350°F.

Bake for 40 to 50 minutes, or until loaf is browned on top and bottom. Turn out of pan and cool on a wire rack.

MAKES 1 LOAF (16 slices).
CALORIES: 144   CHOLESTEROL: 0 mg   SODIUM: 402 mg   FIBER: 4 g

Health tip:
Omit salt; use light beer.
CALORIES: 142   CHOLESTEROL: 0 mg   SODIUM: 2 mg   FIBER: 4 g

Swedish Limpa Bread

In Sweden, this bread is call *vortlimpor* and it's traditionally baked for Christmas. The common denominator in all limpa (sometimes spelled limpe) bread seems to be rye flour, some sweetening, and some form of orange. Variations include the use of beer, caraway seeds, malt, anise, and many types of flour. This recipe is by no means a truly authentic version, as I'm sure that "authentic," in this case, must mean whatever your Swedish mother put into *her* loaf.

> ½ cup very warm water (105–115°F)
> ½ teaspoon sugar
> 2 packages dry yeast
> 3 cups rye flour
> 3 to 3½ cups all-purpose flour
> ½ cup firmly packed light- or dark-brown sugar
> 2 teaspoons salt
> 1 teaspoon ground cardamom (optional)
> 1 cup orange juice
> ½ cup water
> ½ cup butter, melted
> ¼ cup honey
> 2 tablespoons grated orange rind

Grease two baking sheets and set aside.

In a glass measuring cup, stir together the warm water and sugar. Stir in yeast and let stand until ¼ inch of white bubbly foam forms on top. (This is called *proofing*, and if it doesn't happen it means that for some reason or other the yeast has not been activated. Discard this batch and try again, double checking the date on the yeast package and the temperature of the water.)

While yeast is proofing, in a large bowl, stir together rye flour, 1 cup of the all-purpose flour, brown sugar, salt, and cardamom, if using. Stir in proofed-yeast mixture, orange juice, water, butter, honey, and orange rind. Stir in 1¼ cups more all-purpose flour to form a dough that is easy to handle.

Turn dough out onto a floured surface and knead in as much of the remaining 1¼ cups all-purpose flour as necessary to make a dough that is no longer sticky. Place in a large greased bowl. Cover with greased plastic wrap. Set in a warm spot, out of drafts, until doubled in bulk, about 1 hour.

Punch dough down and form into two round loaves. Place on

prepared baking sheets. Cover lightly with greased plastic wrap and let rise until doubled in bulk.

Preheat oven to 350°F.

Bake for 40 to 50 minutes, or until loaves are browned on top and bottom. Remove from sheets and cool on wire racks.

MAKES 2 LOAVES (16 slices per loaf).
CALORIES: 128   CHOLESTEROL: 8 mg   SODIUM: 159 mg   FIBER: 2 g

Health tip:
Omit brown sugar and salt; use unsalted margarine instead of butter.
CALORIES: 128   CHOLESTEROL: 0 mg   SODIUM: 8 mg   FIBER: 2 g

—————— ◇ ——————

Garlic-Rye Crackers

Plan on serving these crisp little crackers soon after they're baked or store in a tightly covered container in the refrigerator. If necessary, you can recrisp them in the oven for a few minutes. These neat little crackers, which will remind you of melba toast, are great to serve with cheese, or are delicious to munch on as is.

2 tablespoons butter, very soft, but not melted
2 cloves garlic, minced
Herbs, as desired
4 very-thin slices rye bread (or you can use melba rye)

Preheat oven to 400°F.

In a small bowl, stir together butter and garlic. You can also stir in any herb that you like: thyme or basil, for instance.

Lightly brush each side of bread with a little of the butter mixture. Using a serrated knife, cut each slice into 8 wedges. Place wedges in a single layer on a baking sheet.

Bake for 5 minutes, then turn bread over and bake for 3 to 5 minutes longer, or until lightly browned and crispy. Remove from baking pans and cool on wire racks.

MAKES 32 CRACKERS.
CALORIES: 13   CHOLESTEROL: 2 mg   SODIUM: 23 mg   FIBER: 0 g

Health tip:
Use unsalted margarine instead of butter.
CALORIES: 13   CHOLESTEROL: 0 mg   SODIUM: 17 mg   FIBER: 0 g

——— ◇ ———

Mini Rye-Soda Breads

This recipe is actually a cross between Irish soda bread and scones. It is slightly denser than soda bread, and has the tenderness of a scone without the sweetness.

1 cup rye flour
1 cup all-purpose flour
½ cup raisins
1 tablespoon sugar
1 tablespoon caraway seeds
1 teaspoon baking soda
1 teaspoon baking powder
1 teaspoon salt
¼ teaspoon cream of tartar
¾ cup buttermilk
3 tablespoons melted butter

Preheat oven to 350°F.

Grease two baking sheets and set aside.

In a large bowl, stir together both kinds of flour, raisins, sugar, caraway seeds, baking soda, baking powder, salt, and cream of tartar. Stir in buttermilk and melted butter. Turn dough onto a floured surface and knead 12 times.

Cut dough into four equal pieces and shape each piece into a round loaf. Place on baking sheets. Using a sharp knife, cut an "X" in the top of each loaf.

Bake for 35 to 40 minutes, or until lightly browned. Remove from baking sheets and cool on wire racks.

SERVES 8.

CALORIES: 195   CHOLESTEROL: 12 mg   SODIUM: 470 mg   FIBER: 3 g

Health tip:

Omit salt; substitute unsalted margarine for butter.

CALORIES: 195   CHOLESTEROL: 1 mg   SODIUM: 172 mg   FIBER: 3 g

———————◇———————

Rye Waffles

These waffles are not crispy, but they are delicious. They also freeze nicely and reheat well in the microwave oven (no small thing).

1 cup all-purpose flour
⅔ cup rye flour
⅓ cup honey-flavored wheat germ
¼ cup cornmeal
1 tablespoon baking powder
1 teaspoon salt
2 eggs, separated
1⅓ cups milk
½ cup butter, melted
⅓ cup honey

Preheat and grease waffle iron as manufacturer directs.

In a large bowl, stir together both kinds of flour, wheat germ, cornmeal, baking powder, and salt. Beat together egg yolks, milk, butter, and honey. Stir into flour mixture.

In a clean, grease-free, medium-size bowl, with clean beaters, beat egg whites until stiff peaks form when beaters are lifted. Fold whites into batter.

Pour about 1 cup of the batter into the waffle iron. Close and bake until steaming stops, about 5 minutes, or until well browned.

MAKES 12 SERVINGS
CALORIES: 202   CHOLESTEROL: 59 mg   SODIUM: 350 mg   FIBER: 2 g

Health tip:
Omit salt; use unsalted margarine instead of butter; substitute 1-percent milk for whole milk.
CALORIES: 195   CHOLESTEROL: 35 mg   SODIUM: 168 mg   FIBER: 2 g

WILD RICE

(Zizania aquatica)

Wild rice is not a rice, or even a grain, for that matter, but a seed from an aquatic grass native to the Great Lakes region of North America. However, I'm including it as a grain in this book because it's cooked and used in many of the same ways as most true grains.

Much of the wild rice available these days is cultivated in paddies, but some of it is still harvested by Native Americans, who gather the grain using canoes the same way they've been doing it for centuries.

Even using the tools and agricultural know-how of the twentieth century, wild rice remains a frustratingly difficult crop to grow and harvest, which is ultimately reflected in the price paid for it. Consequently, wild rice has long been considered a gourmet item to be served on *very* special occasions. More often than not it is mixed with less-expensive rices and eaten at less auspicious meals.

Types of Wild Rice Available

There is only one type of pure wild rice. It is never processed more than removing the hull. Its shape is similar to long-grain rice, but it is usually even longer. The color can range from medium-brown to almost-black, but most wild rice is dark brown.

Wild rice is graded into three categories:

Select: The grains are short, about ⅜ inch or less, are not uniform in size, and will most likely contain some broken grains.

Extra-fancy: The grains are about ½ inch long and uniform in size. Very few of the grains are broken.

Giant: The grains are about 1 inch long, uniform in size, and there are few, if any, broken grains.

As you might guess, the grade determines the price, with select being the least expensive and giant being the most expensive. Packages may be labeled with other terminology, such as "premium" or "finest quality," but you can pretty easily tell which grade you're buying by simply looking at the rice (most is sold in plastic bags or boxes with windows) and checking for size, uniformity, and breakage.

As far as taste and nutrition go, all grades of wild rice are about the same and can be used interchangeably.

The recipes in this chapter were tested with extra-fancy wild rice

Texture and Flavor

Wild rice has a distinct earthy, or woodsy, flavor that is best described as being reminiscent of a walk in the woods just after a rain storm. Some people also perceive a slight nuttiness to the taste, as well.

As it cooks, the grains burst open to reveal a grey-white interior. The texture is dense, a bit chewy, and extremely pleasant.

Compatible Foods, Herbs, and Spices

Wild rice goes especially well with other earthy foods, such as wild game, mushrooms, and beans. The flavor, though very distinct, is also very versatile, so it can also be used successfully with both subtle herbs and pungent spices

Meat, poultry, and fish are also good companions for wild rice, as well as dairy products, fruits, vegetables, and nuts. You can also combine wild rice with other starchy foods, especially white or brown rice.

If you find the flavor of wild rice a little too strong for your taste, or too expensive for your budget, you can subdue the flavor and lower the cost of a recipe by replacing part of the wild rice called for in these and other recipes with white rice.

Availability

Wild rice is now available in most supermarkets. Look in the gourmet-foods section if it is not with the rice. It is also sold in fancy-food stores, some health-food stores, and by mail-order from growers or distributors (see page 21).

Nutritional Content

It's rare when something that is so good is also good for you, but the nutritional profile of wild rice is very impressive. It has more protein and is higher in amino acids, lysine, and methionine than true grains. It is also high in fiber, since only the hull has been removed, and is also a good source of B vitamins, iron, phosphorous, magnesium, calcium, and zinc.

Substitutions

Wehani brown rice: This comes the closest to the flavor and consistency of wild rice, and can be used any time wild rice is called for. However, it's also expensive, and is even harder to find.

White rice: I prefer the flavor of long-grain white rice rather than brown rice as a substitute for wild rice. In recipes calling for raw wild rice, you will have to reduce the cooking time significantly.

Brown rice: Use either the short- or long-grain variety. The flavor of brown rice is close enough to wild rice to be compatible with recipes developed for wild rice. The cooking times are also similar.

Other acceptable substitutes (in order of preference): Oat groats, wheat berries, bulgur, and couscous.

Basic Cooking Instructions

Please read the section *About Cooking Grains* beginning on page 7.

Instructions are given for both 1 cup of wild rice and a 4-ounce package. I have also included instructions for cooking wild rice and brown or white rice together.

The microwave methods for cooking wild rice were tested in a 650-watt oven.

Stove-top method for 1 cup:

2½ cups water
¾ teaspoon salt
1 cup wild rice, rinsed

Bring the water and salt to a boil over high heat in a 2-quart covered saucepan. Stir in rice and return to boiling.

Reduce heat and simmer, covered, for 55 minutes, or until most of the liquid has been absorbed. Remove from heat and let stand, covered, for 10 minutes. Fluff with a fork.

MAKES 2⅔ CUPS.

Stove-top method for 4-ounce package:

1½ cups water
¼ teaspoon salt
4-ounce package wild rice, rinsed

Bring the water and salt to a boil over high heat in a 1½-quart covered saucepan. Stir in wild rice and return to boiling. Reduce heat and simmer, covered, for 55 minutes, or until most of the liquid has been absorbed. Remove from heat and let stand, covered, for 10 minutes. Fluff with a fork.

MAKES 2⅓ CUPS.

Microwave method for 1 cup:

> 2½ cups water
> 1 cup wild rice, rinsed
> ¾ teaspoon salt

Place the water in a 3-quart, microwave-safe bowl. Cover with waxed paper. Microwave on high (100% power) for 5 minutes. Stir in wild rice and salt. Recover with waxed paper and microwave on high for 5 minutes. Microwave on medium (50% power), still covered with waxed paper, for 45 minutes, rotating dish once, if necessary. Let stand 5 minutes. Fluff with a fork.

MAKES 3¼ CUPS.

Microwave method for 4-ounce package:

> 1½ cups water
> 4-ounce package wild rice, rinsed
> ¼ teaspoon salt

Place the water in a 2-quart, microwave-safe bowl. Cover with waxed paper. Microwave on high (100% power) for 3 minutes. Stir in wild rice and salt. Recover with waxed paper and microwave on high for 4 minutes. Microwave on medium (50% power), still covered with waxed paper, for 35 minutes, rotating dish once, if necessary. Let stand 5 minutes. Fluff with a fork.

MAKES 2 CUPS.

To Cook Wild Rice and Brown or White Rice Together

Wild rice and brown rice: Since the amounts and cooking times of wild rice and brown rice are similar, substitute as much brown rice as you like for wild rice. Add rinsed wild rice to the water when it boils and simmer for 15 minutes. Add brown rice and simmer for 45 minutes longer.

Wild rice and white rice: Simmer rinsed wild rice for 30 minutes after adding to boiling water. Add white rice and simmer for 25 minutes longer. Substitute as much white rice for wild rice as you like.

Cooking Note: Since many recipes call for wild rice to be cooked in a flavored broth, you should know that wild rice takes longer to cook in broth than it does in water. Also, use about ¼ cup less broth than water.

Reheating

Wild rice does not stiffen after refrigeration and so does not have to be reheated before adding it to a salad or other recipes that will be served chilled or at room temperature. Steam or reheat in the microwave oven, if desired.

WILD RICE RECIPES

(*indicates easy recipe.)

————————— ◇ —————————

Duck Bouillon with Wild Rice and Mushrooms
Chestnut-and-Wild-Rice Soup
An Omelet with Wild-Rice-and-Mushroom Filling*
Cajun Shrimp*
Creamy Scallops and Leeks with Wild Rice*
Inside-Out Beef Wellington
Wild Oxtail Stew*
Stuffed Cornish Game Hens*
Apple-and-Wild-Rice Stuffing*
Salade de Provence*
Tropical-Fruit-and-Wild-Rice Salad*
Wild Rice with Fennel and Endive*
Wild-Rice Slaw*
Mandarin-Orange-and-Wild-Rice Salad*
Black-White-and-Red Salad (with a Touch of Green)*
Summery Wild-Rice-and-Cucumber Salad*
An Elegant Fruit-and-Vegetable Salad*
Wild Rice and Pasta with a Creamy Tomato Sauce*
Lentils and Wild Rice*
White-and-Wild Rice*
Rice Trio with Peas*
Wild Rice with Summer Squash*
Southern-Style Wild Rice with Mushrooms*
Green Beans, Shiitake Mushrooms, and Wild Rice*
Wild Rice with Red and Yellow Peppers*
Wild-Rice Crêpes with Apricot Sauce

---◇---

Duck Bouillon with Wild Rice and Mushrooms

I can't think of a more elegant starter for a super-festive meal than this bouillon. The duck will not go to waste. Chill it and use it in salads and for sandwiches.

12 cups water
5-pound duck
2 medium leeks, trimmed and thoroughly rinsed
3 ribs celery
3 medium carrots, peeled
2 medium parsnips, peeled
1 large bunch parsley, rinsed
2 cups sliced mushrooms (I use shiitake mushrooms, but you can use
   any exotic mushroom you like, or even cultivated white button
   mushrooms)
¼ cup wild rice, rinsed
½ teaspoon salt

In an 8-quart soup pot, combine the water, duck (include the neck, heart, and gizzard, but not the liver), leeks, celery, carrots, and parsnips. Bring to a boil. Reduce heat and simmer, uncovered, for 1½ hours. Add parsley and simmer for 30 minutes longer.

Remove duck, giblets, and vegetables from pot. Place them in a colander and let the cooking liquid drip back into the pot. Continue to simmer for 30 minutes longer, or until soup is reduced to 8 cups. Skim off fat. (If you have the time, the best way to do this is to chill the soup in the pot overnight, then lift off the congealed fat and continue with the recipe the next day.)

Stir in mushrooms, rice, and salt. Simmer, uncovered, for 1 hour longer.

SERVES 6 TO 8.
CALORIES: 80   CHOLESTEROL: 5 mg   SODIUM: 177 mg   FIBER: .5 g

Health tip:
Omit salt.
CALORIES: 80   cholesterol: 5 mg   SODIUM: 0 mg   FIBER: .5 g

———————————— ◊ ————————————

Chestnut-and-Wild-Rice Soup

This soup was a great hit when I served it last New Year's Eve. It's creamy and has a slightly sweet flavor that my guests found unusual and delicious. The wild rice adds a slightly chewy element, even though the soup is pureed.

2 tablespoons butter
⅔ cup chopped onion
2 cans (13¾ ounces each) ready-to-serve chicken broth or
    3½ cups vegetable broth (see page 19)
1 cup water
1½ cups cooked peeled chestnuts (you can buy these in a can or a jar,
    already cooked and peeled, or you can do this yourself by baking or
    boiling the chestnuts until tender)
⅓ cup wild rice, rinsed
½ cup whipping cream
2 tablespoons dry or medium-dry sherry
¼ teaspoon salt

In a 4-quart saucepan, melt the butter over medium-high heat. Add onion and cook, stirring frequently, until softened. Add broth and water and bring to a boil. Add chestnuts and wild rice. Reduce heat and simmer, covered, for 1 hour and 15 minutes. Remove from heat to cool slightly.

Ladle about one-third of the soup mixture into the container of an electric blender or food processor. (I prefer the blender in this case.) Cover and process until soup is pureed, but the wild rice is still in visible pieces. Pour into a large bowl. Continue processing until all of the soup has been pureed.

Stir cream, sherry, and salt into soup. Reheat before serving.

SERVES 6.
CALORIES: 248   CHOLESTEROL: 38 mg   SODIUM: 337 mg   FIBER: 5 g

---

Health tip:
Use unsalted margarine instead of butter, and half-and-half instead of cream. Omit salt.
CALORIES: 205   CHOLESTEROL: 8 mg   SODIUM: 310 mg   FIBER: 5 g

---◇---

An Omelet with Wild-Rice-and-Mushroom Filling

Wild rice and mushrooms make this omelet-for-two very special. A bottle of champagne to accompany it wouldn't be a bad idea, either. (If you like, the rice-and-mushroom mixture can be used as a savory filling for the crêpes recipe given on page 377.) Although I've designated this recipe as easy, if you've never cooked an omelet before, a little practice may be necessary in order to produce a perfectly gorgeous omelet every time.

3 tablespoons butter, divided
½ cup sliced leek, white and light-green parts only
2 cups sliced mushrooms
⅔ cup cooked wild rice
3 tablespoons herb-and-garlic triple–cream cheese (Boursin)
6 eggs
6 tablespoons water
½ teaspoon salt
¼ teaspoon pepper
Snipped chives, for garnish (optional)

Melt 1 tablespoon of the butter in a large skillet over medium-high heat. Add leek and cook, stirring, until softened. Add mushrooms and cook stirring and tossing, until softened. Stir in wild rice and cheese and continue to cook, stirring, until rice is warm and cheese is melted. Set aside.

Break eggs into a medium bowl. Add water, salt, and pepper. Stir together with a fork until completely blended. *Do not beat the eggs.* Melt 1 tablespoon of the butter in a medium-size nonstick skillet over medium-high heat. When it is foamy, pour in half the egg mixture. As the edges set, tilt the pan and lift eggs with a pancake turner so that the uncooked egg can flow underneath. While the top is still moist, spoon half of the wild-rice filling over the left side of the omelet (if you're right handed, or over the right side of the omelet if you're left-handed). Lift the right (or left) side of the omelet up with the pancake turner and fold it over part of the filling. Tilt pan and turn omelet upside down onto a warm plate. Repeat with remaining butter, eggs, and filling. Scatter a few snipped chives over tops of omelets, if you like.

SERVES 2.

CALORIES: 469   CHOLESTEROL: 695 mg   SODIUM: 1485 mg   FIBER: 2 g

Health tip:
Omit salt. Cholesterol-watchers should skip this dish.

CALORIES: 469   CHOLESTEROL: 695 mg   SODIUM: 419 mg   FIBER: 2 g

---

◇

Cajun Shrimp

Lorraine Klein was one of my primary tasters for the recipes in this book. Although she says she's not too fond of seafood, she did have a second portion of this and thought it was divine.

> 1½ pounds jumbo shrimp, peeled and deveined
> 1 tablespoon plus 1 teaspoon Cajun seasoning or spicy seafood
>   seasoning (or you can use spicy seasoned salt)
> ¼ cup butter, divided
> ½ cup chopped onion
> ½ cup chopped celery
> 2 tablespoons lemon juice
> 2 cups cooked wild rice

In a medium-size bowl, toss shrimp with seasoning. Melt 2 tablespoons of the butter in a large skillet over medium heat. Add shrimp and cook, stirring, until they turn pink and are just cooked through (there's almost nothing tougher than an overcooked shrimp), about 4 minutes. Remove shrimp from skillet and set aside.

Melt remaining 2 tablespoons butter in the same skillet, scraping up all the seasonings that cling to the bottom and side. Add onion and celery and cook, stirring frequently, until softened. Stir in lemon juice. Stir in wild rice and reserved shrimp and cook, stirring, just until heated through.

SERVES 4.

CALORIES: 325   CHOLESTEROL: 203 mg   SODIUM: 2412 mg   FIBER: 3 g

Health tip:
Use 2 tablespoons unsalted margarine instead of butter.

CALORIES: 273   CHOLESTEROL: 172 mg   SODIUM: 2322 mg   FIBER: 3 g

—————◇—————

Creamy Scallops and Leeks with Wild Rice

When I'm not writing cookbooks, I work as a food stylist for magazines and advertisers when they photograph food. Often I bring dishes that I've made to work with me to get the opinion of other food professionals. The day I brought this to a photography session for Parents Magazine, Abby Johnson, the associate food editor, liked it so much that she asked for the recipe. I consider that a very high compliment.

2 tablespoons butter
¾ cup sliced leek, both white and green parts
1½ cups sliced mushrooms
1 pound bay scallops (or sea scallops cut into quarters)
2 tablespoons chopped parsley
Pinch crumbled thyme
¼ cup dry white wine
½ cup heavy cream
⅛ teaspoon salt
Pinch ground red pepper
2 cups cooked wild rice

Melt the butter in a large skillet over medium-high heat. Add leek and cook, stirring, until softened. Add mushrooms and cook, stirring and tossing, until softened. Stir in scallops, parsley, and thyme. Cook, stirring, until scallops are opaque, about 3 minutes. Using a slotted spoon, remove the scallops and vegetables from skillet. Stir wine then cream into juices remaining in skillet. Bring to a boil over high heat and cook until the entire surface of the liquid is furiously bubbling and the cream has turn a light beige, 3 to 4 minutes.

Return scallops and vegetables to skillet. Stir in salt and red pepper. Cook, stirring, until scallops and vegetables are heated through. At this point you can stir the wild rice into the scallop mixture, or you can serve the scallop mixture on a bed of reheated wild rice.

SERVES 4.
CALORIES: 373   CHOLESTEROL: 93 mg   SODIUM: 516 mg   FIBER: 4 g

Health tip:
Omit salt and don't eat too much.
CALORIES: 373   CHOLESTEROL: 93 mg   SODIUM: 250 mg   FIBER: 4 g

— ◇ —

Inside-Out Beef Wellington

Back in the days before we worried about cholesterol and saturated fat, beef Wellington starred at many important events. It was made with a whole beef tenderloin filet (the most tender and pricey part of the beef), which was spread with a pâté de foie gras, covered with puff pastry, and baked. The pastry was lightly browned and flaky, and the pâté-flavored beef was rare and juicy. More often than not, a brown sauce, made with wine and truffles, was served, too. It stands to reason that any recipe that was so popular and so enduring had to be out of this world, and lately this great recipe has enjoyed a comeback. My version of beef Wellington uses a less-costly boneless sirloin steak, and is stuffed with a mixture of wild rice and pâté. Keep the servings reasonably small and expect a lot of compliments.

2 tablespoons butter
2 tablespoons minced shallot or the white part of a scallion
1 cup cooked wild rice
⅓ cup of smooth creamy liver pâté you can afford (This is sometimes
*   called a liver mousse. Any smooth, creamy pâté will work,*
*   and foie gras would be lovely! Just make sure you don't use a*
*   coarse dry pâté, such as a pâté de campagne, for the pâté*
*   must melt in this recipe.)*
1 tablespoon chopped parsley
1¾ pound boneless sirloin steak, about 1½ inches thick
¼ teaspoon salt
⅛ teaspoon pepper

Preheat oven to 350°F.

Heat the butter in a small skillet. Add shallot and cook, stirring, until softened. Remove skillet from heat and stir in wild rice, pâté, and parsley. Set aside.

Working with a long, sharp knife, cut the steak almost in half, lengthwise. (Just imagine that you are cutting the steak into two thinner steaks. Place your hand flat on top of the steak and slice through the meat halfway down between your hand and the cutting surface. Leave about ½ inch uncut so that you can open the steak like a book.) Open the steak and sprinkle the cut surface with salt and pepper. Spread rice mixture over one half of the cut surface, then fold the other half over it, closing the steak back into its original shape. Fasten the cut edge with wooden picks or skewers.

Place the stuffed steak in a shallow roasting pan.

Bake for 40 minutes for rare, or longer for medium-done. Let stand 10 minutes before slicing.

SERVES 6.
CALORIES: 494   CHOLESTEROL: 129 mg   SODIUM: 334 mg   FIBER: 1 g

Health tip:
Omit salt and pâté; use unsalted margarine instead of butter.
CALORIES: 453   CHOLESTEROL: 101 mg   SODIUM: 91 mg   FIBER: 1 g

—————◇—————

Wild Oxtail Stew

There's an old saying that the meat is sweetest closest to the bone. So, even if you think you don't like oxtail, you owe it to yourself to try it, for the flavor of the meat is simply wonderful. Oxtail is difficult to eat. The best way is simply to pick the pieces up in your fingers and nibble the last bits of meat that cling to the bone. Or you can substitute lean short ribs for the oxtail.

2 tablespoons vegetable oil
2½ pounds oxtail (it will be cut in short lengths) or lean short ribs
1½ cups chopped onion
2 cloves garlic, minced
2 cups water
1 cup dry red wine
1 can (6 ounce) tomato paste
1 bay leaf
½ teaspoon crumbled marjoram
¼ teaspoon crumbled rosemary
1½ teaspoons salt
¼ teaspoon pepper
2 cups sliced carrot
¾ cup wild rice, rinsed

In a large heavy saucepan or Dutch oven, heat the oil over medium-high heat. Add oxtail pieces and cook, turning and adjusting heat, until well browned. Add onion and garlic and cook, stirring, until softened. Stir in water, wine, tomato paste, bay leaf, marjoram, rosemary, salt, and pepper. Bring to a boil. Lower heat and simmer, covered, for 1 hour. Stir in carrot and wild rice. Cover and simmer for 1 hour longer. Remove bay leaf before serving.

SERVES 4.
CALORIES: 740   CHOLESTEROL: 128 mg   SODIUM: 679 mg   FIBER: 5 g

Health tip:
Omit salt.
CALORIES: 740   CHOLESTEROL: 128 mg   SODIUM: 140 mg   FIBER: 5 g

———————— ◇ ————————

Apple-and-Wild-Rice Stuffing

Use this stuffing to fill a roasting chicken or 6 to 8 Cornish hens. Double the recipe to stuff a turkey. (And, although I haven't tried it, I expect that this would also be a wonderful filling for duck or goose.)

3 tablespoons butter
2 tablespoons minced shallot
1 cup chopped peeled apple (use a tart crisp apple, such as Granny
    Smith or McIntosh)
1/3 cup finely chopped celery
1/2 teaspoon salt
1/4 teaspoon crumbled rosemary
1/4 teaspoon crumbled thyme
1/8 teaspoon pepper
3 cups bread cubes (about 4 slices of white bread)
1 cup cooked wild rice
2 tablespoons chopped parsley

In a medium-size skillet, melt the butter over medium heat. Add shallot and cook, stirring, until softened. Add apple, celery, salt, rosemary, thyme, and pepper. Cook, stirring, until apple is softened. Remove skillet from heat. Stir in bread cubes, then wild rice and parsley, and toss gently until completely combined.

(Nutrition information is based on 1/2 cup stuffing.)

MAKES 3 1/2 CUPS.
CALORIES: 143   CHOLESTEROL: 15 mg   SODIUM: 428 mg   FIBER: 2 g

Health tip:
Omit salt; use a nonstick skillet, substituting 2 teaspoons unsalted margarine for butter.
CALORIES: 113   CHOLESTEROL: 0 mg   SODIUM: 142 mg   FIBER: 2 g

———— ◇ ————

Stuffed Cornish Game Hens

You can also use this elegant stuffing to fill a 3- to 4-pound broiler-fryer chicken. Or you can double the recipe for an even bigger bird. Just use the liver that comes with whatever poultry you're using when you make the stuffing.

2 slices bacon, cut into 1-inch pieces
½ cup chopped onion
⅓ cup chopped celery
Livers from hens, finely chopped
1 cup cooked wild rice
1 tablespoon chopped parsley
½ teaspoon salt
¼ teaspoon crumbled thyme
¼ teaspoon pepper
4 small or 2 large (total weight should be about 4 pounds) Cornish
*   game hens*
Additional salt and pepper

Preheat oven to 350°F.

In a medium-size skillet, cook the bacon until crisp. Remove bacon and drain on paper towels.

Add onion and celery to the bacon fat left in the skillet. Cook, stirring, until softened. Add liver and cook, stirring, just until cooked through. Remove from heat and stir in rice, parsley, salt, thyme, and pepper.

Skewer the skin at the neck end of the hens to close the opening. Place about ½ cup of the stuffing in the body cavity of each bird, then skewer the skin together to close the vent. (You can use wooden picks for this job.) Sprinkle hens with salt and pepper. Place in a roasting pan that is large enough to hold the hens comfortably.

Bake for 50 to 60 minutes, or until juices run clear when hens are pierced with a fork.

SERVES 4.

CALORIES: 345   CHOLESTEROL: 180 mg   SODIUM: 414 mg   FIBER: 2 g

Health tip:

Omit bacon and liver and use 2 teaspoons oil in a nonstick skillet to cook vegetables. Omit salt.

CALORIES: 322   CHOLESTEROL: 87 mg   SODIUM: 90 mg   FIBER: 2 g

⎯⎯⎯⎯⎯⎯⎯⎯ ◇ ⎯⎯⎯⎯⎯⎯⎯⎯

Salade de Provence

Since the olives contribute so much to the character of this salad, I would advise you to make the effort to find an olive that is a little more unique than the canned supermarket variety. If you can get to a fancy-food store, you will undoubtedly find an interesting selection of bottled, canned and loose olives. Try and find a small French olive, such as a black Nicoise, that is usually oval and slightly tapered at one end. Or you could substitute small Greek or Italian olives. Most, if not all, of these olives will have pits, but that's life.

2 cups cooked and cooled wild rice
½ cup diced or crumbled goat cheese (I use part of a log of Montrachet)
⅓ cup small French olives (see above)
3 tablespoons Provence herb-flavored oil (or olive oil, plus ¼ teaspoon
*   herbes de Provence or fines herbes)*
1 tablespoon Cabernet-wine vinegar or red-wine vinegar
2 teaspoons lemon juice
2 teaspoons minced shallot
1 teaspoon Dijon mustard
Mixed salad greens (as many colors, flavor, and textures and you can
*   find)*

In a large bowl, toss the wild rice with cheese and olives.

In a small bowl, whisk together the oil, vinegar, lemon juice, shallot, and mustard until completely combined.

Pour dressing over rice mixture and toss gently until well mixed. Spoon onto a bed of mixed salad greens.

SERVES 4.
CALORIES: 268   CHOLESTEROL: 33 mg   SODIUM: 610 mg   FIBER: 3 g

Health tip:
Use a low-fat goat cheese and only half of the dressing.
CALORIES: 208   CHOLESTEROL: 26 mg   SODIUM: 352 mg   FIBER: 3 g

————————— ◇ —————————

Tropical-Fruit-and-Wild-Rice Salad

The impact this salad will have depends upon locating exotic fruits to put in it. I like to use a pink Hawaiian papaya, when I can find it, or otherwise I substitute a more ordinary papaya (peak season, May through September). Kiwifruit, from California or New Zealand, is available almost all the time. Finding a feijoa may give you a little trouble, but what you are looking for is a little dark-skinned fruit (the skin is similar to an avocado) that looks something like a kiwi. The feijoa is intensely aromatic, with a flavor that will remind you of a combination of pineapple, pear, and banana. The flesh is creamy-white and has a texture something like a pear.

1 cup cooked and cooled wild rice
1 cup diced papaya
1 kiwifruit, peeled and diced
1 feijoa, peeled and diced (if you can't find a feijoa, use another kiwi)
⅓ cup chopped pecans
1 tablespoon vegetable oil
2 teaspoons red-wine vinegar
¼ teaspoon salt

In a medium-size bowl, combine the wild rice, papaya, kiwifruit, feijoa, and pecans.

In a cup, mix together the oil, vinegar, and salt and pour over wild-rice mixture. Toss gently until well combined.

SERVES 4.
CALORIES: 186   CHOLESTEROL: 0 mg   SODIUM: 237 mg   FIBER: 4 g

Health tip:
Omit salt.
CALORIES: 180   CHOLESTEROL: 0 mg   SODIUM: 4 mg   FIBER: 4 g

———————— ◇ ————————

Wild Rice with Fennel and Endive

Fennel has a distinct licorice flavor that many people love, but some don't. If you fall into the second category, or can't find fennel, substitute celery.

¼ cup sliced almonds
2 cups cooked and cooled wild rice
1 cup sliced fennel
1 Belgian endive, cut into bite-size pieces
½ cup chopped dried fig
1 small red onion, thinly sliced
3 tablespoons olive oil
2 tablespoons lemon juice
1 tablespoon white-wine vinegar
½ clove garlic, minced
¼ teaspoon herbes de Provence or fines herbes
Leaf lettuce (optional)

Preheat oven to 350°F.
Place almonds on a baking sheet. Bake for 10 minutes, stirring once. Set aside.
In a large bowl, combine the wild rice, fennel, endive, fig, and onion.
In a small bowl, stir together the oil, lemon juice, vinegar, garlic, and fines herbes. Pour dressing over wild-rice mixture and toss gently until well combined. Serve over lettuce leaves, if you like, sprinkled with almonds.

SERVES 4.
CALORIES: 288   CHOLESTEROL: 0 mg   SODIUM: 238 mg   FIBER: 7 g

Health tip:
Use half the amount of dressing, diluting it with 1 tablespoon orange juice to make it go further.
CALORIES: 244   CHOLESTEROL: 0 mg   SODIUM: 38 mg   FIBER: 7 g

Wild-Rice Slaw

Wild rice gives this fairly typical slaw a lot of body and infinitely more interest. The parsnip adds a lovely fresh flavor, so please don't be tempted to leave it out.

2 cups chopped cabbage
1 cup cooked and cooled wild rice
½ cup shredded carrot
½ cup shredded parsnip
¼ cup chopped parsley
¼ cup mayonnaise
¼ cup sour cream
¼ cup sliced scallion, both white and green parts
1 teaspoon white vinegar
½ teaspoon salt
¼ teaspoon pepper

In a large bowl, combine cabbage, wild rice, carrot, parsnip, and parsley.

In a small bowl, stir together mayonnaise, sour cream, scallion, vinegar, salt, and pepper. Pour over wild-rice mixture and toss gently until completely combined.

SERVES 6.

CALORIES: 136 CHOLESTEROL: 10 mg SODIUM: 312 mg FIBER: 3 g

Health tip:
Use ½ cup reduced-calorie mayonnaise instead of regular mayonnaise and sour cream; omit salt.

CALORIES: 96 CHOLESTEROL: 5 mg SODIUM: 88 MG FIBER: 3 g

————— ◇ —————

Mandarin-Orange-and-Wild-Rice Salad

Mandarin-orange sections look pretty in this salad, and their sweet-and-sour flavor contrasts nicely with the taste and texture of wild rice.

> *2 cups cooked and cooled wild rice*
> *1 can (10 ounce) mandarin-orange sections, drained*
> *½ cup chopped walnuts*
> *2 tablespoons walnut oil or vegetable oil*
> *2 tablespoons orange juice*
> *1 tablespoon raspberry vinegar or cider vinegar*

In a large bowl, toss the wild rice, orange sections, and walnuts.

In a cup, stir together the oil, orange juice, and vinegar. Pour over wild-rice mixture and toss gently until completely combined.

SERVES 6.
CALORIES: 197   CHOLESTEROL: 0 mg   SODIUM: 138 mg   FIBER: 3 g

Health tip:
Use half the amount of dressing.
CALORIES: 176   CHOLESTEROL: 0 mg   SODIUM: 5 mg   FIBER: 3 g

---

———————◇———————

Black-White-and-Red Salad
(with a Touch of Green)

This salad has just the right amount of crispy stuff and mushy stuff, all in the right flavors. It makes a good main-course salad, as well as a side salad.

1 can (19 ounce) cannellini (white kidney beans), drained
1½ cups cooked and cooled wild rice
1 cup chopped red bell pepper
¼ cup sliced scallion, both white and green parts
2 tablespoons olive oil
1 tablespoon vegetable oil
1 tablespoon cider vinegar
1 tablespoon lemon juice
2 teaspoons spicy brown mustard
1 clove garlic, minced
½ teaspoon salt
⅛ teaspoon pepper

In a large bowl, toss together the beans, wild rice, red bell pepper, and scallion.

In a small bowl, stir together the olive oil, vegetable oil, vinegar, lemon juice, mustard, garlic, salt, and pepper. Pour over wild-rice mixture and toss gently until completely combined.

SERVES 8 (as a side dish).
CALORIES: 140   CHOLESTEROL: 0 mg   SODIUM: 460 mg   FIBER: 6 g

Health tip:
Omit salt.
CALORIES: 140   CHOLESTEROL: 0 mg   SODIUM: 252 mg   FIBER: 6 g

———————— ◇ ————————

Summery Wild-Rice-and-Cucumber Salad

Cucumber, dill, and radish are all fresh, summery flavors, and when you combine them with a light and creamy yogurt dressing, they're guaranteed to make you feel as "cool as a cucumber" on a hot day.

1½ cups chopped peeled or unpeeled cucumber
1 cup cooked and cooled wild rice
½ cup sliced radish
¼ cup sliced scallion, both white and green parts
⅓ cup plain yogurt
2 tablespoons mayonnaise
2 tablespoons snipped fresh dill or
     1 tablespoon dried dill weed
¼ teaspoon grated lemon rind
¼ teaspoon salt
⅛ teaspoon pepper

In a large bowl, combine the cucumber, wild rice, radish, and scallion.

In a small bowl, stir together the yogurt, mayonnaise, dill, lemon rind, salt, and pepper. Pour over wild-rice mixture and toss gently until completely combined.

SERVES 4.
CALORIES: 242   CHOLESTEROL: 4 mg   SODIUM: 866 mg   FIBER: 2 g

Health tip:
Use reduced-calorie mayonnaise instead of regular mayonnaise; omit salt.
CALORIES: 210   CHOLESTEROL: 2 mg   SODIUM: 66 mg   FIBER: 2 g

———— ◇ ————

An Elegant Fruit-and-Vegetable Salad

I originally made this salad during a last-minute emergency. I had some leftover wild rice, so I threw in with it almost anything else I could find in the refrigerator, and, as so often happens in times of "food crises," it turned out to be great.

2 cups cooked wild rice
1 cup cooked asparagus tips (you can use the stems, too, if you like)
1 cup sliced celery
1 cup chopped apple
⅓ cup chopped red onion
2 tablespoons orange juice
2 tablespoons vegetable oil
1 tablespoon olive oil
2 teaspoons Dijon mustard
2 teaspoons lime juice
2 teaspoons balsamic vinegar
1 teaspoon honey
¼ teaspoon crumbled tarragon
¼ teaspoon salt

In a large bowl, combine the wild rice, asparagus, celery, apple, and onion.

In a bowl, stir together the orange juice, vegetable oil, olive oil, mustard, lime juice, vinegar, honey, tarragon, and salt. Pour over wild-rice mixture and toss gently until completely combined.

SERVES 8.
CALORIES: 115   CHOLESTEROL: 0 mg   SODIUM: 82 mg   FIBER: 3 g

Health tips:
Omit salt; use half of the dressing.
CALORIES: 000   CHOLESTEROL: 0 mg   SODIUM: 15 mg   FIBER: 3 g

———————◇———————

Wild Rice and Pasta with a Creamy Tomato Sauce

Although this sauce is easy to make, it's one of the best I've ever eaten. The wild rice mixed with the pasta adds a flavor and texture dimension that makes the finished dish as interesting as it is tasty. In making the sauce, I prefer to use Asiago, an Italian grating cheese with a more delicate flavor than Parmesan.

1 cup tubetti or other small pasta
2 tablespoons olive oil
1 cup chopped onion
2 cloves garlic, minced
1 can (14½ ounce) whole peeled tomatoes
2 tablespoons tomato paste
½ teaspoon salt
⅛ teaspoon ground red pepper
⅓ cup grated Asiago or Parmesan cheese
½ cup heavy cream
1 cup cooked wild rice

Cook the pasta according to package directions; drain.

In a medium-size saucepan, heat oil over medium-high heat. Add onion and garlic and cook, stirring, until softened. Stir in undrained tomatoes, tomato paste, salt, and red pepper. Bring to a boil, reduce heat, and simmer for 20 minutes. Stir in cheese, then cream. Simmer for 10 minutes longer, or until thickened.

In a large bowl, toss together the cooked pasta and wild rice. Pour sauce over wild-rice mixture and toss gently until well combined.

SERVES 8 (as a side dish).
CALORIES: 106   CHOLESTEROL: 23 mg   SODIUM: 348 mg   FIBER: 2 g

Health tip:
Omit salt; use half the cheese; substitute half-and-half for cream.
CALORIES: 134   CHOLESTEROL: 8 mg   SODIUM: 165 mg   FIBER: 2 g

Lentils and Wild Rice

I'm one of those people who think that everything tastes delicious, as long as it has lentils in it, and this recipe is no exception. After she tasted it, my sister Sherry observed that leftovers would probably make a lovely salad if they were dressed with a vinaigrette, and I'm sure she's right.

> 1 can (13¾ ounce) ready-to-serve beef broth or
>   1¾ cups vegetable broth (see page 19)
> ¾ cup water
> 1 medium-size onion, peeled and left whole
> 4 cloves
> ½ cup wild rice, rinsed
> ½ cup lentils, rinsed and picked over
> ¼ cup sliced scallion, both white and green parts

In a 2-quart saucepan, bring the broth and water to a boil. Stud the onion with cloves and add to the broth along with rice. Bring to a boil. Reduce heat, cover, and simmer for 15 minutes. Stir in lentils. Cover and simmer for 35 minutes longer.

Discard onion and stir in scallion.

SERVES 6.

CALORIES: 121   CHOLESTEROL: 5 mg   SODIUM: 214 mg   FIBER: 3 g

Health tip:

Use low-sodium broth.

CALORIES: 121   CHOLESTEROL: 5 mg   SODIUM: 130 mg   FIBER: 3 g

———————◇———————

White-and-Wild Rice

This is a homemade version of the rice mix you can buy in a box—and a lot better. I think that once you've tasted it you may never go back to the packaged version again.

2 tablespoons vegetable oil
1 cup chopped onion
1 can (13¾ ounce) ready-to-serve beef broth or
    1¾ cups vegetable broth (see page 19)
¾ cup water
⅓ cup wild rice, rinsed
⅛ teaspoon crumbled thyme
1 bay leaf
⅔ cup converted white rice
2 tablespoons chopped parsley

In a 2-quart saucepan, heat the oil over medium-high heat. Add onion and cook, stirring frequently, until softened. Stir in broth and water and bring to a boil. Stir in wild rice, thyme, and bay leaf. Reduce heat, cover, and simmer for 30 minutes. Stir in converted rice. Simmer, covered, for 25 minutes longer, or until all of the liquid has been absorbed. Remove bay leaf and stir in parsley.

SERVES 6.
CALORIES: 166   CHOLESTEROL: 0 mg   SODIUM: 208 mg   FIBER: 1 g

Health tip:
Use low-sodium broth.
CALORIES: 166   CHOLESTEROL: 0 mg   SODIUM: 30 mg   FIBER: 1 g

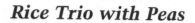

Rice Trio with Peas

I use a combination of wild, brown, and white rices in this dish. And even though it's very tasty, since the cooked long-grain brown rice looks about the same as the white rice. You may want to try and find a dark-brown rice, such as Wahani, and use that instead.

1 can (13¾ ounce) ready to-serve chicken broth or
    1¾ cups vegetable broth (see page 19)
¾ cup water
⅓ cup wild rice, rinsed
⅓ cup long-grain brown rice or Wahani rice
⅓ cup converted white rice
1 cup frozen peas
¼ cup grated Parmesan cheese
¼ cup chopped scallion, both white and green parts
2 tablespoons butter

In a 3-quart saucepan, combine the broth and water and bring to a boil. Stir in wild rice. Reduce heat, cover, and simmer for 10 minutes. Stir in brown rice, cover, and simmer for 25 minutes. Stir in white rice, cover, and simmer for 15 minutes. Stir in peas and simmer for 10 minutes longer, covered, or until all of the liquid has been absorbed. Remove pan from heat. Stir in cheese, scallion, and butter.

SERVES 6.
CALORIES: 171   CHOLESTEROL: 13 mg   SODIUM: 418 mg   FIBER: 1 g

Health tip:
Omit salt; use low-sodium broth. Use unsalted margarine instead of butter, and only 2 tablespoons cheese.
CALORIES: 159   CHOLESTEROL: 1 mg   SODIUM: 153 mg   FIBER: 1 g

―――――――――◇―――――――――

Wild Rice with Summer Squash

Zucchini and yellow squash used to be summertime vegetable treats. Now they're both available all year, so you can enjoy this dish any time.

2 tablespoons vegetable oil
½ cup chopped onion
1 can (13¾ ounce) ready-to-serve chicken broth or
    1¾ cups vegetable broth (see page 19)
¼ cup water
¼ teaspoon salt
½ cup wild rice, rinsed
½ cup converted white rice
1 cup sliced zucchini
1 cup sliced yellow squash
¼ teaspoon crumbled oregano
⅛ teaspoon pepper

In a 3-quart saucepan heat the oil over medium-high heat. Add onion and cook, stirring, until softened. Stir in broth, water, and salt and bring to a boil. Stir in wild rice and return to boiling. Reduce heat and simmer, covered, for 30 minutes. Stir in white rice and simmer, covered, for 15 minutes. Stir in zucchini, yellow squash, oregano, and pepper. Cover and simmer for 15 minutes longer.

SERVES 6.
CALORIES: 165   CHOLESTEROL: 0 mg   SODIUM: 298 mg   FIBER: 2 g

Health tip:
Reduce oil to 2 teaspoons and use a nonstick saucepan. Or, cook onion in a nonstick skillet, transferring to the larger pan to finish cooking. Use low-sodium broth; omit salt.
CALORIES: 145   CHOLESTEROL: 0 mg   SODIUM: 108 mg   FIBER: 2 g

———————— ◇ ————————

Southern-Style Wild Rice with Mushrooms

Southerners almost never cook a starchy dish without some kind of bacon or pork flavoring, but you can leave it out and you'll still have a very delicious side dish.

> 3 slices bacon, cut into ½-inch pieces or
>   2 tablespoons vegetable oil
> ½ cup chopped onion
> ½ cup chopped green bell pepper
> 2 cups sliced mushrooms
> 1 can (13¾ ounce) ready-to-serve beef broth or
>   1¾ cups vegetable broth (see page 19)
> ¼ cup water
> ¼ teaspoon salt
> ½ cup wild rice, rinsed
> ½ cup brown rice

In a 3-quart saucepan, cook the bacon until crisp. Remove bacon and drain on paper towels.

Add the onion and green pepper to bacon fat in skillet. Cook, stirring, until vegetables are softened. Stir in mushrooms and cook, stirring and tossing, until softened. Stir in broth, water, and salt and bring to a boil. Stir in wild rice. Reduce heat and simmer, covered, for 20 minutes. Stir in brown rice. Cover and simmer for 45 minutes, or until most of the liquid has been absorbed. Remove from heat and let stand for 10 minutes. Stir in reserved bacon.

SERVES 8.

CALORIES: 112   CHOLESTEROL: 4 mg   SODIUM: 266 mg   FIBER: 2 g

Health tip:

Omit bacon; cook in a nonstick saucepan with 2 teaspoons of oil. Or, cook onion, green pepper, and mushrooms in a nonstick skillet, transferring them to the larger pan to finish cooking.

CALORIES: 98   CHOLESTEROL: 0 mg   SODIUM: 161 mg   FIBER: 2 g

———————◇———————

Green Beans, Shiitake Mushrooms, and Wild Rice

I first tasted green beans with shiitake mushrooms at the home of my friend, Holly Garrison, and loved the combination. In my adaptation for this book, I added wild rice and, if you'll forgive me, Holly, I think it's even better.

3 tablespoons butter
2 tablespoons minced shallot
1 cup sliced shiitake mushrooms
¼ cup beef or vegetable broth
2 cups green beans, cut into 1-inch pieces
1½ cups cooked wild rice

In a large skillet with a tight-fitting lid, heat the butter over medium heat. Add shallot and mushrooms and cook, stirring and tossing, until mushrooms are softened. Stir in broth. Add green beans, cover, and steam for 10 minutes, or until tender-crisp. Add rice and stir until heated through.

SERVES 6.
CALORIES: 122   CHOLESTEROL: 16 mg   SODIUM: 185 mg   FIBER: 3 g

Health tip:
Use 1 tablespoon unsalted margarine instead of butter and cook in a nonstick skillet.
CALORIES: 88   CHOLESTEROL: 0 mg   SODIUM: 39 mg   FIBER: 3 g

—————————— ◇ ——————————

Wild Rice with Red and Yellow Peppers

If you want to turn this beautiful dish into a full meal, sauté two chicken-breast halves until done, then cut them into strips, and stir them into the wild-rice-and-peppers mixture just before serving. Or, for a more au courant touch, grill the breasts (on a barbecue or under the oven broiler), and serve on top or alongside of the wild-rice-and-peppers mixture.

3 tablespoons butter
½ cup chopped onion
2 cloves garlic, minced
1 cup chopped red bell pepper
1 cup chopped yellow bell pepper
1 cup sliced zucchini
2 cups cooked wild rice
¼ teaspoon salt
⅛ teaspoon pepper

In a large skillet, heat the butter over medium-high heat. Add onion and garlic and cook, stirring frequently, until onion is softened. Add red bell pepper, yellow bell pepper, and zucchini and cook, stirring, until tender-crisp. Stir in rice, salt, and pepper and cook, stirring, until heated through.

SERVES 4.

CALORIES: 203   CHOLESTEROL: 0 mg   SODIUM: 506 mg   FIBER: 3 g

Health tip:

Reduce butter to 2 teaspoons and cook in a nonstick skillet; omit salt.

CALORIES: 163   CHOLESTEROL: 0 mg   SODIUM: 39 mg   FIBER: 3 g

—————— ◇ ——————

Wild-Rice Crêpes with Apricot Sauce

The slight chewiness and subtle flavor of wild rice in these delicate crêpes makes them a luxurious dessert treat. If you leave the sugar out of the crêpe batter, you could also serve these as savory crêpes and fill them with any wonderful mixture you like. For instance, you might want to try using the scallops-and-leeks mixture on page 356, serving it inside the crêpes instead of with wild rice.

Crepes:

> 1½ cups milk
> ¼ cup butter, melted
> ¼ cup sugar
> 2 eggs
> 1 cup all-purpose flour
> ⅔ cup cooked wild rice
> Oil, for greasing skillet

Sauce:

> ¾ cup apricot pouring fruit (This is a relatively new product. Look for it
>   with the syrups or jellies and jams at the supermarket. If you can't
>   find it, use apricot jam.)
> 2 tablespoons hazelnut or orange liqueur

To make the crêpes, combine milk, butter, sugar, and eggs in the container of an electric blender. Cover and blend until thoroughly combined. Add flour, cover, and blend until smooth. Stir in wild rice, cover, and blend until chopped. Let stand for 30 minutes.

Heat a 9-inch, slope-sided, nonstick skillet (the cooking surface should measure 5½ to 6 inches) until a drop of water sprinkled in the bottom of the pan bounces about before evaporating. Brush skillet very lightly with oil. Pour a scant ¼ cup of the batter into the skillet and swirl it around to cover the bottom. Cook until the underside of the crêpe is lightly browned, about 2 minutes. Turn crêpe over and cook until the second side is lightly browned. Remove crêpe by tilting the skillet over a piece of waxed paper. (The crêpe should simply fall out of the pan. If it doesn't, use a wide spatula to assist.) Repeat this procedure with remaining batter, greasing the pan occasionally. Stack crêpes with a piece of waxed paper between each. (This keeps them from sticking, and if you want to you can simply wrap the whole stack tightly and freeze until needed. Thaw crêpes just before using and reheat in the microwave or in a 325°F oven.)

To make sauce, combine pouring fruit and liqueur in the blender container. Cover and blend until smooth. Pour the sauce into a small saucepan to be heated gently just before serving.

To assemble, fold crêpes into quarters and divide among serving plates. Pour a little of the warm sauce over the crêpes and serve remaining sauce on the side.

MAKES 14 CREPES AND 1 CUP SAUCE.
CALORIES: 186   CHOLESTEROL: 42 mg   SODIUM: 53 mg   FIBER: 1 g

Health tip:
Use unsalted margarine instead of butter. Substitute 1-percent-fat milk for regular milk. Eat just one.
CALORIES: 181   CHOLESTEROL: 30 mg   SODIUM: 30 mg   FIBER: 1 g

———◇———

Unusual Grains and Breakfast Cereals: Something Old, Something New, Something Manufactured

———◇———

Amaranth
Job's Tears
Quinoa
Teff
Triticale
Breakfast Cereals

This group of grains ranges from the purest and least tampered with to totally man-made grains and grain products. I consider them to be unusual in a couple of respects. First, they are practically unknown to the general population. Second, most of them do not fit into any of the typical grain generalizations.

When we think of grain, certain qualities come to mind: Grains are starchy and filling with a flavor that is usually described as nutty. With the exception of triticale, the unusual grains have few of these qualities. Teff is seedlike and not at all starchy, although the flavor can be described as a bit like wheat. Amaranth and quinoa have a slippery texture, and the flavor of amaranth is more like a vegetable than like a grain. Job's tears seems closer to beans than grains in both taste and texture. And triticale, since it is a hybrid of rye and wheat, has the qualities of true grains. As for breakfast cereals, we all know that they frequently bear no resemblance to real food at all.

Amaranth and quinoa, which were originally grown in South America, have illustrious histories and similar properties. Both grains have the distinction of having been considered sacred by the Aztec and Inca civilizations. However, as a means of dominating both peoples, the Spaniards forced the Aztecs and Incas to abandon their sacred grains, and amaranth and quinoa fell into disuse for hundreds of years.

It was not until recently that any real interest has been focused on the two grains, and for this reason they have remained *pure* in the sense that agricultural scientists have not had the opportunity to experiment with their gene pools in an attempt to produce heartier or greater-yielding strains. Both amaranth and quinoa are small grains that have most of the bran and germ intact, and consequently most of their nutritional value. Both grains contain unusually high amounts of amino acids, lysine, and methionine, which are generally low in the more common grains.

Teff is another ancient grain. Like amaranth and quinoa, teff has been left virtually untouched by scientific hands. It is native to Africa and is the smallest of all grains. In its flour form, teff is the basis for *injera,* the staple bread of Ethiopia.

Job's tears is a newcomer on the American health-food scene, but it has been used for thousands of years in China and Japan, mainly for medicinal purposes and as a skin beautifier.

Triticale has the distinction of being the newest grain in the world. It is a hybrid of wheat and rye and was engineered by scientists seeking a grain that would be as hearty as rye and as appealing as wheat. It was also hoped that such a grain would have a nutritional value greater than either of the other two, and idealists of the sixties envisioned the grain making a significant dent in world hunger. Unfortunately, triticale is not as hearty as was hoped for, and has never gained anything like overwhelming acceptance. The end result is that much of it is used for animal feed.

Breakfast cereals have the rather sad history of having started out as a healthful product that evolved, in many instances, into nutritional nightmares. A disheartening number are loaded with sugar and saturated fats (palm and coconut oils), sugar, salt, and artificial colors. As a nutritionist, I certainly don't condemn the eating of cold cereals, especially since they do promote milk consumption, but if you're eating this type of cereal with the idea that you're getting a nutritious breakfast, read package labels carefully, or stick with the cooked cereals.

The whole grain scene is currently in a state of frenzied growth. In addition to amaranth, quinoa, Job's tears, and teff, we can look forward to sorghum (an African grain) and newer varieties of quinoa and amaranth making their debut at health-food stores in the near future.

AMARANTH

When Cortez conquered Mexico, the "savages" he found there were actually the advanced Aztec civilization, rich in culture and, more important to their conqueror, *gold!*

The Aztec's diet consisted mainly of corn, beans, and amaranth. The latter, they felt, made them strong (they were probably right about that, since amaranth has a higher protein profile than either of the other two) and they used it as part of their religious ceremonies, and even sent it as a tribute to their emperor, Montezuma.

In addition to stealing the Aztec's gold, the Spaniards also destroyed all the amaranth they could find and forbade the Aztecs from eating it. Eventually the Aztecs themselves cast out the grain from their lives, a real pity, since the nutritional loss was significant to a population who was by then poor and undernourished.

Types of Amaranth Available

Whole-grained amaranth: The whole grain, unhulled.

Amaranth flour: Whole-grain amaranth, finely ground.

Amaranth pasta: Pasta made from amaranth flour and whole-wheat flour.

Texture and Flavor

Amaranth is golden in color with an occasional dark grain, and is as tiny as a poppy seed. As it cooks, the grain becomes transparent, and a miniscule root sprout is visible. The texture will vary considerably depending on the amount of cooking water. If it is cooked according to package directions, the mixture will look like a thick, clear, cornstarch sauce with seeds in it. Cooked with less water, the grain has a mouth feel similar to a crunchy cornmeal mush. It may also remind you of caviar because you are so aware of the many, tiny, individual grains.

Amaranth's distinctive flavor is similar to the aroma of fresh corn silk, and is a taste that may take some getting used to. Stirring butter into cooked amaranth mellows the flavor considerably.

Heating amaranth in a skillet, with or without oil, will pop the grains and they will become little white puffs, which have a milder flavor than the boiled version. If you decide to try popped amaranth, do not be surprised to find that, like corn, it pops high and far, so you may want to have a lid handy to contain it. Popped amaranth can be eaten like popcorn, or used as a kind of miniature crouton in soup or in salads.

Compatible Foods, Herbs, and Spices

The cooked texture of amaranth makes it unsuitable for using in salads or as a vegetable dish. It is best when used in baked goods or, to take advantage of its crunch, stirred into smooth-textured dishes. Combining amaranth and other grains can add a fresh and unusual flavor. The same is true of amaranth flour. Substitute up to one fourth of amaranth flour for the all-purpose flour in most baked goods.

Adding cooked amaranth to some batters (pancakes or waffles, for instance) helps the finished product to retain moisture and gives it a wonderful lightness.

Availability

Amaranth is available in most health-food stores and through mail-order grain catalogs (see page 21). Because of its high nutrition profile, you will find that it has been added to many health-food products, such as breakfast flakes, cookies, breads, and pasta.

Nutritional Content

Because it is so small, amaranth is not hulled as most grains are, so the benefits of all the vitamins and fiber contained in the hull remain. It is one of the few grains that contains significant levels of lysine and methionine, which makes it a high-quality protein. Amaranth is also rich in calcium, iron, fiber, and phosphorous.

Substitutions

Except for teff, there are no substitutions for amaranth because of its unusual texture and flavor.

Teff: Similar to amaranth in many ways, although even smaller in size, and its flavor is milder. However, teff flour can be substituted for amaranth flour.

Basic Cooking Instructions

Please read *About Cooking Grains* beginning on page 000. Also note that when cooking amaranth, <u>salt must always be added *after* cooking,</u> or the grain will not absorb the water. Do not cook amaranth with broth.

Stove-top method:

1½ cups water
1 cup amaranth
½ teaspoon salt

In a 1½-quart saucepan, bring the water to a boil. Stir in amaranth and return to boiling. Reduce heat and simmer, covered, for 20 minutes. Stir in salt.

MAKES 2 CUPS.

Microwave method:

1½ cups water
1 cup amaranth
½ teaspoon salt

Place the water in a 2-quart, microwave-safe bowl. Cover with waxed paper and microwave on high (100% power) for 3 minutes. Stir in amaranth. Recover with waxed paper and microwave on high for 2 minutes. Microwave on medium (50% power), still covered with waxed paper, for 10 minutes. Stir in salt. Let stand for 4 minutes.

MAKES 2 CUPS.

Reheating

If you are going to set the cooked amaranth aside, be sure to place a piece of plastic wrap directly on the surface of the grain. Otherwise, when the air dries it out, which happens quickly, the grains cling together and harden into a skin that is tough and like plastic. Chilled amaranth stiffens considerably, and should be microwaved or lightly steamed to restore its soft texture.

AMARANTH RECIPES

*(*indicates easy recipe.)*

———————◇———————

Curried Fry Bites
Poor Man's Caviar
Chicken with Amaranth Dumplings
Spinach Quiche with an Amaranth Crust
Amaranth-Pasta Tonnato *
Creamy Mashed Potatoes and Amaranth *
Amaranth and Brown Rice *
Scallions and Amaranth *
Bacon-y Corn Bake *
Amaranth Popovers
Amaranth-Walnut Bread
Light-as-Air Amaranth Pancakes *
Amaranth-Mocha Bundt Cake

Curried Fry Bites

Serve these crunchy spicy appetizers with a dipping sauce of pureed chutney or sweet-and-sour duck sauce. Although I think these are best if eaten right after they are fried, you can make the appetizers in advance, if that's more convenient, and freeze them. Reheat in a 350° F oven for 20 minutes. You may also want to adjust the amount of red pepper given here to suit your own taste.

1 can (19 ounce) chick-peas, drained
1 egg
½ cup cooked amaranth
1 tablespoon curry powder
2 teaspoons chopped cilantro (fresh coriander)
1 clove garlic, minced
½ teaspoon salt
¼ teaspoon ground red pepper
¼ cup amaranth flour
¼ cup all-purpose flour
Oil, for deep frying

Place the chick-peas in the container of a food processor. Cover and process until smooth. Add egg and process until thoroughly combined. Add cooked amaranth, curry, cilantro, garlic, salt, and red pepper. Process until well blended. Add both flours and process again until well blended.

Pour enough oil into a deep-fryer or saucepan so that it measures about 2 inches deep. Heat oil until bubbles form when you drop in a bit of the batter. Drop batter by rounded measuring teaspoonsful into the hot oil. Fry until golden on both sides. (It's important that the oil not be too hot, otherwise the batter will brown too quickly on the outside, but the inside will remain uncooked. On the other hand, if the oil is too cool, the bites will be greasy.)

Remove with a slotted spoon and drain on paper towels.

MAKES 30 BITES.
CALORIES: 53   CHOLESTEROL: 7 mg   SODIUM: 39 mg   FIBER: .5gr

Health tip:
Omit salt.
CALORIES: 53   CHOLESTEROL: 7 mg   SODIUM: 10 mg   FIBER: .5 gr

Poor Man's Caviar

The first time I tasted eggplant caviar was at the home of my friend, Robin Gallagher. I must tell you that I spent the entire afternoon glued to the spread, bread, and "caviar." I could not resist adding a little amaranth to my version of the spread and it doesn't hurt it one little bit. This is excellent when served with thinly sliced whole-grain or pumpernickel bread.

1 large (about 1½ pounds) eggplant
¼ cup olive oil
¾ cup finely chopped onion
½ cup finely chopped green bell pepper
3 cloves garlic, minced
1½ cups chopped tomato
⅓ cup cooked amaranth
3 tablespoons water
1 teaspoon white vinegar
1 teaspoon sugar
¼ teaspoon salt
¼ teaspoon black pepper

Preheat oven to 400°F.

Bake the eggplant for 1 hour, or until the outside is charred and the inside is fork-tender.

While eggplant is baking, heat oil in a large skillet over medium heat. Add onion, green pepper, and garlic and cook, stirring, until vegetables are slightly softened. Stir in tomato and cook over low heat, stirring occasionally, until the vegetables are very soft, about 15 minutes. Remove from heat and set aside.

Cut eggplant in half and scrape the flesh out of the shell. Discard shell and chop eggplant finely. Stir into mixture in skillet. Cook over medium heat, stirring occasionally, for 20 minutes. Stir in amaranth until completely blended. Stir in water, vinegar, sugar, salt, and pepper. Cook over medium heat, stirring, until thickened. Cool slightly, then chill until serving time.

MAKES 2¾ CUPS. Nutritional information based on 10 servings.
CALORIES: 95   CHOLESTEROL: 0 mg   SODIUM: 219 mg   FIBER: 3 g

Health tip:
Reduce oil to 1 tablespoon and cook in a nonstick skillet.
CALORIES: 59   CHOLESTEROL: 0 mg   SODIUM: 54 mg   FIBER: 3 g

———————◇———————

Chicken with Amaranth Dumplings

This is a thin stew, but very good, almost like a chicken soup with dumplings.

2 tablespoons oil
1 cup chopped onion
3 cups peeled and cubed butternut squash
1 cup sliced carrot
1 cup sliced celery
2 cups water
⅓ cup chopped parsley, divided
1 bay leaf
1 teaspoon salt, divided
⅛ teaspoon pepper
3½-pound chicken, cut into 8 pieces
⅔ cup all-purpose flour
¼ cup amaranth flour
½ teaspoon baking powder
3 tablespoons solid white vegetable shortening
½ cup milk

In a large heavy saucepan or Dutch oven, heat the oil over medium-high heat. Add onion and cook, stirring frequently, until softened. Add squash, carrot, and celery and stir until lightly coated with oil. Add water, ¼ cup of the parsley, bay leaf, ¾ teaspoon of the salt, and pepper. Bring to a boil, add chicken pieces, and return to boiling. Reduce heat and simmer, covered, for about 45 minutes, or until chicken is tender.

After chicken has been cooking for 30 minutes, prepare the dumplings. In a medium-size bowl, stir together both flours, baking powder, and remaining ¼ teaspoon salt. Cut in shortening with a pastry blender or two knives, until mixture resembles coarse cornmeal. Stir in remaining parsley. Stir in milk to form a soft dough.

Remove bay leaf from stew. Drop dumpling batter into the stew by measuring tablespoonsful. You should have about 8 dumplings. Cook, covered, for 10 minutes. Uncover pan and cook for 7 minutes longer.

SERVES 4.
CALORIES: 645   CHOLESTEROL: 201 mg   SODIUM: 851 mg   FIBER: 5 g

Health tip:
Omit salt; remove chicken skin before cooking.
CALORIES: 505   CHOLESTEROL: 180 mg   SODIUM: 293 mg   FIBER: 5 g

─────── ◇ ───────

Spinach Quiche with an Amaranth Crust

The only thing that makes this different from a classic spinach quiche is the crust, which is crisp, golden, and definitely amaranth flavored. If you prefer, you can substitute Swiss cheese for the Gouda in the filling.

Crust:

> *1½ cups all-purpose flour*
> *½ cup amaranth flour*
> *1 teaspoon salt*
> *¾ cup butter*
> *4 to 6 tablespoons ice water*

Filling:

> *4 eggs*
> *2 cups half-and-half*
> *½ teaspoon crumbled tarragon*
> *½ teaspoon salt*
> *¼ teaspoon crumbled thyme*
> *1 package (10 ounce) frozen chopped spinach, thawed and squeezed dry*
> *1 cup shredded Gouda cheese*
> *⅓ cup sliced scallion, both white and green parts*
> *¼ cup grated Parmesan cheese*

Preheat oven to 400°F.

To make crust, in a large bowl, stir together both flours and salt. Cut in butter with a pastry blender or two knives, until the mixture resembles coarse cornmeal. Stir in ice water, 1 tablespoon at a time, until the dough forms a ball.

Roll dough between two sheets of waxed paper into an 11-inch circle. Fit into a 9-inch pie plate and crimp the edges. Weight the bottom of the crust with uncooked rice, dried beans, or pie weights. (By placing something heavy in the bottom of the pie shell you shouldn't have a problem with the pastry shrinking or puffing up as it bakes. The technical term for baking an unfilled pie shell is "baking it blind.") Bake for 15 minutes, or until lightly browned. Take pie crust out of the oven and remove weights. Reduce oven temperature to 350°F.

To make filling, beat the eggs in a medium-size bowl. Beat in half-and-half, tarragon, salt, and thyme. Stir in spinach, Gouda, scallion and Parmesan. Pour into baked crust. Bake for 35 to 45 minutes, or until a knife inserted in the center comes out clean.

SERVES 6.
CALORIES: 569   CHOLESTEROL: 246 mg   SODIUM: 954 mg   FIBER: 4 g

Health tip:
Omit salt; use unsalted margarine instead of butter; substitute scrambled-egg substitute for eggs. Use milk instead of half-and-half.
CALORIES: 497   CHOLESTEROL: 27 mg   SODIUM: 461 mg   FIBER: 4 g

◇

Amaranth-Pasta Tonnato

In Italian, tonnato means tuna, and it's an important ingredient in the lusty food served in the parts of those countries that surround the Mediterranean Sea. To me, it also means this simple and satisfying dish that I often prepare when I want a quick, substantial meal.

> 2 tablespoons olive oil
> 1 cup chopped onion
> 2 cloves garlic, minced
> 1 can (28 ounce) whole tomatoes in puree
> 2 tablespoons chopped parsley
> 1½ teaspoons crumbled oregano
> 1 teaspoon crumbled basil
> ½ teaspoon sugar
> ⅛ teaspoon crumbled thyme
> ⅛ teaspoon pepper
> 2 cans (7½ ounces each) tuna, drained
> 12 ounces amaranth pasta, cooked according to package directions and
>   drained

In a 3-quart saucepan, heat the oil over medium-high heat. Add onion and garlic and cook, stirring frequently, until softened. Add tomatoes with puree, parsley, oregano, basil, sugar, thyme, and pepper. Bring to a boil, reduce heat, and simmer for 30 minutes. Add tuna to the sauce and cook, stirring, until heated through. Pour sauce over hot pasta.

SERVES 4.
CALORIES: 597   CHOLESTEROL: 15 mg   SODIUM: 628 mg   FIBER: 6 g

Health tip:
Reduce oil to 2 teaspoons and cook in a nonstick skillet.
CALORIES: 372   CHOLESTEROL: 10 mg   SODIUM: 419 mg   FIBER: 4 g

◇

Creamy Mashed Potatoes and Amaranth

Mashed potatoes are a caloric splurge in which I rarely indulge. (The potatoes themselves are somewhat spartan, but if you want really delicious mashed potatoes, you can't be stingy with the butter.) I love the grainy texture that the amaranth adds to the smoothness of mashed potatoes and think it's a nice touch.

*1 pound (about 3 medium-size) boiling potatoes, peeled and cut into
      quarters*
¼ cup butter, divided
¼ cup finely chopped onion
⅓ cup half-and-half
2 tablespoons sour cream
½ teaspoon salt
¼ teaspoon pepper
⅓ cup cooked amaranth

In a 3-quart saucepan, cook the potatoes in boiling water for about 30 minutes, or until soft when pierced with a fork. Drain thoroughly.

While potatoes are boiling, melt 1 tablespoon of the butter in a small skillet. Add onion and cook over medium-high heat, stirring, until softened. Remove from heat and set aside.

Mash hot drained potatoes, in the saucepan, with remaining 3 tablespoons butter, half-and-half, sour cream, salt, and pepper. Stir in amaranth and cooked onion. Stir rapidly over low heat until potato mixture is hot.

SERVES 6.
CALORIES: 181   CHOLESTEROL: 28 mg   SODIUM: 283 mg   FIBER: 2 g

Health tip:
Use unsalted margarine instead of butter, and milk instead of half-and-half. Substitute plain yogurt for sour cream; omit salt.
CALORIES: 165   CHOLESTEROL: 2 mg   SODIUM: 23 mg   FIBER: 2 g

———————— ◇ ————————

Amaranth and Brown Rice

I think these two go well together, the crunchiness and flavor of the amaranth setting off the chewy blandness of the rice.

2¾ cups water
1 cup long-grain brown rice
¼ cup amaranth
1 teaspoon salt

In a 2-quart saucepan, bring the water to a boil. Stir in brown rice and return to boiling. Reduce heat, cover, and simmer for 30 minutes. Stir in amaranth. Cover and simmer for 20 minutes longer. Stir in salt.

SERVES 6.
CALORIES: 139   CHOLESTEROL: 0 mg   SODIUM: 359 mg   FIBER: 2 g

Health tip:
Omit salt.
CALORIES: 139   CHOLESTEROL: 0 mg   SODIUM: 3 mg   FIBER: 2 g

———————— ◇ ————————

Scallions and Amaranth

Since amaranth is dense and filling, it makes a nice side dish for simple meals without too many other accompaniments: a plain roasted chicken and a salad, for instance. You could even serve this for breakfast with scrambled eggs, if you like.

1½ cups water
1 cup amaranth
2 tablespoons butter
1 to 2 tablespoons chopped scallion
½ teaspoon salt

In a 1½-quart saucepan, bring the water to a boil. Stir in amaranth and return to boiling. Reduce heat and simmer, covered, for 20 minutes. Remove from heat and stir in butter, scallion, and salt. Serve immediately.

SERVES 4.
CALORIES: 218   CHOLESTEROL: 16 mg   SODIUM: 319 mg   FIBER: 2 g

Health tip:
Use unsalted margarine instead of butter; omit salt.
CALORIES: 218   CHOLESTEROL: 0 mg   SODIUM: 11 mg   FIBER: 2 g

—————— ◇ ——————

Bacon-y Corn Bake

Serve these squares instead of home-fried potatoes or grits for breakfast, brunch, or supper. This dish is also a nice accompaniment at dinner.

4 slices bacon, cut into 1-inch pieces
1 cup cooked amaranth
½ cup milk
2 eggs
2 tablespoons butter, melted
½ cup whole-wheat flour
⅛ teaspoon pepper
1 can (8 ounce) whole-kernel corn, drained

Preheat oven to 350°F.
Grease an 8-inch square baking pan and set aside.
In a large skillet, cook the bacon until crisp. Remove bacon from skillet and drain on paper towels. Reserve 2 tablespoons of the bacon fat.
In a large bowl, stir together amaranth, milk, eggs, butter, and reserved bacon fat until completely blended. Stir in flour and pepper. Stir in reserved bacon and corn. Spread into prepared pan.
Bake for 30 minutes, or until a knife inserted in the center comes out clean. Cut into 9 squares. Serve warm.

SERVES 9.
CALORIES: 183   CHOLESTEROL: 57 mg   SODIUM: 148 mg   FIBER: 1 g

Health tip:
Eat only half a portion.

––––––––– ◇ –––––––––

Amaranth Popovers

If you've never eaten a popover, you have a treat in store for you. A popover is a very airy muffin, and is so named because, as it bakes, the lightness of the batter causes it to pop over the side of the baking cup. To make certain that popovers "pop," it's important that the batter is poured into *hot*, heavily greased popover cups. The finished popover is somewhat hollow and a little doughy inside, and crisp and brown on the outside. The flavor of the amaranth flour in the popover recipe that follows is a delightful addition.

¾ cup sifted all-purpose flour
¼ cup sifted amaranth flour
½ teaspoon salt
2 eggs
1 cup milk
2 tablespoons melted butter

Preheat oven to 425°F.

Place a popover pan or 6 custard cups (whatever you use, they must be deeper than they are wide) on a baking sheet. Heavily grease each cup with vegetable oil, then place them in the oven to heat.

In a medium-size bowl, stir together both kinds of flour and salt. Set aside.

Place eggs, milk, and butter in the container of an electric blender. Cover and blend until thoroughly combined. Add the flour mixture. Cover and blend until smooth. Remove cups from oven. *Immediately* divide batter evenly among hot popover cups and return to oven.

Bake for 25 to 35 minutes. Remove from oven and pierce each popover with a knife or a fork to vent the steam inside them. Return to oven and bake for 5 minutes longer.

MAKES 6 POPOVERS.

CALORIES: 157   CHOLESTEROL: 85 mg   SODIUM: 253 mg   FIBER: 1 g

Health tip:
Omit salt; use unsalted margarine instead of butter.
CALORIES: 157   CHOLESTEROL: 75 mg   SODIUM: 43 mg   FIBER: 1 g

——————— ◇ ———————

Amaranth-Walnut Bread

If you like the flavor of butterscotch, use pecans instead of walnuts and substitute firmly packed brown sugar for the granulated sugar. However, the walnuts will give you a nuttier-tasting bread.

1⅓ cups all-purpose flour
1 cup ground walnuts
1 cup sugar
⅔ cup amaranth flour
2 teaspoons baking powder
1 teaspoon salt
1 cup milk
1 egg
⅓ cup butter, melted
1 teaspoon vanilla extract

Preheat oven to 350°F.

Grease a 9 × 5 × 3-inch loaf pan and set aside.

In a large bowl, stir together the all-purpose flour, nuts, sugar, amaranth flour, sugar, baking powder, and salt.

In a medium-size bowl, beat together the milk, egg, melted butter, and vanilla. Stir the milk mixture into the flour mixture until well combined. Turn batter into prepared pan.

Bake for 55 to 60 minutes, or until a wooden pick inserted in the center comes out clean. Turn bread out onto a wire rack to cool.

MAKES 1 LOAF (16 slices).

CALORIES: 185   CHOLESTEROL: 25 mg   SODIUM: 219 mg   FIBER: 1 g

Health tip:

Omit salt; use unsalted margarine instead of butter.

CALORIES: 185   CHOLESTEROL: 15 mg   SODIUM: 58 mg   FIBER: 1 g

---◇---

Light-as-Air Amaranth Pancakes

These pancakes are moist and light, not at all cakelike. And, they're good enough to eat without syrup (not that *I* ever do without!)

> ⅔ *cup all-purpose flour*
> ⅓ *cup amaranth flour*
> *2 tablespoons sugar*
> *1½ teaspoons baking soda*
> *½ teaspoon salt*
> *1¼ cups buttermilk*
> *¼ cup butter, melted*
> *1 egg*

In a large bowl, stir together both kinds of flour, sugar, baking soda, and salt.

In a medium-size bowl, stir together the buttermilk, melted butter, and egg until completely combined.

Add milk mixture to flour mixture and stir until blended. The batter should be lumpy.

Heat a large skillet until a few drops of water sprinkled into it bounce about before evaporating. Grease skillet lightly. Drop 2 tablespoonsful of batter for each pancake into the skillet. Cook until bubbles on top of pancake break. Turn and cook until lightly browned on the second side.

MAKES 16 PANCAKES.
CALORIES: 71   CHOLESTEROL: 21 mg   SODIUM: 192 mg   FIBER: 1 g

Health tip:
Omit salt; use unsalted margarine instead of butter.
CALORIES: 71   CHOLESTEROL: 14 mg   SODIUM: 105 mg   FIBER: 1 g

———— ◇ ————

Amaranth-Mocha Bundt Cake

Mocha is a somewhat elusive flavor. A successful mocha-any-thing should not taste too much like chocolate nor too much like coffee, but a subtle blend of each. The first time I made this cake, I couldn't stop myself from cutting slices to munch on, and when I brought the cake to work (to save myself) everyone fell in love with it. I am always amazed that this cake can be so moist *and* feather-light. (Very often if something is described as moist, you can bet your bottom dollar that it is also as heavy as lead.)

1½ cups water
½ cup amaranth
½ cup semisweet chocolate morsels
3 tablespoons heavy cream
1 tablespoon instant espresso powder or
*   1½ tablespoons regular instant-coffee granules*
½ teaspoon vanilla extract
2 cups all-purpose flour
2 teaspoons baking powder
1 teaspoon baking soda
¼ teaspoon salt
1 cup butter
1¼ cups sugar
3 eggs

Preheat oven to 325°F.
Heavily grease and flour a Bundt pan and set aside.
In a 1-quart saucepan, combine the water and amaranth. Bring to a boil. Lower heat and simmer, covered, for 20 to 25 minutes, or until the liquid has been absorbed and the grain has the consistency of a thick sauce. Remove from heat and stir in chocolate morsels, cream, espresso, and vanilla. Set aside to cool to room temperature and don't worry if the ingredients separate.
In a medium-size bowl, stir together the flour, baking powder, baking soda, and salt.
In a large bowl, beat butter and sugar until light and fluffy, about 5 minutes. Beat in eggs. (The mixture may look curdled, but that's okay.)
Beat the flour mixture into the butter mixture alternately with the chocolate mixture, starting and ending with flour mixture. Turn batter into prepared pan.
Bake for 1 hour, or until a wooden pick inserted in the center comes out clean. Turn the cake onto a wire rack and cool. (Because

this cake is so tender, it must be completely cool before slicing, and even then you should use a serrated knife.)

MAKES 20 SERVINGS.
CALORIES: 233   CHOLESTEROL: 59 mg   SODIUM: 191 mg   FIBER: 1 g

Health tip:
Use milk instead of cream; omit salt; use unsalted margarine instead of butter; use scrambled-egg substitute instead of eggs.
CALORIES: 223   CHOLESTEROL: 30 mg   SODIUM: 102 mg   FIBER: 1 g

JOB'S TEARS
(Croix Lacryma-jobi)

Job's tears is a fairly recent entry into the American grain scene. However, it is an ancient grain, highly esteemed in Japan and China. In the Orient, it is valued for its reputed restorative powers. It is also believed that consuming Job's tears will make the skin clear and beautiful.

Job's tears goes by many different names: *hato mugi* (the Japanese name for it), *Juno's tears* (for the Roman goddess), *river grain*, and *jobi*. (I've even seen it labelled pearled barley.) The "tears" refer to the way the grain grows in clusters resembling tears.

Types of Job's Tears Available

Job's tears comes only as a whole grain with the outer husk removed.

Texture and Flavor

Job's tears can best be described as looking like a large pearl barley or a small white coffee bean. It is white and round and has a wide brown indentation that runs lengthwise down one side.

The taste and texture of Job's tears will vary a lot depending on the amount of water in which it is cooked, and the length of time it is cooked. I bring this up because I found that when I followed package directions, the grain had an uncooked flavor and texture that was not at all pleasing—at least to me. By adding half again as much water as called for and cooking the grain longer, it had a much more pleasant, beanlike flavor, and the texture was softer.

Cooked grains of Job's tears are separate and not at all starchy. Please note it is very important that when you rinse the grain before cooking, you also pick out and discard any grains that are tan, rather than white, in color. When the tan grains are cooked they have a very moldy flavor, which makes for a rather unpleasant surprise when you bite into one. (The major importer of Job's tears, Eden Foods, assures me that they are trying new methods of sorting to avoid having the tan grains in the package, so in the near future this may not be a problem. For now, there will always be a few grains that must be discarded.)

Compatible Foods, Herbs, and Spices

Because the flavor and texture of Job's tears is close to that of navy beans, it makes sense that any foods and flavors you would normally combine with the beans are also good with this grain. I think that as a rule of thumb strong flavors work best with Job's tears. Consider using beef, lamb, pork, and ham, rather than poultry or dairy products.

The crunchy texture of vegetables, especially raw or crisp-cooked, are an excellent contrast.

Strong spices and seasonings are, not surprisingly, my first choice to go with Job's tears: curries, chili, and Szechuan or Mexican foods are all good choices in which to include this grain. And since the grain also swells when it is cooked, it makes a good filler for soups and stews.

Availability

Job's tears can be found in health-food stores and through mail-order grain catalogs (see page 21).

Nutritional Content

Job's tears is high in protein, potassium, phosphorous, and magnesium, and it is a good source of dietary fiber.

Substitutions

Navy beans or any small white beans (cooked): You can use either canned or dry beans, substituting them in recipes calling for cooked Job's tears.

Barley: A suitable substitution when used in soups or sautés.

Starchy vegetables: Peas, lima beans, or potatoes can be substituted in stews.

Basic Cooking Instructions

Please read *About Cooking Grains* beginning on page 7.

Stove-top method:

> 1 cup Job's tears
> 3 cups water
> ½ teaspoon salt

Rinse and drain the Job's tears, then carefully pick through, discarding any grains that are tan in color.

In a 2-quart saucepan, bring water and salt to a boil over high heat. Stir in Job's tears and return to boiling. Reduce heat and simmer for 1 hour and 40 minutes, covered, or until almost all of the liquid has been absorbed. Remove from heat and let stand 5 minutes.

MAKES ABOUT 3⅓ CUPS.

Microwave method:

> 1 cup Job's tears
> 3½ cups water
> ½ teaspoon salt

Rinse and drain Job's tears then carefully pick through, discarding any grains that are tan in color.

Place the water and salt in a 3-quart, microwave-safe bowl. Cover with waxed paper and microwave on high (100% power) for 4 minutes. Stir in salt and Job's tears. Recover with waxed paper and microwave on high for 4 minutes. Microwave on medium (50% power), still covered with waxed paper, for 1 hour and 10 minutes. Let stand 5 minutes. Fluff with a fork.

MAKES A SCANT 3 CUPS.

Reheating

As Job's tears cool, the grain becomes more like its under-cooked version. It becomes harder, and develops an underlying flavor that I don't like. I recommend tasting the cold grain and making your own judgement about the flavor. Microwaving or steaming it will return the grain to a softer texture, but I think it is much better to use it freshly cooked.

JOB'S TEARS RECIPES

*(*indicates easy recipes.)*

———————◇———————

Job's Tex-Mex Bean Dip with Guacamole
Sesame Spread *
Escarole-Turkey Soup
Yellow-pea Soup *
Navarin with Job's Tears
Sausage and Tears *
Job's (Brings Tears to the Eyes) Chili
Job's Brussels Sprouts *
Curried Vegetables and Job's Tears
Indonesian Vegetables

————————◇————————

Job's Tex-Mex Bean Dip with Guacamole

You can serve the bean-dip by itself sometimes, or with the gaucamole, as I have done in this recipe. Serve dips with taco or tortilla chips, of course.

Bean Dip:

> ½ cup cooked Job's tears
> ½ cup refried beans (I used Old El Paso brand with green chilies, onion, and garlic)
> 2 tablespoons sour cream
> 2 tablespoons mild or hot salsa

Guacamole:

> 1 medium avocado, mashed (about 1 cup)
> 2 tablespoons sour cream
> 2 tablespoons minced scallion, both white and green parts
> 1 tablespoon mayonnaise
> 1 tablespoon chopped cilantro (fresh coriander)
> 1 tablespoon lime juice
> ⅛ teaspoon ground red pepper

To make the bean dip, in a medium-size bowl, stir together the Job's tears, beans, sour cream, and salsa. Cover and chill until ready to serve.

To make the guacamole, in a medium-size bowl, stir together the avocado, sour cream, green onion, mayonnaise, cilantro, lime juice, and red pepper. (If you aren't serving this immediately, prevent it from turning brown by pressing a piece of plastic wrap directly on the surface. Or you can spread sour cream over the surface. Chill until needed, and stir well just before serving.)

MAKES 1 CUP BEAN DIP; 1⅓ CUPS GUACAMOLE.
Bean Dip per tablespoon:
CALORIES: 19   CHOLESTEROL: 8 mg   SODIUM: 47 mg   FIBER: 1 g

Health tip:
Substitute plain yogurt for sour cream. Omit salt from Job's tears.
CALORIES: 16   CHOLESTEROL: 7 mg   SODIUM: 34 mg   FIBER: 1 g

Guacamole per tablespoon:
CALORIES: 26   CHOLESTEROL: 1 mg   SODIUM: 6 mg   FIBER: 1 g

Health tip:
Substitute plain yogurt for sour cream and mayonnaise.
CALORIES: 19   CHOLESTEROL: 0 mg   SODIUM: 3 mg   FIBER: 1 g

———————◇———————

Sesame Spread

This tastes very much like *hummus,* a tasty Middle Eastern concoction that is usually eaten with or spread on pita bread. Use this as a dip for raw vegetables or as a sandwich filler topped with salad in a pita bread. Tahini, a "butter" made from sesame seeds, is available in health-food stores in jars or in cans.

1 cup cooked Job's tears
⅓ cup tahini (see above)
2 tablespoons lemon juice
2 cloves garlic, minced
2 tablespoons water
2 tablespoons vegetable oil
1 tablespoon Oriental sesame oil
¼ teaspoon salt
¼ teaspoon ground cumin
⅛ teaspoon ground red pepper

Place Job's tears, tahini, lemon juice, garlic, water, vegetable oil, sesame oil, salt, cumin, and red pepper in the container of a food processor. Cover and process until smooth.

MAKES 1¼ CUPS.
CALORIES: 42   CHOLESTEROL: 0 mg   SODIUM: 37 mg   FIBER: 1 g

Health tip:
Omit salt.
CALORIES: 42   CHOLESTEROL: 0 mg   SODIUM: 1 mg   FIBER: 1 g

———— ◇ ————

Escarole-Turkey Soup

You can use more escarole in this soup if you like it, or not as much, or not at all if you don't like it. The soup will still be good.

10 cups water
2 turkey wings (about 3½ pounds)
3 carrots, peeled
3 ribs celery
2 parsnips, peeled
1 tomato, stem removed
1 onion, peeled
¼ cup celery leaves
1 clove garlic
1 teaspoon salt
⅓ cup Job's tears, rinsed, drained, and picked over
1 small bunch parsley
1 small bunch dill
2 cups firmly packed chopped escarole

In a large soup pot, place the water, turkey wings, carrots, celery, parsnips, tomato, onion, celery leaves, garlic, and salt. Bring to a boil and stir in Job's tears. Reduce heat and simmer, uncovered, for 1 hour and 45 minutes. Add parsley and dill. Simmer for 25 minutes longer. Remove turkey and all the vegetables (you can serve these separately with the soup or after it as another course, if you like, or you can throw them out). Skim off all fat. Stir in escarole. Simmer for 5 minutes.

SERVES 8.
CALORIES: 65   CHOLESTEROL: 4 mg   SODIUM: 424 mg   FIBER: .5 g

Health tip:
Remove as much of the skin as you can from the turkey wings before cooking; omit salt.
CALORIES: 65   CHOLESTEROL: 1 mg   SODIUM: 157 mg   FIBER: .5 g

———————— ◇ ————————

Yellow-Pea Soup

This is the kind of soup you can stand a spoon in, but you can add more water, if you like. Serve with croutons, if you like.

10 to 12 cups water
1 smoked pork hock (about 1 pound) or a ham bone
⅓ cup Job's tears, rinsed, drained, and picked over
1 package (16 ounce) yellow split peas
2 ribs celery
2 carrots, peeled
1 parsnip, peeled
1 celeriac, peeled (celery root)
1 teaspoon salt

Place 10 cups of the water, pork hock, and Job's tears in a large soup pot. Bring to a boil. Reduce heat and simmer, covered, for 30 minutes. Add split peas, celery, carrots, parsnip, celery root, and salt. Return to boiling. Reduce heat and simmer, uncovered, for 1½ hours, or until the peas have dissolved. If the soup is getting too thick for your taste, add up to 2 cups more water. Discard meat and vegetables.

SERVES 8.
CALORIES: 221   CHOLESTEROL: 3 mg   SODIUM: 409 mg   FIBER: 8 g

Health tip:
Use a fresh ham bone rather than a smoked one; omit salt.
CALORIES: 221   CHOLESTEROL: 3 mg   SODIUM: 19 mg   FIBER: 8 g

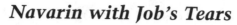

Navarin with Job's Tears

Navarin is a French term meaning lamb stew. This one is thickened with Job's tears and is slightly sweet, just right for a cold night.

1½ pounds boneless lamb, cut into bite-size pieces
3 tablespoons all-purpose flour
¼ cup vegetable oil
1 cup chopped onion
2 cloves garlic, minced
6 to 8 cups water
½ cup dry vermouth
2 tablespoons tomato paste
1 bay leaf
1 teaspoon salt
¼ teaspoon crumbled thyme
⅛ teaspoon pepper
1 cup Job's tears, rinsed, drained, and picked over
2 cups sliced carrot
1½ cups diced rutabaga or turnip

Dredge the lamb in flour, shaking off any excess.

In a large heavy saucepan or Dutch oven, heat the oil over medium-high heat. Add lamb and cook, turning, until lightly browned. Stir in onion and garlic and cook, stirring, until softened. Stir in 6 cups of the water, vermouth, tomato paste, bay leaf, salt, thyme, and pepper, and bring to a boil. Stir in Job's tears, carrot, and rutabaga and return to boiling. Reduce heat and simmer for 1½ to 2 hours, or until lamb is tender. If the stew gets too thick for your taste, stir in as much of the remaining 2 cups water as necessary. During the last 45 minutes of cooking time, you will need to stir the stew from time to time to prevent it from sticking to the bottom of the pan. Remove bay leaf before serving.

SERVES 6.
CALORIES: 498   CHOLESTEROL: 100 mg   SODIUM: 475 mg   FIBER: 4 g

Health tip:
Reduce oil to 2 teaspoons and cook in a nonstick pan. Or, brown lamb in a nonstick skillet, transferring to the larger pan to finish cooking; omit salt.
CALORIES: 471   CHOLESTEROL: 100 mg   SODIUM: 120 mg   FIBER: 4 g

——————— ◇ ———————

Sausage and Tears

Serve this as either a main dish or a hearty side dish.

2 tablespoons vegetable oil
1 cup Job's tears, rinsed, drained and picked over
1 cup chopped onion
½ cup chopped green bell pepper
1 pound sweet or spicy Italian sausage (bulk sausage is preferable)
3 cups water
1 can (8 ounce) tomato sauce
¼ teaspoon salt
¼ teaspoon pepper

In a 2-quart saucepan, heat the oil over medium-high heat. Add Job's tears and cook, stirring, until the grain starts to crackle and pop. Add onion and green pepper and cook, stirring frequently, until vegetables are softened.

If you are using link sausage, discard casing. Add sausage to the pan and cook, stirring, until no longer pink. Stir in water, tomato sauce, salt, and pepper and bring to a boil. Reduce heat and simmer, covered, for 1½ hours.

SERVES 6.
CALORIES: 402   CHOLESTEROL: 64 mg   SODIUM: 1088 mg   fiber: 2 g

Health tip:
Reduce oil to 2 teaspoons and cook in a nonstick saucepan. Or, cook grain, onion, and green pepper in a nonstick skillet, transferring to the larger pan to finish cooking. Cook sausage separately and drain well before adding to other ingredients; omit salt.
CALORIES: 375   CHOLESTEROL: 58 mg   SODIUM: 999 mg   FIBER: 2 g

———— ◇ ————

Job's (Brings Tears to the Eyes) Chili

Serve this chili with cold plain yogurt or sour cream to tame it a little. Of course, you can adjust the spiciness to suit your own taste.

3 tablespoons vegetable oil
1 cup chopped onion
½ cup chopped green bell pepper
½ cup chopped red bell pepper
3 cloves garlic, minced
2 tablespoons chili powder
1 teaspoon paprika
½ teaspoon ground cumin
½ teaspoon ground red pepper
½ teaspoon liquid red pepper (tabasco)
½ teaspoon salt
⅛ teaspoon ground cinnamon
1 can (14½ ounce) whole peeled tomatoes, undrained.
1 can (15 ounce) white beans (I use Goya brand Spanish Style)
1 cup cooked Job's tears
½ cup water

In a 3-quart saucepan, heat the oil over medium-high heat. Add onion, green and red bell peppers, and garlic. Cook, stirring frequently, until vegetables are softened. Stir in chili powder, paprika, cumin, ground red pepper, liquid red pepper, salt, and cinnamon. Cook, stirring, for 30 seconds, or until spices have been absorbed into the oil. Stir in tomatoes and break them up with the side of a spoon. Stir in beans, Job's tears, and water. Bring to a boil. Reduce heat and simmer, uncovered, for 20 minutes, stirring frequently.

SERVES 4.
CALORIES: 344   CHOLESTEROL: 0 mg   SODIUM: 560 mg   FIBER: 13 g

Health tip:
Reduce oil to 1 tablespoon and cook in a nonstick saucepan. Or, cook onion, bell peppers, and garlic in a nonstick skillet, transferring to the larger pan to finish cooking; omit salt.
CALORIES: 274   CHOLESTEROL: 0 mg   SODIUM: 208 mg   FIBER: 13 g

———————— ◇ ————————

Job's Brussels Sprouts

If you're not too fond of Brussels sprouts, you can use almost any vegetable you like better.

1 tablespoon butter
½ cup Job's tears, rinsed, drained, and picked over
1 can (13¾ ounce) ready-to-serve chicken broth or
    1¾ cups vegetable broth (see page 19)
1 pint Brussels sprouts, cut into quarters

In a 2-quart saucepan, melt the butter over medium-high heat. Add Job's tears and cook until the grains begin to crackle and pop. Stir in broth and bring to a boil. Reduce heat, cover, and simmer for 60 minutes. Stir in Brussels sprouts. Cover and simmer for 30 minutes longer.

SERVES 6.
CALORIES: 99   CHOLESTEROL: 5 mg   SODIUM: 233 mg   FIBER: 2 g

Health tip:
Use unsalted margarine instead of butter; use low-sodium broth.
CALORIES: 99   CHOLESTEROL: 0 mg   SODIUM: 46 mg   FIBER 2 g

———————— ◇ ————————

Curried Vegetables and Job's Tears

I usually like my vegetables cooked tender-crisp. Curries are the exception. In a good curry, the vegetables should be cooked until they're mushy.

1 tablespoon vegetable oil
3 tablespoons butter, divided
½ cup Job's tears, rinsed, drained, and picked over
1 cup chopped onion
3 cloves garlic, minced
2 tablespoons curry powder
1 teaspoon salt
½ teaspoon ground cumin
½ teaspoon ground turmeric
½ teaspoon ground ginger
⅛ teaspoon ground red pepper
3 cups water
2 cups cauliflower florets
2 cups green beans, cut into 1½-inch lengths
1 cup peas, fresh or frozen

Heat the oil and 1 tablespoon of the butter in a large heavy saucepan or Dutch oven. Add Job's tears and cook, stirring, until the grains start to crackle and pop. Add remaining 2 tablespoons butter. Stir in onion and garlic and cook, stirring frequently, until softened. Add curry powder, salt, cumin, turmeric, ginger, and red pepper. Cook, stirring, for 30 seconds, or until the spices have been absorbed into the oil. Add water and bring to a boil. Cover and simmer for 1 hour. Add cauliflower, green beans, and peas. Simmer for 45 minutes longer.

SERVES 8.

CALORIES: 137   CHOLESTEROL: 12 mg   SODIUM: 311 mg   FIBER: 3 g

Health tip:

Omit butter and cook in a nonstick saucepan. Or, cook onion and garlic in a nonstick skillet, transferring them to the larger pot to finish cooking. Omit salt.

CALORIES: 99   CHOLESTEROL: 0 mg   SODIUM: 45 mg   FIBER: 3 g

————————◇————————

Indonesian Vegetables

If you're not crazy about vegetables, but you do like spicy, exotic dishes, you'll think this recipe was created just for you. Vary the vegetables as much as you like. And there's probably no reason you couldn't stir in a few cooked shrimp if you like them.

4 shallots, peeled and cut in half (or use the white part of scallions)
2 cloves garlic, peeled
2 tablespoons white vinegar
1 tablespoon water
1 tablespoon coarsely chopped fresh ginger
2 teaspoons paprika
2 teaspoons sugar
1 teaspoon ground turmeric
1 teaspoon salt
¼ teaspoon ground red pepper
3 tablespoons vegetable oil
2 cups julienned carrot
1 cup julienned green or red bell pepper
1½ cup cooked Job's tears

Place the shallots, garlic, vinegar, water, ginger, paprika, sugar, turmeric, salt, and ground red pepper in the container of an electric blender. Cover and blend until the mixture becomes smooth and pasty. (You can use the food processor for this job, but, in this case, I think the blender works better.)

In a wok or large skillet, heat the oil over high heat. Add spice paste and cook, stirring, for 30 seconds. Add carrot and bell pepper and cook, stirring and tossing, until vegetables are tender-crisp. Stir in Job's tears and cook, stirring, until heated through.

SERVES 6.
CALORIES: 171   CHOLESTEROL: 0 mg   SODIUM: 569 mg   FIBER: 3 g

Health tip:
Use 2 teaspoons oil and cook in a nonstick skillet; omit salt.
CALORIES: 125   CHOLESTEROL: 0 mg   SODIUM: 125 mg   FIBER: 3 g

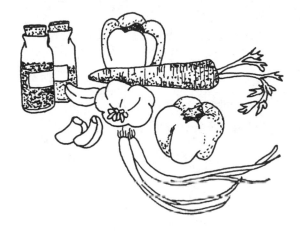

QUINOA

The history and fate of quinoa (pronounced KEEN-wa) is parallel to those of amaranth. It, too, was a sacred "mother grain" to the Incas of Peru. Like the Aztecs, the Incas were also forced to give up eating the grain believed to be the source of their strength by their Spanish conquerors. As time went by, the Incas themselves abandoned the grain.

Today quinoa is regaining some of its past glory, for nowadays both quinoa and amaranth are being touted as the "super-grains" of the eighties.

Although technically an herb, quinoa has an extremely impressive nutritional profile. The amount and quality of the protein this little grain provides is about as high, or higher, than any true grain.

Quinoa is also unique in that it has a built-in insect repellent called *saponin*. Since this substance is bitter and soapy tasting, it would also be a people repellent were it not easily rinsed from the grain in an alkaline water as part of the processing. (In addition to the rinsing it gets before packaging, quinoa should also be thoroughly rinsed before cooking.)

Types of Quinoa Available

Whole-grain quinoa: The grains have been rinsed to remove the saponins.

Quinoa flour: The whole grain that has been ground. If you cannot find the flour, you can easily make it at home. For each cup of flour, place ¾ cup whole-grain quinoa in the container of a blender or a food processor fitted with a steel blade. Cover and process until no whole grains remain and the quinoa is reduced to flour.

Pasta: Made from the quinoa flour, it comes in a variety of shapes and can be used in any recipe calling for pasta or noodles.

Texture and Flavor

Whole-grain quinoa comes in many varieties. The only one that is currently available is creamy beige in color and resembles unhulled sesame seeds in size and shape. The two brands of quinoa that I have found have slightly different characteristics. The Eden brand quinoa, as compared to the Ancient Harvest brand, is slightly smaller, with a few black grains mixed in, and has less residual saponin. Ancient Harvest, on the other hand, has practically no dark grains, but does seem to retain more saponin and requires more rinsing. I found that these differences did not affect the cooked product one way or the other.

The flavor of cooked quinoa will depend largely on how much rinsing you do. The more you rinse, the milder the flavor. The first flavor of the grain is nutty, but the distinct aftertaste is bitter, similar to, but milder than, millet. However, I have been told that people who are fond of quinoa value the bitterness and prefer not to rinse too much of it away, as they feel the bitterness is what gives quinoa its character. My own preference is to rinse the quinoa fairly thoroughly to play down the bitterness. Toasting or sautéing quinoa before adding liquid will also cut down on the aftertaste.

In texture, quinoa is light and fluffy, with an almost melt-in-the-mouth quality. There is very little, if any, of the starchy chewiness usually associated with cooked grains.

As it cooks, quinoa changes from opaque to transparent, first becoming transparent at the edge with an opaque dot in the center. Fully cooked, quinoa is completely transparent and has a small white sprout, or rootlike tail, that surrounds the grain. One sure way to tell if quinoa is cooked is to make sure that the opaque dot is gone.

Compatible Foods, Herbs, and Spices

The flavor of quinoa, and even the bitter aftertaste, is mild. Therefore it can be used with any food or seasoning you choose. The best flavors for quinoa, like millet, are sweet, sour, salty, or spicy.

Availability

Health-food stores and mail-order grain catalogs (see page 21) are the most likely places to find quinoa. But a growing number of gourmet stores and some supermarkets carry it.

Nutritional Content

Quinoa is a veritable powerhouse of nutrition. It has a high percentage of protein, the highest of all grains, in fact. In addition, it has unusually high quantities of lysine, cystine, and methionine—the amino acids lacking in most true grains. All of this makes quinoa a good complement to other grains, as well as beans.

Substitutions

Cooked bean threads: They come the closest to quinoa in texture, and may be used, perhaps cut up, in place of cooked quinoa.

White rice: Can be substituted for quinoa, but the cooking time is almost twice as long and requires a bit more liquid. The texture is also chewier.

Brown rice: Its flavor is similar to quinoa, but the texture and cooking time are very different.

Other acceptable substitutes (in order of perference): Couscous, bulgur, and millet.

Basic Cooking Instructions

Please read *About Cooking Grains* beginning on page 7.

Stove-top method:

> 1 cup quinoa
> 2 cups water
> 1 teaspoon salt

Place the quinoa in a large bowl. Fill bowl with forcefully running cold water (the saponins are what create the sudsy bubbles). Drain the quinoa in a sieve. Put the quinoa back into the bowl and repeat the rinsing and draining for a total of five times.

In a 2-quart saucepan, combine water and salt. Bring to a boil over high heat. Add drained quinoa and return to boiling. Reduce heat and simmer, covered, for 15 minutes. Remove from heat and let stand 5 minutes. Fluff with a fork.

MAKES 3½ CUPS.

Microwave method:

> 1 cup quinoa
> 2 cups water
> 1 teaspoon salt

Place the quinoa in a large bowl. Fill bowl with forcefully running cold water (the saponins are what create the sudsy bubbles). Drain the quinoa in a sieve. Put the quinoa back into the bowl and repeat the rinsing and drain for a total of five times.

Place water in a 3-quart, microwave-safe bowl. Cover with waxed paper and microwave on high (100% power) for 4 minutes. Stir in quinoa and salt. Recover with waxed paper and microwave on high for 4 minutes. Microwave at medium (50% power), still covered with waxed paper, for 9 minutes. Let stand 4 minutes. Fluff with a fork.

MAKES 3 CUPS.

Reheating

Although quinoa clumps slightly as it cools, it can easily be broken up with a fork. Chilled quinoa does not have to be reheated before being used. Should you want to reheat it, steaming or microwaving works fine.

QUINOA RECIPES

(*indicates easy recipes.)

———————— ◇ ————————

Quinoa Eggdrop Soup *
Quinoa Pasta with Fresh Tomato Sauce *
Sesame Chicken with Quinoa and Broccoli
Quinoa Sloppy Joes *
Oriental Liver and Quinoa
Quinoa-and-Cucumber Salad with Cilantro Dressing *
Orange, Almond, and Quinoa Salad *
Quinoa-and-Pear Salad *
Simply Toasted Sesame Seeds and Quinoa *
Cheddar-Zucchini-Quinoa Bake *
Quinoa and Spanish-Style Beans *
Quinoa with Leeks and Asparagus *
Curried Peas and Quinoa *
Mexican Quinoa Stew *
Quinoa Kugel
Cranberry-Quinoa Quick Bread
Pecan-Quinoa Cookies *

Quinoa Eggdrop Soup

Any form of chicken soup is comfort food for me, and this one is no exception. Adding quinoa to eggdrop soup only makes it thicker and more satisfying.

1 can (13¾ ounce) ready-to-serve chicken broth or
  1¾ cups vegetable broth (see page 19)
1½ cups plus 2 tablespoons water, divided
¼ cup quinoa, rinsed five times (see Basic Cooking Instructions)
1 tablespoon cornstarch
2 eggs
2 tablespoons thinly sliced scallion, both white and green parts

In a 3-quart saucepan, bring chicken broth and 1½ cups of the water to a boil. Stir in quinoa and simmer 20 minutes.

In a small bowl, stir together remaining 2 tablespoons water and cornstarch. Gradually stir into the boiling broth.

Beat egg in the same small bowl and gradually stir into the boiling soup. Reduce heat and simmer until egg is completely cooked. Remove from heat and stir in scallion.

SERVES 6.
CALORIES: 65   CHOLESTEROL: 70 mg   SODIUM: 228 mg   FIBER: 1 g

Health tip:
Use reduced-sodium broth.
CALORIES: 65   CHOLESTEROL: 70 mg   SODIUM: 137 mg   FIBER: 1 g

———— ◇ ————

Quinoa Pasta with Fresh Tomato Sauce

I cook this sauce for only 15 minutes, especially when I can use ripe, delicious, summertime tomatoes, at which point the tomato chunks are still intact and the sauce is quite thin. But you can continue cooking the sauce until it reaches the consistency you like. If the sauce is cooked with winter (tasteless) tomatoes, I usually add a tablespoon or two of tomato paste to bolster the tomato flavor.

4 large tomatoes
¼ cup olive oil
1 cup chopped onion
2 cloves garlic, minced
½ jalapeno pepper, minced or
    ⅛ teaspoon black pepper
¼ cup chopped fresh basil
¼ teaspoon salt
1 package (8 ounce) quinoa rotini or macaroni, cooked according to
    package directions and drained
Grated Parmesan cheese

Core the tomatoes and cut in half through the middle (not through the stem end) and squeeze out the seeds. Coarsely chop tomato halves.

In a 3- or 4-quart saucepan, heat the oil. Add onion, garlic, and jalapeno pepper and cook over medium-high heat, stirring frequently, until softened. Add chopped tomato, basil, and salt. Cook for 15 minutes, stirring occasionally. The sauce will be thin and the tomato pieces still quite visible. Cook longer if you prefer a thicker sauce.

Serve sauce over hot pasta, sprinkled with Parmesan cheese.

SERVES 4.
CALORIES: 389   CHOLESTEROL: 4 mg   SODIUM: 373 mg   FIBER: 5 g

Health tip:
Reduce oil to 1 tablespoon and cook in a nonstick saucepan. Or, cook onion, garlic, and jalapeno pepper in a nonstick skillet, transferring to the larger pan to finish cooking. Omit salt.
CALORIES: 277   CHOLESTEROL: 0 mg   SODIUM: 12 mg   FIBER: 5 g

—————— ◇ ——————

Sesame Chicken with Quinoa and Broccoli

Made without the chicken, this casserole can be served as a side dish.

2 tablespoons sesame seeds
2 to 3 tablespoons vegetable oil
1 pound skinless, boneless chicken breast, cut into bite-size pieces
1 cup sliced onion
2 cloves garlic, minced
2 cups broccoli florets
1 tablespoon soy sauce
1 tablespoon mirin (a sweet rice wine available at Oriental grocery stores) or dry sherry
2 cups cooked quinoa
1 teaspoon Oriental sesame oil (or chili oil, for braver souls)

In a dry wok or large skillet, cook the sesame seeds over medium-high heat, stirring, until golden. Remove from pan and set aside.

Heat 2 tablespoons of the vegetable oil in the wok over medium-high heat. Add chicken and cook, stirring, until lightly browned and cooked through. Remove from wok and set aside. If necessary, add the remaining tablespoon of vegetable oil to the wok. Add onion and garlic and cook, stirring and tossing, until softened. Add broccoli and cook, stirring and tossing, until tender-crisp. Stir in soy sauce and mirin. Add reserved chicken and quinoa and cook, stirring, until heated through. Add sesame oil and reserved sesame seeds and toss to mix.

SERVES 6.
CALORIES: 225   CHOLESTEROL: 53 mg   SODIUM: 443 mg   FIBER: 3 g

Health tip:
Reduce vegetable oil to 2 teaspoons and cook in a nonstick skillet. Use reduced-sodium soy sauce. Omit salt when cooking quinoa.
CALORIES: 197   CHOLESTEROL: 53 mg   SODIUM: 68 mg   FIBER 3 g

---◇---

Quinoa Sloppy Joes

This recipe started out as sautéed chicken with quinoa, but sometimes recipes have a mind of their own. This can be eaten like chili (with chopped raw onion and sour cream) or like Sloppy Joes (spooned onto a roll or a bun). Either way, the quinoa acts as a meat extender.

2 tablespoons vegetable oil
½ cup finely chopped onion
½ cup finely chopped green bell pepper
½ cup finely chopped red bell pepper
1 pound ground pork
1 cup water
½ cup bottled barbecue sauce
2 tablespoons light- or dark-brown sugar
1 tablespoon unsweetened cocoa powder
2 teaspoons white vinegar
½ teaspoon ground cinnamon
½ teaspoon salt
½ cup quinoa, rinsed 5 times (see Basic Cooking Instructions)

In a 2-quart saucepan, heat the oil over medium-high heat. Add onion and peppers, and cook, stirring frequently, until softened. Add pork and cook, stirring, until no longer pink. Stir in water, barbecue sauce, brown sugar, cocoa powder, vinegar, cinnamon, and salt. Bring to a boil. Stir in quinoa and return to boiling. Reduce heat and simmer, covered, for 15 to 20 minutes, or until all of the liquid has been absorbed.

SERVES 6.
CALORIES: 269   CHOLESTEROL: 54 mg   SODIUM: 391 mg   FIBER: 2 g

Health tip:
Omit salt. Use ground turkey instead of pork.
CALORIES: 211   CHOLESTEROL: 47 mg   SODIUM: 239 mg   FIBER: 2 g

—————— ◇ ——————

Oriental Liver and Quinoa

If you like liver, you'll love this. Be sure not to overcook the liver. Even if you think you like it well done, liver should be slightly pink in the center to taste its best. Otherwise it will be tough and dry. This is especially true for calves liver, which should be cooked more quickly than beef liver.

¾ cup water
3 tablespoons mirin (sweet rice wine available in Oriental grocery stores) or dry sherry
2 tablespoons Japanese soy sauce (Chinese soy sauce is too dark and salty for this dish)
1½ tablespoons cornstarch
1 teaspoon sugar
¼ to ½ teaspoon crushed red pepper
3 tablespoons vegetable oil, divided
1 pound beef or calves liver, cut into 1-inch-wide strips
2 cloves garlic, minced
1 tablespoon minced fresh ginger
2 cups cooked quinoa
⅓ cup sliced scallion, both white and green parts

In a medium-size bowl, stir together the water, mirin, soy sauce, cornstarch, sugar, and red pepper.

In a wok or large skillet, heat 2 tablespoons of the oil over high heat. Add liver and cook, stirring, until done as you like it. Remove liver from wok and set aside.

Heat the remaining tablespoon of oil; add garlic and ginger to wok and cook, stirring, for 30 seconds. Stir in soy-sauce mixture and cook, stirring, until mixture comes to a boil. Return liver to wok and toss until strips are coated with sauce. Add quinoa and scallion and cook, stirring and tossing, until heated through.

SERVES 4.
CALORIES: 340   CHOLESTEROL: 547 mg   SODIUM: 943 mg   FIBER: 3 g

Health tip:
Use reduced-sodium soy sauce; reduce oil to 2 teaspoons and cook in a non-stick skillet. Cook quinoa without salt.
CALORIES: 290   CHOLESTEROL: 547 mg   SODIUM: 294 mg   FIBER: 3 g

———————— ◇ ————————

Quinoa-and-Cucumber Salad with Cilantro Dressing

The dressing for this salad is very tart, so you can reduce the lime juice accordingly, if you like. If you're an avocado lover, this is the perfect salad in which to include one: small, very ripe, and cut into cubes.

> *2 cups cooked and cooled quinoa*
> *2 cups chopped peeled and seeded cucumber*
> *¼ cup sliced scallion both white and green parts*
> *¼ cup firmly packed cilantro (fresh coriander) leaves*
> *2 tablespoons olive oil*
> *2 tablespoons vegetable oil*
> *2 tablespoons lime or lemon juice*
> *⅛ teaspoon salt*
> *⅛ teaspoon ground red pepper (optional)*

In a medium-size bowl, toss together the quinoa, cucumber, and scallion.

Place cilantro, both oils, lime juice, salt, and red pepper in the container of an electric blender. Cover and blend until cilantro is finely chopped. Pour dressing over salad and toss until well combined.

SERVES 4.
CALORIES: 224   CHOLESTEROL: 0 mg   SODIUM: 445 mg   FIBER: 4 g

Health tip:
Omit salt; cut dressing ingredients in half.
CALORIES: 161   CHOLESTEROL: 0 mg   SODIUM: 3 mg   FIBER: 4 g

——————— ◇ ———————

Orange, Almond, and Quinoa Salad

I find this particular combination of citrus fruit, nuts, quinoa, and a slightly sweetened dressing to be an exquisite combination of refreshing flavors and textures.

½ cup slivered almonds
2 juicy oranges
2 cups cooked and cooled quinoa
½ cup chopped green bell pepper
⅓ cup chopped red onion
1 tablespoon olive oil
3 tablespoons orange juice
1 teaspoon cider vinegar
1 teaspoon honey
½ teaspoon dry mustard
Lettuce leaves

Place almond slivers in a small dry skillet. Cook over medium heat, stirring almost constantly, until slivers are lightly browned and really smell "toasty." Remove from heat and set aside.

Grate enough of the rind from one of the oranges to make about 1 teaspoon. Set aside. Using a small sharp knife or a vegetable peeler, remove the rind from both oranges, as well as the bitter white pith just beneath it. Cut oranges into ¼-inch slices and remove any seeds with the tip of the knife. Reserve any orange juice that accumulates when you slice the oranges to use in the dressing. (This is most easily accomplished if you slice the oranges in a shallow dish, such as a pie plate.) Set orange slices aside.

In a large bowl, toss together the quinoa, green pepper, red onion, and toasted almond slivers.

In a small bowl, stir together the olive oil, reserved orange juice, vinegar, honey, mustard, and grated orange rind. Pour dressing over salad and toss until well combined.

Line four salad plates with lettuce leaves. Place orange slices over lettuce, then top with salad.

SERVES 4.
CALORIES: 262   CHOLESTEROL: 0 mg   SODIUM: 319 mg   FIBER: 7 g

Health tip:
Cook quinoa without salt.
CALORIES: 262   CHOLESTEROL: 0 mg   SODIUM: 12 mg   FIBER: 7 g

———————— ◇ ————————

Quinoa-and-Pear Salad

I enjoy this salad for lunch. Sometimes I stir in some cottage cheese for extra protein.

> *1 can (8½ ounce) pears in syrup*
> *1½ cups cooked and cooled quinoa*
> *½ cup chopped walnuts*
> *¼ cup golden raisins*
> *1 tablespoon vegetable oil*
> *1 tablespoon honey*
> *1 tablespoon lemon juice*
> *¼ teaspoon ground cinnamon*
> *⅛ teaspoon ground ginger*
> *⅛ teaspoon ground nutmeg*

Drain pears, reserving 2 tablespoons of the juice. Chop pears coarsely.

In a medium-size bowl, toss together the pears, quinoa, walnuts, and raisins.

In a small bowl, stir together the reserved pear syrup, oil, honey, lemon juice, cinnamon, ginger, and nutmeg. Pour dressing over salad and toss until well combined.

SERVES 4.

CALORIES: 275   CHOLESTEROL: 0 mg   SODIUM: 236 mg   FIBER: 5 g

Health tip:
Cook quinoa without salt; omit oil.
CALORIES: 250   CHOLESTEROL: 0 mg   SODIUM: 7 mg   FIBER: 5 g

---

———————— ◇ ————————

Simply Toasted Sesame Seeds and Quinoa

Do not be deceived by the few ingredients in this recipe, and the ease of preparation, as it is an absolutely perfect blend of flavors and textures.

> *2 tablespoons hulled sesame seeds*
> *2 cups cooked quinoa (it should still be warm)*
> *2 tablespoons butter*

Place the sesame seeds in small skillet. Cook over medium heat, stirring, until seeds turn golden. Remove from heat.

In a medium-size bowl, combine quinoa, butter, and sesame seeds, stirring until butter is melted.

SERVES 4.
CALORIES: 167   CHOLESTEROL: 16 mg   SODIUM: 356 mg   FIBER: 3 g

Health tip:
Cook quinoa without salt; use unsalted margaine instead of butter.
CALORIES: 167   CHOLESTEROL: 0 mg   SODIUM: 9 mg   FIBER: 3 g

———————◇———————

Cheddar-Zucchini-Quinoa Bake

I usually serve this with roast chicken, for which it is the perfect side dish. You might also serve it as the main dish for a meatless meal.

3 tablespoons butter, divided
2 cups coarsely shredded zucchini
2 cups cooked quinoa
2 cups shredded Cheddar cheese
⅛ teaspoon pepper
⅓ cup unflavored bread crumbs

Preheat oven to 350°F.
Grease a 1½-quart casserole and set aside.
In a large skillet, melt 2 tablespoons of the butter over medium-high heat. Add zucchini and cook, stirring frequently, until softened. Stir in quinoa, cheese, and pepper. Spoon into prepared casserole.
Melt remaining 1 tablespoon butter in a small pan. Stir in bread crumbs. Sprinkle crumbs over casserole.
Bake for 30 minutes, or until heated through and crumbs are golden.

SERVES 4.
CALORIES: 275   CHOLESTEROL: 56 mg   SODIUM: 500 mg   FIBER: 2 g

Health tip:
Use unsalted margarine instead of butter. Cook quinoa without salt.
CALORIES: 275   CHOLESTEROL: 40 mg   SODIUM: 255 mg   FIBER: 2 g

◇

Quinoa and Spanish-Style Beans

You can make this dish as snappy as you like by adding more ground red pepper.

1 tablespoon vegetable oil
½ cup chopped onion
½ cup chopped green bell pepper
1 cup water
1 can (15 ounce) pink beans, undrained (I use Goya brand pink beans
    prepared Spanish style)
½ cup quinoa, rinsed 5 times (see Basic Cooking Instructions)
2 tablespoons chopped cilantro (fresh coriander)
¼ teaspoon salt
⅛ teaspoon ground red pepper

In a 2-quart saucepan, heat the oil over medium-high heat. Add onion and green pepper and cook, stirring frequently, until softened. Stir in water and bring to a boil. Stir in beans and quinoa. Return to boiling. Reduce heat and simmer, covered, for 20 to 25 minutes, or until quinoa is completely transparent and tender. Remove from heat and stir in cilantro, salt, and red pepper.

SERVES 6.
CALORIES: 166   CHOLESTEROL: 0 mg   SODIUM: 92 mg   FIBER: 5 g

Health tip:
Omit salt.
CALORIES: 166   CHOLESTEROL: 0 mg   SODIUM: 4 mg   FIBER: 5 g

—————— ◇ ——————

Quinoa with Leeks and Asparagus

This is a delightful dish to serve in the spring, when both asparagus and leeks are at their best and in good supply.

2 tablespoons vegetable oil
1 cup sliced leek, white and light-green parts only
½ cup quinoa, rinsed 5 times (see Basic Cooking Instructions)
1 cup chicken or vegetable broth, heated to boiling
1 cup asparagus pieces and tips
¼ teaspoon salt

In a 2-quart saucepan, heat the oil over medium-high heat. Add leek and quinoa and cook over medium heat, stirring, until quinoa starts to crackle (it will not have started to brown at this point) and leeks are very soft. Stir in broth and bring to a boil. Reduce heat and simmer, covered, for 10 minutes. Stir in asparagus and salt and simmer, covered, for 5 to 10 minutes longer, or until the liquid has been absorbed and asparagus are tender crisp.

SERVES 4.
CALORIES: 170   CHOLESTEROL: 1 mg   SODIUM: 335 mg   FIBER: 3 g

Health tip:
Reduce oil to 2 teaspoons and cook in a nonstick saucepan. Or, cook leek and quinoa in a nonstick skillet, transferring to the larger pan to finish cooking. Use low-sodium broth and omit salt.
CALORIES: 170   CHOLESTEROL: 1 mg   SODIUM: 116 mg   FIBER: 3 g

————— ◇ —————

Curried Peas and Quinoa

If you've read very far into this book, you know that I like spicy curry very much. If you're not quite as fond of mouth-tingling foods as I am, you may want to omit the red pepper.

¼ cup butter
½ cup chopped onion
3 cloves garlic, minced
1 teaspoon fresh ginger, minced
1 tablespoon curry powder
½ teaspoon ground coriander
½ teaspoon salt
¼ teaspoon turmeric
¼ teaspoon ground cumin
⅛ teaspoon ground red pepper
1 package (10 ounce) frozen peas
1¼ cups chicken or vegetable broth
½ cup quinoa, rinsed 5 times (see Basic Cooking Instructions)

In a 3-quart saucepan, melt the butter over medium-high heat. Add onion, garlic, and ginger and cook, stirring frequently, until softened. Stir in curry powder, coriander, salt, turmeric, cumin, and red pepper. Cook 30 seconds, stirring, until spices have been absorbed. Stir in peas and broth. Cover and simmer for 15 minutes. Add quinoa and return to boiling. Cover and simmer for 15 to 20 minutes longer, or until liquid has been absorbed and quinoa is transparent and tender.

SERVES 6.
CALORIES: 172   CHOLESTEROL: 21 mg   SODIUM: 459 mg   FIBER: 4 g

Health tip:
Use 2 tablespoons unsalted margarine instead of butter. Omit salt and use low-sodium broth.
CALORIES: 139   CHOLESTEROL: 0 mg   SODIUM: 64 mg   FIBER: 4 g

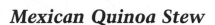

Mexican Quinoa Stew

This recipe started out as a side dish, but after it was cooked it ate more like a stew, since all of the liquid is not absorbed by the quinoa. So, add a loaf of bread, a simple salad, and call it dinner.

2 tablespoons vegetable oil
½ cup quinoa, rinsed 5 times (see Basic Cooking Instructions)
½ cup chopped onion
1 clove garlic, minced
1 can (14½ ounce) Mexican-style stewed tomatoes or plain stewed
  tomatoes, undrained
1 can (15 ounce) whole-kernel corn, undrained
¼ teaspoon ground cumin
¼ teaspoon ground red pepper
¼ teaspoon salt
Shredded Monterey Jack cheese (optional)

In a 2-quart saucepan, heat the oil over medium-high heat. Add quinoa, onion, and garlic and cook, stirring, until quinoa starts to crackle (it will not have started to brown at this point) and onion is softened. Add tomatoes and corn, cumin, red pepper, and salt, and bring to a boil. Reduce heat and simmer, covered, for 20 minutes, or until quinoa is transparent and tender. Remove from heat and let stand 5 minutes. If you like, sprinkle with cheese just before serving.

SERVES 4.
CALORIES: 260   CHOLESTEROL: 0 mg   SODIUM: 550 mg   FIBER: 5 g

Health tip:
Reduce oil to 2 teaspoons and cook in a nonstick saucepan. Or, cook quinoa, onion, and garlic in a nonstick skillet, transferring to the larger pan to finish cooking. Omit salt and cheese.
CALORIES: 208   CHOLESTEROL: 0 mg   SODIUM: 417 mg   FIBER: 5 g

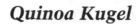

Quinoa Kugel

This fabulous kugel recipe is a variation of an old family favorite that my mother got originally from a cookbook published by her local chapter of The National Council of Jewish Women called "Dining Out at Home." I didn't think that my mother's recipe could be improved upon until I tried it using quinoa noodles, which are *much* more flavorful than ordinary wide noodles. This is as delicious served cold as it is warm.

Pudding:

> 1 package (8 ounce) quinoa flat noodles
> 4 eggs
> ½ cup orange juice
> ½ cup sugar
> ½ teaspoon vanilla extract
> ¼ teaspoon salt
> 1 cup cottage cheese
> ½ cup sour cream
> ½ cup milk
> 2 cups chopped peeled apple
> 1 cup golden raisins

Topping:

> ½ cup apricot jam
> ¾ cup crushed corn flakes
> 3 tablespoons, melted
> 1 tablespoon sugar
> ½ teaspoon ground cinnamon

Preheat oven to 350°F.

Grease a 9 × 13 × 2-inch baking dish and set aside.

To make the pudding, first cook noodles according to package directions. Drain and set aside.

In a bowl, beat eggs. Beat in orange juice, sugar, vanilla, and salt. Beat in cottage cheese, sour cream, and milk. Stir in noodles, apples, and raisins. Pour noodle mixture into prepared baking dish. (The custard will be quite thin.)

To make the topping, in a small saucepan heat jam until melted and pour over pudding mixture. (The jam may also be heated in a small bowl in a microwave oven.)

In a medium-size bowl, stir together crushed corn flakes, butter, sugar, and cinnamon. Sprinkle over top of kugel.

Bake for 1 hour, then cool for 1 hour before cutting into squares. Serve warm or at room temperature.

SERVES 15.
CALORIES: 246   CHOLESTEROL: 70 mg   SODIUM: 161 mg   FIBER: 2 g

Health tip:
Use scrambled-egg substitute instead of eggs; plain yogurt instead of sour cream; and unsalted margarine in place of butter. Use skim milk.
CALORIES: 227   CHOLESTEROL: 3 mg   SODIUM: 149 mg   FIBER: 2 g

———————◇———————

Cranberry-Quinoa Quick Bread

This sweet bread has a very grainy (in the best sense of the word!) texture to it: dense inside with a crisp crust. It tastes good just as it is, but if fat and cholesterol are no problem for you, smear it with cream cheese or butter and serve it with a cup of good coffee.

1¼ cups sugar, divided
1½ cups chopped cranberries
½ cup butter, slightly softened
2 eggs
1½ cups all-purpose flour
¾ cup quinoa flour
1 teaspoon baking soda
1 teaspoon baking powder
½ teaspoon salt
¼ cup milk

Preheat oven to 350°F.

Grease a 9 × 5 × 3-inch loaf pan and set aside.

In a medium-size bowl, combine ¼ cup of the sugar and cranberries. Set aside for 15 minutes.

In a large bowl, cream butter with remaining 1 cup sugar until light and fluffy, about 5 minutes. Beat in eggs.

In a medium-size bowl, stir together both kinds of flour, baking soda, baking powder, and salt. Add to the butter mixture alternately with milk. Stir in cranberries. (The mixture will be thick.)

Turn into prepared pan, smoothing top. Bake for 50 to 60 minutes, or until a wooden pick inserted in the center comes out clean. Turn loaf out of pan and cool on a wire rack.

MAKES 1 LOAF (16 slices).
CALORIES: 186   CHOLESTEROL: 42 mg   SODIUM: 198 mg   FIBER: 1 g

Health tip:
Use unsalted margarine instead of butter; omit salt.
CALORIES: 186   CHOLESTEROL: 42 mg   SODIUM: 89 mg   FIBER: 1 g

———————— ◇ ————————

Pecan-Quinoa Cookies

I was skeptical about how a cookie would taste made with quinoa flour. The answer is: absolutely great!

½ cup butter, slightly softened
3 tablespoons sugar
½ teaspoon vanilla extract
½ cup ground pecans
½ cup all-purpose flour
⅓ cup quinoa flour
Confectioners' sugar

Preheat oven to 300°F.
Grease one or two baking sheets and set aside.
In a large bowl, cream the butter and sugar until light and fluffy. Beat in vanilla, then pecans. Beat in both flours until well combined.
Roll batter into 1-inch balls. Place on prepared baking sheets and bake for 15 to 20 minutes, or until bottoms are lightly browned.
Place confectioners' sugar in a plastic bag. Carefully drop warm cookies into bag and shake to coat them with sugar. Cool on wire racks.

MAKES 16 COOKIES.
CALORIES: 113   CHOLESTEROL: 15 mg   SODIUM: 49 mg   FIBER: 1 g

Health tip:
Use unsalted margarine instead of butter.
CALORIES: 113   CHOLESTEROL: 0 mg   SODIUM: 7 mg   FIBER: 1 g

TEFF
(Eragrostis tef)

Teff means lost, which may refer to the fact that each grain of teff is so tiny that it is easily misplaced, especially during harvesting.

One thing is for sure. Teff is an ancient grain that has been used for ages to make *injera,* a spongy sort of crêpe that is the national bread of Ethiopia. (Millet flour is also referred to as teff sometimes, and injera can be made with it, as well as teff flour.)

Types of Teff Available

Teff: It is the whole grain, and so tiny that it can't possibly be processed, so the germ and bran remain on the grain.

Teff flour: The whole grain ground into flour.

Texture and Flavor

Teff is a tiny reddish-brown seed that cooks up very much like a stiff cornmeal-mush. The grains retain some of their crunch, and the mouth feel can be likened to thick toasted-wheat cereal, better known as Wheatina.

Of all the more unusual grains, I find teff to be the most pleasing. The flavor is pleasant, something like wheat, with a natural sweetness and a hint of malt.

Cooked teff can be used the same way you would use ground nuts or small seeds: to add texture and subtle flavor to baked goods.

Compatible Foods, Herbs, and Spices

Because of its dense texture, teff is not suitable for stews or salads. Its best use is for baked goods, or as a binding agent or a thickener, and its definite texture can be used to advantage in smooth foods. Teff can also be used plain as a hot cereal.

Availability

Teff is available in most health-food stores and through mail-order grain catalogs (see page 21). I think it may be some time before teff makes its debut as a staple supermarket item.

Nutritional Content

Teff is high in calcium, iron, protein, and fiber.

Substitutions

Amaranth: It is the only grain that can be substituted for teff. However, since the flavor of amaranth is a good deal stronger, only use this substitution if the teff is a small part of the recipe.

Poppy seeds: Since teff is frequently called for to add texture to baked goods, whole or ground poppy seeds can just as easily be used in its place.

Ground nuts: They can be substituted the same way and for the same reasons as poppy seeds.

Basic Cooking Instructions

Please read *About Cooking Grains* beginning on page 7.

Stove-top method:

> 3 cups water
> ½ teaspoon salt
> 1 cup teff

In a 2-quart saucepan, bring the water and salt to a boil over high heat. Stir in teff and return to boiling. Reduce heat and simmer for 15 minutes, stirring every 3 to 4 minutes so that the grain does not form lumps.

MAKES 3 CUPS.

Microwave method:

> 2¾ cups water
> ½ teaspoon salt
> 1 cup teff

Place the water in a 3-quart, microwave-safe bowl. Cover with waxed paper. Microwave on high (100% power) for 5 minutes. Stir in salt and teff. Recover with waxed paper and microwave on high 4 minutes. Stir, then recover, and microwave on medium (50% power) for 3 minutes. Stir, then recover, and microwave on medium for 3 minutes. Stir, recover, and microwave on medium for 3 minutes more. Stir and let stand for 4 minutes.

MAKES SCANT 3 CUPS.

Reheating

If you are going to set the cooked teff aside, be sure to place a piece of plastic wrap directly on the surface of the grain. When the air dries it out, which happens quickly, the grains cling together and harden into a skin that is tough and like plastic. Teff binds and tightens considerably when it's chilled. In fact, it gets so stiff that it can be sliced. Steaming and microwaving will restore teff to its softer state.

TEFF RECIPES

(*indicates easy recipes.)

———— ◇ ————

Injera (Ethiopian bread)
Tibs Wot (Ethiopian stew)
Lentil Burgers
Potato-and-Teff Latkes
Teff Spoonbread *
Buttermilk Waffles, Teff-Style
Teff Scones
Molasses-Teff Bread
Teff-Nut-and-Date Bread *
Walnut-Teff Strudel

───────── ◇ ─────────

Injera (Ethiopian bread)

This recipe was developed by Rebecca Wood, spokesperson for the health-food industry. Needless to say, she is an expert on all aspects of the "newer" grains, and she has written two books, "Quinoa the Supergrain" and "The Whole Foods Encyclopedia." Rebecca's injera is an Americanized version of the injera served in Ethiopia, where it is considered the national bread. Injera doesn't look like bread at all, or at least not what we think of as bread, but is more like a large and slightly spongy pancake or crêpe. Although there are only three ingredients in injera, and the actual procedure for making it is not difficult, it does take time, since the batter must ferment for up to a day to activate the natural wild yeast in the teff flour. In Ethiopia, the bread serves the purpose of both plate and eating utensils. Stews are served on top of the injera and then pieces of the bread are torn away and used to scoop up the stew.

2 cups teff flour
4 cups distilled water
⅛ teaspoon salt
Vegetable oil, for greasing skillet

In a large bowl, stir together the teff flour and water. Let stand at room temperature for 12 to 24 hours or until it gives off a slightly fermented aroma.

The following day, when ready to proceed, pour off any excess liquid on the surface of the mixture and stir in salt.

Heat a 9-inch slope-sided skillet over medium heat until a few drops of water sprinkled on the bottom of the pan bounce about before evaporating. Lightly grease skillet with oil. Pour about ½ cup of the batter into the skillet and swirl it around so that the bottom of the skillet is entirely covered with batter. Cover and leave undisturbed for about 3 minutes, or until surface of bread looks dry and bottom is browned. Remove from pan. Repeat this procedure with remaining batter. Serve warm or at room temperature.

MAKES 4 BREADS.
CALORIES: 400   CHOLESTEROL: 0 mg   SODIUM: 33 mg   FIBER: 8 g

Health tip:
These are quite healthy just as they are.

———————— ◇ ————————

Tibs Wot (Ethiopian stew)

A wot is usually eaten, quite literally, with injera (Ethiopian bread), which is broken into pieces and used to scoop up the stew. Wot, which is sometimes spelled *watt* or *wott*, can be made with beef (tibs), chicken, or vegetables. The common denominator is that it is *always* hot. This one is definitely hot, but not fiery. You can make it as hot as your mouth can stand by adding more red pepper.

2 tablespoons vegetable oil
1½ pounds beef cubes
2 cups chopped onion
3 cloves garlic, minced
1 teaspoon minced fresh ginger
2 tablespoons paprika
1 teaspoon salt
½ teaspoon ground red pepper
¼ teaspoon ground cardamom
¼ teaspoon ground coriander
Pinch ground nutmeg
Pinch ground cloves
1 cup water
2 tablespoons lime juice

In a heavy 4-quart saucepan or Dutch oven, heat the oil over medium-high heat. Add beef, onion, garlic, and ginger. Cook, stirring and tossing, until beef is no longer red and onion is softened. Add paprika, salt, red pepper, cardamom, coriander, nutmeg, and cloves, and stir until the spices are absorbed by the oil. Stir in water and bring to a boil. Cover and simmer for 1 hour. Uncover and simmer for 30 minutes longer, or until beef is tender and sauce is thickened. Stir in lime juice. Serve with injera.

SERVES 4.
CALORIES: 620   CHOLESTEROL: 153 mg   SODIUM: 647 mg   FIBER: 2 g

Health tip:
Omit salt. Use only 2 teaspoons of the oil and cook in a nonstick pan. Or, reduce oil to 2 teaspoons and cook beef, onion, garlic, and ginger in a large nonstick skillet, transferring to the larger pan to finish cooking.
CALORIES: 580   CHOLESTEROL: 153 mg   SODIUM: 114 mg   FIBER: 2 g

Lentil Burgers

I make these burgers just firm enough so that they hold together as they cook. If you prefer a firmer burger, add extra bread crumbs to the lentil mixture. These are *very* filling.

2 cups cooked lentils, divided
½ cup cooked teff
⅓ cup chopped scallion, both white and green parts
1 clove garlic, minced
½ teaspoon salt
¼ teaspoon pepper
½ cup dry unflavored bread crumbs, divided
Oil, for frying

Place ½ cup of the lentils, teff, scallion, garlic, salt, and pepper in the container of a food processor. Cover and process until thoroughly blended. Stir in remaining lentils and ¼ cup of the bread crumbs. Shape mixture into 4 patties, then carefully roll in remaining ¼ cup crumbs.

Pour enough oil into a large skillet so that it measures ¼-inch deep. Heat until bubbles form when some bread crumbs are sprinkled on top of the hot oil. Cook burgers until browned on one side. Turn and cook until browned on second side.

SERVES 4.
CALORIES: 503   CHOLESTEROL: 1 mg   SODIUM: 412 mg   FIBER: 13 g

Health tip:
Omit salt.
CALORIES: 503   CHOLESTEROL: 1 mg   SODIUM: 103 mg   FIBER: 13 g

———————— ◇ ————————

Potato-and-Teff Latkes

These are simply potato pancakes with a plus: teff. I serve them with sour cream, but they're also good with applesauce or plain yogurt.

1 cup cooked and cooled teff
1 cup shredded raw potato
1 egg
2 tablespoons grated onion
½ teaspoon salt
¼ teaspoon pepper
Oil, for frying

If the teff is lumpy, mash with the back of a spoon to break up lumps. In a medium-size bowl, stir together teff, potato, egg, onion, salt, and pepper.

Pour enough oil into a large skillet so that it measures ¼-inch deep. Heat until oil bubbles when a small amount of batter is dropped into the skillet. Drop batter into skillet by rounded measuring tablespoonsful, then flatten slightly with a broad spatula. (The more you flatten them, the crispier the latkes will be.) Cook over medium-high heat until potato shreds are a deep golden, then turn and cook the second side the same way, adjusting heat, if necessary. (Make sure that the bottom of the pancake is cooked enough or you will have trouble turning it.)

MAKES 15 LATKES.
CALORIES: 70   CHOLESTEROL: 14 mg   SODIUM: 76 mg   FIBER: 1 g

Health tip:
Omit salt. Use scrambled egg substitute.
CALORIES: CHOLESTEROL: 0 mg   SODIUM: 8 mg   FIBER: 1 g

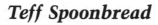

Teff Spoonbread

This is almost identical to traditional spoonbread made with cornmeal, but the teff gives it a slightly crunchier texture, which I find interesting. Serve it like the Southerners do, as a substitute for rice and potatoes, and with a big pat of butter melting on each serving.

2 cups cooked and cooled teff
1 cup milk
2 tablespoons sugar
2 tablespoons butter, melted
3 eggs, separated
2 teaspoons baking powder
1 teaspoon salt

Preheat oven to 350°F.

Grease a 1½-quart casserole or soufflé dish and set aside.

In a large bowl, stir together the teff, milk, sugar, butter, egg yolks, baking powder, and salt.

In a clean, grease-free, medium-size bowl, beat egg whites with clean beaters until stiff peaks form when beaters are lifted. Fold whites into teff mixture. Turn into prepared casserole.

Bake for 50 minutes, or until puffed and browned.

SERVES 6.

CALORIES: 214   CHOLESTEROL: 120 mg   SODIUM: 670 mg   FIBER: 3 g

Health tip:

Omit salt.

CALORIES: 214   CHOLESTEROL: 120 mg   SODIUM: 197 mg   FIBER: 3 g

———————— ◇ ————————

Buttermilk Waffles, Teff-Style

These are moist, chewy waffles, not at all crisp, but they do have a lovely flavor. They also freeze well and reheat nicely in a toaster.

1 cup teff flour
¾ cup all-purpose flour
⅓ cup sugar
1 tablespoon baking powder
1 teaspoon baking soda
1 teaspoon salt
⅔ cup buttermilk
3 eggs, separated
⅓ cup cooked teff
⅓ cup melted butter
1 teaspoon vanilla extract

Heat and grease a waffle iron as manufacturer directs.

In a large bowl, stir together both kinds of flour, sugar, baking powder, baking soda, and salt.

In a medium-size bowl, beat together the buttermilk, egg yolks, cooked teff, butter, and vanilla. Stir the buttermilk mixture into the flour mixture until well combined.

In a clean, grease-free, medium-size bowl, beat egg whites with clean beaters until they form stiff peaks when beaters are lifted. Fold beaten whites into the batter.

Spread about 1 cup of the batter onto the waffle iron. Cook until steaming has stopped and waffles are browned.

MAKES 8 WAFFLES

CALORIES: CHOLESTEROL: SODIUM: FIBER:

Health tip:
Omit salt; use unsalted margarine instead of butter.
CALORIES: CHOLESTEROL: SODIUM: FIBER:

Teff Scones

Teff adds just enough moisture to these scones to make them fairly moist. (Scones are usually a little dry for my taste.) Scones are one of the classic accompaniments to tea, but are also a wonderful breakfast treat. Spread generously with plenty of butter and strawberry jam.

1 cup teff flour
1 cup all-purpose flour
⅓ cup sugar
2 teaspoons baking powder
1 teaspoon baking soda
½ teaspoon salt
⅓ cup butter
½ cup raisins
2 eggs
⅓ cup buttermilk

Preheat oven to 400°F.

Grease a large baking sheet and set aside.

In a large bowl, stir together both kinds of flour, sugar, baking powder, baking soda, and salt. Using a pastry cutter or two knives, cut in butter until mixture resembles coarse cornmeal. Stir in raisins.

In a small bowl, beat together the eggs and buttermilk. Stir into the flour mixture just until the mixture forms a soft dough. Turn onto a floured surface and knead about 10 times. Pat into an 8-inch circle. Cut into 8 wedges and transfer to prepared baking sheet.

Bake for 15 minutes, or until lightly browned.

MAKES 8 SCONES.
CALORIES: 261   CHOLESTEROL: 73 mg   SODIUM: 412 mg   FIBER: 3 g

Health tip:
Omit salt; use unsalted margarine instead of butter.
CALORIES: 253   CHOLESTEROL: 60 mg   SODIUM: 232 mg   FIBER: 3 g

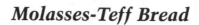

Molasses-Teff Bread

This bread makes exceptional toast. The slight sweetness comes from the molasses, and the teff keeps the bread moist.

½ cup very warm water (105–115°F)
½ teaspoon sugar
1 package dry yeast
3 cups all-purpose flour, divided
1 cup teff flour
1½ teaspoons salt
½ cup milk
⅓ cup unsulphured molasses
1 egg
½ cup cooked teff

Grease a baking sheet and set aside.

In a glass measuring cup, stir together the warm water and sugar, then stir in yeast. Let stand until ¼ inch of white bubbly foam forms on top. (This foaming is called *proofing,* and if it doesn't happen it means that for some reason or other the yeast has not been activated. Discard this batch and try again, double checking the date on the yeast package and the temperature of the water.)

In a large bowl, stir together 1 cup of the all-purpose flour, teff flour, and salt. Stir in milk, molasses, egg, cooked teff, and proofed yeast mixture. Stir in 1 cup of the all-purpose flour. Turn onto a floured surface and knead in as much of the remaining 1 cup flour as necessary to make a smooth dough.

Form dough into a ball and place in a large greased bowl. Cover with greased plastic wrap and set in a warm spot, away from drafts, until doubled in bulk, about 1 hour.

Punch dough down and shape into a round loaf. Place on prepared baking sheet. Cover with greased plastic wrap and let rise until doubled in bulk, about 40 minutes.

Preheat oven to 350°F.

Bake for about 40 minutes, or until top and bottom are nicely browned.

MAKES 1 LOAF (18 slices).
CALORIES: 130   CHOLESTEROL: 12 mg   SODIUM: 196 mg   FIBER: 3 g

Health tip:
Omit salt.
CALORIES: 130   CHOLESTEROL: 12 mg   SODIUM: 9 mg   FIBER: 3 g

—————— ◇ ——————

Teff-Nut-and-Date Bread

My sister loves this bread and eats it like cake. (The teff in the batter will make you think you're eating poppy seeds.)

1 cup teff flour
1 cup all-purpose flour
2 teaspoons baking powder
½ teaspoon salt
¾ cup butter
½ cup sugar
1 egg
1 teaspoon vanilla extract
1 cup cooked and cooled teff
½ cup milk
1 cup chopped dates
½ cup chopped walnuts

Preheat oven to 325°F.
Grease a 9 × 5 × 3-inch loaf pan and set aside.
In a medium-size bowl, stir together both kinds of flour, baking powder, and salt.
In a large bowl, cream the butter and sugar until fluffy. Beat in egg and vanilla, then cooked teff. Add the dry ingredients alternately with the milk, stirring until well combined. Stir in dates and walnuts.
Spoon batter into prepared pan. Bake for 1½ hours, or until a wooden pick inserted in the center comes out clean. Turn loaf out onto a wire rack and cool.

MAKES 1 LOAF (14 slices).
CALORIES: 257   CHOLESTEROL: 43 mg   SODIUM: 243 mg   FIBER: 3 g

Health tip:
Omit salt; use unsalted margarine instead of butter.
CALORIES: 257   CHOLESTEROL: 16 mg   SODIUM: 69 mg   FIBER: 3 g

———————— ◇ ————————

Walnut-Teff Strudel

My Hungarian grandmother never used teff in her strudel, but I'm sure she would have approved of the addition in this case. This recipe makes two small strudels.

1 cup cooked teff
⅔ cup sugar
½ cup sour cream
1 cup ground walnuts
⅓ cup golden raisins
½ teaspoon grated lemon rind
8 sheets phyllo dough (9 × 13-inch), thawed according to package
    directions
¼ cup butter, melted
6 tablespoons corn-flake crumbs
Confectioners' sugar, for sprinkling on strudel

Preheat oven to 400°F.

In a medium-size bowl, stir together the cooked teff, sugar, and sour cream, removing any lumps of teff by pressing them against the side of the bowl with a wooden spoon. Stir in walnuts, raisins, and lemon rind.

Place 1 sheet of the phyllo dough on a work surface with a long edge toward you. (Cover remaining sheets of phyllo with a damp cloth to prevent them from drying out.) Brush sheet with melted butter, then sprinkle with about 1 tablespoon of the corn-flake crumbs. Lay a second sheet of phyllo on top of the first. Brush with butter, then sprinkle with another tablespoon of the corn-flake crumbs. Repeat this procedure with a third sheet. Place a fourth sheet on top and brush with butter.

Spoon half of the teff mixture along the long edge facing you, leaving a 1½-inch border from the edge nearest you and both ends. (You will have a "log" about 2 inches wide of the filling.) Fold the two ends of dough in over the filling, then, starting from the edge nearest, roll the phyllo into a "log," completely enclosing the filling.

Repeat this whole procedure with remaining ingredients. Place both strudels on an ungreased baking sheet and brush tops with any remaining butter.

Bake for 25 minutes, or until golden. Remove from baking sheets and cool on a wire rack for at least 30 minutes before serving. Sprinkle with confectioners' sugar when cool.

MAKES 2 SMALL STRUDELS (10 servings).
CALORIES: 256   CHOLESTEROL: 17 mg   SODIUM: 105 mg   FIBER: 3 g

Health tip:
Use unsalted margarine instead of butter. Omit salt when cooking teff.
CALORIES: 256   CHOLESTEROL: 5 mg   SODIUM: 35 mg   FIBER: 3 g

TRITICALE

Triticale (pronounced tri-ti-CAY-lee), a hybrid of wheat and rye, is the first completely man-made grain.

Research and development on triticale began in the last century, but agricultural scientists of the time were unable to produce consistent results, and the project was abandoned.

In the 1960s, when the hunt was on for high-yielding grain crops with good nutritional value that might help alleviate the third-world food crisis, the triticale project was revived and successfully completed. Triticale has some of the best qualities of each of its parent grains, and, in some cases, even better.

Unfortunately, there's a down side to this success story. Crop yields have never been as great as were hoped for, and there have been some other cultivation problems as well. To top it off, acceptance of the grain has been less than overwhelming.

However, triticale is a high-protein grain with a pleasant flavor and is certainly well worth incorporating into your diet.

Types of Triticale Available

Triticale groats or berries: The whole grain that has been hulled.

Flakes: The whole hulled grain that has been toasted and thinly rolled.

Flour: Triticale that has been finely ground.

Flavor and Texture

Triticale is a rice-shaped, beige-colored grain. It cooks into plump separate grains that have the texture of fresh corn kernels (a chewy skin and a starchy core), as well as a pleasant pop when the grains are chewed.

The flavor is mild and nutty with a very faint rye sourness and a slightly starchy aftertaste. The grain is very filling and has a quality of taste and texture that adds character to any dish.

Triticale flour has a flavor some place between whole-wheat flour and rye flour. Like rye, it is low in gluten, so it should always be used in combination with other flours that are high in gluten.

Compatible Foods, Herbs, and Spices

Because triticale has a mild pleasing flavor, it can be used with almost any food you like. It goes especially well with meats (particularly beef and pork), vegetables, cheeses, and virtually any member of the onion family.

Parsley and dill are the most compatible herbs to use with triticale, although other herbs and spices work well with it, too.

Triticale combines well with other starches, such as rice and potatoes, and is very complementary to dried beans.

Availability

Triticale can be found at health-food stores and can be purchased through mail-order grain catalogs (see page 21).

Nutritional Content

The protein content in triticale is slightly higher than either rye or wheat, its parent grains. Unfortunately, I was unable to find any other nutrition information regarding this grain, but I believe that when this information becomes available it will be similar to rye.

Substitutions

Wheat berries or flakes: The flavor and texture of these two grains are very similar, and can be directly substituted.

Rye berries or flakes: Since this is the other half of triticale, so to speak, the two can be used interchangeably. However, the rye is more sour.

Brown rice: It has a similar nuttiness and chewy texture that would be fine for any recipe calling for cooked triticale. But, since the cooking times differ greatly, that will have to be taken into account.

Whole-wheat flour: Can be substituted for triticale flour.

Rye flour: Can be substituted for triticale flour.

Other substitutes (in order of preference): White rice, barley, Job's tears.

Basic Cooking Instructions

Please read *About Cooking Grains* beginning on page 7.

Whole-grain Triticale (berries/groats)

Please note: When cooking the whole grain, salt must always be added after cooking, or the grain will not absorb the water. Do not cook triticale with broth.

Stove-top method:

> 2½ cups water
> 1 cup whole-grain triticale
> ½ teaspoon salt

In a 2-quart saucepan, bring the water to a boil over high heat. Stir in triticale and return to boiling. Reduce heat and simmer, covered, for 1 hour and 45 minutes, or until almost all of the liquid has been absorbed. Remove from heat and stir in salt. Let stand for 10 minutes.

MAKES 2½ CUPS.

Microwave method:

> 3 cups water
> 1 cup whole-grain triticale
> ½ teaspoon salt

Place the water in a 3-quart, microwave-safe bowl. Cover with waxed paper and microwave on high (100% power) for 5 minutes. Stir in triticale. Recover with waxed paper and microwave on high for 4 minutes. Microwave on medium (50% power), still covered with waxed paper, for 1 hour, rotating dish once, if necessary. Let stand for 5 minutes. Stir in salt and fluff with a fork.

MAKES 2¼ CUPS.

Triticale Flakes

Stove-top method:

> 1¾ cups water
> ½ teaspoon salt
> 1 cup triticale flakes

In a 2-quart saucepan, bring the water and salt to a boil over high heat. Stir in triticale flakes and return to boiling. Reduce heat, cover, and simmer for 40 minutes.

MAKES 1½ CUPS.

Microwave method:

> 1½ cups water
> ½ teaspoon salt
> 1 cup triticale flakes

Place the water and salt in a 3-quart, microwave-safe bowl. Cover with waxed paper and microwave on high (100% power) for 3 minutes. Stir in triticale flakes. Recover with waxed paper and microwave on high for 4 minutes. Microwave on medium (50% power), still covered with waxed paper, for 30 minutes. Let stand for 4 minutes.

MAKES 1¼ CUPS.

Reheating

Triticale gets a little chewier as it chills, but it can still be used without reheating. To restore its fresh-cooked texture, microwave or steam for a short time.

TRITICALE RECIPES

*(*indicates easy recipes.)*

————————— ◇ —————————

Triticale-Carrot Soup *
Parmesan Chicken with Triticale *
Fresh-Salmon-and-Triticale Salad *
Cornish Pasties
Greek Salad *
Succotash Salad *
Fruity Triticale Salad *
Spicy Tofu Salad *
Berries, Beans, and Black-eyed Peas *
Triticale and Cauliflower with Cheese Sauce *
Good-Morning Pancakes
Triticale Yeast Bread
Trail-Mix Bread

—◇—

Triticale-Carrot Soup

The carrots and onions cook down to give this soup a wonderful natural sweetness. It's almost as good as chicken soup when you're feeling low.

8 cups water
2 pounds carrots, peeled and sliced ½-inch thick
1 pound beef short ribs or flanken
2 cups chopped onion
1 cup whole-grain triticale, rinsed
½ cup chopped parsley
¼ cup chopped fresh dill
1 teaspoon salt
⅛ teaspoon pepper

In a large soup pot, place the water, carrots, beef, onion, and triticale. Bring to a boil over high heat. Cover and simmer for 2 hours. Stir in parsley, dill, salt, and pepper. Continue to simmer, uncovered, for 30 minutes longer. Remove beef (make sure you get all the bones) from the soup. Shred meat and stir back into the soup, or serve the beef another time.

SERVES 8. (nutritional values for soup without beef)
CALORIES: 141   CHOLESTEROL: 10 mg   SODIUM: 347 mg   FIBER: 7 g

Health tip:
Omit salt. Skim off any fat from the top of the soup before serving.
CALORIES: 141   CHOLESTEROL: 10 mg   SODIUM: 81 mg   FIBER: 7 g

————— ◇ —————

Parmesan Chicken with Triticale

Don't be deceived by the simplicity of this dish; you can serve it to company on any special occasion. Best of all, it can be made ahead of time, since it reheats beautifully. Needless to say, you can substitute other cooked grains for the triticale. For instance, wild rice would be *wonderful!*

3 tablespoons butter
1 pound skinless boneless chicken breasts, cut into strips
½ cup dry white wine
½ cup heavy cream
½ cup grated Parmesan cheese
¼ teaspoon pepper
2 cups cooked whole-grain triticale

In a large skillet, melt the butter over medium-high heat. Add chicken and cook until lightly browned and cooked through. Remove chicken from skillet and set aside.

Add wine to the skillet, stirring up any brown bits that cling to the bottom and side. Stir in cream, Parmesan cheese, and pepper. Cook over high heat until boiling rapidly. Add triticale and chicken. Cook, stirring, until heated through and sauce is thickened. (If making ahead, cool slightly, then cover and chill until ready to reheat and serve.)

SERVES 4.
CALORIES: 723   CHOLESTEROL: 137 mg   SODIUM: 350 mg   FIBER: 3 g

Health tip:
Eat this only occasionally, and enjoy every mouthful when you do.

———————◇———————

Fresh-Salmon-and-Triticale Salad

I often order main-course salads when I go out to eat, and nowadays I often serve them to company. Everybody seems to enjoy these salads as much as I do, probably because they make a satisfying (and elegant) meal that's not too filling.

2 tablespoons butter
1 pound skinless salmon fillet, cut into ½-inch cubes
1 cup cooked and cooled whole-grain triticale
1 tomato, cut into wedges
½ small red onion, sliced
⅛ teaspoon salt
⅛ teaspoon pepper
⅓ cup mayonnaise
2 tablespoons sour cream
1 tablespoon chopped fresh dill or
   ½ teaspoon dried dill weed
2 tespoons lemon juice
1 teaspoon Dijon mustard
1 clove garlic, minced
4 cups mixed salad greens

In a large skillet, melt the butter over medium-high heat. Add salmon and cook, stirring and tossing, until just cooked through, about 3 minutes. Remove from heat and set aside to cool.

In a medium-size bowl, combine the triticale, tomato, red onion, salt, and pepper.

In a small bowl, stir together the mayonnaise, sour cream, dill, lemon juice, mustard, and garlic.

Divide salad greens among four dinner plates. Top with triticale mixture. Arrange salmon over greens. Spoon mayonnaise dressing over salmon.

SERVES 4.
CALORIES: 469   CHOLESTEROL: 103 mg   SODIUM: 495 mg   FIBER: 3 g

Health tip:
Substitute yogurt for mayonnaise; omit salt.
CALORIES: 389   CHOLESTEROL: 98 mg   SODIUM: 170 mg   FIBER: 3 g

Cornish Pasties

This traditional Cornish recipe for a meat turnover can be served warm or at room temperature, and is typically packed for away-from-home meals for children to take to school or husbands to take to work. The basic ingredients of beef, onion, and potato in a flaky crust rarely vary, but the seasonings can be different from one town, or even one family, to the next.

Crust:

> 1⅓ *cups triticale flour*
> 1⅓ *cups all-purpose flour*
> 1½ *teaspoons salt*
> ⅔ *cup solid white vegetable shortening*
> ½ *package (8 ounce) cream cheese or cream cheese with chives*
> ⅓ *cup ice water*

Filling:

> 1 *tablespoon vegetable oil*
> ½ *pound ground beef*
> 1 *cup* ¼*-inch-diced cooked potato*
> ½ *cup finely chopped onion*
> ¼ *cup sour cream*
> ¾ *teaspoon salt*
> ¼ *teaspoon pepper*

To make dough, in a medium-size bowl, stir both of the flours and the salt together. Cut in shortening and cream cheese with a pastry blender or two knives, until the mixture resembles coarse cornmeal. Stir in the water and form the dough into a ball. Chill for 20 minutes.

While dough is chilling, make filling. In a skillet, heat the oil over medium-high heat. Add beef, potato, and onion and cook, stirring frequently, until beef is no longer pink and onion is softened. Remove from heat and stir in sour cream, salt, and pepper. Set aside to cool slightly.

Preheat oven to 400°F.

On a lightly floured surface, roll dough into an 18-inch circle. Cut out 7 6-inch circles, tracing around a plate, or anything that measures 6 inches in diameter, with the tip of a knife. Place equal amounts of the filling on each circle, leaving a ½-inch border. Brush borders with water and fold one side of the dough over the filling to form a half-moon. (You may find this a little tricky to do as there is quite a lot of filling for each pasty. The best way is to sort of hold the filling back with one finger as you fold the dough over it.) Seal each pasty by pressing the edge with your fingers or the tines of a dinner fork (you may need to dip the fork in flour from time to time to keep it from sticking to the dough). Place pasties on ungreased baking sheets. Cut vents in each pasty, or prick with a fork several times.

Bake for 25 minutes, or until golden. Serve immediately, or cool and serve at room temperature. Pasties may also be chilled and reheated, if that's more convenient.

MAKES 7 PASTIES.
CALORIES: 518   CHOLESTEROL: 52 mg   SODIUM: 833 mg   FIBER: 5 g

Health tip:
Omit salt.
CALORIES: 518   CHOLESTEROL: 52 mg   SODIUM: 72 mg   FIBER: 5 g

Greek Salad

This is a very full-flavored salad. The feta cheese, anchovies, and olives all have strong salty flavors. If you're not fond of or can't eat salty foods, you can omit the anchovies, if you like, and cut back on the feta cheese and olives. However, these ingredients are the heart of a Greek salad, and the anchovies and cheese do make it a complete high-protein dish.

1 cup cooked and cooled whole-grain triticale
1 cup coarsely chopped tomato
1 cup coarsely chopped peeled or unpeeled cucumber
¼ cup sliced scallion, both white and green parts
1 tablespoon olive oil
1 tablespoon vegetable oil
2 tablespoons red-wine vinegar
2 or 3 anchovies, cut into ½-inch pieces (about 1 tablespoon)
¼ teaspoon crumbled oregano
⅛ teaspoon pepper
½ cup crumbled feta cheese
12 pitted black olives, cut in half

In a large bowl, combine the triticale, tomato, cucumber, and scallion.

In a small bowl, stir together both oils, vinegar, anchovies, oregano, and pepper. Pour dressing over triticale mixture and toss gently to combine. Top with feta cheese and olives.

SERVES 8.
CALORIES: 146   CHOLESTEROL: 30 mg   SODIUM: 269 mg   FIBER: 1 g

Health tip:
Omit anchovies; reduce feta cheese to 2 tablespoons; omit olives.
CALORIES: 77   CHOLESTEROL: 1 mg   SODIUM: 126 mg   FIBER: 1 g

Succotash Salad

Chili powder and ground red pepper give this traditional New England dish a real Southwestern flavor. I would certainly think of serving this salad as a nice change from potato salad at a barbecue or a picnic.

1½ cups cooked and cooled whole-grain triticale
1 can (12 ounce) whole-kernel corn, drained
1 package (10 ounce) frozen lima beans, thawed and cooked as package
    directs, and cooled
1 cup sliced celery
½ cup chopped red bell pepper
¼ cup chopped red onion
3 tablespoons vegetable oil
1 tablespoon cider vinegar
½ teaspoon chili powder
¼ teaspoon salt
⅛ teaspoon ground red pepper (optional)

In a large bowl, combine the triticale, corn, lima beans, celery, red bell pepper, and onion.

In a small bowl, stir together the oil, vinegar, chili powder, salt, and ground red pepper. Pour dressing over salad mixture and toss gently to combine.

SERVES 10.
CALORIES: 136   CHOLESTEROL: 0 mg   SODIUM: 296 mg   FIBER: 4 g

Health tip:
Omit salt.
CALORIES: 136   CHOLESTEROL: 0 mg   SODIUM: 100 mg   FIBER: 4 g

—————— ◇ ——————

Fruity Triticale Salad

I think you'll like this sort of strange combination of fruit, cheese, nuts, and grain. I often eat this salad by itself for lunch, but it works just as well as a side salad, with broiled chicken, for instance.

1½ cups cooked and cooled whole-grain triticale
1 cup chopped tart apple (Granny Smith or McIntosh)
1 cup fresh peach slices
1 cup diced Monterey Jack cheese
½ cup chopped walnuts
¼ cup bottled Italian dressing
1 tablespoon fresh lemon juice
1 teaspoon Dijon mustard

In a large bowl, combine the triticale, apple, peach slices, cheese, and nuts.

In a small bowl, stir together dressing, lemon juice, and mustard. Pour over salad ingredients and toss gently to combine.

SERVES 4 (as a light main dish); OR 6 (as a side dish)
CALORIES: 537   CHOLESTEROL: 23 mg   SODIUM: 226 mg   FIBER: 11 g

Health tip:
Use a homemade dressing without salt, cook triticale without salt. Omit cheese.
CALORIES: 432   CHOLESTEROL: 0 mg   SODIUM: 20 mg   FIBER: 11 g

———————— ◇ ————————

Spicy Tofu Salad

I'm very fond of tofu, and the combination of tofu with whole-grain berries is a very healthy and nutritious combination. For my taste, the flavor of this salad is outstanding, but you may want to start with only ¼ to ½ teaspoon of the chili oil. As they say, you can always add more. If you think the chili oil will still be too hot, leave it out altogether and substitute Oriental sesame oil.

1½ cups cooked and cooled whole-grain triticale
1 cup diced tofu
1 can (8 ounce) water chestnuts, drained and chopped
½ cup julienned red bell pepper
¼ cup chopped scallion, both white and green parts
2 tablespoons vegetable oil
1½ tablespoons rice vinegar (available in Oriental grocery stores)
1 tablespoon Japanese soy sauce (if you use a Chinese soy sauce, reduce
*   to 2 teaspoons)*
1 teaspoon chili oil or Oriental sesame oil (both available in Oriental
*   grocery stores)*
1 clove garlic, minced

In a large bowl, combine the triticale, tofu, water chestnuts, red bell pepper, and scallion.

In a small bowl, stir together the vegetable oil, vinegar, soy sauce, chili oil, and garlic. Pour dressing over salad ingredients and toss gently to combine.

SERVES 4.
CALORIES: 165   CHOLESTEROL: 0 mg   SODIUM: 392 mg   FIBER: 3 g

Health tip:
Use low-sodium soy sauce. Omit salt when cooking triticale.
CALORIES: 165   CHOLESTEROL: 0 mg   SODIUM: 66 mg   FIBER: 3 g

———— ◇ ————

Berries, Beans, and Black-eyed Peas

I thought I didn't like either collard greens or kale or black-eyed peas until I cooked this. If you're of the same mind, this dish may make a convert of you, too.

3 slices bacon, cut into 1-inch pieces
2 cups firmly packed chopped collard greens or kale
½ cup chopped onion
2 cloves garlic, minced
1 can (10½ ounce) black-eyed peas, drained
1 cup cooked triticale berries
¼ teaspoon salt
¼ teaspoon pepper

In a large heavy saucepan or Dutch oven, cook the bacon until crisp. Remove bacon and drain on paper towels. Add greens, onion, and garlic to fat remaining in pan. Cook over medium heat, stirring, until vegetables are softened. Stir in black-eyed peas, triticale, salt, and pepper. Cook, stirring, until heated through, about 5 minutes. Stir in reserved bacon.

SERVES 6.
CALORIES: 115   CHOLESTEROL: 3 mg   SODIUM: 440 mg   FIBER: 6 g

Health tip:
Omit bacon. Cook in a nonstick saucepan with 1 tablespoon vegetable oil. Or, cook greens, onion, and garlic in oil in a nonstick skillet, transferring to the larger pan to finish cooking.
CALORIES: 115   CHOLESTEROL: 0 mg   SODIUM: 152 mg   FIBER: 6 g

———————◇———————

Triticale and Cauliflower with Cheese Sauce

When you combine a creamy cheese sauce with cauliflower and triticale, what you get is an indecently rich and delicious side dish. You can also serve this as a meatless main dish, if you like, heeding the health tips below to cut back on the fat and sodium a bit.

4 cups cauliflower florets
3 tablespoons butter
¼ cup all-purpose flour
1½ cups milk
1 cup shredded Cheddar cheese
¼ teaspoon Worcestershire sauce
¼ teaspoon salt
⅛ teaspoon pepper
2 cups cooked triticale

In a 4-quart saucepan, steam the cauliflower in a small amount of water until tender. Drain thoroughly and set aside.

In the same saucepan, melt the butter over medium heat. Stir in flour until absorbed. Using a whisk, quickly stir in milk and cook, stirring, until mixture comes to a boil. Cook, stirring, for 1 minute. Stir in cheese, Worcestershire sauce, salt, and pepper, stirring until cheese is melted. Stir in cauliflower and triticale. Continue to cook, stirring, until heated through.

SERVES 8.
CALORIES: 208   CHOLESTEROL: 31 mg   SODIUM: 411 mg   FIBER: 3 g

Health tip:
Use skim milk instead of whole milk; substitute unsalted margarine for butter; omit salt.
CALORIES: 196   CHOLESTEROL: 14 mg   SODIUM: 114 mg   FIBER: 3 g

—————— ◇ ——————

Good-Morning Pancakes

Pancakes made with cottage cheese are not light and fluffy. In fact, these are moist and heavy with a slighty tangy taste from the cottage cheese and a grainy mouth feel from the triticale. So why eat them? Because they taste good and they aren't too fattening.

½ cup lowfat cottage cheese
2 egg whites
2 tablespoons 1-percent-fat milk
2 tablespoons sugar
¼ teaspoon vanilla extract
Pinch salt
¼ cup triticale flour
¼ cup all-purpose flour
1 teaspoon baking powder
Oil, for greasing griddle

Place the cottage cheese, egg whites, milk, sugar, vanilla, and salt in the container of an electric blender. Cover and blend until smooth. Add both kinds of flours and baking powder to mixture in blender. Cover and blend until combined.

Heat a griddle or a large skillet until a few drops of water sprinkled on the hot griddle bounce about before evaporating. Grease griddle lightly. Drop 2 tablespoonsful of the batter per pancake onto the griddle. Cook until bubbles on top burst. Turn and cook until the second side is browned.

MAKES 10 PANCAKES.
CALORIES: 37   CHOLESTEROL: 1 mg   SODIUM: 130 mg   FIBER: 1 g

Health tip:
Omit salt; reduce sugar to 1 tablespoon.
CALORIES: 32   CHOLESTEROL: 1 mg   SODIUM: 91 mg   FIBER: 1 g

—————— ◇ ——————

Triticale Yeast Bread

This bread is quite similar to a whole wheat bread, but it's a little heavier. It's this very quality that makes this an ideal toasting bread. You can use all-purpose flour if you have trouble finding bread flour, and rye or whole wheat flour if you can't find triticale flour.

½ cup very warm water (105–115°F)
½ teaspoon sugar
1 package dry yeast
1½ cups triticale flour
2½ to 3 cups bread flour
2 teaspoons salt
1 cup milk
2 eggs, beaten
¼ cup butter, melted

Grease a 9 × 5 × 3-inch loaf pan and set aside.

In a glass measuring cup, stir together the water and sugar. Stir in yeast and let stand until ¼ inch of white bubbly foam forms on top. (This foaming is called *proofing*, and if it doesn't happen it means that for some reason or other the yeast has not been activated. Discard this batch and try again, double checking the date on the yeast package and the temperature of the water.)

In a large bowl, stir together the triticale flour and 1½ cups of the bread flour, and salt. Stir in proofed-yeast mixture, milk, eggs, and butter. Stir in ¾ cup more of the bread flour.

Turn dough out onto a floured surface and knead in enough of the remaining ¾ cup bread flour to form a dough that is no longer sticky. (The dough will be soft and not as firm as most bread doughs, but it should not be sticky.) Place dough in a greased bowl and cover with greased plastic wrap. Set in a warm spot, out of drafts, and let rise until doubled in bulk, about 1½ hours.

Punch dough down and form into a 9-inch loaf. Place in prepared loaf pan. Cover with greased plastic wrap and let rise until doubled in bulk, about 45 minutes.

Preheat oven to 350°F.

Bake for 50 minutes, or until loaf is browned on top and bottom. Remove bread from pan and cool on a wire rack.

MAKES 1 LOAF (16 slices).
CALORIES: 148   CHOLESTEROL: 36 mg   SODIUM: 307 mg   FIBER: 2 g

Health tip:
Omit salt; use unsalted margarine instead of butter.
CALORIES: 148   CHOLESTEROL: 28 mg   SODIUM: 20 mg   FIBER: 2 g

Trail-Mix Bread

I didn't start out to make a so-called trail-mix bread. I just thought that a slightly sweet bread with a mixture of nuts and seeds in it would be unusual. Then I got the idea to add the currants. As I struggled to name the bread, I thought about all the goodies I had measured out for it and realized that what I had made was a trail mix. This bread has a lovely kind of crumbly texture, but the slices hold together and are just waiting to be spread with butter, maybe even an exotic butter (like cashew or almond butter), and any kind of jam would be great!

½ cup butter
½ cup firmly packed light- or dark-brown sugar
2 eggs
½ cup currants
⅓ cup chopped cashew nuts
⅓ cup chopped pecans
¼ cup sunflower seeds
1 cup all-purpose flour
¾ cup triticale flour
2 teaspoons baking powder
1 teaspoon baking soda
1 teaspoon salt
½ cup buttermilk

Preheat oven to 350°F.
Grease a 9 × 5 × 3-inch loaf pan and set aside.
In a large bowl, cream the butter and sugar until fluffy. Beat in eggs. (The mixture will look curdled at this point.) Stir in currants, cashews, pecans, and sunflower seeds.
In a medium-size bowl, stir together both kinds of flour, baking powder, baking soda, and salt. Add the dry ingredients to the butter mixture alternately with the buttermilk. Spoon batter into prepared pan.
Bake for 50 minutes, or until nicely browned. Remove from pan and cool on a wire rack.

MAKES 1 LOAF (16 slices).
CALORIES: 171   CHOLESTEROL: 34 mg   SODIUM: 292 mg   FIBER: 3 g

Health tip:
Use unsalted margarine instead of butter; omit salt.
CALORIES: 171   CHOLESTEROL: 26 mg   SODIUM: 141 mg   FIBER: 3 g

BREAKFAST CEREAL

Say "cereal" to the average American and chances are, rather than thinking of any particular grain ("a grain suitable for food" is the first definition of cereal, by the way), row upon row and shelf upon shelf of brightly designed boxes come to mind. The boxes contain flakes, puffs, nuggets, and squares of breakfast cereal, ranging in color from shocking pink to dark brown, and, unfortunately, most of them are a far cry from what their original creators intended.

The story of breakfast cereal is an interesting one. It began in the middle of the nineteenth century, when preachers and doctors started advocating pure plain eating, and a campaign was launched against eating rich foods. Pork, salt, coffee, tea, sugar, and white flour, were only a few of the forbidden foods, and it was believed that consuming them would ultimately lead to physical and moral decay.

The first breakfast cereal was developed by Dr. James C. Jackson, a follower of Sylvester Graham, a Presbyterian minister, who urged his followers to embrace whole-grain flours. Jackson made loaves of bread from graham flour and water, which were baked slowly until they dried out. The loaves were then broken into pieces, baked again, and finally crumbled into even smaller pieces. Graham called his product Granula. It was to be served for breakfast after an overnight soak in milk

The cause of breakfast cereal was subsequently taken up by the Seventh Day Adventists, whose sanitarium in Battle Creek, Michigan was run by Dr. John Harvey Kellogg. Dr. Kellogg also advocated a diet of less meat and more roughage. (It's sort of amazing that Dr. Jackson's and Dr. Kellogg's diet guidelines are about the same as the ones we're hearing so much about today.) To help meet these requirements, Dr. Kellogg came up with a baked biscuit made of oats, cornmeal, and wheat that was ground into a breakfast cereal. He later went on to create the first flaked cereal by cooking wheat, rolling it thin, and baking it until dry. But it was not until he started to make the flakes out of corn and barley malt that his creation would gain widespread acceptance and popularity as—you guessed it—corn flakes.

Dr. Kellogg was not alone in the business of breakfast cereal. There was also Henry D. Persky, who created a wheat biscuit (which he baked, at the suggestion of Dr. Kellogg) that eventually became known as Shredded Wheat. And C.W. Post, who introduced a "scientific breakfast food" known as Grape Nuts, a cereal based on

469

Dr. Jackson's Granula. And so the breakfast-cereal industry, based on the latest principles of nutrition, began to grow.

Now, nearly 100 years later, it's ironic that the words "health food" would be about the last words any nutritionally knowledge- able person would use to describe most of today's array of cold cereals. Even those cereals that include "miracle" foods, such as fiber and oat bran, are also, in many cases, loaded with saturated fats in the form of coconut and palm oils, and sugar.

Hot cereals are more in keeping with the intentions of those pioneers of breakfast cereal. For the most part, cereals that are intended to be cooked and eaten are pure grain products, high in fiber and vitamin and mineral nutrients.

The best advice I can give you about buying cereal is to read, read, read those labels—especially the nutritional information— and make sure that what you take home is, in fact, a reasonably nutritious breakfast food that isn't loaded with saturated fats, sugar, artificial colors, and other additives. Keep in mind that brand names can be deceiving. For instance, a cereal that is named some- thing like "total bran," I assure you, is not, since pure bran can only be compared to sawdust in both flavor and texture.

About Breakfast Cereals

The range of breakfast cereals available nowadays is so vast that it is impossible for me to discuss each product individually.

The recipes that follow, for the most part, use those cereals, which I consider to have at least some redeeming nutritional value, and will give you some ideas to help expand your repertoire beyond pour-into-a-bowl-add-milk-and-eat.

In some cases, you can make cereal substitutions: a corn flake for a wheat flake, for instance. In other cases you will have to use your own judgement, but the substitution should be more or less the same density and flavor. You can be a little more flexible when it comes to crushed cereals that are used for coatings and toppings, for example.

Cereals do have generic names, but they are so long and so ridiculously confusing that I have decided to just go ahead and call them by their familiar brand names.

I had a lot of fun creating these recipes, and I hope you enjoy them.

BREAKFAST-CEREAL RECIPES

*(*indicates easy recipes)*

————————◇————————

Spinach-Stuffed Flounder
Crispy Fried Sole
Spicy Chicken Strips
Crunchy Oven-Baked Chicken *
Stuffed Bell Peppers *
Thursday's Meatloaf *
Kasha Salad *
Mushroom Kasha *
Garlicky Stuffed Tomatoes
Squash-and-Carrot Casserole
Steamed Pudding with Brandied Topping
Honey-Bran Waffles *
Cream-of-Rice Pancakes
Banana-Bran Muffins *
Cereal Dumplings *
Raisin-Bran Oatmeal Cookies
Granola-Cheesecake Squares *
Frozen Maple-Pecan Pie
Viennese Farina
Cinnamon-Toast Bread Pudding *
Corny Apple Fritters
Baked Stuffed Pears à la Mode *
Fresh Peach Strada *
Ice Cream Layer Cake *
Granola Coffee Cake *
Krispie, Crunchy Chocolate Drops *
Maple-Wheat Candy *

471

─────── ◇ ───────

Spinach-Stuffed Flounder

You can substitute almost any fillet that is long and thin and can be easily rolled for the flounder. There are also other cold cereals that are similar to Product 19 that can be used in the stuffing.

4 medium flounder fillets (about 1¼ pounds)
3 tablespoons butter, divided
⅓ cup chopped celery
¼ cup chopped green bell pepper
¼ cup chopped onion
½ cup chopped tomato
1 tablespoon lemon juice
¼ teaspoon salt
¼ teaspoon crushed thyme
⅛ teaspoon pepper
⅔ cup Product 19, crushed
1 package (10 ounce) frozen chopped spinach, thawed and squeezed to
  remove as much of the liquid as possible

Preheat oven to 350°F.

Rinse the flounder fillets, pat dry on paper towels, and set aside.

In a medium-size skillet, melt 1½ tablespoons of the butter over medium-high heat. Add celery, green pepper, and onion and cook, stirring frequently, until vegetables are softened. Stir in tomato, lemon juice, salt, thyme, and pepper. Cook, stirring, until tomato is softened, about 5 minutes. Remove from heat and stir in crushed cereal and spinach.

Place one-quarter of the spinach mixture on the broader end of each fillet. Roll up and fasten with wooden picks. Place in a baking pan that is just large enough to hold the rolled fillets comfortably. Dot fillets with remaining 1½ tablespoons butter.

Bake for 25 minutes, or until fillets are just cooked through.

SERVES 4.
CALORIES: 258   CHOLESTEROL: 91 mg   SODIUM: 456 mg   FIBER: 3 g

Health tip:
Use 1½ tablespoons unsalted margarine in the stuffing only. Omit salt.
CALORIES: 220   CHOLESTEROL: 68 mg   SODIUM: 255 mg   FIBER: 3 g

———— ◇ ————

Crispy Fried Sole

Serve this fried sole (or flounder, or any white-fish fillet) with french fries and what you have is fish-and-chips. An accompaniment of tartar sauce and cole slaw tastes good, too.

4 medium fillets of sole (about 1¼ pounds)
2 eggs
1 tablespoon water
3 tablespoons flour
½ teaspoon salt
⅛ teaspoon pepper
¾ cup corn-flake crumbs (buy them ready-made or briefly process
plain corn flakes in a blender or food processor until flakes
form fine crumbs)
Oil, for frying

Rinse the fillets, pat dry on paper towels, and set aside.
In a wide shallow bowl or pie plate, beat eggs with water.
Place the flour on a piece of waxed paper and stir in salt and pepper. Place corn-flake crumbs on another piece of waxed paper.
Dredge fillets in flour mixture, then dip in beaten eggs. Pat corn-flake crumbs onto fillets.
Pour enough oil in a large skillet until it measures about ¼-inch deep. Heat until the oil bubbles when a few crumbs are sprinkled on it. Add fillets and cook over medium-high heat until browned, then turn with a wide spatula and cook until browned on the second side, adjusting heat as necessary. Drain on paper towels.

SERVES 4.

CALORIES: 302 CHOLESTEROL: 189 mg SODIUM: 682 mg FIBER: 0 g

Health tip:
Use a scrambled-egg substitute; omit salt.
CALORIES: 290 CHOLESTEROL: 85 mg SODIUM: 378 mg FIBER: 0 g

Spicy Chicken Strips

These delicate little strips also make an excellent appetizer, as well as a main dish. Offer honey mustard or honey-mustard mayonnaise for dipping.

1 pound skinless boneless chicken breasts
2 eggs
2 tablespoons water
¼ teaspoon liquid red pepper (Tabasco)
⅓ cup all-purpose flour
½ teaspoon salt
¼ teaspoon ground cumin
¼ teaspoon garlic powder
¼ teaspoon ground red pepper
1½ cups Special K
½ teaspoon spicy seasoned salt
¼ teaspoon pepper
Oil, for frying

Cut chicken breasts into 2 × ½-inch strips and set aside.

In a wide shallow bowl or pie plate, beat the eggs with water and liquid red pepper.

Place flour on a piece of waxed paper and stir in salt, cumin, garlic, and ground red pepper and set aside.

Place cereal, seasoned salt, and pepper in the container of an electric blender or food processor. Cover and blend until the cereal forms fine crumbs. Place crumb mixture on a piece of waxed paper.

Dredge the chicken strips in flour mixture, then dip into beaten eggs. Pat crumbs onto strips.

Pour enough oil in a large skillet until it measures about ¼-inch deep. Heat oil until it bubbles when a few crumbs are sprinkled on top. Add chicken strips and fry over medium-high heat until golden on both sides and cooked through.

SERVES 4.
CALORIES: 322   CHOLESTEROL: 169 mg   SODIUM: 714 mg   FIBER: 1 g

Health tip:
Use scrambled-egg substitute; omit salt.
CALORIES: 311   CHOLESTEROL: 66 mg   SODIUM: 198 mg   FIBER: 1 g

—————— ◇ ——————

Crunchy Oven-Baked Chicken

Coat the chicken early in the day, if that's more convenient, and then chill until ready to cook and serve.

3½ pound chicken, cut into pieces and skin removed
2 cups Grape Nuts, crushed
⅓ cup mayonnaise
¼ cup plain yogurt
1 tablespoon honey mustard
¼ teaspoon salt
⅛ teaspoon pepper

Preheat oven to 350°F.
Rinse the chicken and pat dry.
Sprinkle cereal crumbs on a piece of waxed paper.

In a medium-size bowl, stir together mayonnaise, yogurt, honey mustard, salt, and pepper. Brush chicken generously with this mixture. Roll in crushed cereal to coat. Place chicken on an ungreased baking sheet.

Bake for 50 minutes, or until cooked through.

SERVES 4.
CALORIES: 630   CHOLESTEROL: 180 mg   SODIUM: 878 mg   FIBER: 4 g

Health tip:
Use reduced-calorie mayonnaise; omit salt.
CALORIES: 546   CHOLESTEROL: 175 mg   SODIUM: 740 mg   FIBER: 4 g

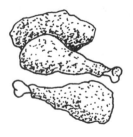

Stuffed Bell Peppers

The microwave oven cooks these to perfection. Cover loosely with plastic wrap and microwave on high (100% power) for 10 minutes.

4 medium-size green or red bell peppers
¾ pound ground veal or beef
1 can (8 ounce) tomato sauce, divided
½ cup 40% Bran Flakes
¼ cup finely chopped onion
½ teaspoon salt
¼ teaspoon pepper
1 can (14½ ounce) Cajun-style stewed tomatoes or plain stewed
    tomatoes

Preheat oven to 375°F.

Cut off tops and remove seeds from bell peppers. Drop peppers into a large pot of boiling water for 5 minutes. Remove from pot. Drain and set aside.

In a medium-size bowl, combine meat, ½ cup of the tomato sauce, cereal, onion, salt, and pepper. Mix gently (I always use my hands to combine meat mixtures) until thoroughly combined. Spoon one-quarter of the meat mixture into each pepper. Stand peppers in a 9-inch-square baking pan. Mix stewed tomatoes and remaining tomato sauce together and pour over and around peppers.

Bake for 50 minutes, or until peppers are tender and meat is cooked through.

SERVES 4.
CALORIES: 268   CHOLESTEROL: 61 mg   SODIUM: 867 mg   FIBER: 4 g

Health tip:
Use ground veal; omit salt.
CALORIES: 268   CHOLESTEROL: 61 mg   SODIUM: 600 mg   FIBER: 4 g

—————— ◇ ——————

Thursday's Meatloaf

Thursday was always my favorite lunch day in the high-school cafeteria. That's when they served the "type A" lunch consisting of meatloaf with mashed potatoes and canned green beans. I freely admit that I still eat this combination any time I'm in need of a little stroking. This is a very simple, down-home meatloaf. It's rather onion-y, but you can adjust that to suit your own taste.

1 egg
1½ pounds ground beef
1 cup spaghetti sauce, divided
½ cup finely chopped onion
½ cup slightly crushed corn flakes
½ teaspoon salt
⅛ teaspoon pepper

Preheat oven to 350°F.

Beat the egg lightly in a large bowl. Add ground beef, ½ cup of the spaghetti sauce, onion, cereal, salt, and pepper. Mix gently until well combined. Shape mixture into an 8 × 4-inch loaf in a baking pan. Pour remaining ½ cup spaghetti sauce over meatloaf.

Bake for 1 hour and 15 minutes, or until cooked through.

SERVES 5.
CALORIES: 422   CHOLESTEROL: 130 mg   SODIUM: 445 mg   FIBER: 1 g

Health tip:
Omit salt. Use extra lean beef.
CALORIES: 354   CHOLESTEROL: 112 mg   SODIUM: 268 mg   FIBER: 1 g

————————— ◇ —————————
Kashi Salad

It was a simple Kashi salad, very much like this one, that was the inspiration for this book. I first tasted Kashi, a whole grain breakfast cereal, and whole-wheat berries) while I was on vacation at a health spa a few years ago and was absolutely bowled over by how delicious grains could be.

1¾ cups water
¾ teaspoon salt
1 envelope Kashi (1 cup less 2 tablespoons)
½ cup chopped red bell pepper
½ cup chopped green bell pepper
3 tablespoons chopped scallion, both white and green parts
2 tablespoons chopped parsley
2 tablespoons vegetable oil
1 tablespoon red-wine vinegar

In a 2-quart saucepan, bring the water and salt to a boil over high heat. Stir in kasha. Reduce heat, cover, and simmer for 1 hour. Remove from heat and set aside to cool.

In a medium-size bowl, combine the red and green bell peppers, scallion, and parsley. Add oil and vinegar and toss to combine. Add cooled kasha and toss again. Chill before serving.

SERVES 6.
CALORIES: 221   CHOLESTEROL: 0 mg   SODIUM: 267 mg   FIBER: 1 g

Health tip:
Omit salt.
CALORIES: 221   CHOLESTEROL: 0 mg   SODIUM: 7 mg   FIBER: 1 g

————————— ◇ —————————
Mushroom Kashi

This is an excellent, easy-to-fix side dish for roast meat or poultry, steak, or chops.

2 tablespoons butter
½ cup chopped onion
2 cups sliced mushrooms
1 can (13¾ ounce) ready-to-serve beef broth or
   1¾ cups vegetable broth (see page 19)

1 envelope Kashi (1 cup less 2 tablespoons)
2 tablespoons chopped parsley

In a 2-quart saucepan, melt the butter over medium-high heat. Add onion and cook, stirring frequently, until softened. Add mushrooms and cook, stirring and tossing, until soft and lightly browned. Stir in broth and bring to a boil. Stir in kasha. Cover and simmer for 1 hour. Remove from heat and stir in parsley. Cover and let stand for 5 minutes.

SERVES 6.
CALORIES: 225   CHOLESTEROL: 10 mg   SODIUM: 244 mg   FIBER: 2 g

Health tip:
Use low-sodium broth. Use unsalted margarine instead of butter.
CALORIES: 225   CHOLESTEROL: 0 mg   SODIUM: 122 mg   FIBER: 2 g

— ◇ —

Garlicky Stuffed Tomatoes

Make these in advance, if you like, and bake them just before serving time.

2 large tomatoes
2 tablespoons butter
2 tablespoons minced onion
1 clove garlic, minced
1 cup crushed Wheaties
¼ teaspoon crushed basil
⅛ teaspoon crushed thyme
⅛ teaspoon salt
⅛ teaspoon pepper

Preheat oven to 400° F.

Cut tomatoes in half, widthwise. Scoop out the centers and chop them. Set aside.

In a small skillet, melt butter over medium-high heat. Add onion and garlic and cook, stirring, until softened. Stir in chopped tomato and cook over high heat until the mixture is a thick sauce. Stir in cereal, basil, thyme, salt, and pepper. Spoon one-quarter of the tomato mixture into each of the tomato halves. Place stuffed tomatoes in a baking pan.

Bake for 15 to 20 minutes, or until tomatoes are heated through and the top of the stuffing is browned.

SERVES 4.
CALORIES: 91   CHOLESTEROL: 16 mg   SODIUM: 208 mg   FIBER: 2 g

Health tip:
Use unsalted margarine instead of butter; omit salt.
CALORIES 91:   CHOLESTEROL: 0 mg   SODIUM: 103 mg   FIBER: 2 g

---

◇

Squash-and-Carrot Casserole

This is an unbelievably delicious way to prepare vegetables, which I like to serve as a nice change from a sweet-potato casserole.

1 large butternut squash, peeled and cut into 1-inch cubes
    (you should have about 4 cups)
3 cups sliced carrot
⅓ cup firmly packed light- or dark-brown sugar
3 tablespoons heavy cream
2 tablespoons butter
2 tablespoons pure maple syrup
1 teaspoon grated orange rind
½ teaspoon salt
¼ teaspoon ground ginger
Pinch mace

Topping:

1 cup slightly crushed Special K
¼ cup butter, melted
2 tablespoons sugar

Preheat oven to 350°F.

In a large pot, boil water over high heat and cook the squash and carrots until tender, about 25 minutes. Drain thoroughly.

Place the drained squash and carrots, brown sugar, cream, butter, maple syrup, grated orange rind, salt, ginger, and mace in the container of a food processor. Process until mixture is smooth. (You can use a blender for this, but in that case you will probably have to puree the vegetables in two or three batches.) Spoon into a 1½-quart casserole.

To make the topping, in a medium-size bowl, stir together cereal, melted butter, and sugar. Sprinkle on top of vegetable puree.

Bake for about 25 minutes, or until casserole is heated through.

SERVES 6.
CALORIES: 294   CHOLESTEROL: 41 mg   SODIUM: 336 mg   FIBER: 5 g

Health tip:
Substitute half-and-half for cream; use 1 tablespoon unsalted margarine instead of butter in the topping, and omit butter in purée; substitute reduced-calorie syrup for maple syrup; omit salt.
CALORIES: 257   CHOLESTEROL: 2 mg   SODIUM: 56 mg   FIBER: 5 g

Steamed Pudding with Brandied Topping

This traditional pudding is just too good to make for holidays only, so serve it anytime you want to serve something a little special—and impressive.

2 cups chopped mixed dried fruits
½ cup apple juice
1½ teaspoons ground ginger
1 teaspoon ground cinnamon
⅛ teaspoon ground allspice
3 eggs
½ cup firmly packed light- or dark-brown sugar
1 cup applesauce
¼ cup unsulphured molasses
2 cups fresh bread crumbs
1⅓ cups finely crushed Cheerios
1 teaspoon baking soda
¼ teaspoon salt
2 tablespoons melted butter

Brandied Topping:

2 tablespoons melted butter
2 teaspoons brandy or orange juice
½ cup confectioners' sugar

Generously grease a 6-cup ring mold and set aside.

In a medium-size bowl, combine the dried fruits, apple juice, ginger, cinnamon, and allspice. Set aside for 20 minutes, stirring occasionally.

In a large bowl, beat the eggs and brown sugar until thick. Beat in applesauce and molasses. Stir in dried-fruit mixture, then bread crumbs, cereal, baking soda, salt, and butter.

Spoon batter into prepared mold. Cover with greased waxed

paper, then two layers of foil. Wrap a piece of string around the mold to hold the foil down tightly and to make the covering waterproof.

Place a wire rack in a large pot. (If you don't have a rack that will fit in the bottom of your pot, you can use three custard cups turned upside down and set the mold on them.) Pour enough boiling water into the pot so that it is just a bit lower than the rack. Place the mold on the rack, cover pot tightly, and steam for 2 hours, checking the pot occasionally to make sure that the water is not boiling away.

Remove mold from pot and cool on a wire rack for 1 hour. Remove waxed-paper-and-foil covering. Run a knife blade around the mold's inner and outer edges. Turn pudding onto a serving platter.

Prepare the topping by stirring butter, brandy, and confectioners' sugar together in a medium-size bowl. Spoon topping over pudding.

SERVES 12.
CALORIES: 285   CHOLESTEROL: 63 mg   SODIUM: 323 mg   FIBER: 2 g

Health tip:
Use scrambled-egg substitute for eggs; omit salt. Use unsalted margarine instead of butter.
CALORIES: 278   CHOLESTEROL: 1 mg   SODIUM: 259 mg   FIBER: 2 g

---

———————— ◇ ————————

Honey-Bran Waffles

These waffles are very moist, and the bran and wheat germ give them a nice texture.

1½ cups milk
⅓ cup butter
¼ cup honey
1 cup All-Bran
2 eggs
1⅓ cups all-purpose flour
¼ cup honey-flavored wheat germ
1 tablespoon baking powder
¼ teaspoon salt

Preheat and grease a waffle iron as manufacturer directs.

In a 2-quart saucepan, combine the milk, butter, and honey. Cook over low heat until milk is scalded (bubbles form around edge of pot, but milk should not actually boil). The butter may not be completely melted. Remove from heat and stir in cereal. Let stand for 15 minutes. Beat eggs into bran mixture, then stir in flour, wheat germ, baking powder, and salt.

Pour about 1¼ cup batter for each waffle into waffle iron. Bake until steaming stops and waffle is browned.

MAKES 12 WAFFLES.
CALORIES: 176   CHOLESTEROL: 52 mg   SODIUM: 277 mg   FIBER: 3 g

Health tip:
Use scrambled-egg substitute instead of eggs; substitute unsalted margarine for butter; use 2-percent-fat milk instead of whole milk; omit salt.
CALORIES: 168   CHOLESTEROL: 3 mg   SODIUM: 202 mg   FIBER: 3 g

—————◇—————

Cream-of-Rice Pancakes

The flavor of the cereal in these pancakes gives them a very special (and comforting) quality. They're light, yet definitely filling.

¾ cup water
¼ cup Cream of Rice
¼ cup butter
½ cup milk
2 eggs
¾ cup all-purpose flour
¼ cup sugar
1 tablespoon baking powder
¾ teaspoon salt
Oil, for greasing griddle

In a 2-quart saucepan, bring the water to a boil over high heat. Gradually stir in cereal. Cook, stirring, for 30 seconds. Remove from heat. Stir in butter until melted. Stir in milk, then eggs, until combined.

In a medium-size bowl, stir together the flour, sugar, baking powder, and salt. Stir into cereal mixture.

Heat a griddle or large skillet until a few drops of water sprinkled on the griddle bounce about before evaporating. Lightly grease griddle. Pour about ¼ cup of the batter for each pancake onto the griddle. Cook until bubbles on top of pancake burst. Turn with a wide spatula and cook until browned on the second side.

SERVES 4.
CALORIES: 302   CHOLESTEROL: 139 mg   SODIUM: 793 mg   FIBER: 1 g

Health tip:
Use unsalted margarine instead of butter, and scrambled-egg substitute for eggs; omit salt.
CALORIES: 290   CHOLESTEROL: 4 mg   SODIUM: 320 mg   FIBER: 1 g

———————— ◇ ————————

Banana-Bran Muffins

Banana adds natural sweetness and moistness to these healthful muffins. Bake a batch when you have a few minutes, then freeze some for any time you'd like a wholesome pick-me-up. Reheat in the microwave oven to restore fresh-baked softness and aroma.

1¼ cups all-purpose flour
1 cup Bran Buds
2 teaspoons baking soda
1 teaspoon baking powder
¼ teaspoon salt
1 cup buttermilk
1 egg, beaten
¼ cup dark-brown sugar
¼ cup unsulphured molasses
1 ripe banana, mashed

Preheat oven to 350°F.
Grease 12 2½-inch muffin cups and set aside.
In a large bowl, stir together the flour, cereal, baking soda, baking powder, and salt.
In a medium-size bowl, stir together the buttermilk, egg, brown sugar, molasses, and banana until thoroughly combined.
Stir the liquid ingredients into the dry ingredients just until blended. Let stand for 5 minutes. Spoon equal amounts of the batter into each muffin cup.
Bake for 15 minutes, or until muffins spring back when lightly touched. Remove from pan and cool on wire racks.

MAKES 12 MUFFINS.
CALORIES: 120   CHOLESTEROL: 18 mg   SODIUM: 282 mg   FIBER: 3 g

Health tip:
Omit salt.
CALORIES: 120   CHOLESTEROL: 18 mg   SODIUM: 240 mg   FIBER: 3 g

——————— ◇ ———————

Cereal Dumplings

I like my dumplings a little on the heavy side, which these are. Drop the dumplings into soups, stews, or just a plain broth.

1½ cups milk, divided
⅔ cup Instant Cream of Wheat or Instant Cream of Rice
¼ cup butter
2 eggs
1 teaspoon salt
3 slices white bread, torn into bite-size pieces
½ cup all-purpose flour

In a 2-quart saucepan, bring 1 cup of the milk to a boil. Gradually stir in cereal. Lower heat and cook, stirring, until very thick. Remove from heat. Add butter and let it melt. Stir in the remaining ½ cup milk, then eggs and salt, then stir in bread and flour.

Bring a large pot of water to a boil. Drop the dumplings into the boiling water and simmer for 10 minutes. Drain thoroughly.

MAKES 24 DUMPLINGS.
CALORIES: 60   CHOLESTEROL: 25 mg   SODIUM: 136 mg   FIBER: .5 g

Health tip:
Use unsalted margarine instead of butter; omit salt.
CALORIES: 60   CHOLESTEROL: 17 mg   SODIUM: 24 mg   FIBER: .5 g

——————— ◇ ———————

Raisin-Bran Oatmeal Cookies

These just may be the best oatmeal cookies I ever ate. However, there aren't too many raisins per cookie, so if you really like them add a few extra.

1 cup butter, softened
½ cup firmly packed dark- or light-brown sugar
½ cup granulated sugar
1 egg
1 teaspoon vanilla extract
1 cup all-purpose flour
½ teaspoon salt
½ teaspoon baking powder
½ teaspoon ground cinnamon
2 cups Old-Fashioned Rolled Oats
1 cup Raisin Bran

Preheat oven to 375°F.

In a large bowl, cream the butter and both kinds of sugars until light and fluffy. Beat in egg and vanilla.

In a medium-size bowl, stir together the flour, salt, baking powder, and cinnamon. Beat flour mixture into butter mixture. Stir in both kinds of cereal until well blended.

Drop by measuring tablespoonsful onto ungreased cookie sheets.

Bake for about 10 minutes. Remove from cookie sheets and cool on wire racks.

MAKES ABOUT 36 COOKIES.

CALORIES: 95   CHOLESTEROL: 20 mg   SODIUM: 91 mg   FIBER: 1 g

Health tip:

Use unsalted margarine instead of butter; omit salt.

CALORIES: 95   CHOLESTEROL: 6 mg   SODIUM: 24 mg   FIBER: 1 g

---◇---

Granola-Cheesecake Squares

Everyone I've ever served these to raves about them and asks for the recipe. Needless to say, they're delighted to find out that the squares are so easy to make. Use any kind of ready-made granola that you like, or use the granola recipe given in this book on page 298.

½ cup butter, softened
¼ cup light- or dark-brown sugar
1 cup sifted all-purpose flour
1 cup granola, divided
1 package (8 ounce) cream cheese, softened
¼ cup sugar
½ teaspoon vanilla extract
1 egg

Preheat oven to 350°F.

Grease an 8-inch-square baking pan and set aside.

In a large bowl, cream the butter with brown sugar until light and fluffy. Beat in flour, then ½ cup of granola. Press into prepared pan and bake for 15 minutes.

While crust is baking, in a medium-size bowl, beat the cream cheese with sugar and vanilla until light and fluffy. Beat in egg. Pour over baked crust. Sprinkle with remaining ½ cup granola. Continue to bake for 25 minutes.

Cool cake on a wire rack, then refrigerate until chilled. Cut into squares to serve.

MAKES 16 SQUARES.
CALORIES: 195   CHOLESTEROL: 44 mg   SODIUM: 97 mg   FIBER: 1 g

Health tip:
Use unsalted margarine instead of butter.
CALORIES: 195   CHOLESTEROL: 28 mg   SODIUM: 66 mg   FIBER: 1 g

---

———————— ◇ ————————

Frozen Maple-Pecan Pie

The filling for this pie is a creamy, rich frozen mousse. Since the pie takes a little time to assemble and freeze, at some point you want a quick version of it. In that case, substitute butter-pecan ice cream (or any ice cream you like) for the mousse.

3 cups Cracklin' Oat Bran
⅓ cup butter
3 eggs, separated
1 extra egg yolk
¼ cup pure maple syrup
2 tablespoons dark corn syrup
2 tablespoons sugar
1 cup heavy cream
1½ cups chopped pecans

Preheat oven to 350°F.

Place cereal in the container of a food processor. Cover and process until cereal forms fine crumbs. (You can do this in a blender in two or three batches.)

Place the butter in a 10-inch pie plate. Place the pie plate in the oven for 4 minutes, or until butter is melted. Stir crumbs into melted butter until completely combined. Press crumb mixture onto the bottom and up the side of the pie plate to form a crust. Bake for 8 minutes, then set aside to cool.

Place the egg yolks, maple syrup, and corn syrup in the top of a double boiler. Beat with a whisk until completely combined. Place over simmering water and continue whisking until mixture is slightly thickened. Remove from heat and fill bottom of double boiler with ice water. Set the top part of the double boiler over ice water and whisk until the mixture has cooled.

In a clean, grease-free large bowl, beat egg whites with clean beaters until foamy. Gradually beat in sugar and continue beating until stiff peaks form when beaters are lifted.

In another large bowl, beat the cream until soft peaks form when beaters are lifted. (There's no need to wash beaters before beating cream.) Add egg-yolk mixture and egg whites to the whipped cream and fold in until completely combined. Fold in pecans. Turn into prepared crust and chill until firm, at least 8 hours.

Cut pie into wedges to serve. If you have a little difficulty getting the slices out of the pan, set the pie plate on a warm wet towel for about 5 minutes.

SERVES 10.

CALORIES: 398   CHOLESTEROL: 132 mg   SODIUM: 208 mg   FIBER: 4 g

Health tip:
Eat only half a serving—about once a year.

Viennese Farina

When I was about 8-years-old, my aunt Annie and uncle Robert came to visit from Vienna. While she was with us, my aunt made a delicious dessert from farina that I have never forgotten, and this is my attempt to recreate it.

3 cups milk
¾ cup farina
⅓ cup sugar
⅓ cup butter
1 teaspoon salt
1 egg
½ cup golden raisins
1 teaspoon vanilla extract
1 can (16 ounce) pitted plums or 1 jar (16 ounce) pitted prunes, or any
*   fruit packed in heavy syrup (optional)*

Grease an 8-inch-square baking pan and set aside.

In a 2-quart saucepan, combine the milk, farina, sugar, butter, and salt. Cook over medium heat, stirring occasionally, until mixture comes to a boil and has thickened. Remove from heat.

In a medium-size bowl, beat egg. Stir ½ cup of the hot farina into the beaten egg, then stir the egg mixture back into the farina in the saucepan. Stir in raisins and vanilla. Pour into prepared pan and chill for 1½ hours.

Preheat oven to 400°F.

Bake the farina for 40 to 50 minutes, or until lightly browned. Remove from oven and let stand for 20 minutes. Cut into 9 squares. Serve topped with fruit, if desired.

SERVES 9.
CALORIES: 213   CHOLESTEROL: 52 mg   SODIUM: 343 mg   FIBER: 2 g

Health tip:
Use unsalted margarine instead of butter; omit salt.
CALORIES: 213   CHOLESTEROL: 34 mg   SODIUM: 57 mg   FIBER: 2 g

---

◇

Cinnamon-Toast Bread Pudding

I'm very partial to bread pudding, and when I feel truly decadent (or depressed) I serve it with a vanilla sauce or vanilla ice cream.

3 tablespoons butter, melted
5 slices soft white bread, cubed
1½ cups Cinnamon Toast Crunch, divided
3 eggs
⅓ cup sugar
1¾ cups scaled milk (bubbles form around the edge of the pan, but the milk should not actually boil)

Preheat oven to 350°F.
Butter a 1½-quart casserole and set aside.
Place the melted butter in a medium-size bowl. Add bread cubes and toss until coated. Place about half of the bread cubes in the prepared casserole. Sprinkle with 1 cup of the cereal and top with remaining bread cubes. Sprinkle with remaining ½ cup cereal.
In the same bowl you used for the melted butter, beat eggs with sugar until combined. Gradually beat in milk. Pour over bread and cereal in casserole. Let stand for 15 minutes.
Bake for 45 minutes, or until a knife inserted in the center comes out clean. Serve warm or chilled.

SERVES 8.
CALORIES: 207   CHOLESTEROL: 97 mg   SODIUM: 230 mg   FIBER: 1 g

Health tip:
Use unsalted margarine instead of butter; use scrambled-egg substitute for eggs; and use 2-percent-fat milk for whole milk.
CALORIES: 191   CHOLESTEROL: 5 mg   SODIUM: 211 mg   FIBER: 1g

———————◇———————

Corny Apple Fritters

Deep-fried apple fritters are always a treat, and make a nice supper dish. The Corn Pops add a nice crunch.

1 cup all-purpose flour
3 tablespoons sugar
1 teaspoon baking powder
½ teaspoon salt
2 eggs
⅓ cup milk
1 tablespoon vegetable oil
½ teaspoon vanilla extract
1½ cups peeled chopped apple
½ cup lightly crushed Corn Pops (the Pops should be broken into pieces,
*   but not actually crushed so finely as to be crumbs)*
Oil, for deep-frying
Confectioners' sugar

In a large bowl, stir together the flour, sugar, baking powder, and salt.

In a medium-size bowl, beat together the eggs, milk, oil, and vanilla. Stir the egg mixture into the flour mixture until well blended. Stir in apple and cereal.

Pour enough oil into a 2-quart saucepan so that it measures about 2 inches deep. Heat oil until it bubbles when a little batter is dropped into it. Drop batter by rounded measuring teaspoonsful into the hot oil. Fry until golden on all sides. Drain on paper toweling. Serve warm, sprinkled with confectioners' sugar.

MAKES 3 DOZEN FRITTERS.
CALORIES: 43   CHOLESTEROL: 12 mg   SODIUM: 45 mg   FIBER: 0 g

Health tip:
Eat just one.

—————— ◇ ——————

Baked Stuffed Pears à la Mode

Although these baked pears are just wonderful as is, when they are served with a scoop of ice cream on the side they are divine.

2 ripe pears
2 tablespoons butter, melted
1 tablespoon brown sugar
2 teaspoons lemon juice
¼ teaspoon grated lemon rind
¾ cup slightly broken up Cracklin' Bran
⅓ cup chopped walnuts
2 cups ice cream

Preheat oven to 350°F.

Cut pears in half and core them. Carefully scoop out about half the flesh in each pear half, leaving a ½-inch shell. Coarsely chop scooped-out flesh and set aside.

In a medium-size bowl, stir together the melted butter, brown sugar, lemon juice, and lemon rind. Stir in pear-cereal and walnuts. Set aside ½ cup of this mixture. Add chopped pear to remaining cereal mixture in bowl and toss until combined. Spoon one quarter of the pear-cereal mixture into each of the pear shells. Top each with 2 tablespoons of the reserved cereal mixture.

Bake 30 minutes, or until pears are fork tender. Serve warm or chilled with a scoop of vanilla ice cream.

SERVES 4.
CALORIES: 348   CHOLESTEROL: 45 mg   SODIUM: 184 mg   FIBER: 4 g

Health tip:
Use unsalted margarine instead of butter; skip the "à la mode."
CALORIES: 213   CHOLESTEROL: 0 mg   SODIUM: 85 mg   FIBER: 4 g

———— ◇ ————

Fresh Peach Strada

Use peaches that are ripe, but still firm, or even slightly under-ripe, otherwise the dessert will be too mushy.

4 cups Sugar Frosted Flakes
¼ cup melted butter
1 teaspoon ground cinnamon
⅛ teaspoon ground nutmeg
2 pounds fresh peaches, peeled and sliced or
    4½ cups frozen peaches, thawed

Preheat oven to 350°F.

In a large bowl, combine the cereal, butter, cinnamon, and nutmeg. Place 1½ cups of the cereal mixture in the bottom of a 1½- to 2-quart casserole. Top with half the peach slices. Sprinkle 1½ cups more of the cereal mixture over the peach slices. Cover with remaining peach slices. Top with remaining cereal mixture.

Bake for 40 minutes, or until fruit is soft. (The time may vary depending on the ripeness of the peaches.)

SERVES 6.
CALORIES: 221   CHOLESTEROL: 21 mg   SODIUM: 254 mg   FIBER: 3 g

Health tip:
Use unsalted margarine instead of butter.
CALORIES: 221   CHOLESTEROL: 0 mg   SODIUM: 198 mg   FIBER: 3 g

———————— ◇ ————————

Ice Cream Layer Cake

You can use any flavor, or combination of flavors, of ice cream that appeal to you. But I found that all chocolate all the way was positively scrumptious.

> *1 cup (6-ounce bag) semisweet chocolate morsels*
> *¼ cup butter*
> *2 cups Nutrigrain Nuggets*
> *½ cup flaked coconut*
> *½ cup finely chopped almonds*
> *2 pints ice cream, slightly softened*

In the top of a double boiler over simmering (not boiling) water, melt chocolate morsels with butter. Stir in cereal, coconut, and almonds.

Pat 1½ cups of the chocolate mixture in the bottom of an 8½-inch springform pan and chill for 10 minutes in the freezer. Spread 1 pint of the ice cream over the cereal mixture. Sprinkle 1 cup of the remaining cereal mixture over ice cream. Return to freezer for 10 minutes. Spread remaining pint of ice cream over crumbs. Top with remaining crumbs.

Cover with foil and freeze until firm, at least 4 hours. Run a knife around the edge of the cake before unmolding.

SERVES 8.

CALORIES: 400   CHOLESTEROL: 45 mg   SODIUM: 180 mg   FIBER: 3 g

Health tip:
Eat only half a serving.

———————— ◇ ————————

Granola Coffee Cake

This is the kind of goodie I like to keep in the freezer for unexpected company.

1 cup granola
1 teaspoon cinnamon
2¼ cups all-purpose flour
½ teaspoon baking powder
½ teaspoon baking soda
¼ teaspoon salt
1¾ cups sugar
1 cup butter, softened
4 eggs
1 teaspoon vanilla extract
1 cup sour cream

Preheat oven to 350°F.

Grease and flour a 10-cup Bundt pan or 10-inch tube pan and set aside.

Stir together the granola and cinnamon on a piece of waxed paper and set aside.

In a medium-size bowl, stir together flour, baking powder, baking soda, and salt and set aside.

In a large bowl, cream the sugar and butter until light and fluffy. Beat in eggs, one at a time, until thoroughly combined. Beat in vanilla. Beat in the flour mixture alternately with the sour cream, starting and ending with the flour mixture.

Sprinkle ¼ cup of the granola mixture into the prepared pan. Spread half the batter over the granola, then sprinkle with remaining granola mixture. Top with remaining batter.

Bake for 1 hour and 10 minutes, or until a wooden pick inserted in the center comes out clean.

MAKES 20 SLICES.
CALORIES: 265   CHOLESTEROL: 72 mg   SODIUM: 165 mg   FIBER: 1 g

Health tip:
Omit salt; use unsalted margarine instead of butter.
CALORIES: 265   CHOLESTEROL: 40 mg   SODIUM: 78 mg   FIBER: 1 g

—————— ◇ ——————

Krispie, Crunchy Chocolate Drops

This is what I consider "junk" candy. If you are a chocolate afficionado, who loves the very expensive brands, this is not for you. But most kids, young and old, adore these make-in-minutes cereal candies.

> 1 cup (6-ounce bag) semisweet chocolate morsels
> ½ cup milk-chocolate morsels
> 1½ cups Rice Krispies
> ½ cup flaked coconut

Combine both kinds of chocolate in the top of a double boiler set over simmering (not boiling) water. Cook, stirring occasionally, until chocolate is melted. Stir in cereal and coconut. Drop by heaping teaspoonsful onto waxed paper. Let stand until hardened.

MAKES 40.
CALORIES: 42   CHOLESTEROL: 1 mg   SODIUM: 18 mg   FIBER: 0 g

Health tip:
Eat just one—if you can.

—————— ◇ ——————

Maple-Wheat Candy

These are something like little popcorn balls. They're not difficult to make, but it does take a little time for the sugar syrup to come up to temperature. And speaking of sugar syrup, remember while you are working with it that there is always the possibility of getting a severe burn if you're not careful. This is *not* a candy-making endeavor in which you will want little kids to help. Although I call for Puffed Wheat, you can use any puffed cereal in this recipe.

> ¾ cup sugar
> ⅓ cup water
> ¼ cup pure maple syrup
> 2 tablespoons butter
> ½ teaspoon white vinegar
> 3 cups Puffed Wheat

Place the sugar in a 2-quart saucepan, then pour water, maple syrup, butter, and vinegar over it. Bring to a boil, stirring occasionally. Insert a candy thermometer in the pan and cook over medium-high heat until the mixture reaches 290°F.

Place the cereal in a greased heat-resistant bowl. Pour syrup over cereal, stirring with a wooden spoon until the grains are well coated. As soon as the mixture is cool enough to handle (the syrup will harden as it cools), quickly form into 3-inch balls. (To protect your hands from the heat of the sugar syrup, keep them coated with butter while you make the balls. Better yet, use clean rubber gloves that are coated with butter.)

MAKES 8.

CALORIES: 120   CHOLESTEROL: 0 mg   SODIUM: 3 mg   FIBER: 1 g

Health tip:
Make balls half size.

Bibliography

Atlas, Nava. *The Wholefood Catalog.* New York: Fawcett Columbine, 1988.

Barrett, Judith, and Wasserman, Norma. *Risotto.* New York: Charles Scribner's Sons, 1987.

Brody, Jane. *Jane Brody's Good Food Book.* New York: W. W. Norton, 1985.

Brown, Elizabeth Burton. *Grains.* Englewood Cliffs, New Jersey, Prentice-Hall, Inc., 1977.

Carroll, David. *The Complete Book of Natural Foods.* New York: Summit Books, 1985.

Claiborne, Craig. *The (Original) New York Times Cook Book.* New York: Harper and Row, Publishers, 1961.

Cohen, Mark Nathan. *The Food Crisis in Prehistory.* New Haven: Yale University Press, 1977.

FitzGibbon, Theodora. *The Food of the Western World.* New York: Quadrangle/The New York Times Book Co., 1976.

Garrison, Holly. *Comfort Food.* New York: Donald I. Fine, Inc., 1988.

Greene, Bert. *The Grains Cookbook.* New York: Workman Publishing, 1988.

Hazan, Marcella. *The Classic Italian Cookbook.* New York: Alfred A. Knopf, 1982.

Hillman, Howard. *The Cook's Book.* New York: Avon Books, 1981.

London, Sheryl and Mel. *Creative Cooking with Grains and Pasta.* Emmaus, Pa.: Rodale Press, 1982.

McGee, Harold. *On Food and Cooking.* New York: Macmillan Publishing Company, 1984.

Robertson, Laurel; Flinders, Carol; and Godfrey, Bronwen. *Laurel's Kitchen.* Berkeley, California: Nilgiri Press, 1976.

Roehl, Evelyn. *Whole Food Facts.* Rochester, Vermont: Healing Arts Press, 1988.

Rombauer, Irma S., and Becker, Marion Rombauer. *The Joy of Cooking.* Indianapolis: The Bobbs-Merrill Company, Inc. 1931 (1981 edition).

Root, Waverley. *Food.* New York: Simon and Schuster, 1980.

Tannahill, Reay. *Food in History.* New York: Stein and Day, 1984.

Townsend, Doris McFerran. *The Cook's Companion.* New York: Crown Publishers, Inc., 1978.

Udesky, James. *The Book of Soba.* Tokoyo: Kodansha International, 1988.

Von Welanetz, Diana and Paul. *The Von Welanetz Guide to Ethnic Ingredients.* Los Angeles: J.P. Tarcher, Inc., 1982.

Wood, Rebecca. *The Whole Foods Encyclopedia.* New York: Prentice Hall Press, 1988.

Index

*indicates vegetarian recipes

501

EASY SHOPPING GUIDE

	(trimmed weight)
up shelled almonds	1 cup + 3 tablespoons chopped (5½ ounces)
medium apple	1 cup chopped or diced (peeled) (4 ounces)
large apple	1 cup shredded (peeled) (5 ounces)
medium asparagus	1 cup asparagus cut into 1-inch pieces (3½ ounces)
pound dried beans	2 cups beans (any kind), dried (16 ounces)
medium bunch broccoli	3½ cups flowerettes (9 ounces)
small head cabbage	4½ cups shredded (9 ounces)
small head cabbage	3 cups chopped (9 ounces)
large carrot	1 cup sliced (6 ounces)
large carrot	1 cup coarsely chopped (6 ounces)
large carrot	1 cup finely chopped (6 ounces)
large carrot	1 cup shredded (6 ounces)
medium head cauliflower	5 cups flowerettes (20 ounces)
2 medium ribs celery	1 cup sliced (4 ounces)
2 medium ribs celery	1 cup chopped or diced (4½ ounces)
2 medium ribs celery	1 cup finely chopped or diced (4¾ ounces)
1 large cucumber	2 cups chopped, sliced or diced (11 ounces)
1 medium eggplant	5 cups cubed (14 ounces)
⅓ pound green beans	1 cup green beans cut into 1-inch pieces (4 ounces)
1 medium green onion (scallion)	3 tablespoons sliced or chopped (white and green parts) (½ ounce)
1 medium green onion (scallion)	2 tablespoons finely chopped (white and green parts) (½ ounce)
1 medium leek	1 cup sliced (white and light green part only) (2½ ounces)
4 medium mushrooms	1 cup sliced or chopped (3 ounces)
1 cup shelled walnuts or pecans	1 cup + 1 tablespoon chopped (4 ounces)
1 medium onion	1 cup chopped or diced (4 ounces)
1 large onion	1 cup finely chopped (7 ounces)
1 small pepper (red, green or yellow)	1 cup sliced (4 ounces)
1 small pepper	1 cup chopped or diced (4½ ounces)
1 small pepper	1 cup finely chopped (5 ounces)
1 medium potato	1 cup cubed (5½ ounces)
1 medium potato	1 cup shredded (4¾ ounces)
1 medium tomato	1 cup diced or chopped (6 ounces)
1 small zucchini	1 cup sliced (3.5 ounces)
1 small zucchini	1 cup shredded (4.5 ounces)